THE INDUSTRIAL ARCHAEOLOGY OF CORK CITY AND ITS ENVIRONS

Colin Rynne

BAILE ÁTHA CLIATH
ARNA FHOILSIÚ AG OIFIG AN TSOLÁTHAIR
le ceannach díreach ón
OIFIG DHÍOLTA FOILSEACHÁN RIALTAIS
TEACH SUN ALLIANCE, SRÁID THEACH LAIGHEAN, BAILE ÁTHA CLIATH 2
nó tríd an bpost ó
FOILSEACHÁIN RIALTAIS, AN RANNÓG POST-TRÁCHTA
4 – 5 BÓTHAR FHEARCHAIR, BAILE ÁTHA CLIATH 2,
Teil: 01-6613111, fo-líne 4040/4045: Fax: 01-4752760
nó trí aon díoltóir leabhar

DUBLIN
PUBLISHED BY THE STATIONERY OFFICE
To be purchased directly from the
GOVERNMENT PUBLICATIONS SALE OFFICE
SUN ALLIANCE HOUSE, MOLESWORTH STREET, DUBLIN 2
or by mail order from
4–5 HARCOURT ROAD, DUBLIN 2,
Tel: 01-6613111, extension 4040/4045: Fax 01-4752760
or through any bookseller

ISBN: 0-7076-6795-X

General Editor: David Sweetman

Copy Editor: Mary Tunney

Design: Ger Garland

Index: Julitta Clancy

Typeset by Wordwell Ltd

Printed in Ireland by Boylan Print Company

CONTENTS

ILLUSTRATIONS

TABLES

WEIGHTS AND MEASURES CONVERSION

	Imperial	**Metric**
Length	1 inch (in)	25.4 millimetres (mm)
	1 foot (ft)	0.3048 metres (m)
	1 yard (yd)	0.9144m
	1 mile	1.6093 kilometres (km)
Area	1 sq in	6.4516 sq centimetres (cm)
	1 sq ft (144 sq in)	0.0929 sq m
Capacity	1 pint	0.5683 litres (l)
	1 gallon (8 pints)	4.5461 l
	1 bushel (64 pints)	36.368 l
Weight	1 pound (lb) (16oz)	0.4536 kilograms (kg)
	1 stone (14lb)	6.35kg
	1 hundredweight (cwt) (112lb)	50.8kg
	1 ton (2240lb or 20cwt)	1016kg or 1.016 tonnes
Power, Energy and Stress	1 foot head (water)	0.434 pounds per square inch (psi) or 2.995 kilonewtons (kN) per sq m
	1 horsepower (hp)	746 joules per second (J/s) or 746 watts (W)

PREFACE

In 1988 a special sub-committee of the Royal Irish Academy (RIA) was established to augment, and indeed initiate, the academic study of industrial archaeology in Ireland. The committee undertook to produce a pilot survey of the industrial archaeology of a region small enough to be satisfactorily investigated with the limited resources available to it. The city of Cork and areas within its immediate environs were chosen for this study and the author was commissioned by the RIA sub-committee to undertake a pilot study. The time-span 1750–1930 was chosen for the survey, as it was largely during this period that the essential fabric of Cork's traditional industries was both woven and worn thin. A preliminary rapid survey of sites established during this period was undertaken in May and June 1988. The finished report, *The industrial archaeology of Cork City and its environs: a pilot study*, was formally launched in 1989. Its principal recommendation was that a fully-fledged industrial archaeological survey of the area defined within it should be undertaken at the earliest possible opportunity. In 1989 and early 1990 the Industrial Archaeology sub-committee of the RIA was able to procure pledges of financial support from the Office of Public Works and Cork County Council. However, it took a generous grant from the National Heritage Council to make the proposed survey a reality, and this subvention comprised the bulk of its resources during its two-year existence.

The area encompassed by the Cork City and Environs Industrial Archaeological Survey (CCEIAS) includes the city of Cork, and the outlying villages of Blackrock and Douglas, areas of which now form part of the conurbation of Cork (Fig. 1). The inclusion of these areas was based on three criteria: firstly, to enable comparisons to be made between the types of industry established within the city and those in what were rural environments, and thus to outline the social, economic, geographical and technological profiles of the main industries found within the survey area; secondly, to give preference to areas which are bearing the brunt of more recent development; and thirdly, to include as many sites as possible of either national or international significance within the environs of Cork, a requirement easily met by these areas. Important exceptions, however, were made in the case of the Ballincollig Gunpowder Mills (**217**) and the Monard and Coolowen Iron Works (**218**). These latter are the most important surviving sites of their type in the Ireland, and while they lie outside the areas mentioned above, they are sufficiently close to Cork to be considered part of its immediate environs. The areas chosen were also important for the ongoing requirements of the Cork County and City planning authorities.

The primary aim of the survey was to make a complete record of all the sites identified by it up to inventory level (as defined by the Office of Public Works), and to survey all of the available documentary evidence. Sites considered to be representative of important industries within the survey area were also selected for detailed recording, and the sites concerned were surveyed in detail in the period 1991–2 by survey archaeologists. This survey was the first of its kind to be undertaken within the Republic of Ireland.

ACKNOWLEDGEMENTS

My thanks to Mr Michael Monk, Department of Archaeology, UCC and Mr Denis Power, Dúchas (former Director of the Cork Archaeological Survey) who initiated and prepared the original proposal for the pilot industrial archaeological survey of Cork City. During the period 1990–92 the industrial archaeological survey was managed by a special committee chaired by Prof. Gordon Herries Davies. The committee also comprised Mr David Sweetman, Chief Archaeologist of the Office of Public Works (latterly Dúchas), Dr Terry Barry, Dept. of Medieval History, Trinity College Dublin, Ms Mairéad Dunlevy, the National Museum of Ireland and Mr Denis Power. I gratefully acknowledge their direction in many matters relating to the conduct of the survey, and am particularly grateful to Mr David Sweetman who provided every encouragement and steered the book through to publication. The survey was financed by a generous grant from the original National Heritage Council along with subventions from the Office of Public Works and Cork County Council. Ms Joan Jennings, formerly of the Royal Irish Academy, expertly administered the survey's finances.

Through the good offices of Dr Michael Mortell, the survey, for its duration, was based in UCC where many individuals smoothed its course. Prof. Peter Woodman and the staff of the Dept. of Archaeology, UCC, in particular Ms Angela Desmond, provided valuable assistance to the survey as did Prof. Ciaran Murphy and his staff in the Dept. of Management Information Systems. The staff of the library UCC, particularly Mrs Pat Connolly, Mrs Helen Moloney-Davis and Mr Max McCarthy, were also very helpful. Ms Anne-Marie Lennon and Mr Flor (Martin) Hurley were employed as survey archaeologists: each made important contributions to the survey. The staff of the Cork Archaeological Survey, Mr Denis Power, Ms Mary Sleeman, Ms Ursula Egan, Ms Elizabeth Byrne, Ms Sheila Lane and Mr Redmond Tobin also gave freely of their time. Ms Virginia Teehan, Archivist, UCC, kindly facilitated access to the University's fine collection of engineering drawings. The Development Plan Section of Cork County Council, through the good offices of Head County Planner, Mr Brendan Kelleher, Mr John Ludlow, Architect and Mr Michael Rice, Senior Draughtsman, provided valuable assistance in our survey of Ballincollig Gunpowder Mills.

The courteous and accommodating proprietors of the many buildings visited during the course of the survey are too numerous to mention. However, the kindness and hospitality of a number of individuals who allowed us long-term access to their property, or buildings in their care, deserves a special mention: Mr George Ellis, Chief Engineer, Beamish and Crawford, Mr Tom O'Byrne, Monard Glen, County Cork and Mr Gerry Duffy, Cork Corporation Waterworks.

Cork-based historians, Mr Colman O'Mahony, Mr C.J.F. MacCarthy, Dr Charles O'Sullivan, the late Mr Seán Daly, Mr Dermot Lucey and Mr Dick Henchion kindly provided important information from their own unpublished researches. Mr Richard Irwin of Irwin and Kilcullen Solicitors, Cork, also brought the survey's attention to important documents on the Glanmire linen-finishing industry. The excellence of the city and county library services and the Cork Archives Institute proved a great boon to the survey. Mr Kieran Burke, Cork City Library, Mr Tim Cadogan, Cork County Library, and Ms Patricia McCarthy, Archivist, Cork Archives Institute, provided an unfailingly courteous and professional service. I would also like to thank Ms Aideen Ireland and the staff of the National Archives, and the staff of Birmingham Central Libraries who facilitated access to the Boulton and Watt Collection. Ms Stella Cherry, Curator, Cork Public Museum, brought a number of important documents to my attention during the course of the survey, and also generated a successful exhibition on Cork's Industrial Past, using material from the survey. Mr Peter Murray, Curator, Crawford Art Gallery, kindly provided copies of material in the gallery's collections.

Dr Fred Hamond patiently read every draft of the book in progress. Its present structure and content owes as much to his outstanding editorial skills, as to his incomparable knowledge of the industrial archaeology of this island. I am also grateful to Dr Andy Bielenberg, Dept. of Modern History, UCC, for his most useful comments on the earlier drafts. The survey's work on the transport history of Cork City owes a special debt of thanks to Mr Walter McGrath, who commented on early drafts of Chapter 7. I am, indeed, very fortunate to be among a second generation of researchers to benefit from his pioneering work on Cork's railway history. Mrs Mary Tunney of the Editing Unit, Archaeological Survey, Dúchas, most skilfully edited the final text. Mr Con Brogan, Staff Photographer, Dúchas, took a series of superb photographs, which feature on the cover and in the main body of this book.

The following individuals also helped the survey in various ways: Mr John Tierney, Ms Martha Hannon, Mr Paul

O'Donovan, Mr Tony Perrott, Mr Tómas Tynan, Mr Martin Byrne, Mr Robert Guinness, Mr Maurice Hurley, Mr Eric Peard, Mr Cormac Scally, Mr Paul Duffy, Mr William Dick, Dr Ron Cox and Mr Jim Hurley. Finally I would like to thank my wife, Stella, for all her encouragement and support.

THE SCOPE OF INDUSTRIAL ARCHAEOLOGY

As a field, industrial archaeology has consistently defied close definition. This has as much to do with the diversity of interests found within the discipline as with the inability of its practitioners to agree on a single definition or, indeed, on the very nature of the discipline itself. The rapid growth in interest in industrial archaeology in the last three decades, particularly in the United Kingdom, has brought together a diffuse agglomeration of interest groups for whom industrial archaeology has become a 'meeting ground where older established disciplines overlap' (McCutcheon 1980, xxxix). As a branch of archaeology or, rather, as a period discipline within it, its ultimate origin lies in a pervasive enthusiasm (in what would otherwise be unrelated disciplines) for the material remains of industrialisation. Clearly, industrial archaeology was not 'born out of a detached academic interest' (Cossons 1987, 11). While this initially spurred its detractors it remains one of its greatest strengths, for the sheer diversity and increasing complexity of industrial monuments between 1750 and 1930 has always encouraged an inter-disciplinary approach amongst its practitioners. And, while industrial archaeologists have recently been urged to consider exactly how more 'conventional archaeological concepts and techniques apply to their own particular field' (Palmer 1990, 276), conventional archaeologists can also learn from the flexibility inherent in industrial archaeology since the 1950s.

The term 'industrial archaeology' was first used in print by Michael Rix in 1955, and while W.A. McCutcheon (1980, 372, n.1) suggested that 'much of the initial unacceptability of the phrase was due to the unnecessarily narrow interpretation of the word "archaeology" then current', the adoption of normal archaeological methodologies has not been as widespread as those coming to the discipline from conventional archaeological backgrounds may have liked. As one recent commentator has noted, the origins of industrial archaeology 'grew from the need to record and preserve standing structures threatened with demolition rather than an inherent desire to understand about the historical period of the monument' (Palmer 1990, 275).

Definitions of industrial archaeology abound, but rarely concur, and curiously much of the debate has centred on the historical period forming the basis for study for industrial archaeologists rather than on how the methodologies employed by them square with those used by archaeologists working in other periods. Industrial archaeology has recently been defined as 'a period study embracing the tangible evidence of social, economic and technological development in the period since industrialisation' (Palmer 1990, 281). But, if industrial archaeology is a period study, does it simply update the physical development of the landscape since the post-medieval period (and thus include agriculture), or is it concerned exclusively with the archaeology of the cultural phenomenon called industrialisation? Most industrial archaeologists, including the present author, would tend to agree with Marilyn Palmer's definition, quoted above, as to the nature and scope of industrial archaeology.

The potential for Ireland to industrialise in the eighteenth and nineteenth centuries remains hypothetical, yet while the greater part of Ireland never experienced the changes which industrialisation wrought in many European regions, industries of both national and international significance became established here. The progress of truly large-scale industrialisation in Ireland during the same period exhibits a pronounced regional bias, and in those regions that experienced it there is a marked trend toward establishing closer ties with industrial regions in other countries than with their own predominantly rural hinterlands (Ollerenshaw 1985, 62). This development has close parallels with developments in contemporary Europe (Trebilcock 1981, 3; Pollard 1986, llff), although the precise reasons for the 'failure' of other Irish regions to experience large-scale industrialisation have yet to be satisfactorily explained. Its predominantly agrarian society also presents rather different challenges to Irish industrial archaeologists in regard to defining the relationships between the pre-industrial elements of the eighteenth- and nineteenth-century Irish landscape and those associated with Irish industry, especially as industry was not the dominant activity in many parts of Ireland well into the twentieth century. In real terms, Belfast was the only Victorian industrial city in Ireland; the economic fabric of both Dublin and Cork was essentially commercial rather than industrial. Small pockets of dispersed industrial activity became established near the ports and larger country towns such as Dundalk, with varying degrees of success, but overall this patchwork of industry can in no way be characterised as large-scale industrialisation.

The components of industrialisation which form the basis for the study of industrial archaeology can be divided into four main categories, two embracing a broad spectrum of industrial activities and two being largely concerned with infrastructure for industry.

EXTRACTIVE or *primary* industries, e.g. mining and quarrying;

MANUFACTURING or *secondary* industries, e.g. textiles and ironworking;

TRANSPORT AND COMMUNICATIONS, e.g. roads, canals, railways, ports and harbours;

UTILITY INDUSTRIES, e.g. water supply, gas and electricity.

A further category suggested by Buchanan (1977) involves agriculture and rural crafts, which, although not included in the present survey, would be of special interest in an Irish context. Service or tertiary activities such as banks, cinemas and hospitals are also of industrial archaeological interest. Other aspects of industrialisation, such as educational establishments (not specifically technical institutes) and housing, are as much a part of the industrial infrastructure as of the culture associated with it, and their study will increasingly be drawn within the ambit of industrial archaeology. Many of the activities included in the categories listed above would have utilised similar sources of energy or, indeed, the same source, as in the case of the water-powered industries established on the River Lee and its tributaries. The categorisation of industry employed here is not intended to show how these activities interacted: it is simply a means of dividing the various types of industrial activity (and associated infrastructure) into their component parts.

THE DEVELOPMENT OF INDUSTRIAL ARCHAEOLOGY IN IRELAND

One of the pioneers of Irish and, indeed, British industrial archaeology, Prof. Rodney Green dismissed the Irish economic historian George O'Brien's *Economic History of Ireland* as 'a highly unsatisfactory work ... strongly southern and protectionist in tone' that clearly ignored the phenomenon of industrialisation of Ulster, which experienced the same nominal statutory disadvantages as the rest of Ireland, but which was evidently not constrained by them (Green 1949, 176; Ó Gráda 1988, 27). Almost forty years on, it appears industrial archaeology in Ireland is predominantly northern in tone, and ostensibly ignores Irish industrialisation outside Ulster. The latter is not a criticism of the valuable work conducted by Green himself or, more recently, by McCutcheon (1980)

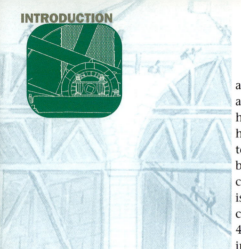

and Hamond (1991). To begin with, the vast bulk of the research into industrial archaeology in Ireland has been conducted within Northern Ireland, and while so much has been achieved in the six counties those who have participated in these achievements have increasingly been drawn to the realisation that so much more has to be done. As to ostensibly ignoring developments in the rest of Ireland, this is not a matter of choice but of the dearth of published comparable data in the Irish Republic. So in this regard circumstances have conspired to make developments in the North appear entirely isolated from those in the rest of Ireland, when in fact their influence in the nineteenth century was felt as far south as the area investigated in the present study (see below Ch. 4). The present monograph can only make a small contribution to redressing this imbalance by encouraging similar regional studies, although it is fair to say that unavailabilty of comparative studies is as much a problem in Britain, the heartland of industrial archaeological studies, as in Ireland (Palmer 1990).

The publication of Green's *The Lagan Valley 1800–1850: a local history of the Industrial Revolution* in 1949 marks the beginning of industrial archaeology in Ireland, and was one of the earliest studies of its type in these islands. Indeed, his *Industrial archaeology of County Down* (1963) was the first survey for any Irish county. In the late 1950s, however, W.A. McCutcheon embarked upon a systematic industrial archaeological study of the six counties funded by the Northern Ireland Department of Finance. The results of his fieldwork, undertaken between 1962 and 1968, complemented by an extensive documentary survey, were published in *The industrial archaeology of Northern Ireland*, (1980). The most recent area survey of Ulster is *Antrim coast and glens industrial heritage* (Hamond 1991). In the late 1960s two important studies on specific aspects of Ulster's industries were published: *The engineering industry of the north of Ireland* (Coe 1969) and *The history of water power in Ulster* (Gribbon 1969). However, no systematic survey of the greater Belfast area, where the largest concentration of industry in Ulster was to be found, was undertaken until the late 1980s. The Greater Belfast Industrial Archaeology Survey (GBIAS) was initiated by the Historic Monuments Branch of the Department of the Environment Northern Ireland and was carried out by Dr Fred Hamond and Cormac Scally. Its primary function was to compile an Industrial Archaeology Record (IAR) or inventory of industrial sites, and to provide planning guidelines for the relevant local authorities (Hamond and Scally 1988, 2). Some 1,160 sites, dating from 1830 to 1930, were identified in a 180 sq km area (ibid., 1). In recent years the National Trust in Northern Ireland has been active in restoring industrial archaeological sites such as Wellbrook Beetling Mill, Florence Court Sawmill, Castleward Corn Mill and Patterson's Spade Mill. Local interest groups and local authorities have also made important contributions to preserving the industrial heritage of Northern Ireland, as in the case of Annalong Corn Mill in County Down and Moneypenny's Lock in County Armagh.

The specific study of industrial monuments in the Republic of Ireland did not really get underway until the late 1960s and early 1970s, although in reality it was already flourishing, albeit under other names. The Irish Railway Record Society (IRRS), established in 1946, with active branches in the larger Irish cities and London, has been responsible for a great number of excellent publications on individual Irish railways, in addition to producing the *Journal of the Irish Railway Record Society*. Conservation and preservation have also figured prominently in its activities, and the establishment of an all-Ireland Steam Preservation Society has resulted in a series of ambitious restoration schemes. An abiding enthusiasm for Irish canals, coupled with a realisation of their enormous potential for amenity use and tourism, led to the establishment of the Inland Waterways Association of Ireland (IWAI), co-founded by Colonel Harry Rice and Vincent Delany in 1954 (Delany 1988, 134, 177). The IWAI has been actively involved in canal conservation projects and scored a notable success in its campaign to save the Dublin section of the Royal Canal. In addition, studies of individual Irish canals — the Grand Canal (Delany 1973) and the Ballinamore and Ballyconnell Canal (Flanagan 1972) — along with general surveys of canals in Ulster (McCutcheon 1965) and in the Republic (Delany and Delany 1966), have also been published in the David and Charles series (see also Delany 1988). Studies of the Royal Canal have also been published by Peter Clarke (1992) and Ruth Delany (1992). One of the most important technological developments in nineteenth-century Irish communications — the evolution of steamship services between Britain and Ireland — has also been covered in a two-volume work by McNeill (1969, 1971).

Unfortunately, the enthusiasm shown for railways and inland waterways in Ireland was slow to spread to other areas. In the early 1970s the Irish Society for Industrial Archaeology was established whose members (notably William Dick, Gavan Bowie and Ken Mawhinney) published a wide variety of short pieces on the more notable Irish sites in *Technology Ireland*. However, by the end of the decade, the society was defunct. The Society for Industrial Archaeology in Munster, a predominantly Cork-based society established in 1986, also sprang from promising origins but eventually met with the same fate. However, in June 1996 a new society, the Industrial Heritage Association of Ireland (IHAI) with a thirty-two county membership, concerned with the preservation and recording of the industrial heritage of Ireland, was established.

Successive governments in the Irish Republic have been slow to realise that industrial archaeology forms an important part of Ireland's historic landscape, a fact all too clearly illustrated by the inclusion of the curious AD 1700 cut-off date in previous National Monuments legislation. Under the earlier acts archaeology officially ended in the year 1700, but under the 1987 Amendment to the National Monuments Acts the Office of Public Works can now use its discretion where post-1700 sites of national importance are involved. In the 1970s An Foras Forbartha commissioned a series of county-based surveys of industrial monuments and sites in the Irish Republic, which were undertaken by Gavan Bowie. It was not until the 1980s, however, with the initiation of the Office of Public Works-sponsored Archaeological Survey of County Cork, that the Irish government became officially involved in the systematic recording of industrial sites and monuments. The recent publication of the first volumes of the Cork Archaeological Survey (Power *et al.* 1992 [vol. 1] and 1994 [vol. 2]) by the Office of Public Works, however, which include inventories of a selection of industrial archeological sites in western, eastern and southern County Cork compiled by Mary Sleeman, are an important development. Future volumes of the County Cork survey will provide the first county-based survey in the Irish Republic. The inclusion of selected industrial sites (mostly windmills) in the *Archaeological Inventory of County Wexford* (Moore 1996), is also a welcome development. A further inventory of industrial archaeological sites for County Galway is currently being prepared by Paul Duffy in conjunction with the Office of Public Works-sponsored Sites and Monuments Record (SMR) for that county. Under National Monuments legislation introduced in 1994 all archaeological sites included in OPW county inventories are now accorded statutory protection. Irish local authorities have also been involved in initiating industrial archaeological survey work. Kilkenny County Council has produced its own county-based IAR, undertaken by Dr Fred Hamond, whilst both Georgina Scally and Mary McMahon have undertaken surveys in the Dublin area.

The Department of the Environment (Northern Ireland) has played an important role in listing and scheduling industrial archaeological sites within its jurisdiction. Indeed, in

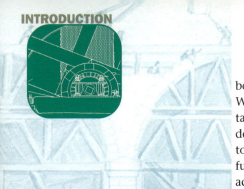

both jurisdictions important industrial archaeological sites such as Ballycopeland Windmill in Northern Ireland and Tacumshin Windmill in County Wexford, have been taken into state care, whilst the Irish and British governments have co-operated on the development of the Erne–Shannon waterway. The large-scale development of heritage tourism in the Irish Republic, fuelled by European Reconstruction and Development funding during the 1980s, enabled a number of important sites to be restored and made accessible to the public. Again, the implementation of many such schemes such as the Blennerville Windmill in County Kerry and Ballincollig Gunpowder Mills in County Cork, could not have come about without the active involvement of local authorities, private interest groups and state-sponsored bodies such as FÁS.

The corpus of published work relating to industrial archaeology in Ireland has increased substantially within the last decade or so. Apart from the works cited above, monographs have also been recently published on aspects of Irish extractive industries (e.g. Dublin granite, Ryan 1992; the West Cork copper mines, R.A. Williams 1991), manufacturing industries (e.g. Locke's distillery, Bielenberg 1993; Dundalk locomotive works, McQuillan 1993), transport and communications (e.g. Irish stone bridges, O'Keeffe and Simington 1991) and utility industries (Irish gas, O'Sullivan 1987; electricity supply, Manning and McDowell 1984; electric tramways, McGrath 1981). Recent legislation regularising the maintenance of local authority archives, many of which are also repositories of important business archives, will also facilitate access to important documentary materials. The establishment of the Irish Engineering Archive in Dublin and the Technological Heritage Archive in University College Galway, are further welcome developments, as is the publication of an excellent guide to the archives of the Irish Board of Works (Lohan 1994). The Mining History Society of Ireland has also been recently established, to cater for a growing interest in the development of Irish mines and their history.

There is, in short, a growing interest in Irish industrial history and archaeology. More recent developments in the 1980s and 1990s have provided a solid base not only for the academic study of industrial archaeology, but also for a wider appreciation for historic Irish industrial buildings and landscapes. As the established groups which cater for the interests of canal and railway enthusiasts clearly demonstrate, these sites have long held a fascination for the public at large — long before they were considered as important archaeological monuments in their own right.

In the text which follows the Sites and Monuments Record number for individual sites, along with features associated with them, will feature as bold-faced numbers in brackets: e.g. St Patrick's Mills (**483**). Where a site involves a large number of buildings or in the case of a linear feature such as a railway, associated features have been assigned suffix numbers e.g. Penrose Quay Station (Great Southern and Western Railway) (**069.1**). If a site's function changes through time, the succeeding use retains the original number e.g. Millfield Distillery (**096**), Cork Spinning and Weaving Company (**096**).

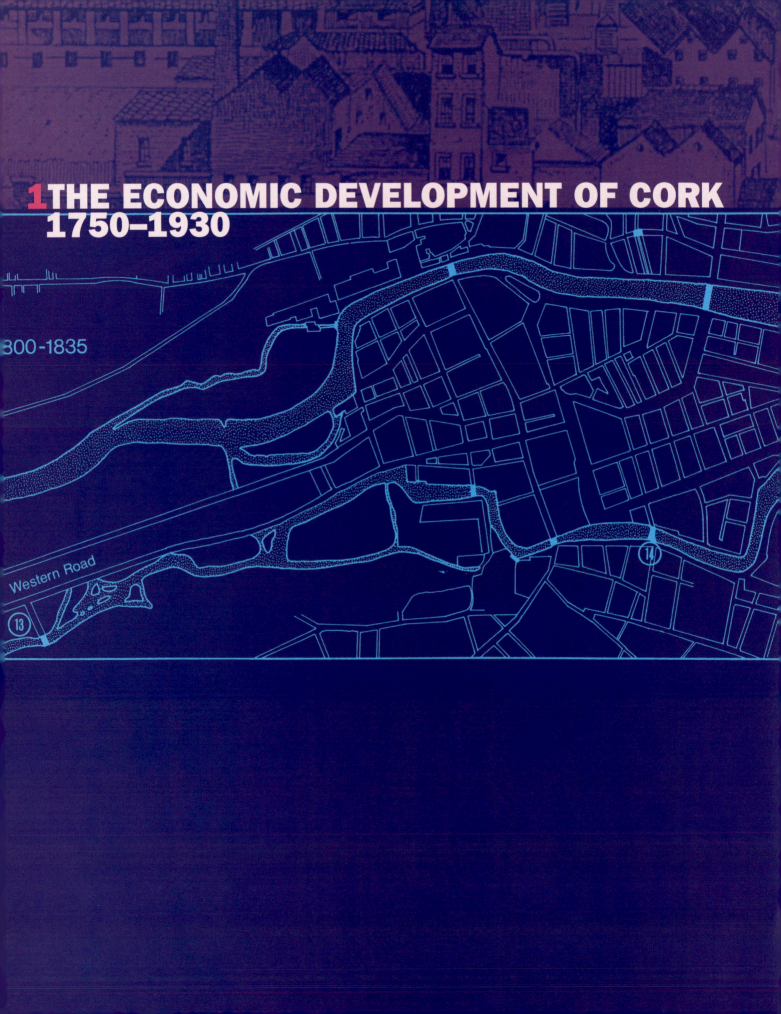

1 THE ECONOMIC DEVELOPMENT OF CORK 1750–1930

ECONOMIC DEVELOPMENT

1

CORN EXCHANGE

GAS WORKS

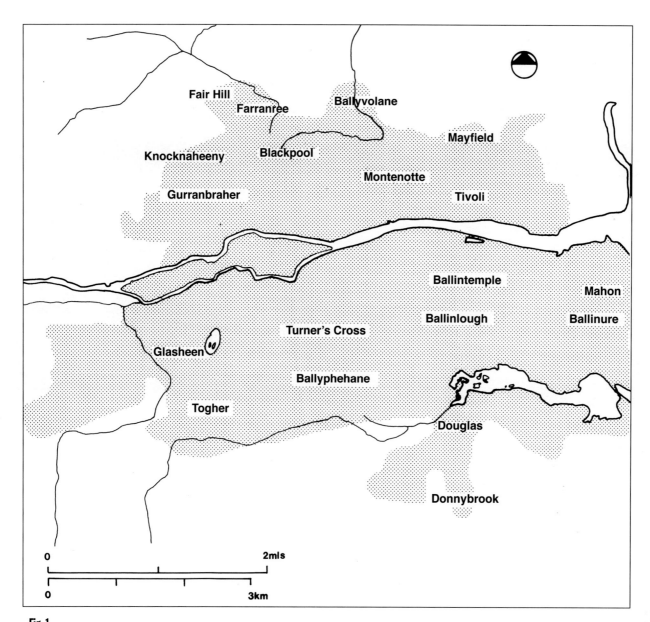

Fig. 1

The survey area.

The origins of the city of Cork lie in the early seventh century, with the establishment of a monastic settlement on the south channel of the river Lee. Between the ninth and the tenth centuries this settlement was drawn into the extensive Scandinavian trade network, and by the twelfth century its population appears to have comprised native Irish and Hiberno-Vikings. By this period the trade of the embryonic city and port of Cork was effectively controlled by the McCarthy kings of Desmond. The fortified town was captured by the Anglo-Normans in 1177, who enclosed it with a wall and defensive towers and created a truly medieval city with quaysides, market and main thoroughfare. For the greater part of the later medieval period, however, Cork was a colonial outpost. Nonetheless, its port was already beginning to serve as an outlet for the agricultural produce of the region, and by the late medieval period ships from Cork were provisioning the English army at Gascony and Bayonne (Rynne 1993, 55). During the sixteenth and seventeenth centuries a nationally important trade in provisions was beginning to become established at Cork. This laid the foundations for its first, although ultimately unsuccessful, steps towards large-scale industrialisation.

At the end of the eighteenth century the port of Cork appeared destined for great things. As the second city of Ireland, Cork's burgeoning trade and industrial development had by this period already eclipsed that of its nearest rivals in the south-west, Waterford, Kinsale and Youghal. Its main textile industries were of national — and in at least one instance international — importance, whilst the largest porter brewery and the largest distillery in Ireland had also been established there. The quality of Cork butter was assured by one of the most innovative and rigorously enforced systems of quality control then known in Europe which laid the foundations for what became the largest butter market in the world. Cork's exports of beef and pig-meat were also of national importance, whilst the non-edible by-products of the slaughterhouses provided the raw material for a plethora of allied trades. But as we shall see below, the city's success as a port was too closely aligned with the provision trade. Foreign markets for Irish provisions had already begun to decline by the turn of the eighteenth century, and the establishment of large industrial units within the city and its immediate environs generated too few spin-off effects to provide a firm base for future industrial development. The optimism of contemporary accounts of Cork's foreign trade is laid bare by the subsequent lack of industrial concentration in the nineteenth century. Brewing, distilling, its principal textile industries, sailcloth manufacture, linen and woollens, along with a number of other important local industries such as shipbuilding, engineering and gunpowder manufacture, were to experience mixed fortunes in the period after 1800.

THE EIGHTEENTH CENTURY

The expansion of Cork's trade in the eighteenth century cannot be simply explained by geographical advantages. Human factors, such as the changing patterns of English and Irish overseas trade, and the military and economic advantages accruing to England from its continued development, are also known to have been important. Nonetheless, Cork harbour was endowed with considerable natural advantages. The lower harbour could easily accommodate the largest transatlantic convoy or naval squadron. From the American War of Independence onwards, British naval facilities became increasingly concentrated in the lower harbour, and between 1777 and 1779 it was claimed that around £90,000 was spent on improvements and on naval repair work at Passage West (Dickson 1977, 527). Britain's American war and the later Napoleonic campaigns were a source of considerable financial gain for Cork merchants. Each of these episodes not only

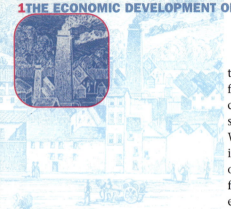

tended to concentrate the greater bulk of transatlantic trade on the port of Cork, but further served to underline the strategic importance of the harbour to the Admiralty. The city of Cork itself, while constructed on a series of reclaimed tidal marshes, was not subject to the same physical restraints of the rival ports of Kinsale, Youghal and Waterford. The approaches from the harbour to the city quaysides were neglected well into the nineteenth century, but there were, technically at least, no physical restraints on the expansion of the city's quaysides (ibid., 424). The fact that Cork was far enough from Dublin not to be threatened by direct competition from the capital city, while close enough to important markets in Britain was also an important factor.

By the end of the seventeenth century Irish provisions, principally salted beef, butter and pork, had become an important factor in the maintenance of the West Indian plantations (Clemens 1976, 214; Nash 1985). Cork and Dublin had by this time already become the most important Irish ports engaged in this trade. The expansion of this trade was a direct result of the preference of British shipowners for victualling their ships at Irish ports, and then transporting this to the continent and the American colonies (Mannion 1988, 210). In the eighteenth century the vessels involved were English owned and registered (Cullen 1968, 21–2), and these were assembled in important naval centres such as Plymouth to be escorted, under convoy, to their destinations in Europe or in the American colonies (O'Sullivan 1937, 148). Both Cork and Waterford each exported the same general range of provisions (Mannion 1988, 212). The difference in the level of trade generated by these ports, however, was considerable. Cork was the seat of the Admiralty's victualling agent in Ireland and its pre-eminence in the Irish provision trade as a whole led to the accreditation of both Spanish and Portuguese consular officials to Cork (Cullen 1968, 16). Furthermore, in certain years Cork's tonnage was in excess of that of Dublin (ibid., 17). Yet although this was a somewhat infrequent phenomenon (and by and large Cork could not hope to realistically compete with Dublin), Cork's outright domination of certain aspects of Irish foreign trade in the same period cannot be disputed. In the first half of the eighteenth century the volume of beef exported from Cork appears to have exceeded the combined total for all the other Irish ports (O'Sullivan 1937, 150). At least one contemporary observer referred to Cork as 'the slaughterhouse of Ireland' (Bush 1769, 42; O'Sullivan 1937, 148), whilst the continental trade in pork was almost entirely controlled by Cork exporters (O'Sullivan 1937, 166). Cork merchants also dominated the export and re-export trade in herring. Imported herrings from Sweden and Scotland were packed in Cork for re-export to the West Indies, the total Cork exports for which in the years 1766–77 accounted for more than half the total Irish volume (O'Sullivan 1937, 170–72).

The high salt content of Cork butter, which was to prove progressively less palatable to English consumers in the nineteenth century, combined with a high degree of expertise in packing it, enabled this distinctively Cork product to be transported over considerable distances in all climates. The secret of the early success of the Cork Butter Market was a rigidly enforced system of quality control. In 1770 inspectors appointed by a committee of Cork butter merchants, constituted in the previous year, began to grade the butter passing through the market in accordance with its quality. Further officers of the committee were employed to inspect each empty cask before it was dispatched to the farmer which, upon its return, was further inspected to ensure that it had been satisfactorily packed. Each cask was branded in accordance with its allotted grade. In order to ensure that casks bearing counterfeit Cork brands were not shipped out, additional inspectors patrolled the city's quaysides. The market itself was also open around the clock to obviate any difficulties arising from unforeseen problems in delivery (ibid., 263–5). Cork Butter Market became the largest in the world, and the system which evolved in the late eighteenth century was to ensure its continued success well into the nineteenth century (Donnelly 1971).

The provision trade enriched the Cork merchant community, and while finance was never really in short supply, Cork entrepreneurs were primarily merchants and not industrialists. In both Dublin and Cork were to be found the largest banking and discount facilities in the Kingdom. Merchants involved in the Cork butter trade were often required to make advance payments to farmers, and ready access to loan facilities was an important advantage unavailable in other south-western ports (Cullen 1968, 13). In theory, at least, these same facilities were available to prospective industrialists. The complexion of Cork business activity, however, tended to favour the provision trade, the existence of which generated many spin-off industries. But as we shall now see, this in no way inhibited the creation of more important industrial concerns within the city and its immediate environs. None of these were directly aligned with the all-important provision trade, but all were created to avail of the commercial infrastructure created by it.

With a population of about 40,000 by the middle of the eighteenth century, increasing to 52,000 by 1793 (albeit mostly unskilled and often unemployed), Cork had a reasonably large working population ready at hand (Dickson 1977). The population of Dublin by the mid-eighteenth century was over three times that of Cork (Dickson 1983, 179). Nonetheless, the ocean-going trade of Cork, which only in certain sectors exceeded that of Dublin, was by no means a reflection of Cork's much smaller size. Immediate access to the port of Cork was probably the main factor in the location of industry within the immediate environs of the city during the eighteenth century. Indeed, while certain large industrial concerns such as brewing and distilling were primarily geared towards a localised market, most of the others (particularly the textile industries) manufactured for export.

Industries in which a large degree of mechanisation was involved needed power, and this, for the vast majority of eighteenth-century Cork industries, meant water power. In the later 1700s many of the tidal marshes upon which the city had been built were in the process of being reclaimed, and the passage of the river Lee through the city was being increasingly confined to a small number of larger channels. The effectiveness of the water flowing through these channels, and particularly of those flowing through the city itself, provided no great inducement to the establishment of water-powered mills, as the tidal reaches of the harbour extended to (and slightly beyond) the built-up area of the city itself. In the medieval and post-medieval periods a small number of grain mills were built on these channels, and it seems quite likely that many of these were tide mills. A water-powered manufactory, however, required a much larger and more dependable source of water; of a magnitude which the tidal channels of the river Lee could not conceivably accommodate. Thus the water-powered industries which utilised the river Lee within the city were few, and all were sited to the west to extract water from stretches of the river beyond its tidal reaches. In consequence, large units of mechanised industry tended to be sited within the immediate environs of the city adjacent to non-estuarine stretches of the river Lee's main tributaries.

From the second half of the eighteenth century onwards the Bride and Glen Rivers (which converged to form the Kiln River in Blackpool), flowing southwards through the northern suburbs of the city, were impounded to power a number of industrial processes. The Blarney, Glasheen and Curraheen Rivers to the north-west and west of the city were also harnessed to serve large industrial units. Only with the arrival of steam power in Cork, in the late eighteenth century, did the location of mechanised industries within

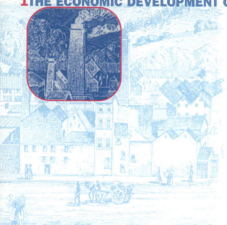

the confines of the city itself become a viable option. In all such cases immediate access to the Welsh coal discharged at the city's quaysides (which reduced transportation costs) doubtless provided a further stimulus to (if not the rationale behind) establishing steam-powered industries within the city.

In the second half of the eighteenth century the woollen, linen and cotton industries established around Cork were becoming nationally important. The setting up of these industries in outlying areas such as Blarney and Douglas provided the focus of later settlements which were, in every sense, 'industrial villages'. Cork county was by this stage the centre of the Irish woollen trade. The Lane family, who had established a large manufactory at Riverstown in the early nineteenth century, and who had created a near monopoly of the manufacture of army clothing, employed upwards on 1,000 workers in their Riverstown and Cork City works (Dickson 1977, 571). The O'Mahony family, who were later to become synonymous with the Blarney tweed industry, also established themselves in the Blackpool area of the city in the 1790s (Dickson 1977, 571; O'Mahony 1984, 84). Approximately one half to two-thirds of Ireland's supply of combed wool was passing through the hands of the city's worsted manufacturers by the early years of the nineteenth century (Dickson 1977, 571). This in itself is a good index of the success of the industry in Cork, but is one that was to a certain extent equalled by those engaged in linen manufacture.

The establishment of linen manufacture within the city dates to the early decades of the eighteenth century. To contemporaries and many later commentators, the Cork industry has been associated with the Besnard family at Douglas. With the development of the port and the subsequent growth in the manufacture of ship's chandlery, the establishment of sailcloth manufacture would appear to have been a natural progression. From its origins in around 1726 the Douglas factory grew to become the largest of its type in Europe. The Besnard family had already acquired the controlling interest in the Douglas sailcloth factory by the early 1780s, which by the turn of the nineteenth century became the first linen factory in Ireland to operate water-powered spindles (ibid., 509).

There were at least two bleach greens within the city in the eighteenth century. One of these was established by Thomas Lee in 1755 near the Pouladuff Road, and survived into the twentieth century (Collins 1958, 101), the other by Francis Price, appears to have become defunct upon his death in 1771 (Dickson 1977, 509). As early as 1769 at least one linen factory established at Blarney by St John Jeffries (through whose endeavours the village of Blarney came into existence) was in operation (O'Mahony 1984, 77). At least two bleach greens were in existence at Blarney by 1782 (ibid., 79), although by the end of the century two of the three main linen concerns established there had failed (Dickson 1977, 594).

In 1755 there were two factories within the city manufacturing both linen and cotton goods (O'Sullivan 1937, 190). The manufacture of cotton was reputedly introduced into Cork City and county in the early 1750s by French prisoners of war. However, the substantial operation begun by Henry and James Sadleir in 1781 drew on the expertise of skilled workers who, along with machines, were directly imported from the Manchester cotton industry. The Sadleir brothers operated 1,606 spindles at their city premises, whilst outside the city at Glasheen a former linen mill became the centre of their finishing and printing operation. In all, the Sadleirs claimed to employ around 1,000 people (Dickson 1978, 104). Important enterprises were also begun at Blarney by Edward O'Donoghue in 1783 and by Thomas Deaves in 1787 (Dickson 1977, 594). By the end of the eighteenth century the various textile industries established in Cork were already in serious decline (Bielenberg 1991). Thomas Deaves was declared bankrupt in 1791, although by the end of the century he had managed to re-establish a foothold in the bleaching end of the business (O'Mahony 1984, 80), whilst the Sadleir brothers enterprise collapsed in the year 1801 with debts of £38,000 (Dickson 1978, 106). The linen industry throughout southern Ireland as a whole experienced a serious decline in the years 1771–3 (O'Sullivan 1937, 191). Sailcloth manufacture was continued in Douglas, but throughout the county the industry declined to the extent that the growing of flax had to be effectively re-introduced into certain areas towards the middle of the nineteenth century (see Ch. 4). The city's woollen and linen industries were to a certain extent revitalised in the second half of the nineteenth century, by which time existing market conditions favoured their success. For the most part, however, the large-scale industrialisation and consequent prosperity which the eighteenth-century textile industries had seemed to promise was not carried over to the twentieth century.

During the eighteenth century the brewing and distilling industries established a firm foothold within the city. A company of brewers was established in 1743 (O'Sullivan 1937, 197), and by the end of the century Cork had a total of 29 breweries, slightly more than half the number then operating in Dublin (Malcolm 1986, 22). Beer was a relatively expensive drink, but beer taxation was abolished in 1794, and its popularity increased (ibid., 25–8). Some years before this the citizens of Cork were beginning to show a marked preference for London porter; an English visitor in the late 1770s found occasion to remark that its consumption in Cork was 'more common than in any part of England outside London' (Campbell 1778, 184; Dickson 1977, 603). However, other contemporaries such as William Dyott were appalled at the quality of the Cork-produced porter which was, in his opinion, 'the very worst'. Cork porter drinkers apparently found few grounds for dissenting from Dyott's conclusion, for there appears to have been little popular support tor the restriction of English beer imports (Dickson 1977, 605). The output of the largest 15 breweries in the 1770s was relatively small (ibid., 604) and, if we are to take contemporary accounts at face value, of poor quality. Towards the end of the century, however, the units of production tended to be larger. Beamish and Crawford's porter brewery, established in 1792, became the largest in Ireland by the early years of the nineteenth century. Nonetheless, the main Cork breweries in the late eighteenth century were locked into an extremely localised market, and were unable to focus attention on the national market (and thus attain sustained growth) until the establishment of a national rail network in the nineteenth century.

The first large distillery in the city was built on the quayside adjacent to the North Mall in 1779, and from about 1782 onwards was to be controlled by the Wise family. Three further large distilling enterprises were, along with three smaller ones, established between the years 1789 and 1796 (Dickson 1977, 609–10). By 1796 the total for the city was ten, which accounted for more than four fifths of the Cork region's still capacity: two of these were the largest in Ireland, each with a capacity of 2,000 gallons (O'Sullivan 1937, 247; Dickson 1977, 610). Early in the nineteenth century the proprietor of the Crosses Green distillery, Thomas Walker, is said to have been 'the greatest distiller in the kingdom' (Wakefield 1812, vol. 1, 732; O'Sullivan 1937, 247). Indeed, as early as 1808 the Crosses Green distillery was considered to be the largest in Ireland, and was certainly the first to utilise steam power (see Ch. 3). Yet Cork's commercial success in the latter half of the eighteenth and in the early decades of the nineteenth centuries could provide no solid foundation for industrial success. Indeed, Cork was never to become an industrial city (Murphy 1981, 126) and the aftermath of the Napoleonic Wars served only to highlight the fragility of the port of Cork's commercial and industrial base.

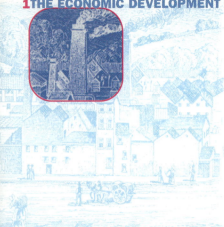

THE NINETEENTH CENTURY

The Napoleonic Wars were boom times for the port of Cork. 'Considerable fortunes' wrote Thomas Crofton-Croker (1798–1854):

> ...have been amassed during the late war by some speculative individuals, with much credit to themselves. The convenience of Cork harbour in time of war rendered it the rendezvous where all vessels trading with the new world assembled for convoy, and the victualling of such fleets alone created an extensive consumption for its staple commodities (Crofton-Croker 1824, 203).

But in aftermath of the war in Europe came the end of the lucrative contracts for provisions and munitions and 'few cities', Crofton-Croker remarked, 'felt the transition to peace more severely, being without manufactures, and solely dependent on trade for the support of its inhabitants'. 'To those who remember what the city was previous to 1815', he opined, 'its present appearance is extremely cheerless' (ibid., 203–4). For at least one industry in the locality, the Ballincollig Gunpowder Mills (then under the control of the Board of Ordnance), the end of hostilities brought about its almost immediate closure in 1815. In other areas the decline, though gradual, was irreversible. The provision trade was seriously undermined by the end of government contracts, which was followed by a general depression in British and Irish agriculture (O'Brien 1993, 704). However, the more important food-processing industries such as brewing and distilling continued to develop apace. When the commercial clauses of the Act of Union began to be implemented after 1824, English textiles were dumped on the Irish market, with truly devastating consequences for the Cork-based textile industries (Murphy 1980, 32; O'Brien 1993, 704–5; Cronin 1993, 737). The failure of Cork's textile industries to adopt new technology also contributed significantly to their decline in the early nineteenth century (Bielenberg 1991, 118–19). Indeed, the manufacture of linen yarn within the immediate environs of the city was not re-attempted until the 1860s, whilst the fortunes of the city's woollen industry was not successfully revived until the closing decades of the nineteenth century.

The expansion of the city's principal food-processing, engineering, shipbuilding, tanning and gunpowder industries in the period 1780–1840 has recently been charted by Andy Bielenberg (1991), who has also documented their decline in the second half of the nineteenth century. Yet despite some notable successes, large-scale industrialisation did not occur within the survey area, whilst rapid technological change in some areas (e.g. the woollen textile industry) was equally matched by technological stagnation in others (e.g. tanning) and even active technological regression as in the distilling industry. Resistance to technological modernisation has been recently cited as one of the principal reasons for Cork's poor industrial performance during the nineteenth century (ibid., 118–24). There was certainly no shortage of capital in the region with which to modernise (ibid., 132), and this is in no small way reflected in the success of the city's brewing and woollen industries. Even the region's gunpowder manufacturing industry, whose base was eroded by more powerful chemically manufactured alternatives, was no laggard in terms of the technology used to manufacture gunpowder.

But it is all too easy to exaggerate the extent to which technological stagnation affected industrial growth in the Cork region, especially if one considers that the rate of technological change within this region during the nineteenth century, in certain key areas, compares quite favourably with that of contemporary England. This is particularly true where industrial motive power is concerned. The early technological leadership of Cork City distilleries in the adoption of steam engines (generally as supplements to water-powered prime movers), for example, was of national importance. Three of the four Boulton and Watt rotative beam engines known to have been installed in Irish distilleries before 1812 were in Cork City.[1] This was, of course, a fair reflection of the Cork region's importance within the Irish distilling industry at that time and, in the main, Cork distillers kept abreast of technological changes within the industry up until the latter half of the nineteenth century. Indeed, some of the earliest patent stills, which included the earliest recorded example of a Saintmarc still in Ireland, were operated in Cork City distilleries. Compound and horizontal steam engines were quite common in steam-powered flour mills within the city by the 1850s. The practice of compounding beam engines was frequently employed in Cork City steam engines around this time whilst in the period 1857–61 there were at least three horizontal engines at work in flour mills within the survey area. By way of contrast, the earliest recorded example of a horizontal engine in a Yorkshire textile mill dates to *c.* 1864–5 (Giles and Goodall 1992, 135) whilst similar engines in the cotton mills of the greater Manchester area did not become common until the 1870s (Williams and Farnie 1992, 114). However, Cork's early successes were not sustained, and in the second half of the nineteenth century both Dublin and Cork were eclipsed by Belfast.

Irish millwrights and iron foundries played an enormously important role in the development and adoption of the water turbine in both Britain and Ireland. In Cork, largely through contacts in the Irish linen industry, local foundries were manufacturing water turbines for use in local industry by the early 1850s. At least four water turbines were employed throughout County Cork by 1855, which included one of the earliest-known Jonval turbines used in either Britain or Ireland, manufactured by the city of Cork's Hive Iron Foundry (see Ch. 5). In qualitative terms, therefore, technological change in important areas of Cork industry during the nineteenth century certainly did not lag behind similar developments in England.

Yet the Cork region, like so many others within Ireland during the nineteenth century failed to industrialise. Other factors such as a general erosion in the region's economic base caused by a declining home market, shrinking population after the Great Famine of the 1840s and its geographical isolation from important English industrial regions all militated against the industrialisation of the greater Cork area, as Bielenberg has recently documented (1991, 124–6). Indeed the general lack of large-scale industry within the survey area by the end of the nineteenth century was not so much a symptom of general decline as of the simple fact that Cork had never, at any stage of its development, been an important industrial city (Murphy 1981, 128). In 1841 some 40% of the males employed within the city were engaged in manufacturing; in 1901 this figure was 19%. A similar decline is discernible in the employment figures for women (ibid., 127) — and all this in a period when the population always outran the amount of gainful employment available to it (Murphy 1980, 28).

Even by working to its strengths the Cork region was unable, in the long term, to develop industries which could successfully exploit the raw materials produced within its agricultural hinterland. In the 1860s and 1870s the Cork Butter Market controlled around 30% of the Irish butter trade (Donnelly 1971, 130). However, Cork butter failed to compete with butterine and factory-blended butter imported into England (its main market) from Europe. As in the case of the local distilling industry the Cork Butter Market failed to respond to market conditions and its strict regulations, formerly a hallmark of its quality, became an excessive force of restraint on innovation (Donnelly 1971 and 1975).

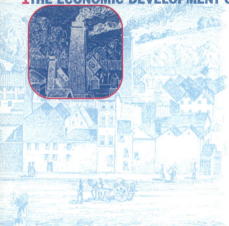

As late as the early 1870s large ships, owing to the undeveloped nature of the approaches to the city's quaysides, were forced to tranship part of their cargoes at Passage West. Despite the best efforts of the Cork Harbour Commissioners, the single most important artery of communication linking the city with its international markets remained underdeveloped for the greater part of the nineteenth century, adding significantly to the cost of importing goods into Cork. Furthermore, vital physical links between the city's main railway terminals were not brought about until the early twentieth century.

There can be little doubt that the nineteenth-century development of the port of Belfast, which overcame similar difficulties to those experienced by shipping in contemporary Cork, was critical to its industrial success. Belfast enjoyed the advantage of access to the open sea via the Pool of Garmoyle, but did not have a superb natural harbour like that at Cork. Nonetheless, improved access to the port and quayside development, which allowed its shipbuilding yards to develop with few restrictions, proved essential to the development of heavy industry in the Belfast region (Sweetman 1988).

THE EARLY TWENTIETH CENTURY

By the early decades of the twentieth century the port of Cork served mainly as a conduit for imported goods. Local industry had, by and large, failed to rise to the challenge of foreign competition, and while industries such as porter brewing and textiles continued to expand, the essential fabric of local industry had worn very thin. Even the establishment of the Ford tractor works at the Marina in 1919 was largely a philanthropic gesture by the founder of the Ford empire. 'Cork', wrote Henry Ford in 1926, had 'no real industry' (Anon. 1977).

During the First World War the city's textile and engineering industries received a temporary boost. But in the aftermath of the war and immediately before Partition, the city's textile and food-processing industries continued to be the main employers but, as in Dublin, the work force in manufacturing industries had effectively halved in the second half of the nineteenth century. Local initiative in the form of the Cork Industrial Development Association, established in 1902 to promote Cork industry, could do little to reverse this trend. The entire Irish economy was depressed after the boom years of the Great War, although it was still very closely tied to Britain, its principal export market (Daly 1992, 3–13). Even the presence of the Ford Motor Works at Cork, which in 1923 was employing up to 1,600 workers, was not enough to attract further large-scale foreign investment (Jacobson 1977, 55).

Nonetheless, the more important city industries in the period under review, such as brewing, distilling and bacon curing, followed by certain textile industries were, in varying degrees, able to survive up until recent times. Murphy's and Beamish and Crawford's Breweries continue to make important contributions to the city's economy whilst the flour-milling industry enjoyed a revival, but other industries such as shipbuilding, gunpowder manufacture and tanning have long since disappeared. Many important industries with eighteenth-century roots were severely battered by adverse international economic conditions which prevailed in the aftermath of the Napoleonic Wars. The impact of the commerical clauses of the Act of Union in the later 1820s, the Famine of the 1840s, along with localised effects of Father Matthew's Temperance Campaign, all took a heavy toll on Cork industries. However, as only Belfast could lay claim to being a Victorian industrial city, Cork, when compared to Dublin and even smaller towns like Waterford and Limerick, was by no means exceptional in failing to work to its strengths.

2 EXTRACTIVE INDUSTRIES

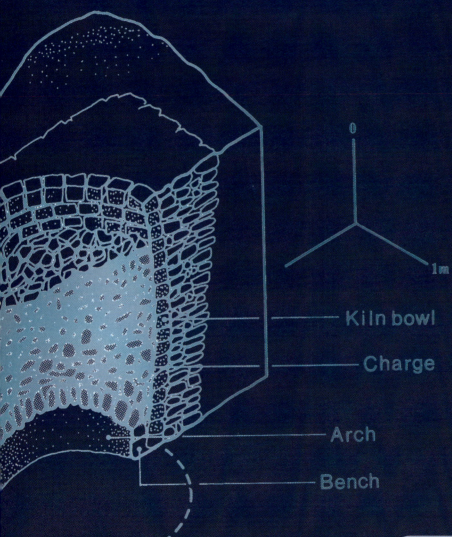

0

1m

Kiln bowl

Charge

Arch

Bench

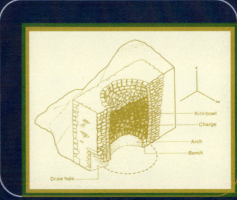

EXTRACTIVE INDUSTRIES

2

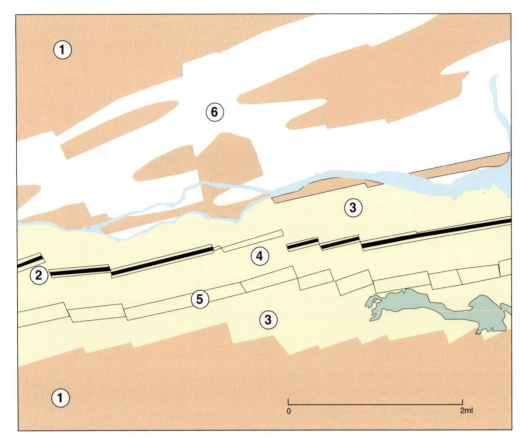

Fig. 2

Geology of the city and its environs.
1 Ballyandreen Formation, green and grey sandstone. 2 Cork 'red marble' Formation (indicated by black line). 3 'Walsortian' Formation, massive pale grey limestone (biomicrite). 4 Little Island Formation, massive pale grey limestone (biomicrite). 5 Lough Mahon Formation, poorly bedded grey limestone. 6 Kiltorcan Formation, green, grey and red sandstone, purple and red siltstone (after Geological Map of Cork District, UCC 1988).

Fig. 3 BELOW

Distribution of main quarries, brickfields and sandpits in survey area.

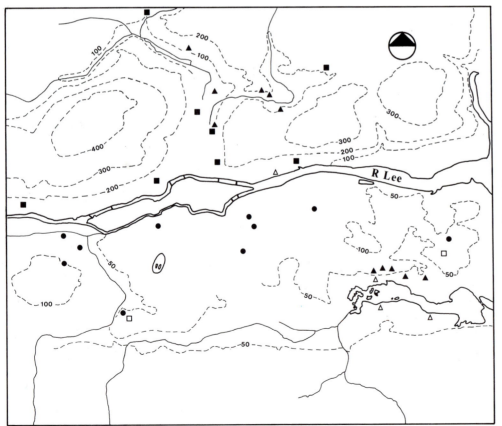

- ● *Limestone quarry*
- ■ *Sandstone quarry*
- △ *Brickfield*
- ▲ *Gravel pit*
- ▢ *Sand pit*

With the exception of certain non-ferrous ores such as copper, County Cork, like the greater part of Ireland, was poorly endowed with mineral resources. It did, however, possess some of the finest building stones in Ireland, which continue to be quarried (although rarely for architectural purposes) throughout the Cork Harbour region to the present day. Clay was also quarried for the manufacture of pottery, tile and brick within the greater Cork area. For the most part, however, these were relatively small-scale industries attuned to localised markets. Certain industries, indeed, such as the brickyards of the Douglas slobs, were seasonal in nature, and by the early decades of the twentieth century, brickmaking around Cork Harbour had ceased.

METALLIFEROUS ORES

From about 1810 onwards copper ores were mined in the west Cork region at locations such as Berehaven/Allihies, Ballydehob and Cappagh, and were shipped directly by schooner to Swansea.[1] In national terms the output of the west Cork copper mines was by no means insignificant, but the economic impact of this activity on Cork City was minimal. Indeed, this was the case with all mining activity involving either metallic ores or mineral fuels in the Cork area during the eighteenth and nineteenth centuries. West Cork mine owners such as John Cavallin Puxley preferred to order their steam plant from English manufacturers such as Harvey and Co. of Hale in Cornwall (Williams 1991, 70) and the Neath Abbey Iron Co. in Wales (Ince 1984, 103, 105). Norwegian conifers were also imported for timbering the mines through west Cork ports and the only industry within the environs of the city to really benefit from the west Cork mining activity was Ballincollig Gunpowder Mills (Williams 1991, 75).[2] Barytes (Barium Sulphate), which was used in the manufacture of rubber, paper, paint, pottery and as a filler in linoleum, began to be mined in the Bantry district from the mid-1850s onwards. During this period the Bantry district was the largest producer of barytes in these islands, but again there were virtually no economic benefits for the port of Cork, the barytes being processed near the site and eventually shipped from a jetty near Dunmanus Bay directly to Liverpool, London and Glasgow (Cole 1922, 17; O'Brien 1994a, 17). Similarly, other non-ferrous metals such as lead ore (argentiferous galena), which was mined at Ringabella near Cork Harbour as early as the 1750s,[3] were also extracted during the nineteenth century without bringing any lasting economic benefits to the port of Cork. (Lewis 1837, vol. 2, 639; Cole 1922, 128; Power 1994, 350).

COAL

In the first half of the eighteenth century coal was discovered in the north of the county at Dromagh near Kanturk (Smith 1750, vol. 1, 294). The coal pits in the Kanturk area formed part of the Munster coalfield, an anthracite area, where the coal seams which had originally been laid horizontally, were thrown up vertically by later geological movement. This activity had also twisted and contorted the coal measures and made them both difficult and expensive to work.[4] Nonetheless, in the early eighteenth century the discovery of this coal raised such expectations that the construction of a canal which was to link the Kanturk coalfield with the River Blackwater — and ultimately with the sea at Youghal — was begun in 1755 under the supervision of William Ockendon. However, only a short section between Mallow and Lombardstown was ever built and the canal never reached the Dromagh colliery (Jackson 1987, 22–9). By the early years of the nineteenth century this section of canal appears to have been defunct. In view of Richard Griffith's improvements to the local road network during the 1820s, the

likelihood is that the transportation of any coal raised in the area during this period was by road. In 1853, the opening of the Killarney Junction Railway linking Killarney with Mallow and, ultimately, with the Dublin–Cork section of the Great Southern and Western Railway, brought a national rail link within two miles of the Dromagh collieries (Murray and McNeill 1976, 28). The Mining Company of Ireland's Duhallow Colliery was adjacent to the Rathcoole siding of the Killarney line in 1882,[5] but despite the accessibility of such an important national rail link — a service which the majority of other Irish coalfields could not avail of as late as 1922 — the development of the Kanturk coalfield never expanded to serve a truly national market.[6]

Indeed, the economic effects of the Kanturk coalfield, like its counterparts throughout Ireland, were very localised. Apart from the difficulties often encountered in mining coal in Ireland, most Irish coalfields were poorly served by transit facilities. In consequence, coal and *culm* (anthracitic slack) were generally only utilised by industries within about a 20 mile radius of a coalfield for activities such as lime-burning or malting, in forges and as domestic fuel. Nonetheless, within a very short time after their discovery, pits in the locality appear to have been supplying coal and culm to the city of Cork.[7] Coal from the Kilkenny field was also imported into the city of Cork,[8] but most of the coal used by the city's industries during the nineteenth and early twentieth centuries was imported from either South Wales or Scotland.[9]

QUARRYING

The earliest stone buildings uncovered by archaeological excavation within the city date to the late thirteenth century, a period during which (particularly when the city walls were under construction) a number of limestone and sandstone quarries are likely to have been opened within the immediate environs of the city. The rock on the north bank of the river is almost exclusively red and green sandstone, whilst that on the south bank is of the finest quality limestone. Not surprisingly, the architecture of the city over many centuries has tended to include an attractive mixture of both. The slob mud of the Lee and Douglas estuaries has also been used for brickmaking from at least the late eighteenth century, and this also (but to a much lesser extent) has been a characteristic of certain Cork buildings.

In the main, the public buildings of Cork City, built during the eighteenth and nineteenth centuries, were built of limestone quarried either within the immediate environs of the city or within the greater Cork Harbour area. Many of the bridges constructed within the survey area and, indeed, the city's imposing and extensive nineteenth-century quaysides were also built of limestone. The availability of good-quality sandstone also led to a distinctive polychrome style, characteristic of both industrial and domestic buildings. Stressed quoins, when employed on multistorey buildings, tend to be of limestone, whilst in more formal buildings, built of dressed sandstone, limestone was nearly always used for more ornamental features such as window mouldings and tracery. The vast majority of the eighteenth- and early nineteenth-century buildings within the survey area were built of rubble stone either randomly laid (i.e. without any particular order or direction), brought to courses (levelled up to form courses) or laid in regular courses. More formal buildings were finished with *ashlar* masonry, in which either blocks of finely dressed stone, or thinner slabs (used to face brickwork or rubblestone masonry) were laid in regular, finely pointed courses.

Limestone

The main lower carboniferous limestone formation within the survey area is situated immediately to the south of the river Lee. It is a massive pale grey carboniferous limestone, which forms part of a formation extending in an east-west band across Cork Harbour (Fig. 2). All of the main limestone quarries described below, including the Carrigmore, Diamond, Rocksavage, Windmill Road, Gillabbey and Deanrock quarries (Fig. 3) were situated on this formation. There are two relatively thin bands of this formation within the environs of the city which are separated by an east-west band of limestone of the Little Island formation which was exploited at the Lawn Quarry in Ballinlough.

A thin band of the Cork 'red marble' formation (a well-bedded, red coarse-grained breccio conglomerate) also extends across the survey area, but is only known to have been quarried at Boreenamanna (Kinahan 1889, 135). The principal Cork red marble[10] quarries within Cork county, however, were at Little Island in Cork Harbour, Johnstown near Fermoy, near Midleton and near Buttevant (Kinahan 1889, 135; Coakley 1919, 64). Little Island 'reds' were used in the Liverpool and Manchester exchanges and in St John's College, Cambridge, whilst Little Island and Fermoy 'reds' were also used in St Finbarr's Cathedral (Coakley 1919, 64). Marble from Churchtown and Little Island was also used in the balustrades of Manchester City Hall.[11] In 1777 amethysts were discovered in a limestone quarry on the Blackrock Road, which subsequently became known as the 'Diamond Quarry' (Tuckey 1837, 175). Crofton-Croker (1824, 215) described these as being of 'an inferior quality to those produced in foreign countries'.[12] Charles de Montbret who became French Consul in 1789 and who visited Cork in 1790, remarked that he found Cork marble far superior to imported Italian marble from Leghorn, which he called *dove d'Italie*. The typical Cork grey marble which was sold in polished slabs 1ft square and 1in thick sold at up to three shillings a slab, whilst Leghorn marble sold at prices in excess of five shillings simply because it was considered to be more exotic (Ní Chinnéide 1973, 9–10).

Surprisingly little is known about the quarrying techniques employed within the environs of the city, despite the former importance of the stone-cutting and allied trades. Rock blasting appears to have been under way by at least the first decade of the nineteenth century, presumably in the quarries on the outskirts of the city.[13] Indeed, the use of cut limestone in almost all of the city's public buildings, bridges and quaysides during the late eighteenth and throughout the nineteenth centuries, called for enormous amounts of limestone from quarries within the Cork Harbour area, though these activities receive only passing references in contemporary sources. The quarries on the Mahon peninsula, however, are often referred to, principally because stone from the Carrigmore Quarries in Ballintemple (Fig. 4) was used in the construction of important public buildings such as St Finbarr's Cathedral, the Cork Savings Bank (1842) and the Court House (1835). In the late nineteenth century the limestone of the Ballintemple area was described as 'light grey, close even grained, and compact; works well and freely' (Kinahan 1889, 168) and was known locally as Ballintemple grey marble or 'Beaumount Dove'[14] (Coakley 1919, 64). Local masons and stone-cutters found limestone of this variety much easier to work with than the local sandstones. Indeed, even in buildings such as St Vincent's Church in Sunday's Well where the dressed red sandstone blocks are of superlative quality, the quoins, doorways and window mouldings are made of dressed limestone.

Apart from architectural stonework such as ashlar blocks, cornices, window mullions, lintels, sills, coping, string courses, corbels and pier caps, the quarries around the city

would also have produced flagging, kerbing and sets. At the Spring Assizes of 1793, for example, Grand Jury presentments were made for repairs to a total of 5.96 miles of roads within the immediate environs of the city, and for a total of 19,316 sq yds of flagging for streets within the conurbation. Some 2,361 sq yds of flagging alone were required for Great Britain Street.[15] For the most part the limestone quarried within the immediate environs of the city was ideally suited for ashlar work. However, the stone from certain quarries within the Cork Harbour area was also used for specialist tasks or, indeed, because it may well have been cheaper. Many of the city quaysides, for example, which were built by the Harbour Commissioners in the early nineteenth century, were constructed with either Little Island or Rostellan limestone. Many quarries would also have been equipped with forges to enable the quarrymen and stonecutters to be able to make and sharpen tools (Ryan 1992, 128–9).[16] Throughout the nineteenth century the erection of public buildings in stone in the city of Cork, guaranteed a livelihood for a large number of stonecutters, a development which led to the establishment of the Stonecutters Union of Ireland in Cork in 1884, a union which later became established in Dublin (ibid., 44). With the introduction of concrete in the early years of the twentieth century, many items previously hewn from stone were substituted with this material. Cut stone became an expensive item and the craft of stonecutting went into decline. The present Cork City Hall was the last large public building in the city to be built in stone, in the 1930s, the construction of which involved stonecutters from all over Ireland. The limestone used in its construction was quarried at Castlemary, near Cloyne and at the Little Island Quarries, and the stone for its entrance columns was from Ballinasloe (Murphy 1986, 200).

In many cases, the lime and salt works situated within limestone quarries on the outskirts of the city, changed hands over relatively short periods of time during the nineteenth century. However, most of the limestone quarries on the Mahon peninsula appear not to have done so. The 'superior limestone quarry' at Ballinlough, which was advertised to let or for sale in Cork press in 1858,[17] is a rare exception. It appears to have been owned by James Joyce, a salt and lime manufacturer of South Terrace,[18] who also owned a brickyard at Douglas. The Carrigmore Quarries, which were owned by the firm of William Carroll, a salt, lime and brickmaker of Douglas Street, covered a total area of some 120 acres. In 1892 these were the largest limestone quarries in Ireland (Stratten and Stratten 1892, 223).[19] The limestone of the Carrigacrump quarries near Cloyne which, while retaining the same basic properties as Ballintemple stone, could also be raised in large blocks and was preferred in certain instances for steam engine beds.[20] A good example of the latter is Wallis and Pollock's Douglas flax spinning mill (**554**), whose engine beds incorporate both Carrigacrump limestone and stone from Foynes, County Limerick (see Ch. 4). Stone from Foynes was also incorporated into the reservoirs of the Cork Corporation Waterworks in 1858.[21] Thus, while the quality of the limestone available within the environs of the city was never disputed, it was clearly not seen as the solution to every architect's or builder's needs. What may be termed *ad hoc* quarries were also opened specifically to meet the needs of a particular building project, as was the case with Queen's College of 1848, now University College, Cork, where stone was quarried on the site.[22]

Sandstone

The sandstones quarried within the survey area are of two varieties. The first and most widely exploited being the Kiltorcan formation green, grey and red sandstone, as at Flaherty's or the Brickfield Quarry, Sunday's Well Road, and the Lee Road; the second, a small pocket of the Ballytrasna formation minor fine-grained sandstone (Figs. 2 and 3). This latter appears only to have been quarried at Richmond Hill and the Back

Watercourse Road. Needless to say, the sandstone quarries within our present ambit of interest are confined to the area north of the River Lee. John Rocque's map of 1773, shows the 'old quarry' near Peacock Lane, which Holt in 1832 shows as a 'brownstone' (i.e. sandstone) quarry, but generally speaking sandstone quarries are not marked on early maps. Despite the extensive use of these stones in Cork buildings during the eighteenth and nineteenth centuries there is, as in the case of the limestone quarries, very little information on the techniques used in their extraction. In 1832 a 'good stone quarry' on Sunday's Well Road was advertised in the Cork press,[23] around which time the principal sandstone quarries within or immediately adjacent to the city appear to have been the Brickfield, Back Watercourse, Richmond Hill and Lee quarries. However, during the excavation of the Great Southern & Western Railway tunnel between 1847 and 1855 (see Ch. 7), thousands of tons of stone were blasted out of the adjacent hillside, most of which was used for building around the city. But with the opening of the Cork and Queenstown Railway in 1860 the most important sandstone quarry in the environs of the city at Brickfields ('Flaherty's'), was effectively closed as blasting operations could no longer be undertaken (Fig. 5). Thereafter, building with local sandstone was curtailed (Hill 1943, 96). A number of important buildings, including St Peter and Paul's Church and Convent, the North Cathedral, St Vincent's Church (Sunday's Well), the Dominican Convent (Pope's Quay), St Mary's of the Isle Convent New Orphanage and the Incurables Hospital, were all built with stone from the Brickfield Quarry (Kinahan 1889, 323).

SALT AND LIME WORKS

Limestone was also used to manufacture quicklime which was used in building work (as a bonding agent), in render, in whitewash and as a fertiliser. But within the city, in common with many other Irish ports, this activity was normally combined with the manufacture of salt; the expedient being to economise on the use of coal by using the heat of the lime kiln in the purification of imported rock salt (Sproule 1854, 76). Upwards of eleven salt and lime manufactories were at work within the survey area throughout the nineteenth century, although the proportion of these which continued to produce quicklime was reduced to four by 1893.[24]

In a process called calcining, the calcium carbonate in the limestone is subjected to high temperatures to form calcium oxide or *quicklime*. This was then slaked in pits with water, with which it acted exothermically to form hydrated or *slaked* lime. A further chemical reaction with carbon dioxide and moisture in the atmosphere, which caused it to revert to calcium carbonate, enabled it to be used as a cement (*lime putty*) mixed with sand. The resulting mortar does not 'go off' in the conventional sense but continues to harden in an hydraulic set when exposed to the air over a number of years. Up until the 1820s lime-based mortar was the only bonding material available for most purposes, and it is not until the early 1840s that there are any indications that Roman cements were manufactured in the city.[25] J. Parker's Roman cement was patented in 1796 and was made from septaria, a natural cement rock which was calcined. It was used in stucco and was eventually superceded by early forms of Portland cement, originally patented by Joseph Aspidin in 1824. Portland cement is, of course, one of the principal constituents of concrete, in which it was mixed with sand and gravel. By 1840 Wilson and Company, of South Friary Lane in the city, were importing lump alabaster and preparing plaster of Paris in their mills, which was used both in the preparation of stucco and in the manufacture of composite millstones.[26] The type of quicklime used as fertiliser, on the other hand, while generally unslaked into a fine powder, could be incorporated into the soil in a number of different ways (Bell and Watson 1986, 37). Lime was also used in the

Fig. 4

Carrigmore Quarries, Ballintemple. (Con Brogan, Dúchas)

Fig. 5

Brickfield ('Flaherty's') Sandstone Quarry, Lower Glanmire Road, closed *c.* 1860.

purification of town gas, in the production of bleaching powder and of soda from common salt, and in de-hairing hides in the tanning process.

The vast majority of the lime kilns identified within the survey area were generally situated within limestone quarries, or immediately adjacent to them to minimise transport costs. In the larger quarries lime kilns were continually in use. The majority of the lime kilns within the environs of the city were probably used intermittently but a small number, such as the 'large lime kiln with quarry' available for leasing in 1840 at Lower Glasheen (**534** near Glasheen Bridge)[27] may well have been used on a regular basis. These were often imposing structures built into the side of hills to allow the kiln to be easily charged with stone from the rear. However, in some of the smaller kilns, a dome, springing from a bench or ledge at the base of the kiln pot, was constructed in the interior to form a receptacle for the fire. The stone charge was fed in above this, the end product normally being raked out from the draw or stokehole at the base of the kiln (Fig. 6). Such kilns were more attuned to the agricultural cycle than perhaps to the continuous needs of the building trade. Larger kilns, however, such as those at the Windmill (formerly Quarry) Road (**517**) and the Rocksavage Salt and Lime Works (**212**) were continuously charged with intermediate layers of fuel and lime, which could be raked out at intervals, the end product being used either for mortar and render, or for agricultural purposes. Smaller kilns, such as that surviving within the grounds of Bishopstown house (**62**, Power *et al.* 1994, 334) were used to fire little more than a cartload of stone at a time, mostly for fertiliser. This was a long-established practice in the Irish countryside up to recent times (Davies 1938, 80; Bell and Watson 1986, 36). At Spillane's Salt and Lime works on Leitrim Street in the late 1880s, lime-burning in the kiln took two days, the slack lime being mixed with sand from the Blarney area to make mortar.[28] Part of a large kiln used for calcining lime for the Brookefield Chemical Works (**002**) also survives within the survey area on the present-day Orchard Road.

The combination of salt and lime manufacture appears to be unique to Ireland, but as the only area in Ireland with deposits of rock salt is situated in the Carrickfergus area of County Antrim (which were only discovered in the 1850s), nearly all of the rock salt refined in Ireland was imported (Ludlow 1989, 1–5). There was a five-fold increase in the importation of rock salt into Ireland in the second half of the eighteenth century (ibid., 5), a development which in the greater Cork area corresponds to the expansion of the provision trade. Salt was, of course, one of the principal ingredients of butter, a commodity in which Cork had a premier international profile, but both the rock salt and the culm used in its manufacture had to be imported. During the seventeenth century the rock salt imported into Cork came from a European source (O'Sullivan 1937, 128), but by the second half of the eighteenth century most of this was imported from England. For the greater part of the eighteenth and the early decades of the nineteenth centuries, salt manufacture in Ireland received special treatment under English legislation. But in 1825 salt duties which had hitherto favoured the Irish salt industry were abolished and the industry went into decline (Ludlow 1989, 10). In the mid-1840s very little refined English salt was imported into Cork, and by 1847 almost all of the city's salt and lime manufacturers had, by general agreement, stopped importing it. The principal reason for this was because Cork proprietors of salt and lime works believed that it produced inferior quality butter owing to the way it was boiled on coal fires, whilst the salt boiled on Cork lime kilns was believed by Butter Market Inspectors and local manufacturers alike to produce a salt which would not interfere with the flavour of the butter. After 1847, however, most manufacturers appear to have overcome their objections to it.[29]

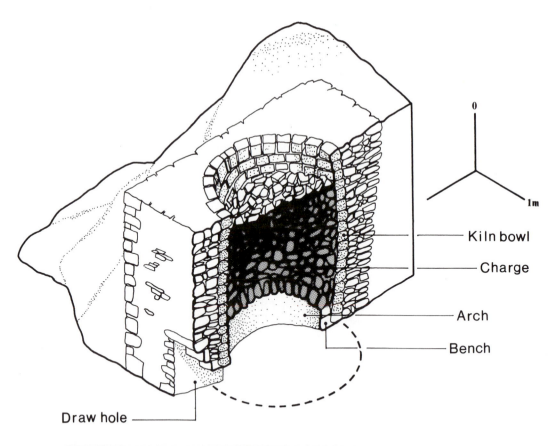

0

1 m

Kiln bowl

Charge

Arch

Bench

Draw hole

Fig. 6 ABOVE
Lime kiln.

Fig. 7
Imported dutch brick, South Mall.

The earliest known salt and lime works within the survey area were established south of the river Lee in the 1760s, but in the Mallow Lane and Blackpool areas of the city other sites were set up, well away from limestone quarries on the south bank of the river, before the end of the eighteenth century.[30] In these and other north-side salt and lime works the manufacture of lime for the many tanneries in the area may well have been the main business for certain salt manufacturers, although there can be little doubt that in most instances the production of dairy or butter salt was of primary importance. The availability of running water is also likely to have been a primary locational consideration, but in certain instances access to water transport also appears to have figured prominently. As in the case of the John Street salt and lime works (**583**), metal salt pans and water reservoirs were needed for refining the salt, using the heat from the lime kilns, whilst force pumps were also necessary for filling the reservoirs.[31] Similar water requirements existed in the north-side tanneries, and it is not really surprising to find salt and lime works situated at Old Chapel Lane (**469**, latterly Cathedral Walk), Clarence (Gerald Griffin) Street (**016**) and Great Britain (Great William O'Brien) Street (**552**), areas in which there is a sizeable concentration of tanneries. William Daly's John Street works also had the added advantage of access to water transport, rock salt being delivered by lighters via the Kiln River at the rear of the works, whilst the storage space for 500–600 tons of rock salt and a large yard capable of holding the same amount of limestone was also available on the other side of John Street.[32] Daly also owned a large salt warehouse (**407**) at Clarke's Bridge[33] where rock salt was also, perhaps, delivered by lighter. However, at least one north-side salt and lime works was established in a sandstone quarry (025) on the Back Watercourse. The site is shown on the first edition of the OS as a lime works and appears to have begun processing salt about 1845.[34]

Very little is known about the physical arrangements of salt and lime works within the city, many of which appear to have changed hands at regular intervals. The Maylor Street salt and lime works, for example, was leased out in 1801, 1832 and 1839 and was certainly under different management again by 1856.[35] This appears to be a Cork manifestation of a national trend where works of this type were generally family concerns which went out of business on a regular basis (Ludlow 1989, 1). Business records are, in consequence, difficult to come by but a sketched ground plan of a salt and lime works on Morgan's Lane off South Main Street provides what may prove to be a vital clue to the basic layout of many of the Cork works.[36] The South Gate salt and lime works (**125**) were owned by William Deane in 1802[37] and by a partnership of Mark Collins and Richard F. Waddy in the early 1840s. This partnership was dissolved in 1843 when Collins took over the business.[38] The surviving drawing of the works is undated but appears to date to the early nineteenth century, and depicts four keyhole-shaped kilns built in a continuous block with a west-facing frontage. This arrangement was probably quite common. The Maylor Street works in 1801, for example, had three kilns and three pans along with 'rocking cisterns',[39] the kilns being presumably built in a continuous block with a salt pan to each. Michael and Thomas Daly's works on Old Chapel Lane (latterly Cathedral Walk) had a 'tiled' kiln in the late 1840s,[40] which would suggest that the interior of the kiln pot was tiled to enhance its reverberatory properties and thus its efficiency. There is even a reference to a 'salt kiln' at Richard Sherrard's works on the Watercourse Road during the same period.[41] The output from the Cork works could also be substantial, as at Shine's at Windmill Road/Summerhill South, which in 1848 had the capacity to produce 25,000 barrels of lime per annum along with 200 tons of salt.[42] Thus far, however, it is impossible to say how typical this performance was within the survey area.

By the end of the nineteenth century at least two city salt manufacturers, McCauliffe's

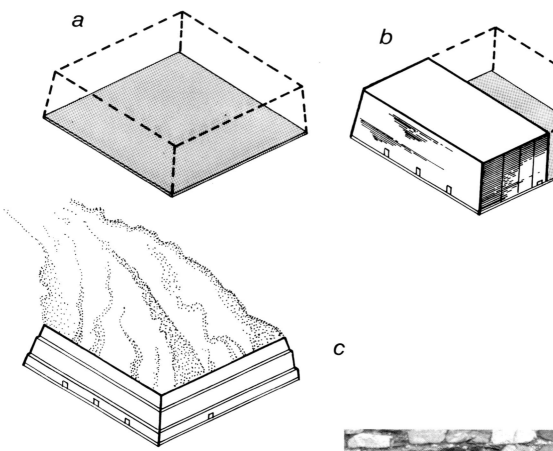

a

b

c

Fig. 8

Reconstruction of brick firing clamp (after Brunskill 1990);

(a) preparation of clamp base; (b) clamp under assembly; (c) clamp while burning.

Fig. 9

Use of slob brick in window arches of eighteenth-century granary on Rutland Street.

of Watercourse Road and Spillane's of Leitrim Street (**588**) were buying salt from the Earl of Downshire's estate at Carrickfergus.[43] In 1903 Spillane's works kept two large lime kilns constantly working, burning limestone transported by horse and cart from the Douglas Road area, and refining salt from Carrickfergus rock salt in $1^{1}/_{2}$ ton lumps. The salt was reduced to brine in three large cisterns, 40–50ft in diameter made of stout planks bound together with iron bands. The rock salt was laid on top of perforated platforms surmounting the cisterns, upon which the rock salt was dissolved into brine using spring water. The perforated floor served as a filter for the removal of impurities, and once the brine had passed into the cisterns it was conveyed via pipes to one or other of four large boiling vats. The final quality and texture of the refined salt was largely determined by the duration and extent of the heat applied to the boiling vats. If a coarse salt was required — the type generally used for curing meat — a slow heat was applied to the vat. But if salt of a finer texture was required a more moderate heating was applied. The salt collected after the boiling process was ready for immediate use, and was removed from the cisterns by shovel. The Leitrim Street works employed some 20 men in 1903, who were engaged in both lime-burning and in the manufacture of dairy salt and curing salt.[44]

BRICKMAKING

The use of locally manufactured brick within the survey area appears to have been more widespread than has been previously thought. Its generally coarse texture almost invariably precluded its use as a facing brick, although it was used for finishing windows in early industrial buildings. But despite this, there are a large number of late eighteenth and nineteenth-century buildings in the greater Cork region in which it was employed in stud walls or even in the principal load-bearing walls, although in all cases it was plastered over. Throughout the nineteenth century higher-quality brick, beginning with the Youghal brickworks, began to successfully compete with brick imported from the Staffordshire region of England (see below).

The first bricks used in Cork buildings appear to have been Dutch imports, which were normally brought into the port as ballast, examples of which can be seen in a number of surviving eighteenth-century structures on the South Mall (Fig. 7). Local manufacture commenced in the second half of the eighteenth century on the Brickfield slobs on the north bank of the river where, it was claimed, some three million bricks were being manufactured annually (O'Sullivan 1937, 199). In common with many Irish coastal towns in the early eighteenth century, many houses within the city were beginning to be built with local brick, which under Pearce's Act of 1729 was beginning to be manufactured to more or less standard sizes.[45] Surviving examples of eighteenth-century Cork-made brick are generally similar to those manufactured on the Cork slobs up until the present century.[46]

The extent of brickmaking operations at Brickfield slobs in the 1770s was such that the smoke from the firing clamps had become a public nuisance, and in 1778 an act was passed declaring that 'no bricks shall be burned or any clamp of bricks set to burn within two miles of English Statute measure, computed from the Exchange of the City of Cork'.[47] In 1782 Cooper Penrose (1736–1815), a Quaker merchant from Waterford engaged in the timber trade,[48] bought two large plots of land in the North Liberties of the city. The first of these, purchased from Adam Newman, extending over 27 acres adjacent to the Strand (latterly Lower Glanmire) Road and including about 1,000ft of river frontage, was described as a brickyard and marsh. The second property, described

as land in Monatiny, a 13 acre plot bounded by the Strand Road at its northern extremity, was described as a brickfield, and Cooper Penrose acquired rights to quarry brick earth from it (Read 1980, 91). There is no surviving evidence that he ever chose to do so, but if he did he would probably have had to use clamp sites lying outside the limits set out in the act of 1778.

In Ireland during the late eighteenth and early nineteenth centuries brickmaking was often a seasonal occupation and remained so in certain areas up until very recent times. The clay pits were first pumped out with wooden, manually operated double-acting pumps, the excavated clay being then heaped on a specially prepared piece of ground. Stones were then picked out of it by hand before the clay was mixed to the right consistency for moulding (Dowling 1972, 43; Brunskill 1990, 21–2). The next process, tempering, in which the mud was generally macerated mechanically into a more plastic consistency, was carried out by a machine called a pug mill. This mill was normally powered by a horse, jennet or mule, and consisted of an inverted metal cone with a series of knives set into a vertical axle for chopping and mixing the clay (Dowling 1972, 43–4; Brunskill 1990, 22). Tempering had traditionally been carried out by men and animals trampling the mud underfoot, a process which was still undertaken by temperers in the Glenmore Brickyards of County Kilkenny in the late nineteenth century (Dowling 1972, 43–4). After tempering, the clay was ready for moulding in to the desired form, and this was undertaken by a moulder in a wooden mould at a moulding table. Depending upon the skill of the moulder anything between 3,000 and 5,000 bricks could be manufactured per day and from this it is easy to see how a number of crews could have manufactured three million bricks on the Brickfield yards near Cork over a single year. The moulded bricks were then carried off in special barrows or by hand to a drying platform, where they were left for at least a week to dry out before the all-important clamp firing could commence (Dowling 1972, 45; Delaney 1990, 31–62).

The clamp site was carefully chosen in order to facilitate access to water transport by barge or lighter, and was always well drained. The clamp itself was a rectangular construction consisting of alternate courses of stretchers and headers, which were battered externally. Approximately every 3ft along its entire length, a series of fire-setting holes placed at right angles to the long axis of the clamp, were built through it, into which the fire-setting materials were placed and ignited (Fig. 8). Coal or culm were the basic fuels used in this operation, during which large amounts of white smoke were given off. On the Glenmore Brickfields the clamp was allowed to burn for about five days, but in England, traditional clamp-firing could take anything from 2–12 weeks depending on the size of the clamp (Dowling 1972, 46–7; Brunskill 1990, 27).

Brickyards were in operation on the opposite bank of the river at Blackrock in the 1820s[49] which had ceased to exist by the 1840s, but the main centre of the Cork industry became centred upon the slobs of the Douglas estuary (Fig. 3). These were in operation from at least the late 1820s[50] and on the first edition of the six-inch OS (1842) map there were three brickfields shown on the banks of the Douglas channel, the largest of which had been established on the north bank. According to Lewis (1837, vol. 1, 485) 'A large quantity of bricks of a bright ash colour, is made in the vicinity of the village, [i.e. Douglas] and sent to a considerable distance inland; and great numbers are conveyed to the port of Cork.' A few years later N.L. Beamish (1844, 87) noted that some 56 people were employed as brickmakers in the locality, although all of these were only employed for about three months of the year (Cadogan 1988, 32). The Cork Clayworks Company, which commenced the manufacture of bricks at Belvelly in 1858, was highly critical of the quality of Douglas brick in the Cork press: 'there is at Douglas from the river slob, certain articles, so irregular in shape, so ill burnt and altogether so inferior that they can only be used for rude work, and must be cemented over'.[51] The high proportion of plastered-over slob brick visible on demolition sites within the environs of the city in recent years, clearly demonstrates that many nineteenth-century Cork builders concurred in this appraisal (Fig. 9).

In 1852 James Joyce, salt and lime manufacturer at South Terrace, Cork[52], quarry owner (see above) and brickmaker at Douglas (and grandfather of the novelist James Joyce), became bankrupt (Ellman 1983, 12). The subsequent auction of his brickfield provides an important insight into the scale of operations on the Douglas brickfields up to this period and into the type of equipment in use. The 'Goat Island' concerns had two lighters, one hooker, four large-sized mud boats and two skiffs in addition to an entire stock of 150,000 bricks. All of the moulding tables, moulds, barrels and the pug mill were also put for auction, plus two horses which were presumably used for powering the pug mill.[53]

Douglas brick, like most slob bricks was poorly fired, and its mottled reddish/yellow colour made it unsuitable for external facing purposes. In 1889 it was stated that the 'clay if washed, will not burn, but when dried and unwashed it burns into a desirable brick'. It was available in a size $8^{3/4}$ x 4 x $2^{1/4}$ in, and cost anything from 11–14s per thousand (Kinahan 1889, 372). In 1892 John Barry, a lime manufacturer and brickmaker of Douglas Street in the city, owned a 10-acre brickfield at Douglas with 'extensive clay pits' employing a 'large number of hands'. Barry's family had been in business since the 1840s, but it is not clear when they became involved in brickmaking at Douglas (Stratten and Stratten 1892, 185). William Carroll of Anglesea Street, whose business was founded in 1830, was also involved in brickmaking at Douglas in the early 1890s, his works being 'fully equipped with necessary plant and machinery for producing a sound quality of building bricks' (ibid., 223). There are no indications that anything other than traditional clamp-firing was undertaken at Douglas during this period, although a Hoffman-type kiln was at work at the Belvelly brickworks on Great Island in the period 1858–c.1914 (Cadogan 1988, 35). The Hoffman kiln, patented by Friedrich Hoffman in Austria in 1856, enabled bricks to be continuously fired in a circular kiln. Many of the problems associated with the traditional seasonal manufacture of bricks in Ireland, in clamps or in intermittently fired kilns, were now overcome and enabled brick manufacturers at Youghal and Belvelly to meet the increased demand by the local building trade from the early 1860s onwards.

English Bridgewater bricks were imported in large quantities during the nineteenth century principally because most County Cork brickworks could not produce good quality facing brick. Youghal brick, which was fired in Hoffman kilns from the second half of the nineteenth century, and which was used in large quantities,[54] was generally unsuited for facing work, and from its inception in 1858 the Belvelly works began to make up for this defect where Cork-made brick was concerned. There was also an attractive cost differential for Cork builders, Bridgewater brick cost 21s per 1,000 at source in 1858, and 50s at Cork.[55] It was used in the Union Quay Constabulary Barracks and in the extension to the Cork School of Design, latterly the Crawford Art Gallery (Cadogan 1988, 37).[56] Belvelly brick did, nonetheless, have a tendency to 'sweat', that is, exude a white salt after a period of time (Kinahan 1889, 372), and from the 1860s onwards it had a solid competitor in the brick made at Ballinphellic, which was also fired in a Hoffman kiln from around the late 1890s. Ballinphellic brick was first used to effect within the city in the construction of the Model School on Anglesea Street in 1864.[57]

POTTERY AND CLAY PIPE MANUFACTURE

During the nineteenth century a small pottery operated on North Abbey Street (**210**)[58] using clay shipped into the city from Youghal (Kinahan 1889, 372), with other small potteries operating at Knapps Square[59] and Merchants Quay.[60] Pottery manufacture within the city, however, was no longer carried out by the early 1880s (ibid.).

Upwards of six clay pipe manufactories were established in the city during the nineteenth century, with a notable concentration in Adelaide Street (Lane 1980, 118), the most durable of these being John Fitzgerald's Clay Pipe Factory on Adelaide Street. The clay used in these works was formerly brought into Cork from Clare, but later in the nineteenth century all of the clay was imported from England (Kinahan 1889, 372). In 1903 the raw clay blocks were purchased in 28lb blocks, which were first kiln-dried and then mechanically pulverised and reduced to a powder which was then steeped in large vats. The clay was then taken out and beaten before being lumped into a stiff dough.[61] Accounts of the same process during the later operation of this factory, however, indicate that the clay was puddled in tubs on the ground floor of Fitzgerald's three-storey building (Lane 1980, 16). Indeed, later accounts of the *modus operandi* of Fitzgerald's factory accord quite well with those of English clay pipe factories. A visitor to the works in 1903 was informed that the round clay pans used to hold the pipes in the firing kiln was called a *saggar*, a term which clearly derives from English practice.[62] The clay was also imported from Devon and Cornwall (ibid.), the principal source for many English works (Ayto 1987, 19). The pipes were fired in a brick-lined kiln for eight to nine hours and the finished product was exported to New York, London, Liverpool and to most of Wales, especially Newport, Tredegar and Cardiff.[63]

SAND AND GRAVEL

Immediately to the north of the city there are large glacial deposits of sand and gravel, the full extents of which encompass the area from New Inn to the east and Kilnap to the west, and as far north as Ballincolly. In all, some 4 million cubic yards of gravel sand and shingle are estimated to have been deposited here (Lamplugh 1905, 71). Extensive quarrying began in the Goulding's Glen area in the second half of the nineteenth century and continued up until recent times. In the late 1860s large pits were opened in the Goulding's Glen area in Ballyvollane and Cahergal, with a sizeable pit being opened immediately to the north of Hewitt's Distillery on the Watercourse Road. Most of this gravel was probably used as road-surfacing material.

Sand was also quarried within the environs of the city and a quarry near Blarney railway station supplied much of County Cork. According to Kinahan 'some of an inferior quality' was 'got in the neighbourhood of Bishopstown'. The sand used for casting in the city's many iron foundries and engineering works, presumably because of its superior quality, was brought from the Lagan Valley area near Belfast (Kinahan 1889, 245).

3 FOOD-PROCESSING INDUSTRIES

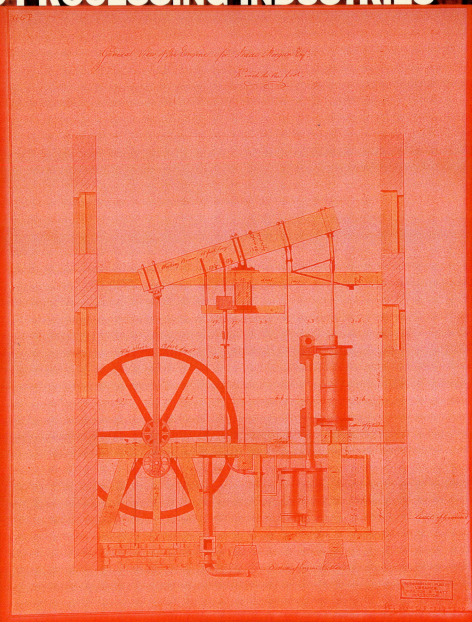

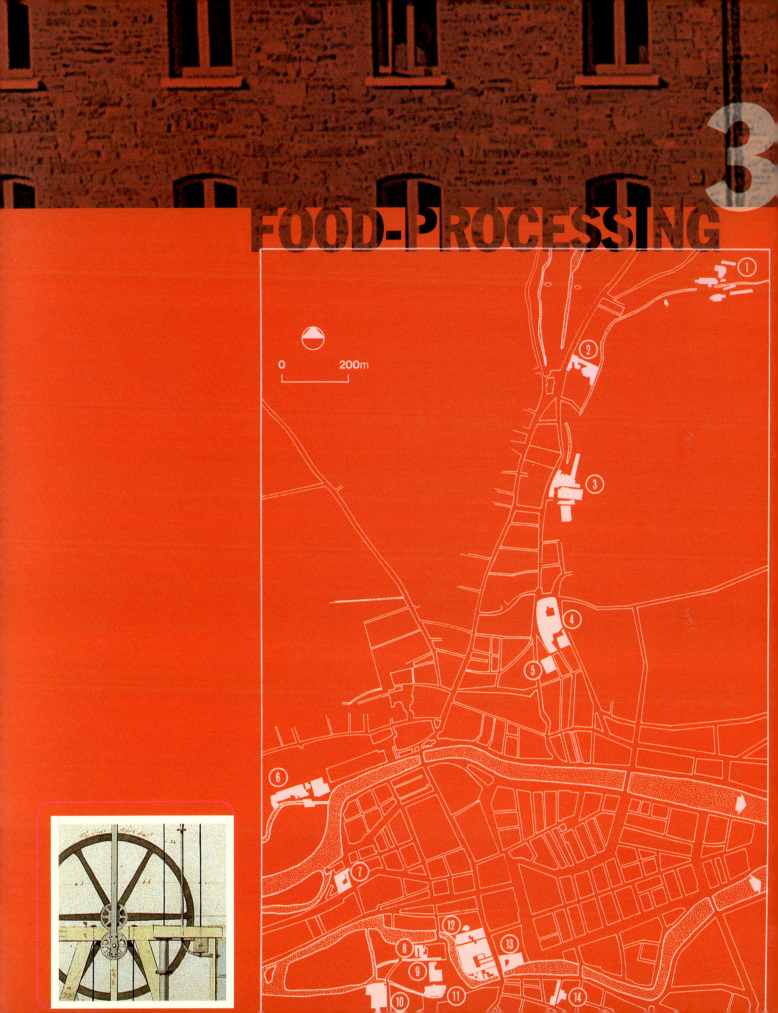

FOOD-PROCESSING

3

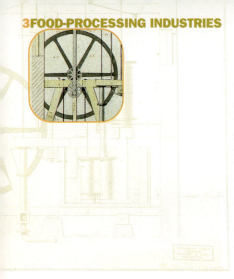

The most important food-processing industries in and around Cork — brewing, distilling, malting and grain milling — involved those which processed cereals crops. In the first half of the nineteenth century oats was the main cereal crop in County Cork, followed by wheat and barley (Donnelly 1975, 33). During the Napoleonic Wars the increased demand for wheat led to the expansion of the local flour-milling industry and between 1815 and 1825 flour exports from Cork actually doubled (Donnelly 1975, 34; Bielenberg 1991, 42). In 1851 County Cork, followed by Tipperary and Wexford, was the most important wheat-growing area in Ireland, although by 1900 this figure was only 11% of its 1851 level. Cork was also the principal barley-producing county in Ireland by the middle of the century, some 46,000 acres were under barley in the 1850s, but again this had declined significantly by the beginning of the present century (Kennedy 1981, 183). Most of the barley was, of course, malted for use by the distilleries and breweries in the region, some of which were of national importance (see below).

MALTING

The Cork region was one of the principal malt-producing regions of Ireland for the greater part of the nineteenth century. Some 18% of the entire national output of malt was produced in Cork malthouses in 1829, almost four times that produced in Dublin (Bielenberg 1991, 67). The expansion of the railway network enabled Cork distillers to acquire malt from other Munster counties. Thus, while the acreage under barley in County Cork declined after 1851 (see above), the quantity of malt used by Cork breweries increased fourfold in the period 1844–98 (Ó Gráda 1994, 304).

As one of the principal constituents of beer and whiskey, the manufacture of malted barley from the late eighteenth century onwards was generally brought into line with the more scientific methods increasingly applied in the brewing and distilling industries. In its essentials the malting process involved the artificial germination of the barley, with the degree of sprouting being arrested at a critical point in order to conserve the saccharine in the budding grain. The sugar was then chemically transformed into alcohol in the fermentation process. Four basic processes were involved in the manufacture of malted barley — *steeping, couching, flooring* and kiln-drying — two of which were closely monitored by excise officials.

Kiln-drying is normally associated with the final stage of malting when the germination process is deliberately halted (see below). However, towards the end of the nineteenth century it became common for barley to be kiln-dried before germination. Barley harvested using traditional methods was left to stand and mature, but with the introduction of steam threshing the crop was no longer encouraged to sweat, and so kiln-drying at a steady temperature of around 100° F over a 12–24 hour period (which effectively imitated this process) became a priority (Callan MacArdle and Callan 1902a, 461). The first stage in the malting process involved the immersion of the kiln-dried barley in a wooden cistern called a *steep*, in which it was thoroughly soaked under controlled conditions. The temperature of both the barley and the water was carefully monitored throughout the process. Seeds and other extraneous matter tended to float to the surface where they could be skimmed off, whilst the heavier cereal grains sank to the bottom. Failure to remove all of the unwanted debris would result in the payment of extra excise duty (which was based on volume) and, worse still, the germination process would be impaired (Donnachie 1979, 101). The water in the steep was drawn off after a period of 54–60 hours, during which it would be inspected a number of times by an excise officer, after which the swollen barley was *couched*. The *couch* or *couch frame* was normally a wooden-framed receptacle, the size and construction of which was controlled by excise regulations (ibid., 102). The swollen barley was allowed to lie here for about 24 hours, before being spread on the malthouse floor in a layer about 12 inches thick to enable the *flooring* process to proceed.

Over the next 8–10 days the germination process was encouraged, the maltster turning the barley regularly with a large wooden shovel, up until the point he considered that germination should be arrested. The grain was then removed to a kiln where the introduction of strong heat, over a period of up to three days, expelled all residual moisture and prevented further germination taking place.[1] Finally, the malt was stored in air-sealed bins where it was allowed to mature for a number of weeks (Callan MacArdle and Callan 1902a, 462).

Brewery Malthouses

The preferred option for all of the city-based breweries would have been to have all of their maltings within the brewery complex, immediately adjacent to their malt mills (see below). In smaller breweries this presented few difficulties, particularly in the eighteenth century before large-scale brewing became the norm and when animal-powered malt-milling plant could be relied upon to handle the brewery's needs. Allen's Brewery on Cremer's Square, for example, which formed the nucleus of Beamish and Crawford's Cork Porter Brewery (**040**), had its own maltings on site, the kiln of which is shown on the earliest large-scale survey of Cork Porter Brewery of 1802.

Cowperthwaites's Brewery (**127**) on Wandesford Quay (Fig. 10), the only independent malthouse of note within the city during the nineteenth century[2] and Drinan's Brewery (**145**) on Drinan Street also had their malthouses on site. However, there were also a number of independent maltsters within the city, although many of these began to be subsumed by Beamish and Crawford from the late eighteenth century onwards. Beamish and Crawford were in control of eight city malthouses by the end of the 1830s (see below), which accounted for slightly more than a quarter of the maltings situated throughout the county (Donnelly 1975, 34). In the early 1860s the number of malthouses controlled by Beamish and Crawford had been reduced to five (Gibson 1861, vol. 2, 314), and from about 1888 onwards their malting operations became concentrated in the Lee Maltings (**036**) and in the Morrison's Island Maltings (**348**) (Cosgrave 1989, 101–2).

Many of the malthouses taken over by Beamish and Crawford had been established in the eighteenth century (Fig. 11). The Morrison's Island malthouse which was in existence in 1785, was the first large malthouse within the city to be acquired by Beamish and Crawford.[3] A ground plan of the site, dated 29 June 1866, shows two malt floors, a boiler house, a kiln and a *droppings room*.[4] The drying kiln was a substantial structure and had a drying floor supported on cast-iron stanchions.[5] A steep, of modern construction, with bolted cast-iron sections, was positioned on the first floor, and each of the three storeys had cast-iron supports.[6] The Rutland Street maltings (**130** and **131**), which they acquired in 1813, had been in existence since at least 1753.[7] A detailed ground plan of this complex dating to around 1860, shows malthouses on either side of Rutland Street complete with at least two kilns.[8] The main malthouse at Rutland Street had a quadrilateral ground plan and a 13-bay malt floor.[9] Sections of the original malthouses have survived on either side of Rutland Street and include a range of two and three-storey buildings with sack-hoist lucams facing the street (Fig. 12).

Beamish and Crawford's Hanover Street Maltings, which dates to around 1790, appears

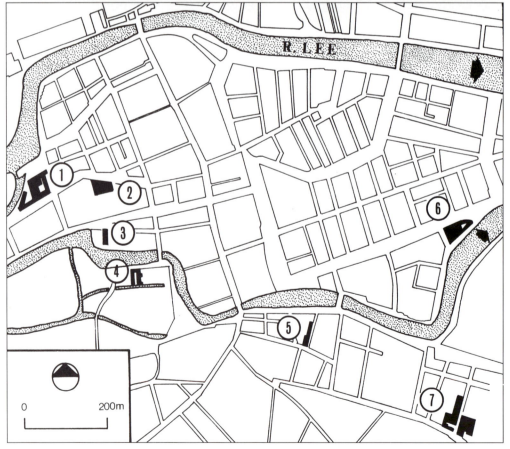

Fig. 10 OPPOSITE ABOVE

Cowperthwaite's Brewery, Wandesford's Quay; late eighteenth century.

Fig. 11 OPPOSITE BELOW

Principal maltings in survey area.

1 Nile Street ('Lee') Maltings. 2 Fenn's Quay. 3 Hanover Street.
4 Wandesford's Quay. 5 Cobh Street.
6 Morrisson's Island. 7 Rutland Street.

Fig. 12 ABOVE

Rutland Street Maltings.

Fig. 13 RIGHT

Ground plan of Lee Maltings in 1890 (redrawn from survey in collections of Cork Archives Institute).

1–5 Kilns. 6 Office. 7 Dwelling. 8 Malt store. 9 Droppings room.
10–11 Malt floors. 12 Courtyard.

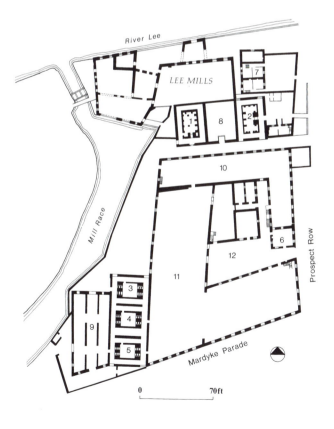

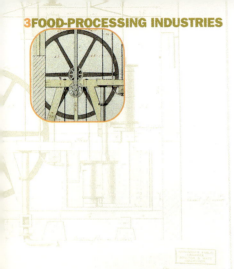

to have been originally controlled by Walker's Distillery at Crosses Green (see below), until it was sold to the brewery in 1808. [10] The Hanover Street premises had two kilns and a malting floor, with a single steep at the southern end of the malthouse.[11] It was demolished in 1993. Beamish and Crawford also controlled two further eighteenth-century malthouses on Fenn's Marsh (**561**, on latter day Sheares Street, which later became Woodfood Bourne's wine vault) and Francis Street (Grattan Street).[12] By far the largest maltings controlled and operated by them, however, were the Nile or Lee Maltings (**036:2**) on Prospect Row.

The Lee Maltings

Up until the end of the nineteenth century the complex of buildings on Prospect Row–Mardyke Walk, known today as the 'Lee Maltings', consisted of a large, independently run flour mill, the former Lee Mills (**036:1**), and Beamish and Crawford's Nile Street ('Lee') Maltings. In 1813 Beamish and Crawford acquired the former River Lee Porter Brewery, which the company converted for use as a maltings and storehouses. For the greater part of the nineteenth century the maltings operation here was concentrated in the converted River Lee Porter Brewery complex, with the addition of two cellars adjacent to the headrace channel of the Lee Mills (Fig. 13).[13] These are clearly shown on a ground plan of the complex dating to the early 1840s[14] and this is how they are depicted on the first edition of the OS of 1842.

The former River Lee Porter Brewery complex operated three steeps by the mid-1860s. Each steep was positioned within a cast-iron framework made by Perrott's Hive Iron Foundry (**285**), which survived *in situ* until its removal by University College Cork in June 1991.[15] Two wooden-framed wagons on iron bogeys, running on wooden rails, were used to service the individual steeps, with a weighbridge positioned over the crossing point between the two main lofts. A trapdoor at the base of the wagon was positioned over the main feeder chute, from which were led three subsidiary chutes feeding (by gravity flow) the individual steeps.[16] The steeps were positioned at the Prospect Row end of the malthouses, and the remainder of each storey served as growing floors.

By 1866 three substantial kilns and a droppings room (into which the kiln-dried malt was dropped from the kiln's drying floor) had been built onto the malthouses at their south-western extremity. Two further kilns, with an intermediate malt store and droppings room, had also been added. The construction of one of these kilns involved substantial modifications to the late eighteenth-century miller's house associated with Hayes' (i.e. the Lee) mills, which was effectively cut in half to form an office and a smaller dwelling.[17] Alfred Barnard (1890, vol. 2, 353) who visited the Lee Maltings in the late 1880s, described them as:

> ... a picturesque block of buildings, erected around three sides of a square court, the front of which is devoted to malt offices, gatekeeper's house and dormitories for the maltmen. The maltings, which cover nearly an acre, are entirely enclosed, and are built upon the banks of the north channel of the River Lee, over which there is a bridge to the island opposite [i.e. Love's Island].

From this period onwards, as we have already seen, Beamish and Crawford began to concentrate their malting operations here and at Morrison's Island. The Lee Maltings at this period were clearly the largest in the city, and their capacity was further expanded with the conversions of the Lee Mills to malthouses at the turn of the century. Malthouses 1 and 2 each had two barley stores on the ground and first floors respectively, and four working floors.[18] The largest surviving kiln, which post-dates the infilling of the headrace of the Lee Mills, was constructed in or around 1903.[19] The other two surviving kilns appear to date to around 1867.[20] Kiln no. 2 is a three-storey structure, the first and second storeys of which served as drying floors. The firing kiln, subsequently removed, was positioned on the ground floor.

Other nineteenth-century Cork breweries such as Lane's South Gate Brewery on South Main Street (**306**) also acquired control of city maltings. Lane's Maltings (Measom 1866, **328**), which were situated immediately across the River Lee at Drinan Street, originally formed part of Drinan's Brewery. Of these, the Drinan Street premises included an extensive malt store and two kilns.[21] In 1889 Murphy's Brewery (**060**) erected a large five-storey maltings on their premises, designed by the local architect T. Hynes. The lower two storeys were used for grain storage and the upper three served as malt floors. The steep was situated at the northern end of the building, whilst the sweating and malting kiln at the southern extremity of the building was equipped with an elaborate furnace. Coal for the latter was stored in the adjacent yard (Stratten and Stratten 1892, 148). The bucket elevators within the malthouse were powered by a horizontal engine by Roby's of Lincoln.

BREWING

Porter, a dark beer originating in England (McDonagh 1964), has been known by many names. 'Stout', 'stout ale', 'stout porter' or simply 'porter', was traditionally stronger and darker than either brown or pale beers. Its also had a creamy head which lasted much longer than that of other beers, its characteristically darker colour resulting from the use of heavily roasted malt. Cork breweries have been traditionally associated with the manufacture of porter, but ale, including weak table beer or small beer, was also produced by Cork breweries, and even Beamish and Crawford (see below) became involved in its manufacture towards the end of the nineteenth century (Cosgrave 1989, 131). Arnott's Brewery on Fitton Street, for example, produced both porter and Indian pale ale, whilst Lane's South Gate Brewery manufactured both stout and bitter ale.

The second half of the eighteenth century witnessed a marked trend towards increased industrialisation in the Cork brewing industry. Some 30 'common' or commercial breweries had been established within the city by 1791, and as the greater part of the city's porter production became concentrated in larger commercial breweries, English imports became drastically reduced (Dickson 1977, 605; Malcolm 1986, 22). By the end of the eighteenth century Cork had already become an important centre of the Irish brewing industry. So much so that Thomas Newenham, writing in the first decade of the nineteenth century could assert that the Cork porter breweries 'almost vie in extent with some of the principal ones in London' (Newenham 1809, 277). Most of the production from city breweries was consumed within the city, but there was also a small export trade to the West Indies in the early decades of the nineteenth century. Exports to England increased in the second half of the nineteenth century, particularly by Murphy's Brewery, while the arrival of railways enabled Cork City breweries to further expand throughout the nineteenth century (Bielenberg 1991, 50–53).

The main locational considerations for the city's larger late eighteenth and early

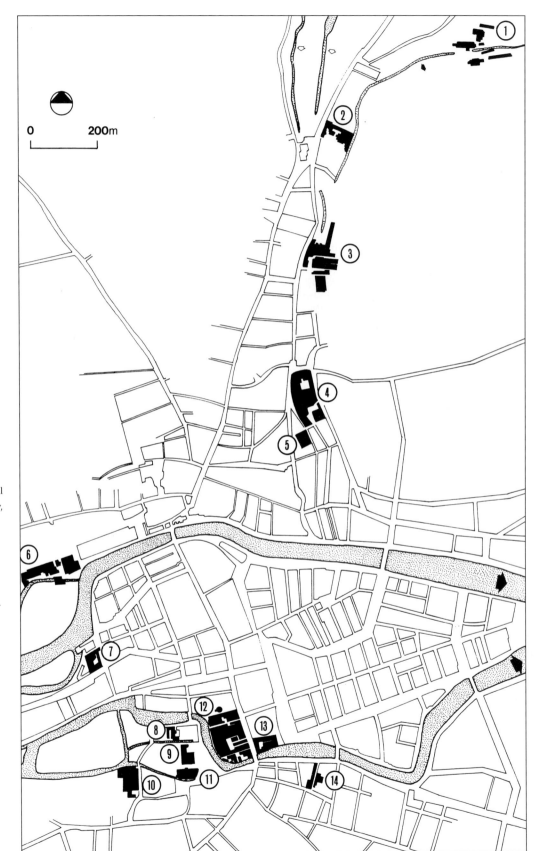

Fig. 14

Distribution of main Cork City breweries
and distilleries in the nineteenth century,
with dates of establishment (when known).

1 Dodge's Glen (Callaghan's) Distillery, c.
1803. 2 Green Distillery, 1796.
3 Watercourse Distillery, 1794. 4 Lady's Well
(Murphy's) Brewery, 1856. 5 Daly's Distillery,
1820. 6 North Mall Distillery, 1779. 7 Lee
Porter Brewery, 1797. 8 Cowperthwaite's
Brewery, eighteenth century. 9 Crosse's
Green Brewery, early nineteenth century.
10 St Finn-barre's (Arnott's) Brewery, 1805.
11 St Dominick's (Walker's) Distillery, 1789.
12 Cork Porter Brewery (Beamish and
Crawford), 1792. 13 South Gate Brewery,
1758. 14 Drinan's Brewery, eighteenth
century.

nineteenth-century breweries appear to have been immediate access to a navigable channel of the River Lee, the availability of a pure water supply on site and demand for beer in the city. Riverside location substantially reduced the cost of transporting bulk cargoes such as coal (imported from Wales and Scotland) and dried hops (ibid., 57). Beamish and Crawford's Cork Porter Brewery, Lane's Southgate Brewery (on opposite sides of South Main Street), St Finn-barre's Brewery on Fitton Street and Cashman's Brewery at Crosses Green, are associated with the South Channel of the Lee (Fig. 14).

As enormous volumes of water were used in the brewing processes, the maintenance of the quality and quantity of water for breweries was extremely important, particularly when many Cork breweries began to expand their output in the second half of the nineteenth century. In all cases, the water supply was originally provided by either artesian wells or rainwater cisterns, which in certain instances was supplemented by the piped municipal supply from about 1859 onwards. Arnott's Brewery appears to have relied principally on the municipal water supply (Anon. 1873, 12). A similar pattern, indeed, can be observed in English breweries during the second half of the nineteenth century, which by this period were drawing large supplies from water companies (Gourvish and Wilson 1994, 49). The Cork porter breweries' principal rival, Guinness of Dublin, obtained most of its supply from the rivers Poddle, Dodder and from the Grand Canal and, after 1870, from the Vartry reservoir (Lynch and Vaizey 1960, 240).

Brewing Processes

The type of malted barley preferred by porter brewers was generally drier than that used in the manufacture of ale. Many of the Cork breweries, especially Beamish and Crawford's, preferred to run their own malting concerns, although a number of these continued to purchase malt from independent maltsters.[22] After kiln-drying it was lightly screened in the *malt loft* then bruised between millstones (and later between roller mills) to form grist. The bruised malt or grist was then immersed in water in a *masher*, a vessel with internally mounted revolving arms which mixed the grist and water in a cylinder outside the mash tun. Patent mashers, such as Steel's, were introduced into Cork breweries in the second half of the nineteenth century by which time the necessity of carefully mixing malt and water prior to its immersion in the mash tun was fully understood. The *mash tun*, a false-bottomed vessel was then filled with the contents of the masher. Internally mounted revolving arms within the mash tun assisted the infusion of the grist and water. In the mash tun the enzyme diastase, which is cultivated in the malting of the barley, was released, and transformed the starch in the malt into maltose. The resulting mixture, the *goods*, was then allowed to stand for about two hours. After mashing — a process common to both brewing and distilling — had been completed, the residue from the bruised malt, now termed *spent grains*, was collected on the false bottom of the mash tun (Callan MacArdle and Callan 1902a, 462). Small or table beer was produced from mashing the grist for a second time, to produce a much weaker but cheaper beer, which was produced by a number of Cork breweries. The spent grains — an important by-product of ale breweries and whiskey distilleries — were generally sold as cattle feed.[23]

The liquid drawn off from the mash tun was called *worts*, which at this stage in the process would have a light head. When the average strength of the wort was stronger than that required by the brewer, a process called *sparging* was undertaken. In sparging the mash tun was mechanically sprinkled with hot water, an action which reduced the strength of the wort (Callan MacArdle and Callan 1902a, 462; Donnachie 1979, 108). After mashing and sparging the worts were conveyed to a large, domed copper vessel called a *copper*, in which the liquor was boiled for a couple of hours with dried hops and

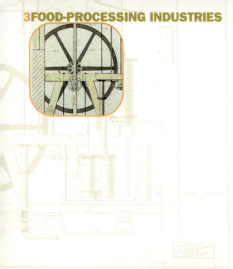

sugar. In the boiling process the flavour of the hops was extracted, imparting to the beer its bitterness. After boiling the worts were then conveyed into a vessel called a *hop back*, a false-bottomed receptacle which collected the spent hops and allowed the now clear liquor to pass into the coolers. The liquor was cooled in refrigerators, originally shallow wooden vessels usually erected in the top floor of the brewery, where louvred windows enabled the coolers to take full advantage of cold currents of air, particularly in the winter months. Good examples of this type of arrangement have survived in Beamish and Crawford's Brewery, which still retains louvred ventilators along the ridge of the mashing loft. Nonetheless, as it was important to cool the wort quickly in order that fermentation could be begin, the summer months still presented problems for breweries until refrigerators which used ether as a refrigerant were introduced (see below).

After the worts were allowed to cool they were then conveyed to a fermenting vat in which fermentation was induced by the addition of yeast which converted maltose into alcohol. During fermentation the yeast reproduced itself and had to be continually skimmed off. The yeast thus acquired was formed into solid cakes, the surplus of which was commonly sold to distilleries. The brewer would check the specific gravity of the liquor (the level of which fell as the wort was converted into alcohol) to determine the progress of the fermentation.

After fermentation had proceeded to a satisfactory degree, the porter brewer would run the beer straight to the vats in order that it would be naturally conditioned through secondary fermentation in the cask. This gave the beer a creamy head and induced natural carbonation (i.e. the formation of carbon dioxide) which prevented the beer from becoming flat. The final process, called *fining* involved the addition of finings, a gelatinous substance made from the swim bladder of a sturgeon, which cleaned the beer by dragging particles of sediment to the bottom of the cask. Depending upon the quality and strength of the brew required, the beer was either casked in wooden barrels and racked in stillions, or stored if it was intended for export rather than immediate consumption (Callan MacArdle and Callan 1902a, 464; Donnachie 1979, 110). Nearly all of the larger Cork breweries and distilleries maintained cooperages in which large numbers of coopers were employed in the manufacture and repair of casks. In the second half of the nineteenth century most of the Cork breweries had special bottling plants installed.

Cork City Breweries

Lane's Southgate Brewery (306)
Established in 1758 (Bielenberg 1991, 54), this was reputedly the first Cork enterprise in which a steam engine was installed. It was said to be a Cork-made 16hp engine, which Lane had installed in 1798 (Barnard 1890, vol. 2, 322). 'Pirated' versions of Boulton and Watt beam engines were manufactured elsewhere in Ireland during the late eighteenth century (Bowie 1978, 171), and it may well be that the engine installed in Walker's Distillery around this time was a pirated copy. However, there is no evidence which would indicate that any of the Cork City foundries were manufacturing rotative beam engines before 1800, or indeed before the expiry of Boulton and Watt's patents. As there is no independent confirmation of this claim and as Barnard is generally not reliable on facts he cannot establish with his own eyes, on present evidence the earliest authenticated use of a steam engine in a Cork brewery is that installed in Beamish and Crawford's Cork Porter Brewery in 1818 (see below).

The northern and southern extents of Lane's Brewery were defined, respectively, by Old

Post Office Lane and the South Channel. Its capacity was expanded in 1802 and by 1837 it was the second largest unit of brewing within the city (Lewis 1837, vol. 1, 416–17). The main range of buildings were effectively sandwiched between the offices and commercial buildings fronting Grand Parade to the east and South Main Street to the west.[24] One of the most curious features of this brewery was a series of seven slate tanks, contained within one of the largest buildings in the complex.[25] These were used as reservoirs for water used in the 'working off' (i.e. reducing its strength during fermentation) of beer and porter, and were capable of holding 550 barrels (Measom 1866, 328). There were two vat rooms on the northern side of the central courtyard, the eastern room holding six vats (average capacity 200 gallons), and the western one five vats (average capacity 300 barrels). In 1866 the brewery was equipped with two mash tuns, each with a capacity of 100 quarters of malt, and four coppers (ibid.). Lane's premises were also equipped with Morton and Wilson refrigerators (capable of cooling 50 barrels per hour), five fermenting tuns, hop stores and a large cooperage (ibid.). Motive power was provided by two beam engines, the second (a 16hp model) by McSwiney's of Cork which seems to have been erected *c.* 1860 (Barnard 1890, vol. 2, 325). The Goad Insurance Plans of 1897 show a large chimney and two boilers near the well and pump cellar, and it is evident that by this period only one engine was in use. In 1901–2 the Southgate Brewery was bought out by Beamish and Crawford (Cosgrave 1989, 104) and thenceforth used as a tradesmens' and materials stores. By 1906 both the steam engine and its exhaust chimney had been removed, along with the greater part of the original plant.[26] The entire site has now been cleared from Old Post Office Lane to the riverside wall.

Beamish and Crawford's Cork Porter Brewery (040)

This is perhaps the city's most enduring large-scale industrial concern. Its nucleus was a brewery and maltings in Cremer's Square converted by Aylmer Allen in 1782, the lease of which was purchased by William Beamish and William Crawford in 1791. They commenced porter production in 1792, in line with improvements made in the London industry (Lynch and Vaizey 1960, 89; Dickson 1977, 604–5). Beamish and Crawford's output was of national importance, and it was the largest Irish brewery until 1833 when its output was exceeded by Guinness's of Dublin (Lynch and Vaizey 1960, 89).

A large-scale survey by P. Aher dated January 1802 shows the brewery in embryonic form with its full extent lying between Lamley's Lane to the north and Morgan's Lane to the south.[27] The old kiln shown on the south riverside of the complex was probably part of Allen's maltings. There were three vat rooms during this period, each containing four vats each, one large tun room (adjacent to the west riverside wall), a malt mill, and a cooperage and a cellar on Morgan's Lane. The earliest prime movers installed in the brewery were a series of horse whims.[28] In 1818 these were supplemented by a steam engine, the housing for which still survives.[29] From surviving plans of the complex dating to 1839, there can be little doubt that animal-powered engines were in use after 1818 and that these were used in conjunction with a steam engine. However, the installation of the second engine is likely to have allowed the horse whims to be dispensed with.[30]

In 1802 there were two large tuns and some 16 vats.[31] This latter figure was increased to 18 (which were contained in two vat rooms) in the period before 1837.[32] The total area of the complex was now 73,700 sq ft, and by 1839 the southern extremity of the brewery extended beyond the south side of Morgan's Lane, where cask stores, a cooperage and a gasometer had been erected.[33] The expansion and reorganisation of the brewery between the years 1802 and 1839 is clearly shown in two lithographs by Unkles of Cork dated 1839.[34] The physical development of the brewery before 1865 has largely been

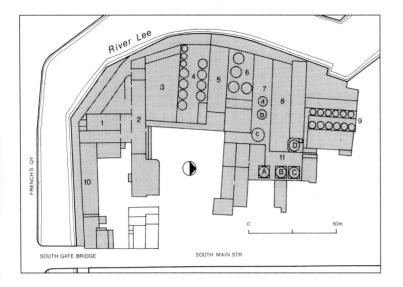

Fig. 15 LEFT

Ground plan of Beamish and Crawford's Cork Porter Brewery (redrawn from Goad Insurance Plans of 1897).

1 Cooperage store. 2 Delivery cellar. 3 Porter stores 1, 2, 3 and 4. 4 Vat room no. 1. 5 Cleansing cellar no. 1. 6 Cleansing cellar no. 2. 7 Mash loft (a-c, mash tuns). 8 Cleansing cellar no. 4. 9 Vat room no. 2. 10 Cooperage. 11 A, B, C, and D, coppers 1–4.

KEY TO FIG. 16 CENTRE

1 Hanover Street Glassworks cone. 2 Original engine house (1818). 3 Cooperage. 4 Malt-milling tower. 5 Malt lofts with porter store. 6 Vat room. 7 Fermenting cellar. 8 Mash loft with refrigerators in roof. 9 'Sky cooler'. 10 Delivery yard. 11 Bottling plant. 12 Cask store. 13 South Gate Bridge.

Fig. 16 BELOW

Late nineteenth-century panorama of Cork Porter Brewery.

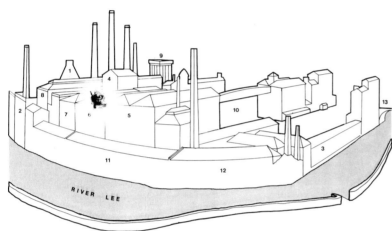

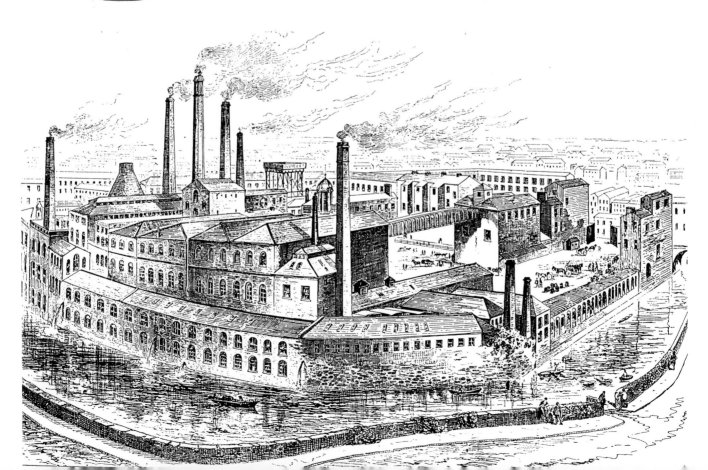

ignored in more recent accounts, where greater emphasis has been placed on the period subsequent to the refit of 1865–8. However, a large-scale survey of the brewery dated 1863 clearly indicates that further significant development occurred before 1865.[35] There is, for example, substantial development in the southern half of the complex, where three cooperage stores have been built on the south quayside, whilst the malt loft is now connected by a tramway to a series of five new malt bins. Furthermore, the coal tramway described by Alfred Barnard in 1890 linking the coal stores in the northern section of the brewery with the coppers, was already in existence in 1863, while a further tramway is shown connecting the boiler house of the northern steam engine.

The period 1865–8 witnessed a further period of refurbishment and redevelopment, during which it is claimed that some £100,000 was invested in modernisation (Cosgrave 1989). Doubtless important changes were made in the layout of the brewery during the 1860s, but its overall configuration at the turn of the twentieth century cannot be wholly ascribed to the developments undertaken in the 1860s. From the mid-1860s onwards the existing range of buildings was extended back onto the south-western riverside quay, with the construction of twin-storey cleansing and barrel-washing cellars, along with a bottle-washing facility (Fig. 15).[36]

Most, though by no means all, of the plant described by Barnard in 1890, dates to the late 1860s, but there had been notable areas of improvement. In 1889 the Cork Porter Brewery, according to Barnard, was using Siebe and West ice-making or refrigerating machines, which used ether as a refrigerant (Corran 1975, 201).[37] A series of Steel's Mashers, were also installed around the same time (Barnard 1890, vol. 2, 325). The existing coppers[38] were also replaced with two cone-headed coppers by Llewellyns and James of Castle Green, Bristol and two dome coppers by Murphy's of Dublin.[39] Measured survey drawings of the setting of these coppers, made in 1884, have survived.[40]

By the early 1880s the brewery complex had reached its greatest extent. All of the intervening east-west laneways on the south side of South Main Street had now been subsumed by its expanding mass, and the area to the riverside wall to the south of Morgan's Lane was occupied by its cooperage, the cooperage stores and yard. The Goad Insurance Plans of 1897 show two 40hp steam engines, one in the north-west corner of the site where the brewery's first engine was originally installed, the other in the engine house near the coppers loft. A panorama of the site dating to the early 1880s (Fig. 16) and a late nineteenth-century photograph taken from the adjacent sixteenth-century Elizabeth Fort (which shows more or less the same view), show a further engine house and chimney at the south-west corner of the site. The Goad Fire Insurance Plans of 1897 show two boilers in this same position, but the mechanism involved is not expressly marked as an engine. Most of the impressive cast-iron superstructure of the main mashing loft dates to the period 1870–83. Details of the cross girders are shown on a drawing dated 14 March 1870, which provides a *terminus post quem* for the installation of the coolers in a special roof compartment above the main mash loft.[41]

The remains of the eighteenth and nineteenth-century brewery buildings now form a central block, demarcated by the former grains yard to the east (which has a mock-Tudor frontage) and the former vat room to the south-west. The areas to the north and south of this central block are now occupied by more recent additions. These include a kegging facility in the area formerly occupied by the Glass Works cone (Fig. 16) and the brewery's main coalyards. The southern area of the complex is now largely taken up by Beamish and Crawford's modern fermentation plant.

Most of the surviving buildings in the western half of the complex are eighteenth century, the principal exceptions being the malt-milling tower, the mash loft and the range of two-storey buildings abutting the western river wall. Where the main load-bearing walls of the late eighteenth-century range of buildings have not been rendered, it is clear that these are a mixture of sandstone and coursed limestone rubble.

The three-storey malt-milling loft (Figs. 16 and 17), which has a relatively light framework sandwiched between wooden interior panelling and exterior corrugated ironwork, continues to dominate the skyline of the brewery. It is also probably unique in Ireland in that it still retains its entire range of late nineteenth early twentieth-century screening and milling plant. The upper floor of the tower contains the separator screens and a large wooden hopper (Fig. 17), from which emanate wooden subsidiary chutes which feed the roller mills on the floor below.

The substance extractor/separator was used to extract unwanted grains and foreign matter such as stones from the malt before it was fed into the roller-milling apparatus. Beamish and Crawford's extant screening machinery is by Nalder and Nalder; the primary drive was by an electric motor, made by Hugh J. Scott of Belfast. The roller mills were fed by drop chutes from the screening machinery on the upper deck of the loft (Fig. 18).[42] A survey drawing dated October 1906 shows three sets of roller mills powered by electric motors via line-shafting.[43]

The roof of the former cleansing cellar no. 2 building, which abuts the malt-milling tower to the west supports a remarkable survival: an enormous cast-iron plate water-storage reservoir. This feature covers the entire surface area of this particular roof, and is clearly shown both in a panorama of the brewery dating to the early 1880s and on the Goad Insurance Plans of 1897. In the main foyer of the modern brewery is a series of 27 mash tun base plates, believed to date to the 1880s, by Robert Morton and Company of Burton on Trent. One mash tun, complete with an enormous hopper, masher and electric motor has survived *in situ*. This was also made by Morton's but dates to 1896. It is entirely encased in wooden panelling and is surmounted by an I-section girder framework supported by cast-iron columns (by Robert Merrick of Cork), which support a small electric motor by Scott & Co. of Belfast. This latter also powers the hopper control on the lower end of the enormous hopper suspended over the tun (Fig. 19). The decking above the main mash loft, immediately east of mash tun contains the remains of four coppers, two of which are complete (Fig. 20). These were made by Llewellyns and James of Bristol England and according to Barnard (1890, vol. 2, 362) the capacity of these was coppers was 1,560 gallons.

The River Lee Porter Brewery (036)

The second surviving, though long defunct, eighteenth-century Cork porter brewery, is the River Lee Porter Brewery on Prospect Row (Fig. 21), which was later incorporated into Beamish and Crawford's Nile Street ('Lee') Maltings Complex (036). The River Lee Porter Brewery was built between 1796 and 1797 (Dickson 1977, 606), and by 1799 had passed into the ownership of the Cork banker and proprietor of Ballincollig Gunpowder Mills (217), Charles Henry Leslie.[44]

The brewery buildings are built around a quadrilateral courtyard, the eastern and southern sides of which originally faced out onto open channels, now culverted. A series of late eighteenth or early nineteenth-century drawings of the brewery, which provide valuable insights into the physical organisation of Beamish and Crawford's early rivals, have recently been discovered amongst the Beamish and Crawford collections held at the Cork Archives Institute.[45] From the latter it is clear that the west wing of the brewery contained most of the plant. The northern end of this wing contained two coppers and two mashers, with an underback set between the mashers. Immediately south of these is a large *tun and stilling* room with seven double stillions and two 'working' tuns. The building to the right of the main Prospect Row entrance is called a 'vat storehouse', a term also used to describe the south wing of the brewery facing Dyke Parade. The River Lee Porter Brewery also appears to have operated water-powered machinery, which was possibly employed in the preparation of malt. The outfall sluice for the brewery's mill-stream was blocked up by 1833.[46]

In areas where there is no exterior render on the brewery buildings it is clear that a mixture of sandstone and some limestone rubble (mainly coursed) was used. All of the buildings around the courtyard have three storeys, and in nearly all cases the roofs are hipped all round. Many of the original eighteenth-century window opes have survived, the majority of which have segmental brick arches. In 1813 the brewery was sold by Leslie to Beamish and Crawford[47] and was used as a storage area for its malting operation. The interiors of three of the wings have been entirely modernised by University College Cork, but in 1992 it became possible to fully investigate the south-east Prospect Row and southern Dyke Parade sections which, apart from addition of an ironwork for supporting a series of steeps in the mid-nineteenth century, proved to have been relatively undisturbed. The timber joists of the first floor are supported on pitch pine longitudinal beams, the opposing ends of which rest on cast-iron brackets, which are supported by stout upright timbers resting on stone pads. Most of the joists are notch-lapped to the cross beams and the floorboards carried by them have been covered with small, square clay tiles, set into a loose mortar and sand mix. The loft or third floor of this wing has an asymmetrical M-shaped roof profile, with steeply pitched king post trusses.

St Finn-barre's Brewery (056)

Situated on Fitton (latterly Sharman Crawford) Street, 'Abbott's', later 'Arnott's' Brewery was one of the largest ale breweries in the city. It was established in 1805 by Samuel Abbott,[48] and was capable of making up to 600 barrels of ale per week when the distiller George Waters (see below under 'Distilling'), who had purchased the brewery in 1858,[49] put it up for auction in 1860.[50] The brewery was bought by Sir John Arnott (1814–98), a prominent expatriate Scottish businessman, philanthropist and one-time Lord Mayor of Cork, in 1861,[51] and was extensively refurbished by him in 1863 and 1870 (Anon. 1873, 11). Hitherto the brewery had largely been involved in the manufacture of table beer (ibid., 6) but by 1876 the brewery was producing up to 50,000 barrels of stout per year.[52] In the early 1870s St Finn-barre's Brewery operated three large mash tuns (each with Steele's patent mashers), three Irish-made coppers, two Morton's patent refrigerators and seven fermenting tuns. The brewery's cooperage was situated on the opposite side of Fitton Street and the bottling stores adjoining the brewery (Fig. 22) were equipped with four bottling machines made by William Dunn of Glasgow. The malt mills were equipped with special screens invented in Cork by Thomas and Edward Lane. Three steam engines were used within the brewery, one of which was manufactured by Caird and Company of Greenock in Scotland, although it is possible that the other two engines were manufactured locally (ibid., 7–11). The greater part of St Finn-barre's Brewery was demolished in *c.* 1909 to make way for the Crawford Technical Institute, latterly the Cork School of Art, although part of the original porter stores appear to have been incorporated into the college buildings.

Fig. 17 OPPOSITE

Main screens in malt loft, Cork Porter Brewery, by Nalder and Nalder of Wantage. *

Fig. 18 ABOVE

Roller mills for malt, by Henry Stopes & Co. of London with Shaeffers Patent Magnetic Apparatus *c.* 1906, in Cork Porter Brewery.*

Fig. 19 CENTRE

Mash tun by Robert Morton & Co. of Burton on Trent, 1896, in Cork Porter Brewery.

Fig. 20 BELOW

Copper by Llewellyns and James of Bristol, *c.* 1883, Cork Porter Brewery.*

*(Con Brogan, Dúchas)

Fig. 21

Lee Porter Brewery, Prospect Row, built between 1796 and 1797. (Con Brogan, Dúchas)

Fig. 22

Ground plan, St Finn-barre's Brewery (Redrawn from Goad Insurance Plans, Cork, 1897).

1 Engine house. 2 Malt mill. 3 Coolers and refrigerators. 4 Racking cellar. 5 Cask washing. 6 Casks. 7 Porter store no. 1. 8 Porter store no. 2. 9 Porter store no 3. 10 Mash loft. 11 Bottling store.

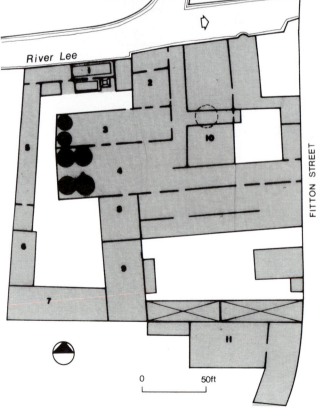

River Lee

FITTON STREET

0   50ft

Murphy's Lady's Well Brewery (060)

This was the last major porter brewery to be established in the city. Built in 1856 within the grounds of the eighteenth-century Foundling Hospital on Leitrim Street it was, after Beamish and Crawford's Cork Porter Brewery, the second largest porter brewery within the city, but by the 1880s it was clearly the largest. Most of the original plant was replaced in the early 1880s (Callan MacArdle and Callan 1902a, 476). A beam engine was still in operation on the ground floor of the brewhouse in 1892, which was worked alternately with a more recent horizontal engine (100hp between both engines, Stratten and Stratten 1892, 146). The 200ft chimney for so long associated with these engines, on the north side of the complex facing Watercourse Road, was demolished in the early 1980s (Fig. 23). The late nineteenth-century Lady's Well Brewery had metal mash tuns made by William Spence of Cork Street, Dublin, each of which was equipped with a cast-iron grist hopper. This was one of the largest mash tuns to be installed in any Irish nineteenth-century brewery (Corran 1970, 24). The brewery's screening room was situated immediately over the malt mills which, like those operating comtemporaneously in Beamish and Crawford's Brewery, were made by Nalder and Nalder of Wantage (see above). Morton's horizontal refrigerators were also installed in the brewery (Stratten and Stratten 1892, 146–8).

The engine and boiler house associated with the former cask washing house was at one time fitted with a horizontal engine by Roby of Lincoln, and had two steel boilers by Adamson's of Hyde. This latter engine actuated the elevators of the three-storey malthouse built in the late 1880s, and a dynamo which provided electric light for the southern end of the brewery (ibid., 148). The malthouse is an impressive structure with a multi-floored kiln at its southern end, which was renovated for modern use in 1992 (Fig. 24). An ammonia cooling plant, fitted out by Pontifex and Wood of London was built on the east side of Leitrim Street, directly opposite the main brewery complex in the late 1880s (Fig. 25) (ibid., 149). The brewery also had sophisticated cask-washing and filling machinery (Fig. 26). All of the brewery buildings on the east side of Leitrim Street, which also included craftsmen's shops and extensive stables, have recently been demolished. Until the early 1980s two small inverted vertical single cylinder engines survived *in situ*. One of these engines was a Tangye (of Birmingham) model, which drove a series of chains (through a series of shafts and bevel gears) in a nearby copper (Cooper 1986, 56).

DISTILLING

By the close of the eighteenth century, Cork had established itself as the centre of the Irish whiskey industry. In the period 1801–23, some 43% of Irish whiskey exports were distilled in Cork, while as early as 1807 Cork distilleries controlled just over 32% of Ireland's registered still capacity. Reliance on the home market increased as the export markets declined, while declining consumption by the middle of the nineteenth century could only partially be addressed through the establishment of national and county-based rail links, an increased export trade and the amalgamation of Cork City's main distilleries. However, by the 1880s Cork's former pre-eminence in the Irish whiskey trade had already been eclipsed by Ulster-based manufacturers of patent still whiskey. The amalgamation of the city's main distilleries and the Midleton distillery in 1867–8, which resulted in the North Mall distillery (see below) becoming the only operational distillery in the city, could only temporarily arrest this decline. Amalgamation, to a certain extent, enabled the Cork Distillers Company to regulate output and respond more flexibly to market fluctuations, but the continued preference by most Irish distillers for more

Fig. 23
Late nineteenth-century panorama of Murphy's Lady's Well Brewery.

Fig. 24 OPPOSITE ABOVE
Malthouse of 1889, designed by T. Hynes of Cork, at Murphy's Lady's Well Brewery. This structure was re-adapted for modern use in 1992. (Con Brogan, Dúchas)

Fig. 25 OPPOSITE BELOW LEFT
Ammonia cooling plant by Pontifex and Wood of London, Murphy's Brewery in early 1890s (from Stratten and Stratten 1892).

Fig. 26 OPPOSITE BELOW RIGHT
Cask-washing machinery, Murphy's Lady's Well Brewery in early 1890s (from Stratten and Stratten 1892).

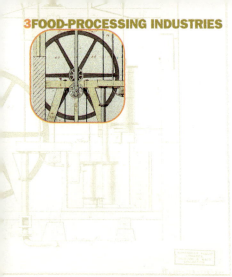

expensively produced pot still whiskey made them increasingly uncompetitive (McGuire 1973, 375; Bielenberg 1991, 61–9; Ó Gráda 1994, 297–8).

The Distilling Process

During the eighteenth century, whiskey distillers were also generally involved in rectifying and compounding, in which small pot stills were employed to manufacture spirits of wine (a purified strong spirit used for scientific and industrial purposes) from raw spirit, along with drinks flavoured with ingredients such as coriander seed and aniseed (Wilson 1975, 56). Between 1807 and 1828 the law made a distinction between the rectifier and the compounder, the compounder being solely engaged in the manufacture of sweetened drinks using sweeteners such as sugar and honey. As early as 1805, however, whiskey distillation, rectifying and compounding had become separate activities (McGuire 1973, 24–5). Some 13 rectifiers were operating within the city in 1813, when Cork was the most important rectifying centre in Ireland (Dickson 1977, 612).

Traditionally, whiskey in Ireland has been distilled from malted barley mixed with a certain amount of raw barley and other cereals such as oats and later maize, the grain being first being reduced to grist and then mixed with the ground malt in a mash tun, in which it is infused with water as in the brewing process (see 'Brewing'). The wort or saccharine-enriched fluid is then run off from the mash tun into an underback, whilst the grains in the mash tun are continually re-mashed to extract as much saccharine matter as possible. The spent grains, as in breweries, were sold off as cattle feed. After cooling, the wort is then run off into a fermenting vat, to which yeast (also called *barm*) is added to enable the fermentation process to begin.

Whereas the brewer endeavoured to retain the aroma of his hops and malt, and to convert only a certain amount of the sugar in the wort to alcohol, the aim of the distiller was the exact opposite. In it essentials, distilling involves the separation of alcohol from fermented wort or *wash*. Alcohol has a lower boiling point than water and is thus given off first, and the still converts the wash into a vapour which is then condensed into a liquid. The condensate is then collected in a vessel called a receiver. Two basic varieties of still were used in Cork, the *pot still* and the *patent* or *continuous still*, the former type being the more common. The pot still was a flat-bottomed copper vessel, from the head of which ran a *worm*; a spiral copper tub which ran around inside an adjacent wooden vessel called a *worm tub*. The worm tub was filled with water which acted as a condenser. The spirit collected at this stage was by no means pure, and it was necessary to purify it in a series of successive re-distillations. The first of these was called the *low wines*, which passed on to the *low wine receiver* and from thence to the *low wines still*, where it was re-distilled. The resulting distillate was then passed on to the *feints receivers*, and the purest of the feints was then conveyed to a third still from which it emerged as whiskey (Callan MacArdle and Callan 1902b, 501–3).

The development of the patent still arose out of a desire to reduce the amount of fuel needed to perform the various distillations involved in the use of the pot still, by achieving continuous distillation from wash to spirit in a single process. Cork-based distillers such as Joseph Shee of the Green distillery and Sir Anthony Perrier of the Spring Lane distillery were amongst the first in Europe to effect significant improvements to traditional distilling apparatus. Although not technically a continuous still, Shee's apparatus directly addressed the fuel consumption problem of the traditional pot still, by employing a succession of four connected pot stills. The lowest still was heated by a fire, the steam from which passed upwards to the second still immediately above it and thence to the third and fourth stills, each positioned at successively higher levels. As the wash entered the fourth and highest still, it flowed against the steam down to the first still, the rising vapours absorbing alcohol, which was condensed and tapped off from the fourth still. The entire arrangement was kept going by vapours from the exhausted wash from the first still (McGuire 1973, 376–7). However, Sir Anthony Perrier's apparatus, patented in 1822, was one of the earliest continuous stills to be developed in Europe. Perrier's still allowed the wash to flow over a heated surface equipped with baffles. Steam was then blown through it, the steam lifting the spirit-laden vapours (ibid., 38).

The still patented in 1830 by Aeneas Coffey (1780–1852), a former Inspector General of Excise in Ireland (Rothery 1968; Davis 1985), was a significant advance in the technology of distillation. In the pot still process strong spirit could only be obtained from repeatedly distilling individual batches, which was wasteful of fuel. In the Coffey still, however, the distilling process is continuous, where cold wash was continuously fed into the still, from which it was discharged as spirit. The Coffey patent still was the first successful heat exchanger. It consists of a pair of fractionating columns, one of which, the analyser, stripped the wash of spirit, and a second column called the rectifier which consolidates and purifies the spirit. Within the still the outgoing hot vapour is allowed to come into contact with the incoming wash awaiting distillation, the greater part of the heat from the hot vapour thereby being exchanged before it was conveyed to the condensor. A very strong spirit of upwards of 95% alcohol could be obtained using this process with significant fuel savings, although the main casualty was the flavour (Callan MacArdle and Callan 1902b, 503; McGuire 1973, 39; McCutcheon 1977, 56–9; Davis 1985, 22–3). In Ireland only the larger distilleries serving expanding urban markets tended to convert to patent still production, but in the main most Irish distillers regarded patent still whiskey as an inferior product and proved reluctant to adopt it even in the face of increased competition from patent distillers with lower cost bases (Ó Gráda 1994, 298). There were only eight patent stills in Ireland in 1833 and two of these were in Cork (see below) (Weir 1978, 138–9).

Cork City Distilleries

The North Mall Distillery (035)

The traditional date for the founding of the North Mall distillery is 1779, a date which has never been satisfactorily documented. In the nineteenth century the enterprise can be closely associated with the Wise family, but no-one of this name is known to have an association with distilling until 1782 (McGuire 1973, 375).[53] Nonetheless, the Wise's were well established at the North Mall by 1802 by which time they were working a new 1,112 gallon still, replaced by a 1,516 gallon still in 1807 (ibid.). The North Mall site was the only distillery in the city to draw its water-power requirements from the north channel of the river Lee, via a diversion dam or weir which directed water into the distillery's millrace. In 1833 'Wise's Weir' was some 230ft long,[54] and in 1863 its sill was 10ft 6in OD,[55] which made it the second largest hydro-power dam on the north channel of the Lee. The site of the weir and the mill channel are probably medieval, having a long association with the site of the Dominican Abbey mill.[56] From 1809 onwards the distillery's cooling pipes were laid in the mill channel,[57] a practice recorded at most of the other distilleries within the city (see below), but the primary uses of this channel are likely to have been for the operation of the malt mill and for the mashing machinery.

Relatively little is known about the early physical development of the North Mall distillery, despite the fact that it was the longest continually operated distillery in the city (Fig. 27). A 20hp Boulton and Watt beam engine was installed in 1808[58] which made

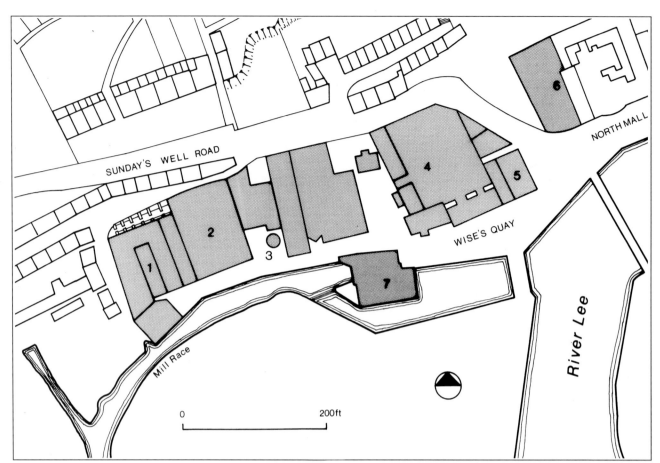

Fig. 27   OPPOSITE

Ground plan, North Mall Distillery in 1869.

1 Still house. 2 Stores. 3 Worm tub.
4 Grain stores. 5 Dwelling. 6 Bonded warehouses. 7 Malt mill.

Fig. 28   OPPOSITE BELOW

Eighteenth-century grain stores, North Mall
Distillery. (Con Brogan, Dúchas)

Fig. 29   BELOW

Late nineteenth-century panorama of North
Mall Distillery.

Fig. 30

Ground plan Millfield Distillery, redrawn from survey of Thomas Holt, dated 6th August 1836, which Holt based on original survey by Sir Thomas Deane.

1 Malthouse. 2 Coach house. 3 Stables. 4 Workers' housing. 5 Cooperage. 6 Malthouse. 7 Coal linneys. 8 Stone water cistern. 9 Barm house. 10 Fermenting house. 11 Office. 12 Still house. 13 Mash house. 14 Kiln. 15 Mill. 16 Corn stores. 17 Flour mill. 18 Wash house.

Fig. 31

Glen Distillery mills in 1869.

1 Kiln. 2 Flour mill. 3 Malt mill. 4 Intake sluice.

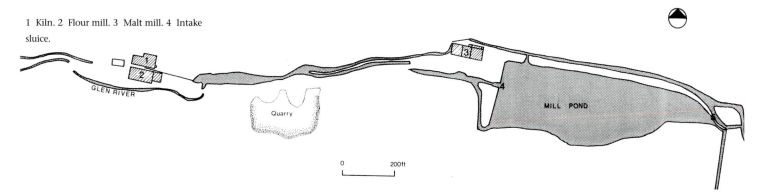

Owner	Cylinder Diam. (inches)	Stroke (feet)	Nominal HP	RPM	Date
THOMAS WALKER & CO.	31½	4	40	18	1805
WILLIAM AND THOMAS WISE	20 ¾	5	20	21.5	1808
THOMAS HEWITT & CO.	28 ⅓	6	30	19	1811
Small side lever independent engine			6	40	1811

Table 1 — Boulton and Watt beam crank engines in Cork City distilleries. (Source: Boulton and Watt Archive, Birmingham City Library, official listing).

it the second distillery in the city to use steam power (see Table 1). In 1848 the malt mill was powered by an 11ft 6in diameter undershot waterwheel with 32 floats which were capable of powering four pairs of Irish stones, which were presumably all used for grinding malt.[59] The entire site, which by the 1880s covered some 23 acres and had a frontage of 684ft, was described in detail by Alfred Barnard in 1887 (Barnard 1887, 406–7). The granaries, which were built against a sandstone escarpment, enabled access from Sunday's Well Road (Figs. 27 and 28), where doubtless some of the sandstone used in their construction was quarried. Barnard states that these had a capacity of 30,000 barrels. The barley was first passed through cleaning machinery before being conveyed to one of the four drying kilns, after which it was removed to the grain deposit rooms and thence via bucket elevators to the malt mill. The malt mill, which replaced the earlier structure described above, and which itself was demolished in 1985, was constructed in or around 1850. This was a five-storey structure with hipped roofs on each main division, tied internally with cast-iron bars, the individual floors being supported on cast-iron columns (Ryan 1985). The mill straddled arches built immediately over the mill channel, one of which enclosed a 25ft diameter undershot waterwheel which drove six pairs of stones. The upper floors of the building functioned as storage lofts (Barnard 1887, 406).

The power requirements of nearly all of the North Mall's machinery in the 1880s were met by two steam engines, of 60hp and 40hp respectively, by John Rowan & Sons of the York Street foundry, Belfast,[60] with six Galloway patent steam boilers. The principal advantage of the Galloway boiler, patented by William and John Galloway of Manchester in 1851, was the design of its twin fire tubes 'which improved the circulation of the water and the increased heating surface as the hot gases passed around them' (Hills 1989). In the panorama of the North Mall distillery published in Barnard's account five chimney stacks are shown (Fig. 29), but in 1877–8 the Cork Distilleries Co., who bought the distillery in 1867, demolished these and connected all of the main flues to a single stack 160ft high. The butt of this can still be seen on Sunday's Well Road complete with its foundation plaque.

The greater part of the North Mall premises was destroyed by fire in the 1920s after which the manufacture of pot still whiskey ceased. The malt mill was demolished in 1985 and up until 1988 the remains of the distillery's bonded stores survived at the foot of Wise's Hill. At the present showing the only surviving structures associated with the distillery are the corn stores fronting onto Wise's Hill and a twin-arched stone bridge allowing access to the adjacent island which currently houses some of Irish Distillers

bonded stores and an early twentieth-century cooperage.

The Millfield Distillery (096)

Established in 1783 by Morgan Coldwell on the site of the Kilnap mills of William Furlong,[61] the adjacent river Bride provided what was probably the best hydraulic head available within the environs of the city, equivalent to about 60hp.[62] However, although the distillery was in operation from the early 1780s Coldwell did not acquire control of the Kilnap mills until 1790.[63] The complex of buildings at Millfield appears to have been expanded in 1824,[64] reaching its greatest extent by 1831, by which time it ceased to function as a distillery and was put up for auction.[65] Water power was used to actuate a 30ft diameter patent metal kieve or mash tun in the mash house, the pumps in the still house and two mills. The range of distillery buildings included a bonding store, a mash house and a large grains house (Fig. 30).

The still house had a wash charger, spirit receiver, pumps and a Saintmarc patent still with which it was possible to manufacture 180,000 gallons of whiskey in a season. Jean-Jacque Saintmarc's still, patented in the early 1800s, was one of the first continuous stills. In its essentials this was a fire-heated pot still equipped with rectifying chambers, in which pure spirit could be produced continuously. However, although it was capable of producing more than a conventional pot still it is only known to have been used in three Irish distilleries (McGuire 1973, 39; Weir 1995, 23). The Millfield example is the only one known to have been used in a Cork distillery, and appears to be the earliest recorded example used in Ireland.[66] Connected to the still was a 'hewn stone' cooling cistern, the cold water of which was supplied by the millstream, in which the distillery's cooling pipes were laid (Fig. 30). The double acting pumps in the still house appear to have been powered by an overshot waterwheel.[67] The Millfield distillery was under the control of James Daly, owner of the John Street distillery (see below), in 1836, and thereafter only the flour mills were utilised until the purchase of the site by the Cork Spinning and Weaving Company in 1862.[68]

The Dodge's Glen (Spring Lane) Distillery (015)

From at least the early 1800s the Glen River was used for a distillery at Dodge's Glen which, like the Millfield distillery, was purposely sited just outside the municipal boundary to avoid rates. The exact date for its establishment, which is also confusingly referred to as the Glen distillery (see below), is not known.[69] The 'New Distillery' at Spring Lane, Blackpool was in existence as early as 1803, when it was run by one Robert Vincent,[70] and in the following year was referred to as the 'Spring Lane and Glen Vale Lane Distilleries'.[71] In 1805 Sir David Perrier is listed as owner of the 'Spring Lane Distillery', and in the following year a Sir Anthony Perrier was operating a 1,555 gallon still there (McGuire 1973, 355).[72] Sir Anthony Perrier patented his own continuous still in 1822, although the design was apparently not a success (ibid., 38). Control of the distillery seems to have passed to the Callaghan family by at least 1818 (ibid.) and remained so up until its closure in the late 1840s.[73]

The section of the Glen River immediately to the west of the former sailcloth and rope manufactory at Cahergal (**010**) was formed into a series of interconnected mill channels and millponds (Fig. 31) for the use of the distillery and its associated mills (**013** and **014**). The distillery's 'East Mill' had three lofts and a wooden waterwheel driving two pairs of stones for grinding malt. The 'West Mill', which had four lofts, was slightly bigger, originally driving three pairs of stones, and also had a kiln.[74] In 1846 the 'Glen Distillery Mills' were advertised in the local press (as were other Cork mills during the famine period see below) as 'ready for grinding Indian and other corn'.[75] By 1848 the West Mill was seldom worked, whilst the East Mill was said to grind rarely and only then for the distillery.[76]

Callaghan's Distillery was the third largest in the city environs in 1828 (Bielenberg 1991, 64). At least part (if not all) of the distillery's power requirements were met by two steam engines of 4 and 12hp respectively.[77] However, it is likely that the water power was used exclusively when the site was established. The only surviving traces of the Glen distillery are sections of the original millraces, most of which have been modified during the laying out of the current Glen park. All traces of the east and west mill buildings had been obliterated by the early 1980s, but many buildings appear to have been incorporated into Goulding's Chemical Works (**445**).

The Green Distillery (018)

The desire for distillers to exploit the higher available falls of water on the river Bride and the Glen Stream led to the establishment of four distilleries in the Blackpool/Watercourse Road area in the north liberties of the city. At least two of these — the Green distillery (**018**) on York Street (Thomas Davis Street) and the Watercourse distillery (**024**) — were established in the late eighteenth century. The exact location of Ring's Blackpool Distillery (**562**), built in or around 1828, could not be ascertained. What is clear, however, is that some of its machinery was water-powered.[78] Given the known dispositions of the other water-powered industrial sites within the Blackpool area during the early nineteenth century, this would suggest that it drew its water from the Back Watercourse. [79]

The Green distillery, originally known as the 'Blackpoole Distillery' (which should not be confused with Ring's distillery of the same name), was established by Robert Allan and Denis Corcoran in 1796, on the site of a malthouse (O'Keefe 1974, 58).[80] Its water power was presumably drawn from the canalised section of the Glen River flowing past its western boundary, which effectively became the outfall from Callaghan's distillery from the early 1800s onwards. The distillery was sold in 1801, by which time it was operating two stills. It also controlled two malthouses, one of which adjoined it, and was also in control of the two mills at Wherland's Lane called 'Waters Mills'.[81] In 1812 this distillery was under the ownership of Thomas and Joseph Shee (McGuire 1973, 376), and by 1828 it was amongst the four smallest distilleries within the city, accounting for less than 7% of the city's annual production (Bielenberg 1991, 64, table 7.1), although by 1844 its capacity had been greatly expanded.[82] Joseph Shee, however, was an innovator, patenting his own still, one of which was operated at the Green Distillery in 1850 (Underwood 1935, 24; McGuire 1973, 377).

In 1836 the distillery along with its 'corn mill and stores' was put up for auction,[83] the corn mill being no other than Water's Mills in Wherland's Lane (**019**).[84] These latter, like most of the distillery mills in the city, also ground flour and oats when the need arose. By 1844 the Wherland's Lane Mills were supplemented by a steam mill, which was presumably situated within the distillery proper.[85] In 1850 the distillery was taken over by George Waters, formerly of the John Street distillery (see below) and in 1851 the distillery plant was modified for the production of traditional pot still whiskey,[86] up until the closure of the distillery after its amalgamation with the Cork Distilleries Co. in 1868 (McGuire 1973, 377). It was used as stores by the Cork Distilleries Company throughout the later nineteenth century, and by the turn of the century functioned as bonded warehouses.[87] The greater part of the Green distillery buildings were demolished in 1989. However, the remains of what appears to have been the original eighteenth-century store house have partially survived. The greater part of the cast structural work

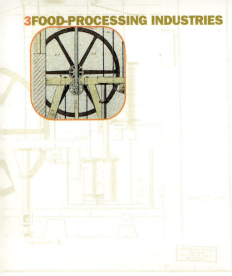

(mostly cast-iron supporting columns and an open-framed roof in the central area of the complex) was manufactured by John Steele's Vulcan Foundry (see Ch. 5).

The Watercourse Distillery (024)

In the closing decade of the eighteenth century the outfall from the Green distillery was directed to the Watercourse distillery, which had been established by the partnership of Hewitt, Teulon and Blunt in 1792 and constructed in 1793–4 (McGuire 1973, 377–8; Bielenberg 1991, 72). The scale of operations at the Watercourse site required that the foundations be excavated into the adjacent hillside, in order that the ground area be maximised and also, perhaps, that the available head of water be increased.[88] The Watercourse Distillery was a relative latecomer in an area where the available heads had previously been utilised by small flour and meal mills, and the availability of suitable heads was to become a serious problem in the later physical development of the site (see below). Production began in earnest in November 1793[89] with two large capacity stills.[90] The construction of the stills, condensers and worms was undertaken by Edgar Curtis of Bristol[91] during the early years of production, because the necessary expertise was unavailable locally (Bielenberg 1991, 72).

The Back Watercourse, an extensively canalised section of the Glen River, was used by the Green Distillery (see above) and later by the Blackmiller's Lane (Watercourse Mill–Assumption Road) flour mill (**061**, see below). A large stretch of the Glen Stream in Dodge's Glen, from at least the 1800s onwards, was harnessed for the use of Callaghan's Distillery (see above). The availability of water power, while nominally an important consideration in the choice of site, could hardly have been one of the Watercourse distillery's main attractions, because while the available fall appears to have been reasonable enough, without extensive quarrying it would not have been possible to satisfactorily impound it. Indeed the scarcity of water *per se* both for energy and for cooling purposes was considered by the valuation office surveyors of the late 1840s to be amongst the distillery's main disadvantages.[92] Water- and horse-powered machinery were originally used in the distillery (ibid., 73) but by themselves these were insufficient to ensure its continued expansion. In 1810 the distillery sought the permission of the owners of the evidently disused St John's Mills to divert water from it for their own use.[93] However, when the latter mills were put for auction in 1811,[94] the company passed over the opportunity of acquiring them. It was not until 1830, by which time it had been converted to a sawmill,[95] that the company actually did so. The company then set about disabling this mill (ibid.). In 1825 the company acquired Waters Mill (**059**, also known as Archdeacon's Mills, see below under 'Grain Milling'), situated immediately south of it on the same channel, which it used for grinding malt. In the late 1840s this was operating an 18ft diameter breastshot, metal waterwheel with 48 buckets on a 15ft fall.[96]

Continuing problems with its water power requirements forced the distillery to invest in steam-driven prime movers, and in the period 1811–12 they installed two Boulton and Watt engines, one a 30hp beam crank engine, the other a small side lever independent engine of 6hp (see Table 1).[97] The more powerful engine was used in the distillery's mill and the smaller engine for pumping and for the stills and coppers. A 20hp engine by Maudslay, Sons and Field of Westminster Road, Lambeth,[98] was purchased in 1823, but despite the firm's strong reputation the engine needed regular packing (presumably to minimise the escape of steam), and could only be used for mashing two weeks in each month.[99]

In 1836 the Watercourse distillery was described as 'the most extensive in Ireland', with bonded stores for 2,000 puncheons of spirits, and an annual output of 800,000 gallons.

The Maudslay engine drove two 30ft diameter cast-iron mash tuns. Two water-powered mills were also controlled by Hewitt's, one of which (presumably the malt mill acquired in 1825, see above) had been recently modified and could 'be made to grind most of the grain wanted'.[100] In 1833 the company purchased a Coffey's patent still — the first of its type to be used in the city — which was worked by a steam boiler, with which it was possible to distill 3,000 gallons of wash every hour.[101] The Watercourse distillery accounted for 56% of the city's distilling capacity in 1808 (Dickson 1977, 610), and by 1828 it was the second largest producer in the city after Wise's North Mall Distillery.[102]

A panorama of the site in 1870 indicates that it had already, by this date, reached its largest extents (Fig. 32). The buildings facing Watercourse Road were mostly taken up with the distillery's stores and offices, whilst the maltings, grain stores, mash houses, and still houses occupied the three main blocks of buildings at the rear (Fig. 33). Four large circular coolers were located to the north of the mash house adjacent to the distillery's feeder stream, from which they presumably drew water. The stream was culverted underneath the mash house, re-emerging immediately south of the steam-powered flour mill (Fig. 33).[103] In 1887, by which time the Watercourse distillery had been closed by the Cork Distilleries Co., there were three corn stores holding some 40,000 barrels of barley, and seven bonded warehouses (Barnard 1887, 408). Between 1915 and 1917 the Watercourse distillery was converted for the manufacture of yeast and industrial spirit, in which all of the machinery was powered by electric motors (Coakley 1919, 155–6).

The Watercourse distillery is currently the best-preserved eighteenth-century example within the city and its environs. All of the surviving buildings are mostly built of sandstone, with the use of brick generally being confined to the early twentieth-century additions. The original mash house has effectively been cut in half by a later access road and the steam mill has been demolished. The eighteenth-century granaries, however, and part of the original maltings have survived (Fig. 34).

St Dominick's Distillery (438)

The only large distillery to be sited to the south of the north channel of the river Lee — St Dominick's Distillery — was established by Thomas Walker in 1789 at Crosses Green (Dickson 1977, 610). The distillery is shown on Thomas Holt's map of 1832 on the site believed to be that of the Dominican Abbey mill (see below), which raises the question of the relationship of the present St Dominick's Mills to the preceding St Dominick's Distillery. The site certainly was in use as a mill site in 1753[104] and there can be little doubt that Walker was primarily interested in site's potential for water power and its ready access to the south channel. But in adapting the site for the use of his distillery, to what extent did he adapt the existing buildings? This latter question, in the present state of our knowledge cannot be satisfactorily answered. However, the recent discovery of a drawing of the distillery made in 1805 now leaves little doubt that the buildings currently called St Dominick's Mills are none other than those of Walker's Distillery.

In 1799 Thomas Walker and Company had formally approached Boulton and Watt about the installation of a steam engine at its St Dominick's Distillery.[105] Few details of this engine have survived, although it is clear that an engine was already in existence in the distillery by 1805 when Walker proposed to have a larger and much more powerful engine installed by Boulton and Watt. The earlier engine is likely to have been installed sometime before 1800, and appears to be, along with an example installed in a Dublin distillery around the same time, one of the earliest known examples of steam power at work in an Irish distillery (Archer 1801, 203–4; Bowie 1978, 171). Walker engaged a Dublin engineer called Alex Johnston to oversee the various modifications to the

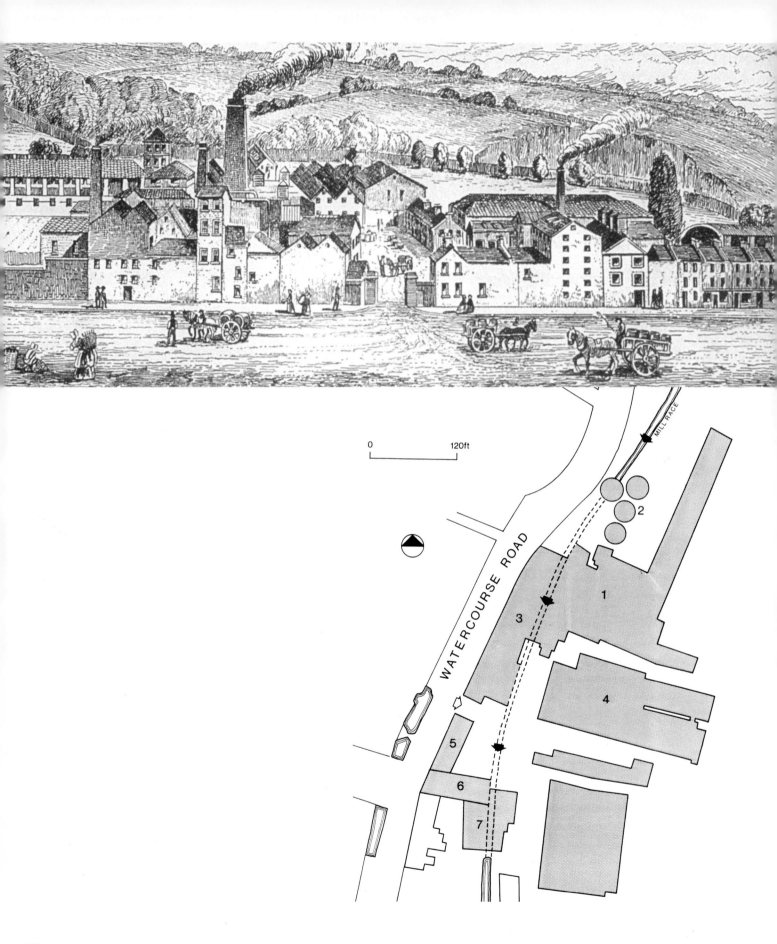

0   120ft

MILL RACE

WATERCOURSE ROAD

1

2

3

4

5

6

7

Fig. 32 OPPOSITE ABOVE
Late nineteenth-century panorama of
Watercourse Distillery.

Fig. 33 OPPOSITE
Ground plan, Watercourse Distillery in
1861, redrawn from Landed Estates
Court Map by Frederick A. Klein,
courtesy Cork Archives Institute.

1 Mash and still houses. 2 Coolers.
3 Distillery stores. 4 Grain stores.
5 Offices. 6 Stores. 7 Flour mill.

Fig. 34 ABOVE
Eighteenth-century granaries (on
extreme right), Watercourse Distillery.

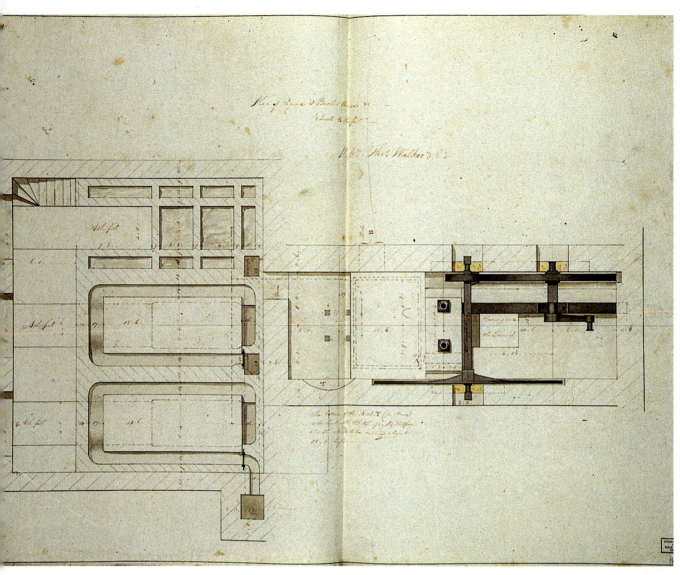

Fig. 35 ABOVE

Boulton and Watt Engine in St Dominick's Distillery in 1805 (Courtesy Birmingham Central Reference Libraries).

Fig. 36 RIGHT

Daly's Distillery, John Street est. 1820. (Con Brogan, Dúchas)

existing distillery buildings, which would both enable the new engine to be adequately housed and ensure that a series of additional distilling processes could be powered by it. Johnston proposed to work the new engine from both sides, by means of transmission shafting to millstones erected in a room to the east of the engine, to power three mashing kieves and two pumps.[106] A sketch of the distillery by Johnston, dated 20 February 1805, shows a smaller beam engine with a single boiler, which is annotated 'small engine to be removed after the large one [i.e. the new engine] is at work'. The new engine (see Table 1) was a 40hp Boulton and Watt double-acting beam crank engine (Fig. 35), the first engine of its type to be installed in an Irish distillery, and in its day the most powerful Boulton and Watt engine in any Irish industrial installation. The engine was at work by the end of 1805 and was described by the Rev. James Hall, who visited Cork in 1812, as 'the only one of its kind in this part of the country' and powered 'four pairs of millstones for grinding malt and other grains' (Hall 1813, vol. 1, 156–7).[107] Johnston's sketch also establishes beyond reasonable doubt that Walker's Distillery later became St Dominick's Mills after the distillery was sold in 1831. The mill canal, now culverted, is shown to the south of the distillery building, with the main sluice gate at the south-western corner: the same location as that shown on an undated early nineteenth-century plan of the area. This area of the building is called the 'water mill' on Johnston's sketch, and it appears that the mash tuns were actually powered by it. Water power appears to have continued to play an important role in the power requirements of the distillery, because in 1810 Walker brought a successful action against William Lumley of the Pipe Water Company, for interfering with the supply of water allowed into the south channel of the Lee (Tuckey 1837, 235). In 1802 Walker was using a 2,179 gallon still which was considered to be the largest then in use in Ireland (Dickson 1977, 610). By 1831, when the distillery was put up for auction, it had two cast-iron kieves with mashing machines, three large coppers, two large stills with worms, 'numerous' fermenting backs, and its copper cooling pipes were laid in the river (cf. the Millfield and North Mall distilleries).[108] The distillery was bought by the O'Keefes in 1831, and shortly afterwards was converted for use as a flour mill (see below). In 1843 the remains of the distillery utensils had been auctioned off.[109]

The John Street Distillery (190)

James Daly and Company's Distillery in John Street was established in 1820 (Measom 1866, 307).[110] Daly was originally a rectifying distiller who had set up a business in 1798 in Blarney Lane, and he later appears to have entered into a partnership with George Waters to run the John Street distillery.[111] The distillery was powered by three steam engines, the oldest of which, a 30hp beam engine by Robinson of Dublin, drove the machinery of the brewhouse. An 80hp compound engine by Neilson and Hyde of the Park foundry in Glasgow, which was used to power most of the other machinery within the distillery and its associated mill, was installed sometime before 1866. The distillery also had eight duty-free warehouses on Leitrim Street, John Street and Watercourse Road, along with maltings on John Street and granaries on Leitrim Street (ibid., 308). James Daly was in control of the Millfield distillery by 1836 and probably bought the Millfield premises when they were put up for auction in 1831. Daly's ownership of the Millfield complex effectively prevented it from ever being operated as a distillery again.[112] The surviving multistorey distillery/steam mill building on John Street (Fig. 36) originally had a pitched roof (ibid.) which was later converted to a flat roof to enable a cast-iron water cistern to be emplaced. James Daly died in 1850 whereupon George Waters withdrew from the John Street distillery to become involved in the Green distillery.[113] The distillery continued to function up until the incorporation of the Cork Distillers Company in 1867 (McGuire 1973, 379) and thereafter functioned as a steam-powered flour mill.

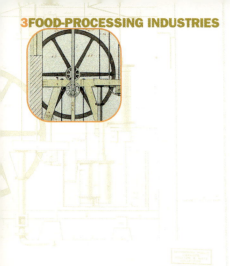

The Glen Distillery (646)

The last whiskey distillery to be established within the environs of the city was the Glen distillery, run by the Glen Distillery Co. Ltd at Kilnap.[114] The former Glen Flour Mills owned by John Power were converted into a distillery premises in 1882, but in 1884 the entire premises was put up for auction after a legal dispute between the partners John Warren and Christopher Woods.[115] An inventory of the buildings and plant made in 1884 provides a detailed account of the Glen distillery at that time, one of the most striking features of which was an iron overshot waterwheel, 40ft in diameter.[116] In 1887 the distillery's mill drove only four pairs of stones powered by the same, large overshot waterwheel, which was fed by an aqueduct drawing from the adjacent Kilcully River. The granaries, which intercommunicated with a kiln, had a capacity of 7,000 barrels (Barnard 1887, 412). The distillery's cooling pipes, as at the North Mall, St Dominick's and Millfield distilleries (see above), were laid in the bed of the adjacent river (ibid., 412–13). The Glen distillery ceased production in the 1920s.

GRAIN MILLING

The spread of merchant milling in the second half of the eighteenth century, which was actively encouraged by a government bounty between 1758 and 1797 on flour brought to Dublin, provided the impetus for widespread structural and technological changes in the Irish grain-milling industry (Cullen 1977). The traditional, small-scale oatmeal and flour mills of the Irish countryside were gradually replaced by larger units of production in which the various milling processes had become almost fully mechanised. The adoption of steam power in grain mills also greatly reduced the traditional reliance on water power. Large-scale milling could now be undertaken on the quaysides of Ireland's ports, where grain could be unloaded into adjacent granaries, reduced to flour in nearby mills and directly conveyed from the latter to outgoing ships. After 1846 the Irish grain-milling industry began to contract in the face of a decline in tillage due to an increase in pasturage, American competition and new technology (Ó Gráda 1994, 304–5). Towards the end of the nineteenth century large quantities of maize for provender (i.e. animal foodstuff) milling began to be imported into the city (Coakley 1919, 163), an activity to which many city-based millers changed as the demand for flour in the Irish domestic market declined (Bielenberg 1991, 49).

Water-driven prime movers continued to be used for milling within the city and its immediate environs well into the second half of the nineteenth century. With the exception of the main channels of the river Lee, which lay within the harbour's intertidal zone, the hydrological conditions favouring the establishment of water-powered installations were generally good. Steam-driven plant was introduced into many of the larger mills, but as late as the 1870s it continued to be used, in many instances, as back-up rather than an alternative to water power (see below).

From about the 1830s onwards, the city's wholly steam-powered flour mills tended to become established on the south channel of the river Lee, when direct access to the city quaysides became an important locational consideration, and increasingly so when the city's flour-milling industry came to rely on imported grain. The capacity of these mills greatly exceeded that of their more traditional water-powered counterparts, and their storage requirements alone necessitated larger kilning facilities and separate warehousing. The construction of corn and flour stores was an important, although often neglected, aspect of the infrastructural development of the Irish flour-milling industry, and no less so in Cork than in any other Irish port.

Grain Storage and Preparation

The French Consul Charles de Montbret, who visited Cork in 1790, remarked that wheat was exported from Cork in bulk and that grain-drying kilns were widely available. Cork bakers generally kiln-dried their grain before having it ground, the drying process taking about six hours (Ní Chinnéide 1973, 9). From the late eighteenth century onwards multistorey 'corn stores' or granaries became an increasingly common feature of the city's quaysides. Many of these became established along the south channel of the river Lee. From 1833, when the new corn exchange was constructed on Albert Quay (**094**), the quaysides immediately south of it became favoured locations. The cornmarket, which cost £17,460 with a government advance of £4,615 towards the cost of the adjacent bridge over the south channel, had 13 carriageways for unloading grain and 12 covered walks for those engaged in buying and selling (Lewis 1837, vol. 1, 413). The majority of the granaries situated either on the city's quaysides or on the sidestreets leading to them were quite extensive, and were also equipped with drying kilns and coal storage yards. The drying of the grain preparatory to milling, as we will see, was essential, and while the vast majority of the city's grain mills appear to have had kilning facilities, it is also clear that this task was undertaken by corn merchants.

In 1829 Benjamin White's corn store on Lavitt's Quay covered 10,580 sq ft, with a quayside frontage of 80ft, which extended inwards from the quay for a distance of 136ft. The premises had seven lofts 80–120ft long, along with 'a convenient kiln for drying corn and plenty of good water'.[117] One corn store in Deane Street in 1830 was 102ft deep and had a 74ft street frontage[118] and by 1845 had five lofts and two grain-drying kilns.[119] William Crawford's corn store on Fish Street was 256ft long, with a 62ft quayside frontage to Merchants Quay, and was equipped with a single drying kiln.[120] Apart from their multi-floor storage capabilities these were clearly purpose-built structures. J. Gould and Company's corn stores adjoining Clarke's Bridge, for example, had three grain lofts, the first of which was divided into four compartments which were skirted with sheet iron to counteract damp. The floors of its droppings room were, in addition, surfaced with Shanakiel flags laid on clinker.[121] The corn stores situated directly upon the city's quaysides also provided berthage facilities. In 1834 a corn store on Morrison's Quay was advertised as being 'so close to water that large vessels can load and discharge without cartage', and also boasted 'two powerful windlasses'.[122] In most cases the capacity of the city's quayside corn stores was quite large, but very few of these appear to have exceeded that of the corn stores attached to, or directly associated with, the city's steam mills (see below). J. Gould and Company's corn stores at Clarke's Bridge,[123] for example, could hold 5,000 barrels of prepared oats, whilst the corn stores at Union Quay could hold 6,000 barrels.[124] The Queen Street corn stores, however, which in 1848 had a capacity of some 15,000 barrels (which greatly exceeded that of the city's larger mills) were clearly exceptional.[125] The kilning facilities associated with these corn stores appear to have been quite substantial. The Morrison's Quay corn stores (see above) was operating a patent kiln in 1834, which was capable of drying three varieties of grain simultaneously.[126] Unlike country kilns where the principal fuels included peat, wood or culm, the city-based grain-drying kilns used imported fuel (Dickson 1977, 473). J. Gould and Company's drying kiln attached to their corn stores at Clarke's Bridge required one ton of coal to dry 1,000 barrels of oats.

The largest surviving corn store within the city, situated on Charlotte's (present-day Father Matthew) Quay (**143**), has six storeys (Fig. 37). Appropriate ventilation in the form of either multi-level fenestration (i.e. closely spaced windows on each floor) or louvred vents, was an important feature of all grain-storage buildings in the city. The more typical nineteenth-century Cork grain stores had three to four storeys, with central

Fig. 37

Corn store, Father Matthew Quay.

Fig. 38

Young's Steam Mills, Crosses Green. (Con Brogan, Dúchas)

or near central loading bays on each storey facing the quayside or the street frontage. In most cases the loading doors were situated on the gable end of the building with a projecting overhead sackhoist (complete with a ridge canopy or *lucam*) positioned at the gable's peak. Good examples of the latter can still be seen on the corn stores at St Paul's Avenue (**284**), Beasly Street (**345**) and on the corn lofts of Young's steam mills at Crosses Green (**117**), (Fig. 38).

As the presence of foreign matter in a stock of grain to be milled could both adversely affect the colour of the flour and worse, cause damage to the millstones or chilled iron rollers used to reduce them, it was essential that all cereal grains passing through them were carefully cleaned beforehand. From the second half of the eighteenth century onwards the means by which this could be achieved became increasingly more sophisticated. In the more basic varieties of corn cleaners the separation of dirt and other extraneous matter was carried out using mechanically agitated sieves. The use of hand or mechanically operated winnowing fans, which utilised a draft of air for this purpose, were introduced in the second half of the eighteenth century. In the nineteenth century rotary cleaners were introduced, which consisted of a wire mesh drum equipped with internal rotating brushes. Any grain fed into the drum was forced up against the wire mesh by the brushes, which forced out any smaller particles of dirt. *Cockle cylinders*, for separating foreign seeds from the grain, rubble reels, for removing dirt and stones and magnets for screening out metal fragments, were also introduced in the nineteenth century (Watts 1983, 13–15).

The relatively damp climate of Ireland required that after cleaning, any home-produced grain had to be kiln-dried to reduce its moisture content to facilitate milling. This was particularly important where oats was concerned, as the removal of the husks became more difficult if they where not rendered sufficiently brittle by kiln-drying. The kilns themselves were generally exactly the same as those used for malting. Indeed, as it became necessary to dry barley before malting, many kilns may well have been used for terminating the sprouting process and for drying grain preparatory to milling.

Milling with Stones

Most of the grain mills within the city and its environs ground both wheat and oats and from the late 1840s onwards, indian maize (see below). After cleaning and drying, oats were first passed through a pair of *shellers* or *shelling stones*, set at a distance equivalent to the width of one grain apart, to remove the husks. In the contemporary nineteenth-century accounts these are commonly referred to as 'Irish' stones, being generally cut from conglomerate sandstone, but without the elaborately dressed working surfaces of grinding stones. Shelling stones were usually manufactured in sizes of 3ft 6in, 4ft 6in and 5ft in diameter. The groats or cereal berries and the husks were then passed through a sieve to remove dust and the husks (shells) were then blown off by a mechanical fan. Mechanical bucket elevators were employed to lift the shelled oats up to the grinding stones and, having passed through these, the resultant meal was then dressed with mechanically agitated sieves and fans to produce grades of coarse, medium and fine oatmeal (Bowie and Jones 1978, 260).

Throughout the nineteenth century *French* or *French burr* stones were extensively used for grinding oats and wheat in the Cork region, which leaves little doubt that white flour was main product of Cork flour mills. The stone itself, which is quartz-like and had superior grinding surfaces was quarried at La Ferte-sous-Jouarre and Bergerac near Paris. The millstones produced from it are called composite stones, as the stones themselves are normally manufactured from dressed blocks of the stone set in plaster within an iron

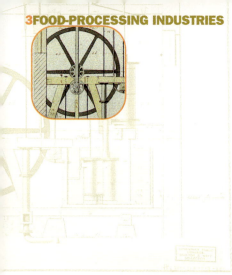

hoop, in sizes up to 4ft 6in in diameter. All of the available evidence suggests that French burr stones were either imported directly into Cork from France or via English millstone manufactories.[127]

Most of the large later eighteenth-century flour mills and all of the nineteenth-century examples were equipped with mechanically driven flour-dressing machinery which was used to sieve and grade the flour. The mechanical bolter was the first of a series of power-driven devices employed in mills for more efficient flour dressing and it is from its widespread application in early industrial mills that the contemporary eighteenth- and nineteenth-century term 'bolting mill' originates.[128] A textile mesh was drawn over a cylindrical wooden framework, which was rotated by an auxiliary drive from the waterwheel. The meal, which was fed in at one end of the drum thus formed, was graded by being forced through the mesh from which only flour of the desired grade could emerge. From the late eighteenth century onwards wire machines, which enabled different grades of flour to be separated simultaneously, became available, and from the mid-nineteenth century onwards silk reels, which produced higher quality flour than either bolters or wire machines, began to be used in Irish and English mills. By 1796 there was at least one specialist machine maker in Cork at Fishamble Lane, William Mozly, who manufactured bolting machines, wheat cylinders, winnowing and screening machines. Mozly had supplied bolting machinery to Hayes' Mills (the Lee Mills, see below) and to William Clarke's mills at Crosses Green (see below).[129]

Cork foundries became agents for patent English flour-dressing machinery, whilst English millwrights and foundries (at least in the first half of the nineteenth century) undertook work for Cork millowners. In 1820 the Scottish engineer John Rennie (1761–1821) designed the machinery for Thomas Walker's flour mill at Crosses Green, whilst in 1835 the English firm of Peele, Williams & Peele fitted out the Lee mills (see below).[130] By the early 1830s Cork foundries had established agencies for British patented milling plant. In 1833 John Steele of the Vulcan foundry on Lancaster Quay was agent for Smith's patent flour machinery,[131] and in 1855 Richard Perrott of the Hive Iron Works had the 'sole agency' for Hennicart's flour-dressing silks.[132] Cork-based foundries also manufactured waterwheels, steam engines and power transmission systems for local grain mills (see below).

Water-powered Flour and Meal Mills on the River Lee and its Tributaries

A number of water-powered grain mill sites on the main channels of the River Lee have medieval antecedents, and in the case of the Fishamble Lane (Liberty Street) mill (**073**) it is possible to document the almost continued use of this mill site from the fourteenth century onwards.[133] 'Droop's mill', the only water-powered installation to be constructed within Cork's medieval town walls, was built on the natural watercourse separating the two islands upon which the medieval citadel became established. The section of the watercourse within the city walls was probably canalised at a relatively early period. With the gradual reclamation of the marshes to the west of the city from the eighteenth century onwards, the natural watercourse outside the city walls supplying the mill became a more or less regularised channel, running between Fenn's Marsh to the south and Hammond's Marsh to the north. A lease of 1712, which refers to 'Droop's mill pond',[134] and a newspaper account of 1754 which refers to 'mill dam near Fishamble Lane',[135] provide clear indications that the watercourse servicing the mill was impounded to the west of Fishamble Lane. However, the nature and ultimate fate of this reservoir are somewhat obscure, for by the end of the eighteenth century the mill channel running approximately from the corner of Prospect Row to the western end of Liberty Street had been culverted. At the Spring Assizes of 1793 a presentment was made

SMR No.	TD/ Street	Waterwheel(s) No.	Type	Diam.(s)	No. Buckets	HP	Millstones Type	Diam.
002	Orchard Rd.	-----	-----	-----	-----	-----	2(U)	-----
010	Cahergal	1	OS	15ft 6in	40	-----	1FB, 1SH	-----
013	Ballyvolane	-----	-----	-----	-----	-----	2SH	-----
019	Wherland's Lane	2						
	(1)		OS ?(W)	15ft	40		1FB, 1SH	1 @ 4ft, 1 @ 4ft 6in
	(2)		OS ?(W)	14ft	40		3SH	2 @ 4ft 6in; 1 1 @ 4ft
021	Kilnap	1	OS ?	-----	-----	-----	5(U)	-----
036:1	Prospect Row	3						
	(1)		US	20ft			15(U)	4ft 6in
	(2)		US	20ft				
	(3)		US	20ft		60 (total)		
059	Backwatercourse Rd.	1	BS ?(M)	18ft	48	------	4SH	------
061	Assumption Rd.	2						
	(1)		OS	-----	-----	10–12	3(U)	
	(2)		OS	18ft 6in	-----	10–12	2(U)	-----
073	Liberty Str.	1	US(M)	18ft	-----	30	4(U)	2 @ 4ft; 2 @4ft 6in
096	Millfield	2						
	(1)		BS(M)	30ft	-----	30	6(FB?), 1SH	-----
	(2)		(BS?)W	-----	-----	-----	2(FB?) 1SH	
117	Crosses Green (St Dominick's)	1	BS	18ft 6in	32	-----	2FB;2SH	4 @ 4ft 6in

KEY OS (Overshot); BS (Breastshot); US (undershot); W (wooden); M (metal); FB (French Burr); SH (Shelling); U (Unknown)

Table 2—Waterwheel types and millstones, Cork City and environs flour and meal mills. (Source: Valuation Office Housebooks 1849–51). Note: all dimensions are given in imperial units as in original surveyors' notebooks.

for arching over a 66½ft length of Fenn's Quay dock, an area immediately to the west of the mill,[136] and in 1799 the remainder of Nile Street was culverted (Tuckey 1837, 212). A brewer called Edward Fenn acquired a lease to 'two grist mills under one roof and one waterwheel commonly called Droop's mill' in 1714.[137] Little is known about its subsequent physical development up until the late 1840s, by which time it had an 18ft diameter, 30hp undershot waterwheel which powered four pairs of millstones, and two barley screens.[138] As one might expect, its waterwheel was affected by backwatering caused by the rising tide, a problem it shared with other mills sited within the tidal reaches of the river Lee (see below).[139] Indeed, almost all of the similarly located mills within the city employed undershot waterwheels because of the low head available. The tailrace of the Fishamble Lane mill, according to a city engineers' report of 1866, was an open sewer and they recommended that 'the uncovered portion of the tailrace at the back of the houses in Fishamble Lane and Liberty Street should be arched over as soon as possible and the space thus formed over the arch may be used as back yards to the houses at each side of the stream'.[140] The mill is clearly shown on the OS 1:1056 survey of 1869, by which time the tailrace had been completely culverted: by 1878 the mill buildings had been entirely demolished (MacCarthy 1983, 116, n. 2).

The sites of St Francis' Abbey Mill (035) and St Dominick's Mills (118) also appear to have been in continuous use from the medieval period onwards. The St Francis' Abbey mill is shown on Rocque's map of 1773, and came into the possession of Wise's Distillery

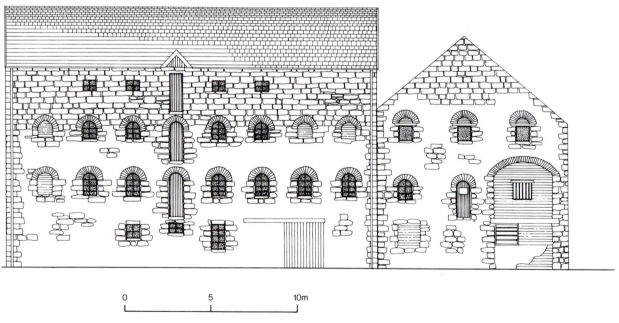

Fig. 39 OPPOSITE ABOVE
Crosses Green. This entire
eighteenth/nineteenth-century industrial
complex was demolished in 1993.

Fig. 40 OPPOSITE BELOW
Elevation of St Dominick's Mills,
demolished in 1993.

Fig. 41 LEFT
St Dominick's Mills, demolished in 1993.

Fig. 42 BELOW
Eighteenth-century flour mills at Crosses
Green, demolished in 1993.

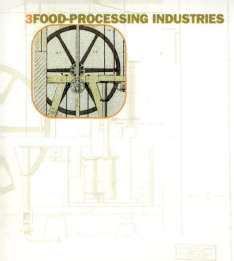

in 1804 (see above). It is said to have been a 'tide mill' with a 4ft (1.21m) wide undershot waterwheel,[141] and its millrace was later reused to power Wise's malt mill. St Dominick's Mills appears to have been built near the Dominican abbey ('the Abbey of the Isle'). The mill is depicted on at least two of the earliest maps of the city, where it is shown on the channel immediately south of the abbey and if the present mill is not exactly built on the same site (which seems likely) it at least utilised the same water source as its predecessor.[142] In the late 1840s the mill employed an 18½ft diameter breastshot waterwheel to drive four pairs of stones, three elevators and a bolting machine (see Table 2).[143]

As in the case of the Fishamble Lane and Franciscan Abbey mills, St Dominick's Mills suffered from tidal backwatering. Nonetheless it still managed to operate two sets of millstones and its bolting machinery for up to six months in the year, except when interrupted by the daily movement of the tides.[144] Its water supply appears to have been interfered with by improvements to the Corporation Waterworks weir in the late 1850s, by which time the installation of a steam engine (see below) enabled the mill's continuous 24-hour operation.[145] The present mill is clearly a reused distillery complex, to which many additions were made from the middle of the nineteenth century onwards (see above).[146] The current St Dominick's Mills is a five-storey structure with a slated, half-hipped roof (Figs. 39, 40 and 41). Its head and tailrace channels were culverted early this century, although the tailrace outlet can still be clearly seen exiting beneath Proby's Quay bridge. The western end of the mill contained the main mill drives and the millstone sets, and as late as 1869 this was still a separate building, the mill stores and main lofts being in a separate building immediately to the west.[147] The Crosses Green mill (**117**), which was fed by a second mill leat immediately north of St Dominick's (Fig. 42), was one of three water-powered mills within the city to benefit from the inland bounties available on flour and corn transported to Dublin. These bounties became available from 1758 onwards (Cullen 1977, 9), and from at least 1771 William Clarke's mill at Crosses Green was sending flour to Dublin (O'Sullivan 1937, 199).[148] 'Clarke's Mills'[149] came under the control of Thomas Walker early in the nineteenth century, who arranged for the Scottish millwright, John Rennie (1761–1821), to refurbish the mill's machinery in 1820.[150] In 1839 the Crosses Green mill had a 45hp waterwheel[151] which, given the relatively low-lying location of the mill and the power of the waterwheel itself, was presumably an undershot or low breastshot wheel.[152] By the late 1840s, however, water power appears to no longer have been used for driving the stones.[153] The headrace and tailrace channels for this mill have now been entirely culverted: the tailrace outlet arch (now blocked up) is still visible on Crosses Green Quay wall.

The Lee Mills (036:1)

 This was the largest water-powered flour-milling installation to become established on the north channel of the river Lee and, indeed, within the immediate environs of the city. The original mill complex was established on the site by Atwell Hayes in 1787, on a natural channel separating what was called the 'Middle' or 'Love's Island', near Hammond's Marsh, from the marshland immediately south of the Mardyke.[154] 'Hayes's Mill' operated with three wooden undershot waterwheels, the largest of which was only 7ft in diameter.[155] The mills were sold in 1803 and Beamish and Crawford, who had purchased the adjacent Lee Brewery in 1813 (see 'Malting' above), became tenants of the mills in the period 1813–15. [156] In the period 1815–20 the mills ground only for toll,[157] and it was not until 1825 that Beamish and Crawford made any moves to acquire a long-term interest in the mills.[158] The greater part of the existing six- and seven-storey mill buildings were entirely rebuilt on the site of Hayes's mills by Beamish and Crawford in the period 1825–31.[159] The original iron waterwheels were erected by Steele's Vulcan

Iron Works,[160] and the machinery driven by these, which by 1835 included two flour machines, one wheat (cockle) cylinder, bucket elevators and at least five pairs of french burr stones, were erected by Peele, Williams and Peele of Manchester.[161] Henry Inglis, who visited Cork in the early 1830s, was very surprised by the sheer size of the Lee mills along with the 'perfection of everything connected with them' (Inglis 1834, vol. 1, 190). A sketch by W. Roe dated 1838 (Fig. 43) shows the north-facing elevation of the mills with the outfall arches open. By the late 1840s three 20ft diameter undershot waterwheels were powering 15 pairs of stones (see Table 2), the waterwheels developing around 60hp. By this period the mills were operated intermittently.[162] Ground plans of the Lee mills complex from the early 1860s onwards (Fig. 44) suggest that the three waterwheels were by this period of the suspension type.[163] The headrace wheel arches are still clearly visible on the south-facing elevations of the mills 1, 2 and 3 (Fig. 45).

The Lee mills were primarily flour mills but from 1847 they began grinding Indian corn (maize).[164] They were the last flour mills within the city to rely solely on water power (see below), which continued to drive 15 pairs of stones for flour and Indian corn after the Cork Milling Company was founded by Reuben Harvey Jackson in 1877.[165] In 1881, when the Cork Milling Company was in liquidation, two waterwheels were at work. By this stage 'The Lee Tide Watermills' comprised two mills. The first had six lofts with storage for 6,000 barrels of corn and an annual output of some 20,000 barrels. The second working mill also had six lofts, but with a storage capacity of 10,000 barrels and an annual output of 20,000 barrels.[166] As far as can be seen, the Lee mills became fully incorporated into Beamish and Crawford's adjacent maltings operations shortly after 1881.

Water-powered Flour and Meal Mills on the Rivers Kilnap and Bride

Water-powered mills on the tributaries of the river Lee such as the Kilnap, Bride and Glen Rivers generally had more reliable water sources than those situated on the main channels of the river Lee (Fig. 46). Topographical conditions favoured higher heads than those available on the tidal reaches of the Lee, and as a direct consequence of this more efficient potential energy waterwheels could be employed. The natural watercourses immediately north of the city were extensively utilised for hydro-power before the industrial period. 'Water's Mills' (**056**) and St John's Mills (**566**) in Blackpool are listed in the Civil Survey of 1663–4 (Simington 1942, vi; MacCarthy 1985, 189–90), the former being described as 'two grist mills', which suggests that these were *double mills* (i.e. mills situated on opposing sides of a common watercourse). In 1690 the mills featured in the siege of Cork when Major General Scravemoer was encamped on the high ground to the east of them (Ó Murchadha 1990, 5), and in 1703 they were acquired by the Hollow Sword Blades Company (MacCarthy 1985, 189). Water's Mills are again referred to as a 'double grist mill' in 1755.[167] Their water supply appears to have been originally drawn from the River Bride, but by the end of the eighteenth century it appears to have been taken from the Back Watercourse.[168] St John's Mills, which drew their supply from the Kiln River, also appear to have been a double mill, and were sufficiently large in 1811 to operate three grain-drying kilns.[169]

Extensive use was also made of the river Bride in the Millfield–Kilnap area by the second half of the eighteenth century. An eighteenth-century survey of the lands in the north liberties of Cork by James Reilly shows a double mill adjacent to the latter-day Redforge Road, with two undershot waterwheels, with a further undershot mill situated on its tailstream.[170] The mills themselves were incorporated into the Millfield distillery in 1783 and, as early nineteenth-century surveys of the distillery complex clearly indicate, the relative positions of each of these mills correspond exactly to those of the later

Lee Mills

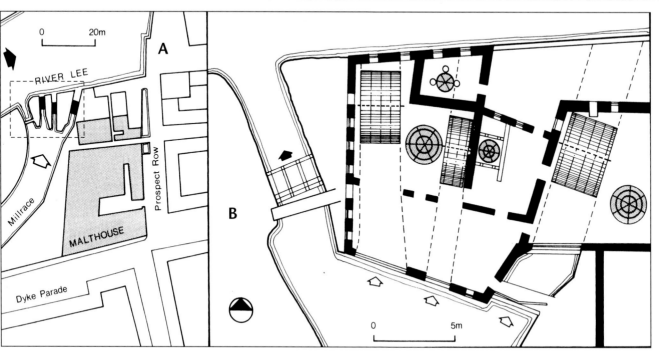

A

RIVER LEE

Millrace

MALTHOUSE

Prospect Row

Dyke Parade

0   20m

B

0   5m

84

Fig. 43 OPPOSITE ABOVE
Sketch of Lee Mills by W. Roe in 1838.

Fig. 44 OPPOSITE
A) Ground plan, Lee Mills in 1870.
B) Detail of area indicated by dotted lines on
A). (Redrawn from survey signed by O.E.
Edwards, 10th July 1870, Cork Archives
Institute.)

Fig. 45 ABOVE
The Lee Mills today, after restoration.

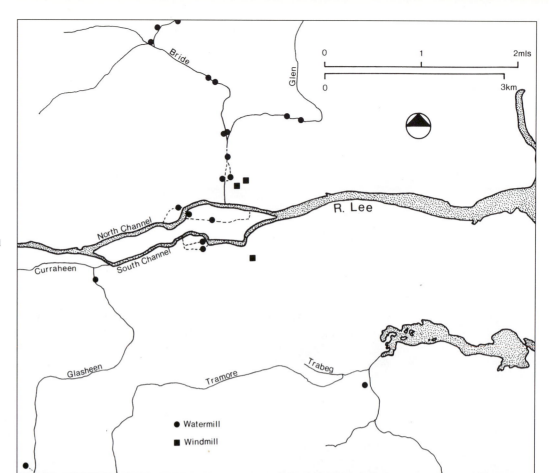

Fig. 46

Water-powered flour mills in Cork City and its immediate environs.

Fig. 47

Kilnap Mill, Co. Cork.

Within the map:

Bride

Glen

0   1   2mls

0   3km

R. Lee

North Channel

Curraheen

South Channel

Glasheen

Tramore

Trabeg

● Watermill

■ Windmill

Millfield flour and oat mills (**096**, see Fig. 30). The complex ceased to function as a distillery in 1831 and in 1836 its flour and oat mills were leased, separately, to Thomas Dawson and Frederick Lyons.[171] By the late 1840s the Millfield flour mill operated six pairs of grinding stones and one pair of shelling stones driven by a 30ft diameter metal waterwheel which developed some 30hp. The oatmeal mill immediately east of it was equipped with a wooden waterwheel which drove three pairs of stones (two grinding, one shelling) as in 1836.[172] Two of the former distillery's malt kilns appear to have been used for drying both wheat and oats.[173]

The section of the Kilnap River lying within the survey area serviced three grain mills during the nineteenth century (Fig. 46), which included the Glen mills (**021**) and Shaw's Kilnap Mills (**022**). In the late 1840s the Glen mills (which by the 1880s was converted for use as a distillery, see above) drove five pairs of stones powered a by a large overshot waterwheel.[174] George Shaw's mills at Kilnap (Fig. 47), which originally consisted of separate flour and oatmeal mills, were built early in the 1820s by the Scottish engineer, Robert Thom, who was later to act as a consultant to Cork Corporation on the city's waterworks (see Ch. 8).[175] By 1861 less than half of the French burr stones were water-powered, whilst the oatmeal mill was powered by a separate waterwheel.[176]

After the closure of the Glen distillery in Dodges Glen (**015**) its malt mills began to be used for grinding oats and Indian corn from at least 1846 onwards (see above).[177] But by the late 1840s the 'East Mill' (**013**) and the 'West Mill' (**014**) were rarely used and their feeder channels and ponds were becoming run-down. Indeed, neither mill was fitted out with meal-dressing machinery.[178] However, by around 1855 at least the West Mill had been equipped with elevators for meal and corn, along with four new pairs of stones (the original arrangement involved three sets) all driven by a 25ft diameter waterwheel. The East Mill continued to drive two pairs of stones, but one of these appears to have been replaced with a pair of grinding stones. Oatmeal-processing machinery had also been installed and the entire arrangement was actuated by a wooden (overshot) waterwheel.[179] The grain-drying kiln of the West Mill, which was originally used in the manufacture of malt for Callaghan's Distillery, was 30ft square.[180] Two further grain mills drew water from the Glen River immediately east of the Glen Distillery mills: William Lambert's mill whose overshot waterwheel appears to have driven a forge hammer and two pairs of millstones,[181] and Joseph Shee's Springfield Mill at Cahergal.[182] In the 1840s the Cahergal mill had a relatively limited capacity,[183] but by 1855 at least six pairs of grinding stones were at work.[184]

Windmills

There were at least three windmills at work within the city in the second half of the eighteenth century and the first half of the nineteenth century, at Lady's Well and Patrick's Hill on the north side of the city and on Windmill Road on the south side. Very little is known about their physical development, but it seems likely that they were all tower mills. The earliest evidence for their use within the city is J. O'Connor's *Map of the city and suburbs of Cork* (1774), which shows a windmill (**568**) on the high ground in the Patrick's Hill area of the city. Charles de Montbret noted in 1790 that the best available view of the city of Cork was from the 'old windmill' on the north side of the city (Ní Chinnéide 1973, 2). A further windmill (**211**) is depicted on the 1st edition of the OS 6-inch map to the west of the Patrick's Hill windmill near Lady's Well which was clearly a substantial structure. The latter, and the tower mill at Windmill Road (**567**) illustrated in F. Calvert's *The first series of select views of Cork and its environs*, published in 1807, had ceased to exist by the late 1840s. The Windmill Road tower mill was owned by Isaac Morgan in 1824 and had a bakehouse attached to it.[185]

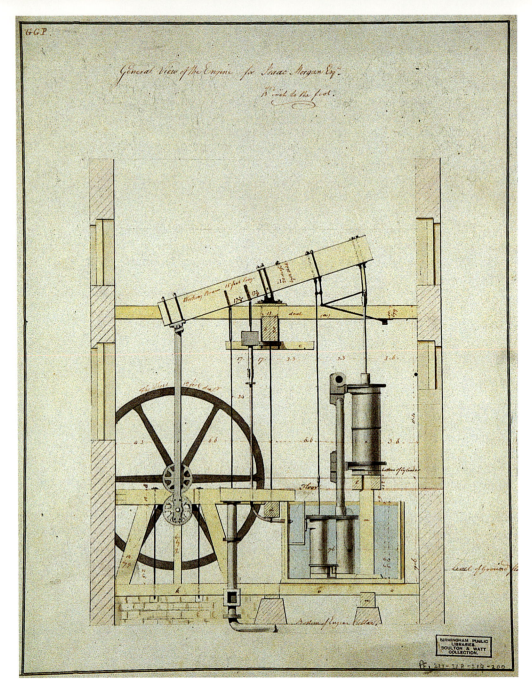

Fig. 48
Boulton and Watt 'sun and planet' engine at Isaac Morgan's mill in 1800, (Courtesy Birmingham Central Reference Libraries).

Fig. 49
Furlong's Mill, Lapp's Quay. Built in 1852, refitted as roller mill in 1874.

Steam-powered Mills

From the middle of the nineteenth century onwards it became all too obvious to mill owners, with even the most favourably situated water-powered mill sites, that they could only hope to compete with the more modern steam-powered mills established on the city quaysides by acquiring steam-powered prime movers. At mill sites where the engine was intended as a back-up for water-powered plant the engine was either housed in a separate building and linked independently to its own set of millstones, or even housed at opposite ends of the same building as the water-powered plant, as in the Springfield mill at Cahergal. Most of the engines used, particularly in the first half of the nineteenth century, were probably manufactured by Cork-based foundries, although this appears to have changed when compound engines were introduced (see below). Cork millers adopted steam power with great alacrity and by the early 1850s almost every water-powered flour mill within the environs of the city had installed a back-up engine. This is a remarkable development if one considers that as late as 1870 two thirds of the 90,000hp available for the processing of cereals in Britain was supplied by water power (Kanefsky 1979; von Tunzelman 1978, 122).

The earliest-known steam-powered flour mill to be erected within the city was also a first in terms of the engine used to drive it. The engine installed in Isaac Morgan's flour mill on George's Quay in November 1800 was the first, and last, of its kind ever to be used in an Irish flour mill. Morgan's engine was a 12hp Boulton and Watt beam engine (Fig. 48), with a Watt's patent 'sun and planet' gear and a rocking spindle valve gear (Bowie 1978, 173).[186] This type of valve gear was a feature of early double-acting engines, and consisted of a lever connected by a link to a lever on the rocking spindle which sets the valve in motion (Dickinson and Jenkins 1927, 184). The sun and planet gear was essentially Watt's attempt to get around the patent obtained by James Hickard in 1780 for the use of the crank in rotative beam engines. It was an epicyclic gear linkage which consisted of two cog wheels held in mesh by a link, one of which was attached to the beam's connecting rod and the other to the flywheel (Crowley 1986, 12). The motion of this type of gearing enabled the output shaft to rotate at twice the speed of the engine. This was found to be particularly advantageous not only in textile mills where line shafting was used, but also in terms of the improved performance of the piston (Hills 1989, 63). Furthermore, as the speed of the flywheel was twice the speed of the engine it could be made more lightweight (Crowley 1986, 12). Isaac Morgan's bakehouse and flour mill were destroyed by a fire in November 1802. The exact location of the mill is unknown, but as it was clearly near Morgan's house at Buckinghamshire Place on George's Quay it seems reasonable to conclude that the mill was either on George's Quay or immediately adjacent to it. A contemporary newspaper account stated that 'the ingenious machinery of the fine steam engine' was destroyed in the fire,[187] but this was clearly an exaggeration. In point of fact the engine was bought by the Dublin distiller Nicholas Roe in 1811 and later installed at his distillery in the Dublin district of Pimlico.[188]

In 1834 William Dunbar obtained the lease to a steam mill on George's Quay (**332**), a prime location for a flour mill given its ready access to both the river and the Cornmarket.[189] By 1844 his plant consisted of a 35hp engine which worked eight pairs of stones in one mill and three pairs in an adjacent one, which apparently processed oats. The mill's engine was supplemented with the power of a second engine by the late 1840s.[190] The mill also had a corn store capable of storing 10,000 barrels.[191] In May 1876 the George's Quay mill was severely damaged by a fire which broke out in the screen room, spreading to the kiln and eventually gutting the screen room.[192] Later that year a high-pressure beam engine was advertised for sale at the mill, presumably as part

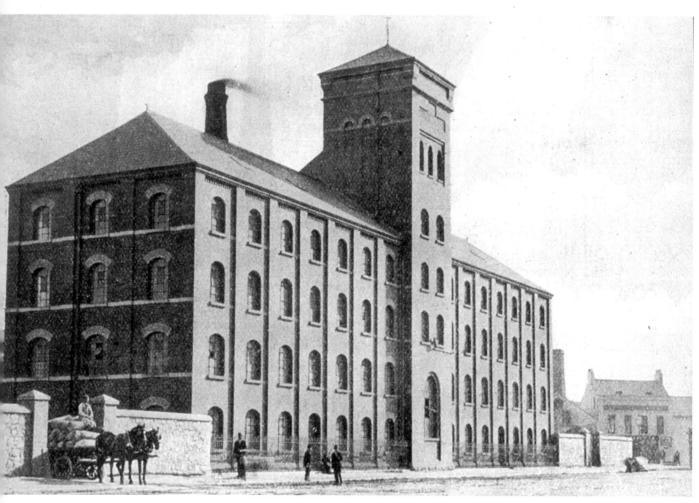

Fig. 50

Marina Mills, Cork, built in 1891.

Fig. 51

Marina Mills, ground plan (redrawn from Goad Insurance Plans of 1897).

1–5 Grain silos. 6 Steam dryers. 7 Roller mill. 8 Engine house. 9 Boiler house. 10 Flour warehouse (former offices of City Park terminus of Cork, Blackrock and Passage Railway). 11 Wheat cleaning. 12 Chimney. 13 Grain and flour warehouse (former City Park terminus of Cork, Blackrock and Passage Railway). 14 Grain warehouse.

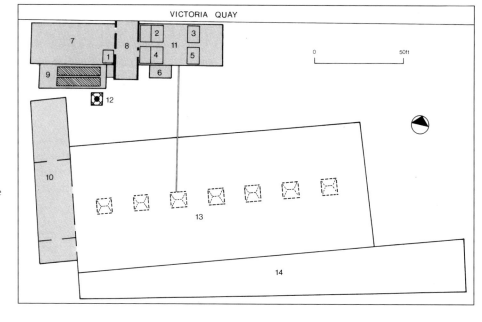

of a fire damage sale.[193] The George's Quay mill was one of the largest steam mills driving millstones in the city during the nineteenth century and appears to have been one of only a handful of mills which successfully made the transition to grinding with rollers (see below).

St Dominick's Mills, which succeeded Thomas Walker's Distillery as a water and steam-powered mill (see above), was working 12 pairs of stones with a 46hp engine in 1841, the engine itself possibly being a modified version of the Boulton and Watt engine installed in 1805 (see above). At any rate this engine, which was clearly intended to supplement the water power available at the site, had been replaced by the late 1840s by a 12hp engine, which worked three pairs of stones at a time. The fate of St Dominick's Mills as a water-powered site clearly illustrates the fate of many similar sites within the environs of the city. In a court action of 1865 taken by the owners of St Dominick's Mills against Cork Corporation, the Corporation deposed that :

> of late years, since large steam mills had been built convenient to the [city] quays where lighters could come up and discharge their corn at the very door, watermills less favourably circumstanced had of course become seriously depreciated.[194]

By the late 1840s most of the water-powered flour mill sites within the environs of the city had been equipped with auxiliary steam engines. Most of these are likely to have been rotative beam engines, but in the late 1850s compound beam engines and horizontal engines appear to have been widely adopted by Cork flour mill owners. At Thomas Dawson's Millfield mill, for example, a 30hp engine was worked in 1849,[195] which was replaced in *c.* 1857 with a compound engine, which was worked in conjunction with a 25hp horizontal engine.[196] The steam mill at Douglas was also working a compound engine, in this instance a 35hp model, by 1858.[197] Both the Kilnap mill (see above) and the Great Britain Street steam mill were operating with horizontal engines by 1861, the Kilnap engine being a 30hp model with a multitubular boiler by Ormond and Son of Manchester.[198] Indeed, only Sir John Arnott's bakery on Fitton Street at which two new beam engines (total 40hp) were erected in 1862, appears to have moved on more traditional lines, but these may well have been McNaughted.[199] By the 1870s high-pressure engines were being used in a number of Cork steam mills. A high-pressure beam engine was at work in the George's Quay mill by this period (see above), whilst Capwell Steam Mills and St John's Steam Flour Mills were both employing high-pressure engines by the mid-1870s. The Capwell steam mills on Douglas Street (**587**) was operating with a pair of high-pressure engines made by Steele's Vulcan Foundry (see Ch. 5) in 1874.[200] St John's Steam Flour Mills (**190**), which occupied the former John Street distillery's premises (see section on 'Distilling') had a 40hp horizontal condensing engine made by Rowan and Sons of Belfast.[201] By this period even Droop's Mill (see above) had a 10hp back-up engine,[202] but the same period also witnessed the introduction of new technology into the city's flour-milling industry, the steam-powered roller mill.

Roller Mills

The use of millstones for manufacturing flour tended to produce more coarse household grades than fine white flour, whilst the keeping quality of the flour manufactured in this way was limited. In consequence, even the larger steam mills within the immediate hinterlands of Irish and British ports tended to supply local rather than national markets. In the late 1870s, however, a new system of flour milling, more mechanically efficient than that involved in stone milling and capable of producing a larger quantity

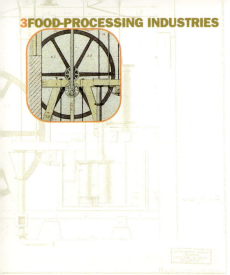

of fine, white, patent flour was introduced into Britain and Ireland. The system called roller milling, in which the different components of the wheat were carefully reduced and separated between sets of rollers, was developed in Hungary and improved upon in the USA and Europe (Perren 1990, 4234). However, although the system had been employed in one Manchester flour mill as early as 1878, some ten years later only 20 British flour mills out of an estimated 10,000 or so were using it (Storck and Teague 1952, 201; Perren 1990, 424). The first large-scale application of the roller system in Ireland was at Shackleton's Mills in Carlow in 1879 (Bowie 1975; Tann and Gwyn Jones 1996, 49) and it seems that at least one mill (see below) may even have converted to roller milling as early as 1874. By 1889 MacMullen's Mills on George's Quay and even long-established mills such as Shaw's at Kilnap had converted to the roller system.[203]

In the roller process the wheat is gradually reduced by being passed between pairs of metal rollers. The grain passes, successively, between three main types of rollers, each set of which has individual rollers which revolve at a different speed: one roll to hold the stock for another roll rotating at faster speed whose function is to cut the grain. The stock is first passed through break rolls, whose fluted surfaces help to tear open the grain, whilst scraping the endosperm from the bran skin. It is then passed through scratch rolls which reduce the size of the semolina granules and remove any residual bran skin. The stock is then passed through reduction rolls, with smooth surfaces, which reduce the granules to flour (Lockwood 1962, 277; Watts 1983, 22).

J.W. MacMullen's Cork Steam Mills, the successor of William Dunbar's Mill (see above), and John Furlong's Lapp's Quay Flour Mill (**204**), originally built as a steam flour mill in 1852, were probably the first stone mills to change over to the roller process in 1874. Furlong's mill (Fig. 49) was operating 19 sets of rollers, worked by 220hp engines by 1897 and has the only surviving stack (some 80ft high) of any steam-powered flour mill within the environs of the city.[204] The Cork Steam Mills operated with 17 sets of rollers worked by 160hp engines with twin Lancashire boilers.[205] The first custom-built roller mills within the city, however, were not built until the early 1890s, by which time the approaches to the city quaysides had been considerably improved and additional wharfage had enabled ships of large tonnage laden with American wheat to dock at Cork (see Ch. 7). John Furlong's Marina Mills (**072**), completed in 1891, were the first custom-built roller mills within the city which directly took advantage of the new deep-water berthage (Fig. 50). Furlong had obtained a lease on the former Cork Blackrock and Passage Railway terminus at City Park (**067.12**, see Ch. 7) in 1889, which was later to become incorporated into the Marina Mills complex as grain stores. The Marina mills consisted of two four-storey wings divided by a central tower 78ft high which contained the engine room.[206] The building was faced with bricks made at Ruabon by Edwards of North Denbighshire, Wales (Brunskill 1990, 72), with some granite dressings being supplied by Blessington Quarries in County Wicklow. The limestone dressings for the plinth and sub-plinth along with the heavy stone blocks for the engine bed were supplied by Fitzgerald's Quarries at Carrigacrump near Cloyne, County Cork.[207] The ground floor of the mill was equipped with grain elevators, the first floor with 13 break and reduction rollers and the second floor with four rotary scalpers, four purifiers and four cyclone dust collectors. The upper storey of the mill housed wheat sieves, four centrifugal dressing machines and one single rotary grader and reel. All of the original machinery was supplied by the firm Simon and Company of Manchester, and indeed, Lancashire firms appear to have been the principal beneficiaries of the contracts for machinery and plant. The Rochdale firm of John Petrie and Company[208] built 200hp power horizontal compound tandem engines for the mill, complete with rope drives, boilers and a Green's Economiser.[209] The former Cork and Passage railway terminus, which was now used as a grain store for the Marina mills was linked to the main mill buildings by a band conveyor (Fig. 51). A second, much larger grain store was constructed to the east of the mills sometime before 1906 and was linked to the mills with a band conveyor.[210] The Marina mills were demolished in 1986.

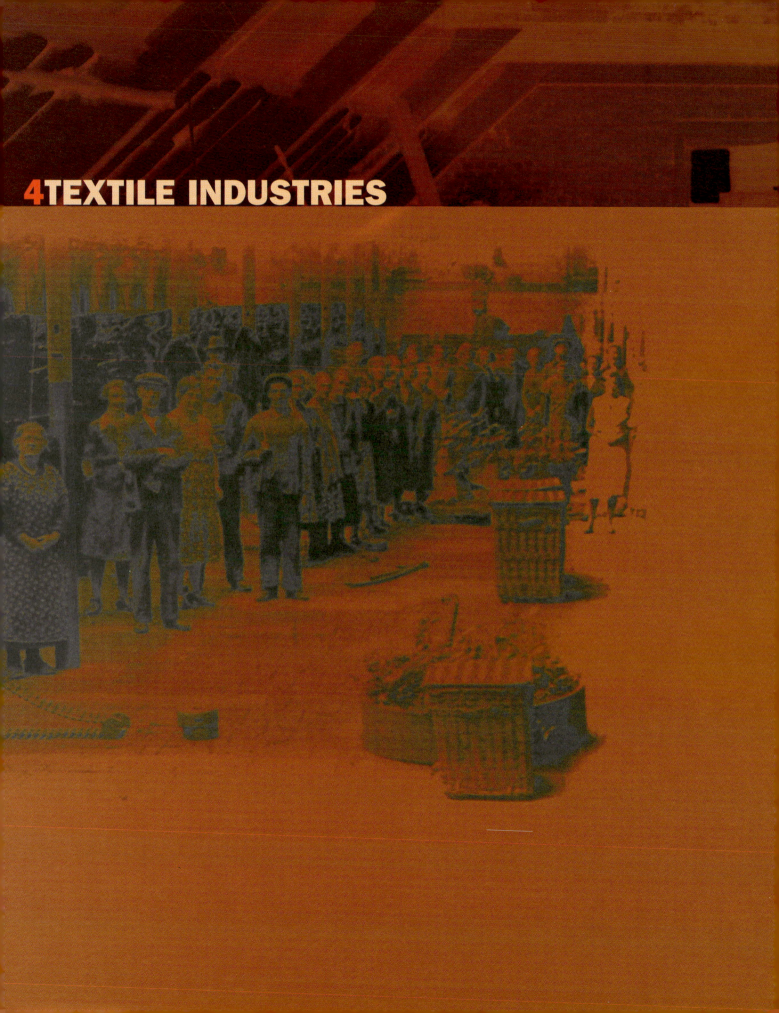

4 TEXTILE INDUSTRIES

TEXTILE INDUSTRIES

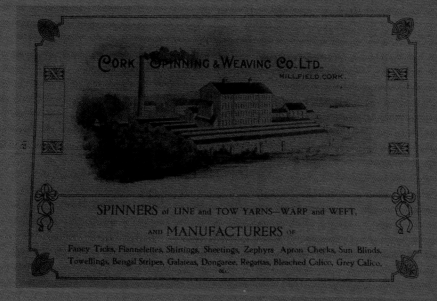

CORK SPINNING & WEAVING Co. Ltd.
MILLFIELD CORK.

SPINNERS of LINE and TOW YARNS—WARP and WEFT,

AND MANUFACTURERS OF

Fancy Ticks, Flannelettes, Shirtings, Sheetings, Zephyrs Apron Checks, Sun Blinds,
Towellings, Bengal Stripes, Galateas, Dongaree, Regattas, Bleached Calico, Grey Calico,
&c.

Linen, wool and cotton were the principal textile industries in the Cork region in the period under review. Of these the local cotton industry, although very much a passing phase of industrial activity, was briefly of national importance. The manufacture of sailcloth also made a significant contribution to the local economy. Its manufacture was, however, over-reliant on wartime demand during the Napoleonic period, so much so that by 1820 its manufacture and indeed the mechanised spinning of linen yarn had all but died out. Bold iniatives were taken in the early 1850s to revitalise the linen industry within the county, but only one of the four new spinning mills erected between 1850 and 1866 continued in production into the twentieth century. The woollen industry, on the other hand, had established international markets by the end of the nineteenth century and continued to expand well into the present century. With exception of the cotton industry, many of the more important sites associated with textile production (particularly those established during the second half of the nineteenth century) have survived. Sites associated with the finishing processes of linen, however, such as bleach greens, have not been as fortunate.

LINEN

The processing of flax into linen involved six basic processes, *retting*, *scutching*, spinning, weaving, *bleaching* and *beetling*. In the main flax-growing areas retting dams or flax ponds were constructed for the immersion of bundles of flax. After being soaked in water for around two weeks the flax fibre, the useful part of plant, was loosened from the *shous* (as it was known in Ulster), the waste or non-usable portion of the plant. The retted flax was then removed by hand using a scutching blade and later, from the eighteenth century onwards, in water-powered scutching mills, where the flax fibre was separated from the shous by the action of rapidly rotating wooden scutching blades. In Ulster scutching was generally undertaken in the flax-growing area. The scutched flax made up approximately 10% of the entire plant. When the plant was divested of its shous the flax fibre could then be transported more economically to the spinning mill. Up until the beginning of the nineteenth century, the domestic spinning of linen yarn by women using spinning wheels and the weaving of the yarn into brown linen cloth by their menfolk, was the universal means of producting coarse and fine linens. By the beginning of the eighteenth century water-powered spinning machinery, suitable for producing coarse yarn, was introduced into Ireland. The introduction of the wet spinning process in the late 1820s, however, which enabled finer yarns to be produced by machinery, effectively killed off the domestic linen industry. By passing the fibre through a trough of hot water the binding gums in the fibre could be dissolved, which enabled finer yarns to be drawn off than was possible in the dry spinning process. This was a crucial technological development for the Irish linen industry, enabling as it did the large-scale industrialisation along the lines of the cotton industry.

Most of the weaving undertaken in Cork during the period under review was undertaken by handloom weavers working at home. As early as 1812 however, and up until 1814, Robert Honner was operating water-powered looms in Cork. This is the first recorded use of power looms in Ireland, and it seems likely that this development was influenced by the wartime expansion of the sailcloth industry. But ultimately Honner's attempt to introduce such machinery proved to be unsuccessful, owing to the rapid contraction in the industry after 1814 (Gribbon 1969, 99).

In the eighteenth century linen bleaching was a time-consuming process. The cloth was first steeped in a *keeve* (*kieve*) filled with cold water for a period of up to nine hours and then spread out on the ground (*grassed*) for up to four days, a period during which it was sprinkled with water to keep it wet. The next stage, in which the cloth was bucked, involved the boiling of the cloth in an akaline solution called *lye*, which was made with potash made from wood ash. Charles Smith's account of the Douglas sailcloth manufactory (see below) refers to a *buck house* and a mill for grinding wood ash for making lye. Bucking was undertaken for 12 hours with ten hours between each bucking. The cloth at this stage in the process was once again grassed, in this instance for two days. It was then steeped in buttermilk *sour*, weighed down with heavy objects and after being allowed to ferment in the mild acid or sour, the cloth received a further bucking and was grassed yet again for a further two days and nights. All of these processes were repeated until such time as the cloth had been whitened, after which the cloth was washed (McCutcheon 1980, 292). A smooth finish was then imparted to the cloth by *beetling*, during which the cloth was pounded by vertical wooden fallers or beetles (ibid., 250). *Calendering*, a finishing process which involved rolling the cloth between cylinders, appears to have been introduced into the Cork region during the early 1800s. During the nineteenth century, specialist bleachworks, similar to those established in Ulster, were quite rare and only that established by William Thorley at Poullacurry near Glanmire bears any comparison. Thorley's works was powered by no less than five waterwheels and two 30hp steam engines in 1863,[1] and is, at the present showing, the only cloth-finishing works within the immediate environs of the city to have employed beetling engines.[2]

Bleachgreens for linen had been established at Douglas (see below), Glasheen (mixed cottons and linens, Dickson 1977, 595 and 1978, 104), Pouladuff (see above) and in the Hammond's Marsh area of the city, where calenders were also at work (Bielenberg 1991, 13) by the end of the eighteenth century. The scarcity of bleach greens within the region would suggest that most of the yarn was bleached before it was woven into cloth, a process clearly implied in an early description of the Douglas sailcloth factory (see below). Yarn bleaching was also pre-eminent in the Drogheda linen industry in the period 1780 to 1820 (Fitzgerald 1981, 36).

A white linen hall had been built at Dublin between 1721 and 1723 (Gribbon 1978, 78) and at Drogheda in 1770 (Fitzgerald 1981, 39), whilst the growing influence of the linen industry in Ulster led to the establishment of linen halls in Newry in 1783 and at Belfast in 1785 (McCutcheon 1980, 292). A 'Linen Hall' is also marked on Joseph Connor's map of Cork of 1774 and Daniel Murphy's map of 1789 on Reilly's marsh immediately east of the North Mall distillery, but according to de Montbret who visited Cork in 1790 it appears not to have functioned as one, although he did note that a lot of textiles (presumably linen) were washed and laid out to dry in the vicinity. However, the Cork-based industry was not large enough to sustain a linen hall on a permanent basis. The Cork Linen Hall could have been either a brown (i.e for unbleached cloth) or white linen hall, but despite the importance of linen finishing near the city up until the early years of the nineteenth century, there are no firm indications as to which it was.

The Origins of the Cork Linen Industry

Cork county was the focal point of the Munster linen industry in the eighteenth and nineteenth centuries. Over half of the total acreage of flax within the province was grown within the county in 1814. The Irish Linen Board not only financially assisted the development of the Cork industry, but also provided direct access to Dutch expertise in sailcloth manufacture, by bringing personnel skilled in weaving and bleaching from Holland to Cork in 1718 (Bielenberg 1991, 14). In 1801 the board also granted the first mechanical spinning frames erected in Ireland to Julius Besnard of Douglas (see below).

At the beginning of the nineteenth century, largely through initiatives taken by local landlords, colonies of Ulster weavers became established in County Cork. Settlements such as those at Dunmanway, Inishannon and Donnybrook near Douglas, laid the foundations of an important domestic linen industry which, by the early decades of the nineteenth century, was employing up to 60,000 people engaged in the cultivation of flax and in the various processes involved in its manufacture into linen (ibid., 8–11). However, the removal of support premiums on flax growing in 1828 led to a 50% reduction in the national acreage by the early 1840s (Smyth 1988, 240). In the Cork region this decline was further compounded by the removal of bounties on coarse yarn — the raw material of sailcloth manufacture in 1825 — and the general lack of mechanisation in the Cork linen industry (Bielenberg 1991, 18). As a consequence of this the area around Fermoy, by 1850, was the only important centre of flax cultivation in County Cork (Smyth 1988, 244).[3] However, in 1841 the main linen manufacturers in the north of Ireland established the Royal Flax Improvement Society of Ireland (Bell and Watson 1986, 156), whose principal aim was to give 'every facility to those entering upon the cultivation of the flax crop'.[4] By the early 1850s flax societies had been established at Bandon and Riverstown near Cork, both of which established contacts with the main producers in Ulster and Belgium. In 1848 George Robinson engaged Belfast workmen to supervise the construction of his flax-scutching mill at Drimoleague,[5] whilst two years later work was underway on a flax mill at Kildinan for Lord Fermoy and the railway contractor William Dargan.[6] A further flax-spinning mill was completed at Trabolgan, on the eastern side of Cork Harbour in 1852 (Maguire 1853, 374). In 1853 a scutching mill, powered by a water turbine, was erected near Ballineen by Edward Smyth of Newry, who was credited with the introduction of flax production in this neighbourhood through the good offices of the Earl of Bandon.[7] However, attempts to promote flax growing during the early 1850s met with little success, largely because there were no proper flax markets and a scarcity of scutching mills, this latter deficiency not being satisfactorily addressed until the early 1860s. In 1860 there were only four scutching mills within the county — half of the total for the entire province of Munster — with the only example within the immediate environs of the city being at Riverstown.[8] The Riverstown scutching mill was part of William Thorley's Glanmire and Riverstown Bleachworks, which was described by J.F. Maguire in 1853 as 'the most extensive in the South of Ireland' (Maguire 1853, 161). In 1863 the Riverstown scutch mill was powered by one of the complex's five waterwheels and was equipped with both breaking rolls and scutching handles (see below), and steps were already underway to not only double the number of scutching handles in the existing building but to erect a second scutching mill.[9] The development of a city-based linen industry was to quickly follow.

Spinning Mills

The period 1852–66 witnessed the almost complete reintroduction of the manufacture of linen yarn to the greater Cork area. As shall be outlined below the *modus operandi* of the Cork spinning mills was copied directly from existing Ulster mills, from the design and arrangement of the buildings and machinery to the employment of skilled workers from Ulster and the continent in supervisory positions.

The Cork Spinning and Weaving Company (096)

The first industrial linen yarn spinning mill to be modelled along the lines of Ulster examples, was the Millfield mill of the Cork Spinning and Weaving Company, built between 1864 and 1866.[10] This mill was built near the then extant eighteenth-century distillery and adjacent flour mills (see Ch. 3). The site for the mill was carefully chosen so as to be just outside the municipal boundary in order that the company could avoid paying rates to Cork Corporation. The mill was designed by the Belfast architects Boyd and Platt,[11] and is a five-storey, brick-built structure (Figs. 52 and 53), with fireproof jack-arched floors throughout, supported on cast-iron columns supplied by the King Street Iron Works in Cork. A local contractor, Richard Evans successfully tendered for the main mill building, whilst Richard Brash (the architect of Wallis and Pollock's Douglas mill, built shortly afterwards; see below) built the mill chimney.[12] At a meeting of the Munster Flax Improvement Society in December 1864, John Francis Maguire, acting Chairman of the company stated that the mill was 'rapidly rising towards its fourth storey'.[13] The directors of the company confidently predicted that the mill would be operational in the spring of 1865.[14] However, by late 1865 the mill was still not fully operational, although the company could boast that the first fine linen yarn ever to be spun by machine in Cork had been produced in its special training facility. This latter was fitted out in one of the existing buildings on the site and was used to train prospective employees.[15] The delay in getting the mill operational principally lay with Combe Barbour, the suppliers of the spinning machinery. Nonetheless, the mill got underway on the 15 February 1866, operating with 900 spindles, and by the beginning of July in the same year some 5,180 spindles were at work.[16] In a city with no tradition of modern flax spinning the company made great efforts to ensure that its future workforce acquired the necessary skills from experienced Belfast mill hands. In 1867 the company was employing 70 Belfast linen workers along with 630 local women, girls and boys,[17] under the general management of a former Belfast mill manager, J.R. Mulholland.[18] Yet despite its best efforts, the fledgling company did not have the resources to survive the slump experienced by the Irish linen industry in the aftermath of the American Civil War, and after barely five years of operation the Millfield mill was put up for auction in October 1871.[19] It was reopened in the mid 1870s by William Shaw and Co.,[20] who tried to sell the mill in 1881 by which time it was operating 13,000 spindles.[21] Shaw exhibited at the Cork Exhibition of 1883 when he was buying up to 450 tons of flax and producing about 350 tons of yarns per year.[22] Before the closure of the mill in 1885 the Millfield and Douglas factories were very much the most important flax-spinning mills outside Ulster. In 1884 there were some 847,788 spindles operated in Ireland of which 31,508 were worked outside Ulster, the majority of which were 'in the neighbourhood of Cork.'[23]

The Millfield factory was to be reopened under new management in 1889. In this period of its use its operation was significantly expanded, and for the first time since 1814 linen cloth was woven in Cork on power looms.[24] In 1917 the mill was operating 20,000 spindles,[25] but for our present purposes the period after 1890 is particularly important, because contemporary accounts of the operation of the mill highlight the extent to which linen manufacture in Cork continued to be carried out using northern Irish and foreign expertise. In 1889 the company began to experiment with flax growing on the continental system, in which the flax seed was removed prior to retting (a process called debolling), and had rented up to 200 acres of land from local farmers to enable this process to be carried out. The company brought a Dutch specialist called Snaaw over to Cork to supervise the growing, retting and scutching of its own flax crop, and to pass on his skills to local employees of the company.[26] Flax supply was an important concern for the company as only some 265 acres of flax were grown in Munster in the period 1889–90, whereas over 100,000 acres had been planted in Ulster in the same period. At least 4,000 acres of flax were required to produce the company's annual 7–800 tons of raw flax, and so considerable amounts of Russian, Dutch and Belgian flax were used in addition to native flax.[27]

CORK SPINNING & WEAVING Co. LTD.
MILLFIELD. CORK.

SPINNERS of LINE and TOW YARNS—WARP and WEFT,
AND MANUFACTURERS OF

Fancy Ticks, Flannelettes, Shirtings, Sheetings, Zephyrs Apron Checks, Sun Blinds,
Towellings, Bengal Stripes, Galateas, Dongaree, Regattas, Bleached Calico, Grey Calico,
&c.

Fig. 52
Early twentieth-century panorama of
Millfield Spinning Mill.

Fig. 53
Millfield Spinning Mill, designed by Belfast
architects Boyd and Platt and erected
between 1864 and 1866.

Scutching was carried out within the Millfield complex. The original Millfield scutchmill, built in 1866, had 12 water-powered scutching handles, and was replaced by a corrugated-iron structure in the late 1880s. This latter had iron scutching blades of Dutch manufacture which were powered via an auxiliary drive from the main mill building. A section of the eighteenth-century distillery buildings within the complex were modified for use as flax stores, which were also used to house the company's supplies of flax seed.

At Millfield, the *roughing room* was a separate building from the main spinning mill, in which the ends of the flax fibre were given a rough combing and were effectively squared off at the root end to facilitate their suspension on the holders of the hackling machine. *Hackling* was the process by which the flax fibres were carefully combed out, first by machine in the machine or hackling room, and later by hand in the sorting shop. In the combing action of the hackling machine the short fibre or *tow* was separated from the long fibre or *line*, the former being processed separately before being spun into coarser yarn (McCutcheon 1980, 299). The Millfield hackling frames were built by George Horner's Clonard Foundry and Stephen Cotton's Brookfield Foundry, both of Belfast. The tow was housed separately at Millfield in the *tow store*, where it was made up into batches of 1 ton before its removal to the *card room* on the ground floor of the main spinning mill. The machine-hackled line was then removed to the sorting shop, which at Millfield was situated in a loft above the roughing room. The flax fibre was then manually hackled by highly skilled men called *hacklers*, many of whom would have served long apprenticeships (Messenger 1988, 83). After this additional combing the hacklers would then sort the flax fibre in accordance with its quality, after which it was removed to the dressed line store where it was allowed to mature for up to three months.[28]

The ground floor of the Millfield spinning mill served as the *tow preparing room*, which had six *carding machines* and six systems (i.e. production units), of drawers and rovers each consisting of two spreaders, three *drawing frames* and one *roving frame*. This was exactly the same arrangement as that found in contemporary Belfast mills (McCutcheon 1980, 299). The second floor of the mill was the line preparing room which consisted of ten systems. Female operatives placed pieces of fibre on the spread boards, slightly overlapping each new piece to form ribbon-like strands called *slivers*.

The next stage of the preparing process involves the passing of the slivers through *drawing* and doubling frames, the former process elongating them, the latter process evening them out (ibid., 299). Each of these processes were repeated until the requisite count (i.e. recognised weight per unit length) was achieved. The count was based on the length of fibre it took to make one pound in weight, where if one *cut* or *lea* at the standard length of 300 yards took 25 cuts to the pound (i.e. 25 x 300 = 1lb) the count was said to be '25s'.[29] In its first period of use the Millfield mill spun tow and line yarns from 16s to 100s lea,[30] but by the 1890s this ranged from 16s to 180s lea. The slivers were then passed through a roving frame which, in addition to further drawing out the sliver, imparted to it a slight twist to form a roving, which was then wound onto wooden bobbins and removed to the *wet spinning rooms*.[31]

The second and third floors of the mill were taken up by wet spinning rooms, between which there were some 67 spinning frames with 13,000 spindles[32] made by Combe Barbour of Belfast.[33] As in northern spinning mills the spray from the spindles left the spinning room floors permanently wet, and the spinners wore long leather aprons. Female *doffers*, under the control of a forewoman doffer called the doffing mistress (the

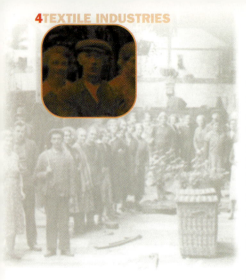

terms themselves clearly borrowed from northern usage, Messenger 1988, Ch. 3), removed and replaced the flyer bobbins when necessary.[34] Once spinning had been completed the yarn was taken to the *reeling room* on the top floor of the mill, where it was wound or *reeled*, on collapsible *reels* (McCutcheon 1980, 300) into *cuts* and *hanks* (3,600yd lengths). The yarn was then transferred via a sloping wooden chute (as in Belfast mills) connecting the reeling room with the *drying room* situated over the boiler house in a building immediately below it. Steam pipes were also fitted in the drying room to facilitate the drying process, in which the hanks of yarn were hung on poles about 4ft above the floor for up to 12 hours. After drying the hanks of yarn were taken to the cooling room and left to lie for 24 hours, and were then removed to the *bundling room*, and arranged in bundles each containing 60,000 yards. A hydraulic press was then used to form the bundles into bunches in accordance with the fineness of the yarn involved.[35]

In the 1890s the adjacent Millfield weaving factory consisted of two weaving sheds. Its overall capacity was for 100 looms and this was expanded early in the present century. The drive for the looms and the spinning mill machinery was provided by two Hick Hargreaves single cylinder condensing engines, with three Lancashire boilers; power transmission to the main mill building was by rope drive.[36] Rope driving was first developed and used in Belfast by James Combe of the Falls foundry in 1863 (Hills 1989, 209), and its use in the Millfield spinning mill would appear to be one of the earliest examples outside Belfast. The transmission arrangement involved a series of heavy cotton ropes which fitted into grooves formed on the engine's flywheel. Individual ropes powered line shafting on each of the mill's floors, the ropes themselves being accommodated in a vertical chamber called a *rope-race* set at one end of the mill building (Watkins 1971, vol. 2, 102ff). In terms of mill design, the adoption of rope-driving eventually led to engine houses (as at Millfield, Fig. 54) being built alongside the mill building (Hills 1989, 211).

The Donnybrook Spinning Mill (554)

In 1863 Wallis and Pollock's Douglas Patent Hemp Spinning Company, the largest ropeworks in the south of Ireland, which had been established within the former Douglas sailcloth factory, erected scutching machinery. This was one of the first steps the company made towards establishing flax cultivation in their immediate locality.[37] Wallis and Pollock also began to import Riga flax seed in the same year, for sale to local farmers to encourage flax growing in the locality, although ultimately the company's flax-spinning mill, which was soon to be constructed, and that at Millfield could never rely upon locally produced flax (see above). The company's scheme to build its own flax-spinning mill was to reintroduce mechanised flax spinning into the Douglas area after a lull of some forty years.

Nothing survives of the original Douglas sailcloth factory and all of the eighteenth and early nineteenth-century buildings associated with the rope and cordage works appear to have been destroyed by later building work on the site. The five-storey flax-spinning mill which survives at Donnybrook, Douglas (Fig. 55), was designed by the Cork architect Richard R. Brash (1817–88)[38] and its style of architecture and the organisation of spinning operations conducted within it were clearly based on contemporary Belfast models. Brash had been the contractor for the chimney of the Cork Spinning and Weaving Company's spinning mill at Millfield (see above), where he doubtless came into contact with their Belfast architects. Indeed, he is also known to have travelled to Belfast to examine some of its more recently constructed spinning mills, sometime before work on the Donnybrook mill commenced.[39]

The foundation stone for Wallis and Pollock's mill was laid, after long delays in preparing the foundations, in March 1866 and by December in the same year the mill was at work. According to contemporary accounts the spinning mill was near the hemp spinning mill, and a large excavation into the adjacent hillside was necessary to accommodate its foundations. Each of the internal floors of the mill consists of a matrix of brick segmental jack arches, which are supported on four tiers of cast-iron girders. Jack-arched floors were the principal means by which textile mills of this period were rendered fireproof, and the individual floor surfaces at the Donnybrook mill were also finished with fire-clay tiles. The girders, in nearly all multi-storied textile mills of this period, are connected by wrought-iron tie rods, and are supported along the central long axis of each floor on cast-iron columns. The cast-iron columns and the girders were supplied and installed by the Vulcan foundry in Cork. The wet spinning rooms, as in contemporary Belfast mills, were provided with metal drains running along the inner edge of the main walls, while the floors sloped downwards from the centre to allow moisture and condensate falling from the wet spinning frames to be collected. The contents of the drains were then discharged into pipes positioned on the outer walls.[40]

The main enclosing walls are built with Youghal brick and are externally faced with Ballinhassig (Ballinphellic) brick, whilst the jack arches, window dressings and quoins are finished with patent facing bricks. The engine beds and most of the other cut stone work was supplied by a quarry in Foynes, County Limerick, although a certain amount of local limestone was quarried at Carrigacrump quarries near Cloyne.[41] Before the mill was seriously damaged by fire in 1919 (see below) the roof was double-ridged and hipped. In its current state it has been appreciably lowered, and appears to have segmental trusses, whilst the original moulded eave cornice has also been removed.

The engine and boiler houses are at the east gable of the mill, and each are essentially two-storey buildings with high lofts (Fig. 56). Unlike most Belfast mills the main windows on these buildings are, relatively speaking, quite small and narrow, although the drying loft in the Donnybrook mill (like the former) is situated over the boiler house. The reeling room was almost invariably accommodated in the top floor of the mill building, while any intercommunication between the engine house and the spinning mill would generally have been to facilitate power transmission. The mill engine, built by Hick, Hargreaves and Co. of Bolton, was an Inglis Corliss engine with 40 nominal horse power and a Spencer-Corliss valve gear. John Frederick Spencer and William English were largely responsible for the adoption of Corliss-type engines in Britain. Inglis became involved with Hick Hargreaves in the mid-1860s and used Spencer's release mechanism (patented in 1865) and his double ported slide or Corliss valve in many of the engines made by him for Hick and Hargreaves (Hills 1989, 183–4), including that installed in Wallis and Pollock's spinning mill. One of the main advantages of the Corliss engine where textile mills were concerned was that it allowed close speed control in power transmission (Law 1986, 22). In choosing such an engine for their Donnybrook mill, Wallis and Pollock were clearly in line with what was then the most up to date textile mill technology available. Indeed, this appears to have been, if not the first, then certainly one of the earliest mill engines of its type used in Ireland.[42]

The preparing and spinning machinery was mainly supplied by Belfast foundries. Combe Barbour of the Falls foundry, Belfast, who also supplied the preparing and roving frames, and Lawson and Son of Leeds supplied the spindles, whilst George Horner's Clonard Foundry (also of Belfast) supplied the hackling frames. All of the latter appears to have been shaft- rather than rope-driven. A 2,500 gallon cast-iron tank was also

Fig. 54
Engine house, Millfield Mill.

Fig. 55 OPPOSITE ABOVE
Wallis and Pollock's Spinning Mill,
Donnybrook, Co. Cork, designed by Richard
Rolt Brash and built in 1866. (Con Brogan,
Dúchas)

Fig. 56 OPPOSITE BELOW
Engine and boiler house, Donnybrook
Spinning Mill.

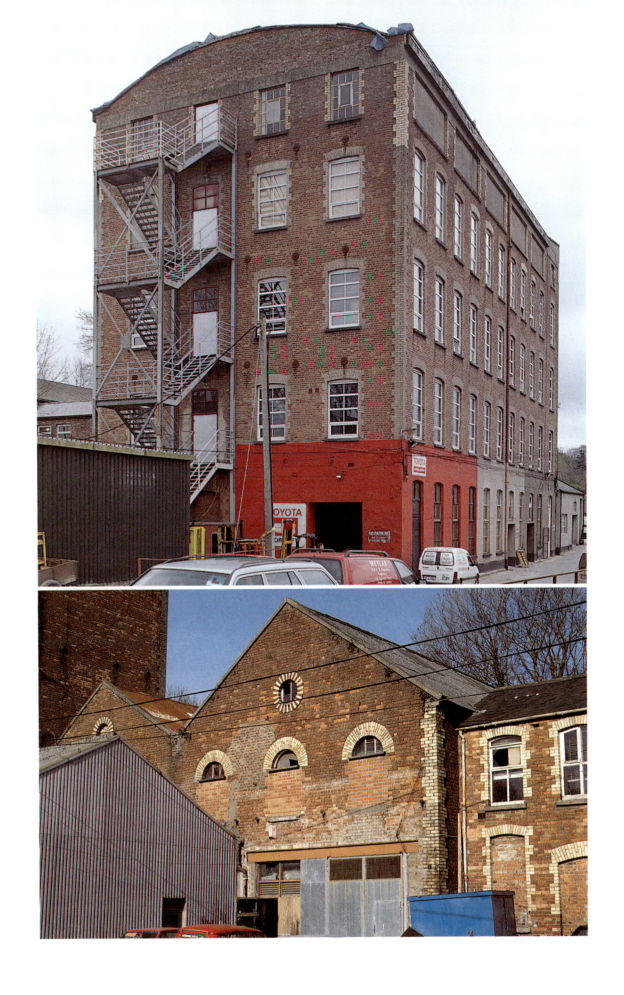

installed in the attic, which was used to fill the water troughs of the wet spinning frames. Early in 1867 some 5,000 spindles were being operated.[43] As far as can be seen, the organisation of the processes carried out within the mill were the same as those of contemporary Belfast, with the tow and line preparing rooms being situated, respectively, on the ground and first floors. The second and third floors are likely to have served as wet spinning rooms, and the fourth floor probably served as the reeling room. Wallis and Pollock also built some 50 worker's housing within the immediate vicinity of the mills, examples of which can still be seen on the Grange Road.[44] The Douglas flax spinning mill was closed by Wallis and Pollock in 1885, but was reopened in 1890 after being refitted as a woollen mill (see below).

The Cork Sailcloth Industry

The origins of the Cork sailcloth industry can be traced to the early decades of the eighteenth century, the traditional date for the establishment of the sailcloth factory at Donnybrook, near Cork, (commonly referred to as the Douglas sailcloth factory, **554**) being 1726. Beginning with 40 hand-operated looms the factory operated with 100 by 1750, the entire establishment, according to Charles Smith, 'being the largest in the kingdom':

> about 250 persons [are] constantly employed in hackling, bleaching, warping, weaving, &c. and more than 500 spinners, many of whom come above seven miles for work... There is a magazine for the hemp, yarn, &c. a fine water-mill, for pounding the hemp and ashes, and convenient buck house and bleach yard, in the middle of which is a large dry-house for the yarn, in bad weather. There are houses and gardens for the master-workmen, for which they do not pay rent... (Smith 1750, vol. 1, 358).

When Robert Stephenson visited the Douglas factory in 1755 there were 'about 100 Looms, with Boylers, Cesterns, Kieves and every Apparatus for preparing the Yarn.' The boilers, cisterns and kieves indicate that the yarn was bleached before it was woven into cloth. However, in the prevailing economic climate only 50 looms were being operated by Perry, Carleton and Co.[45] By 1783 Julius and John Besnard had taken over the business and thenceforth the name of Besnard became closely associated with the Cork sailcloth industry (Dickson 1977, 589). Imported hemp appears to have originally been the principal raw material used in the Douglas sailcloth factory, although this was gradually replaced, first by hand-spun and later by mechanically spun coarse linen, particularly during the Napoleonic Wars when access to Baltic hemp was regularly interrupted. The organisation of the Douglas industry was also very different from that of the rural linen industry of the greater Cork region. As Charles Smith's description clearly indicates, the Douglas factory had already become a vertically integrated unit by the middle of the eighteenth century. On present evidence this was Cork's first factory, in which all of the processes associated with the manufacture of a given commodity had been integrated, with a workforce of over 500 spinners working within a single complex.

As has been noted in Chapter 1, limited mechanisation in the Douglas sailcloth manufactory had already been achieved early in the nineteenth century. In the late 1790s mechanically dry-spun flax, through the efforts of John Marshall of Leeds, had become a viable proposition. The coarse yarn spun in this fashion was viewed a future competitor with Irish yarn in the British market, and so the Linen Board began to take steps to encourage the adoption of mechanical spinning frames in Ireland (Gribbon 1969, 90). In 1796 the Board came to an agreement with W.H. Stevenson of Edinburgh for the erection of a water-powered spinning mill in Ireland. This latter scheme was not brought to fruition, but through a strange compromise horse-powered spindles were installed in the Dublin Linen Hall in 1797. However, Julius Besnard of the Douglas sailcloth manufactory had pre-empted the Linen Board's efforts, when he built a water-powered spinning mill at Douglas. Later, in 1801, he was able to persuade the Board to grant him the machinery that Stevenson had installed in Dublin (ibid., 91). Initially the Douglas mill was beset with mechanical problems, but Besnard was able to get it into production in 1801 using a spinning frame built by John Drabble of Leeds (a former employee of John Marshall) and machinery based on that introduced into Ireland by Stevenson (Takei 1994, 28–30).[46]

The subsequent development of the Douglas linen industry can be linked to the Napoleonic Wars, and to the increased demand for sailcloth and other goods manufactured from coarse, machine-spun yarn. The importance of its output was duly recognised, and in 1805 Lord Dundonald brought a millwright over with him to Ireland to make adjustments to the plant at Douglas and other Irish installations. In 1806 Peter and John Besnard established a larger mill in nearby Ravensdale, with locally made machinery, which by 1809 was operating with 1,214 spindles. Barnes and Atkinson of Cork had been responsible for some of the machinery erected in the original late eighteenth-century Douglas spinning mill, shortly before 1807, and it is likely that either they or Drabble manufactured and erected the machinery for the Ravensdale mill (ibid., 30).

'At Douglas, two miles east from Cork', wrote the Rev. James Hall, 'there are two factories which go by water [where] Mr Besnard cards and tow hands, and spins all kinds of linen yarn, but particularly coarse, in the same way they do cotton and woollen' (Hall 1813, vol. 1, 181). William Shaw Mason, who visited the Douglas factory around the same time, described the works as a 'sailcloth, rope and raven duck manufactory', which gave employment to 'about 100 looms and 300 persons. In this manufactory are four mills, two of which, for order and perfection of machinery, may well arrest the traveller's attention' (Shaw Mason 1814, vol. 1, 137). Sailcloth was generally made of coarse linen yarn and canvas of unbleached cloth made from either hemp or flax. Duck, however, was generally a heavy-duty, untwilled linen fabric from which small sails or sailors' clothing were manufactured.

The importance of the Douglas sailcoth industry (like that of the Ballincollig gunpowder industry; see Ch. 6), was too closely linked to the demand for its products occasioned by hostilities with France, and with the withdrawal of war contracts only two of the five spinning mills in the Cork region were in operation in 1815 (Bielenberg 1991, 17). Flax-spinning mills had also been established at Blarney, Springville and Tower Bridge in the first decade of the nineteenth century, but not one of these continued in operation after 1811 (ibid., 16). The Besnard family's involvement in flax spinning ended sometime before 1820, and as early as 1818 they already appear to have been concentrating more on cloth finishing (Foley 1991, 14; Bielenberg 1991, 17).

The other recorded sailcloth factories within the survey area have proved notoriously difficult to locate. Denis Connor's Springville factory, however, which was in operation in 1807 (Bielenberg 1991, 16) and which was one of the only two remaining Cork spinning mills in 1817 (Foley 1991, 14) is shown on the first edition of the Ordnance Survey as an 'old sailcloth factory'. Around the same time the factory, which by this period was equipped with a steam engine, was put up for auction, some £10,000 having been spent on its buildings.[47] A description of the Springfield mill (sic.) at Cahergal written in 1850, which by this period had been converted for use as a flour mill, states

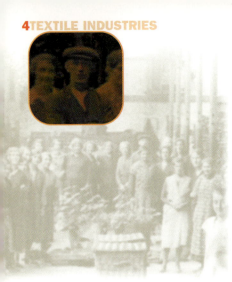

that it was 'used some years since as a canvas and rope manufactory'.[48] By the late 1840s the sailcloth factory had definitely been converted for use as a flour mill (see Ch. 3), but there can be little doubt that the original sailcloth factory was sited there because of the excellent head of water available from the Glen stream in a location immediately outside the municipal boundary. However, the fact that the factory had a steam engine in 1841 can only indicate that at least some of its machinery was powered by steam prior to its closure.

WOOL

The basic processes involved in the manufacture of the various types of woollen cloth can be grouped together in four stages: preparation, spinning, weaving and finishing. On arrival at the woollen mill, the raw wool had to be carefully sorted, after which it was washed to remove grease and dirt. In many nineteenth-century Cork mills such as St Patrick's mills at Douglas, Bantry and Dripsey the next preparatory stage involved the dying of the wool (*stock-dying*), a practice generally employed in the manufacture of patterned cloth.[49] The fibres were then *willeyed*, on willeying machines which beat the wool and separated the fibres, gently teasing out the wool preparatory to carding. Woollen cloth was manufactured with short fibre or short staple wool, the fibres of which had to be *carded* prior to spinning. *Carding machines*, in which the the fibres were teased out by wire rollers to form loose threads or *slivers* suitable for spinning, were generally available from the late eighteenth century onwards. Worsted cloth manufacture, on the other hand, involved the use of long staple wool, which had to be separated from the short staple wool in a process called *combing*. In this latter process heated combs were used to form slivers from the long woollen fibres or *tops*, which were wound into a ball called *top* prior to being drawn and spun. Combing, however, was not successfully mechanised until the 1840s.

At the spinning stage the fibres were first drawn out as slivers, which were twisted together to form yarn. During the early mechanisation of the Cork woollen industry the woollen and worsted yarns were generally spun on jennies. This device, which was originally developed for the spinning of cotton yarn, was developed by James Hargreaves in 1769 and was the first successful spinning machine employing multiple spindles. The technology of the jenny and Richard Arkwright's water frame (a roller spinning device) were later successfully married in Samuel Crompton's mule, an automatic version of which was widely used in Cork mills by the end of the nineteenth century.

The third stage of manufacture involved weaving. All of the Cork mills described below used power looms, which were generally erected in spacious loom shops, although unfortunately few technical details of these have survived.

The final stage of manufacture involved the finishing of the cloth, in which both woollen and worsted cloth were first scoured, that is, washed and pounded in a soapy solution in order to thicken it (a process called *fulling* or *milling*, the latter term being commonly used in the Douglas mills, see below). After milling the cloth was then *tentered*, a process during which the fabric was stretched under tension and then dried. In the manufacture of woollen cloth the object was to disguise the weave under a smooth nap, to which end the short fibres of the cloth were raised and then *sheared*, i.e. cut to the required even finish. In worsted cloth manufacture, in which the cloth's pattern was important, the desired effect was to expose the weave and hence the raising of the nap was dispensed with. At Morrough's Mills at Donnybrook it was common practice for the cloth to be dyed as part of the finishing process, which was termed dying in the piece, a practice generally associated with the manufacture of plain cloths (see below).

Both woollen and worsted cloth were manufactured in the greater Cork area, although in the eighteenth century import duties tended to favour the cheaper worsted cloths. Most production was for the home market but by the 1760s a strong export trade in woollen yarn had been established with Norwich, and in camblets with Portugal. In 1776 Arthur Young noted that the carding and combing of half of the Irish wool production was carried out in County Cork (Young 1780, vol. 1, 34; Dickson 1977, 561). The vicissitudes of the woollen industry within the greater Cork area were such that by the 1780s it was in the middle of a severe depression, but by the end of the eighteenth century the industry within the city of Cork experienced an upturn. Cork manufacturers such as Lane and the Mahoney brothers also acquired substantial army clothing contracts and experienced a boom period in these during the Napoleonic Wars. An unsuccessful attempt had been made by at least one Cork manufacturer to adopt power-driven machinery in the late 1790s, but by the early decades of the nineteenth century at least two city-based woollen manufacturers were using mechanised jennies and carding machinery (Bielenberg 1991, 34–5). For the greater part of the eighteenth century, therefore, the only process in the manufacture of woollen cloth which had experienced any degree of mechanisation was fulling. *Fulling* or *tuck* mills were in use in Ireland from the Anglo-Norman period onwards (Lucas 1968). They were quite common throughout County Cork, but very few examples have been noted within the Blackpool area of the city, where the importance of woollen production was clearly represented by the number of people employed in the industry during the eighteenth century. The number totalled 2,500 in 1800 (Bielenberg 1991, 34). In 1755 a tuck mill and a 'water engine for napping broad cloths and satteens' (sateen was a cotton fabric with a glossy surface woven like satin) was at work near Water's Mills (see Ch.3.) in the Watercourse Road area of the city.[50] However, the canalised watercourses in this area, in the vast majority of documented cases, were clearly harnessed for the benefit of distilleries and flour mills and where later mechanised woollen manufactories have been recorded it has not been possible to either pinpoint their exact locations or any remains which may be associated with them. By 1841 there was only one water-powered spinning and carding mill within the survey area, at Lower Glasheen. This was run by John Bransfield and appears to have been established in the Sadlier Brothers' former cotton spinning mill (**003**).[51] However, in the second half of the nineteenth century a number of large, modern woollen mills became established in the Cork region. Many of the latter, like the two to be described below, captured important export markets in the United States whilst collectively expanding to dominate the home market.

Cork Woollen Mills

St Patrick's Mills (483)

In 1883 the O'Brien Brothers St Patrick's mills in Douglas village, designed by the Glasgow architect Richard Murray, was in operation.[52] The buildings consisted of three main blocks, of which the engine house occupied the central position flanked, on each side, by the preparing, carding and spinning rooms in one block and the weaving and finishing shops on one other. The buildings, which had an original frontage of 300ft and a depth of 150ft, were mainly built with cut limestone, with brick used at gable ends to facilitate future additions. In the preparing house there was a large wool washing machine with a drying machine in an adjacent room, which opened onto the dyehouse. A door from the dyehouse gave access to the *willey* house. The carding house could accommodate up to seven sets of carding machines, some of which were to be set for

Fig. 57 **OPPOSITE ABOVE**
O'Brien Brothers' woollen mill, Douglas, designed by Glasgow architect Richard Murray and completed in 1883. (Con Brogan, Dúchas)

Fig. 58 **OPPOSITE BELOW**
Engine house, O'Brien Brothers' Woollen Mill, Douglas.

Fig. 59 **ABOVE**
Carding room, O'Brien Brothers' Woollen Mill, Douglas.

Fig. 60 **BELOW**
Yarn lofts, O'Brien Brothers' Woollen Mill, Douglas.

Fig. 61

Loom shop at Morrough's Mill in 1933
(Courtesy, *Cork Examiner*).

Australian and New Zealand wool and others for home-grown wool. The yarn was spun on mules. Although the weaving shop could house up to 50 looms only 20 were operated in 1883, owing to the scarcity of skilled labour. The scouring and milling house contained washing and milling machines, a hydro extractor and napping and tentering machines. The woollen cloth was then conveyed to the finishing room where cropping, brushing, pressing and shrinking were undertaken. All of the machinery was powered by a 100hp high-pressure steam engine in 1883, to which a second example was to be added as the mill expanded.[53] The mill was extended in the closing decades of the nineteenth century, and by 1903 it operated with some 80 looms and employed 300 workers, many of whom lived in company-owned houses in Douglas village.[54]

A large number of the original buildings survive (Fig. 57). The engine and boiler houses are entirely built of finely pointed, well-dressed limestone blocks (Fig. 58), which present a stark contrast to the severity of their brick-built counterparts at Millfield and Donnybrook (see above). The roof of the engine house has been modified by the addition of a water tank, but it still retains its original venetian-style windows. In recent years the economiser house has been removed although the brick arches for the connection of the economiser (a device which saved fuel by using the engine's exhaust gases to heat the boiler feed-water prior to their expulsion through the chimney) to the Lancashire boilers are still visible in its west-facing gable wall.

The southern range of the surviving buildings, which housed the carding machinery (Fig. 59), still retain their original saw-tooth profile roofs, which are supported by thin cast-iron columns made at the Hive iron works (**285**). A total of six, 60ft long carding machines were operated between the bays formed by these columns up until quite recent times, along with six mules in the adjacent building to the east. The weaving sheds were situated in the range of buildings to the north of the carding shop and like the latter had steeply pitched roofs with north- and south-facing skylights. The original ridge ventilators are also in position on the main surviving weaving shop building. The lofts above the main weaving shop, which still retain their original shelving for the reels of yarn, have also survived (Fig. 60).

Morrough Bros. Woollen Mills (554)

In 1883 the first indications of the transfer of Wallis and Pollock's Flax Spinning Mill to woollen manufacture become apparent, when the mill was producing Cork tweeds.[55] The mill was entirely given over to the manufacture of woollen cloth by 1885[56] and in 1889 the mill was bought by James and Patrick Morrough and R.A. Atkins, the High Sheriff of Cork.[57] The Morrough brothers engaged the Cork architect W.H. Hill to make the necessary modifications to the existing structures for their own customised mill, which involved the creation of a 170ft long weaving shed from an existing annexe to the main five-storey mill building. This annexe ran parallel to the main mill building, but a single-storey extension to the spinning mill was adapted for use as a carding room. The existing 250hp engine on the premises was used to actuate all of the machinery, along with an electric generator set. By the end of 1890, however, the mill's new carding room had not been completed.[58] By 1903 the mill was employing 300 people, many of whom were housed in the 100 company-owned cottages in Douglas.[59] The original steam engines were replaced sometime before 1917 by two 130hp gas engines which powered everything from milling to tentering machines.[60] By 1933 the mill operated with 60 looms (Fig. 61).[61]

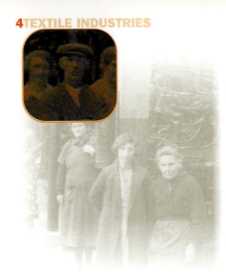

COTTON

In the context of the survey area cotton manufacture was essentially a passing phase of industrial activity. Mixed cottons in which cotton weft was woven with a linen warp became an important branch of the Cork textile industry towards the end of the eighteenth century, with the linen component being supplanted by machine-spun cotton by the 1790s. Indeed, by the closing decades of the eighteenth century the cotton industry within the city had superceded the linen industry in terms of importance (Bielenberg 1991, 12–13). The cotton industry in the Belfast played an important role in the introduction of the factory system to linen manufacture in Ulster, but in Cork this system had already been introduced into the sailcloth industry by the middle of the eighteenth century (see above). The success of the city's cotton industry was a short-lived affair and by 1801 all of the principal manufacturers had been become bankrupt, having fallen victim to, amongst other factors, English competition, a severe shortage of coinage and difficulties in advancing credit (Bielenberg 1991, 24–5).

As was noted above, machinery used in the manufacture of linen, woollen and woollen worsted cloths had been widely adapted from that originally developed for the cotton industry. Again, the same four basic processes were involved. Individual bales of raw cotton varied considerably and at the preparing stage it was necessary to blend a number of bales to ensure consistency in the quality of the yarn. Prior to being cleaned the cotton had to be disentangled from the bales, after which the resulting tufts or *lap* were then carded. As in wool processing, carding had originally been carried out by hand, but from the 1770s onwards carding machines were widely used. The carding machine produced a continuous roll of cotton, which was then fed into drawing and roving machines, which prepared the fibres for spinning. In the Cork City area most of the yarn was spun on jennies, the first water-powered spinning mill was established at Blarney in 1787 (ibid., 22). All of the yarn was woven on hand looms, the city-based industry never developing to the stage where power looms could be profitably introduced, simply because the city's principal cotton manufacturers became bankrupt in 1801. The cloth was finished by bleaching in much the same way as white linen, by exposure to the air and through immersion in alkaline leys. The cloth could then be printed using blocks or machinery, or by Calico printing, which was essentially a form of localised dyeing.

The first large-scale, cotton-spinning enterprise within the city was established by Henry and James Sadlier on Lawton's Quay in 1781 and at Glasheen (**003**) outside the city. In 1783 they were operating 1,606 spindles and by this period appear to have been the second largest manufacturers in Ireland.[62] The Sadlier brothers empire, however, collapsed in 1801 (Dickson 1978, 106) and their mill at Glasheen was later converted to a carding and spinning mill for wool.[63] Some remains of the original spinning mill complex survived around the turn of the present century, but all traces of it have now gone.

There were two cotton manufacturers in the Blackpool/Watercourse Road area of the city using spinning jennies in the 1790s, but again these were relatively short-lived enterprises and by the early years of the nineteenth century cotton manufacture within the city of Cork had effectively ended (Bielenberg 1991, 24). There was a brief attempt to revive cotton weaving in the city at Albert Quay in 1868 by the firm of Nash, Harty and Company. But again this was a short-lived affair which ended in 1871 with the firm's bankruptcy.[64]

5 SHIPBUILDING AND ASSOCIATED INDUSTRIES, IRON FOUNDRIES AND ENGINEERING WORKS

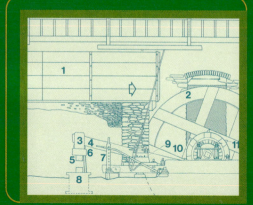

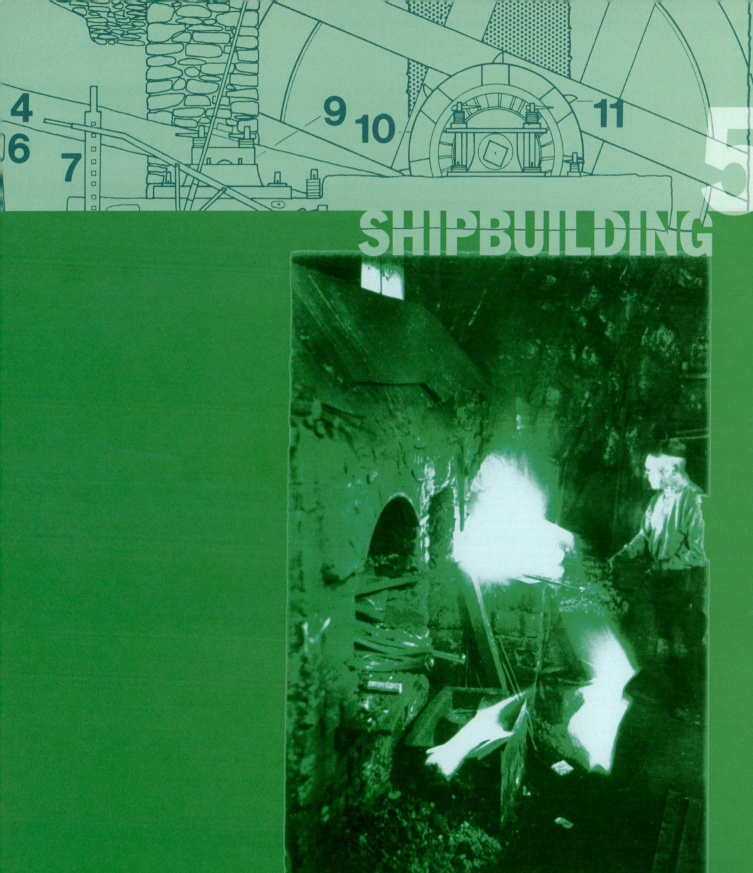

SHIPBUILDING

Cork's shipbuilding yards were the most extensive in Ireland during the first half of the nineteenth century. A number of the local foundries and engineering works were also important in their own right, making significant contributions to the adoption and development of both prime movers and manufacturing technology in the Cork region. At least ten spade and shovel mills were in operation near the city in the period 1790–1960, one of which — the Monard and Coolowen iron works — is the best-preserved example of its type in Ireland. The city also became the site for Henry Ford's first European venture, which progressed from the manufacture of tractors to motor cars.

SHIPBUILDING

In the closing decades of the eighteenth century there were at least three shipbuilders at work in the Leitrim area of the city, and one in the vicinity of Drawbridge Street.[1] The upper reaches of the Kiln River (which have only recently been culverted near its discharge point into the north channel of the Lee) would have been readily accessible for small vessels where presumably basic facilities for both the manufacture and repair of small boats could have easily been provided.[2] Nonetheless, it is unlikely that these enterprises were capable of handling any vessel that could not be conveniently beached on a slob during low tides. Indeed, the earliest references to such activity within the environs of the city, with the exception of an attempt to provide proper facilities at Dundanion, would suggest that in most cases such facilities were extemporised (O'Mahony 1989, 74). By the end of the eighteenth century, however, the expansion of Cork's maritime trade along with the growing British naval presence in the lower harbour, brought with it a need for proper shipbuilding and repair facilities.

The first real dockyards on the river Lee were established on the Brickfield slobs, on the north bank of the river Lee, in the early decades of the nineteenth century. The extent to which technological factors may have hastened the move of Cork shipbuilders towards updating their graving dock facilities and slipways remains obscure. Shipbuilding had always been a technologically conservative industry, although the Cork City yards were in many key respects quick to take advantage of the opportunities which the port of Cork's expanding trade presented to them. The fastening of copper sheathing to wooden hulls, to counteract the effects of Toredo worm, was becoming an increasingly common feature of shipping from the 1780s onwards. It seems likely that many of the ocean-going vessels manufactured in the Cork Harbour area during the early nineteenth century would have been copper-fastened but the earliest references to copper-bottomed vessels being built in the Cork City yards date to the early 1820s (ibid., 75). Cork City shipyards built and repaired a wide range of sea-going vessels, including schooners, barques and West Indianmen, along with iron-hulled vessels such as steamers and passenger vessels (Anderson 1984).

By 1815 there were at least two shipyards in operation on the Brickfield slobs, Joseph Wheeler's on the Strand Road and John and Edward Moloney's, on the Glanmire Road, which appears to have been taken over by John Knight in or around 1817.[3] According to contemporary accounts their facilities were quite primitive and ultimately dangerous to those charged with carrying out the work, with the tradesmen often working on stages erected in the river. But in 1828 Cork became, along with Dublin and Waterford, one of the first Irish ports to have a dockyard equipped with a patent slip, when John Knight had one constructed at his Brickfields yard. Patent slipways enabled ships to be mechanically hoisted out of the water, using a steam hoist, for repairs without the use of a dry or graving dock. Knight's slipway was 320ft long, and could accommodate two vessels of up to 500 tons. It had a manually operated 120ft carriage with which it was possible for a handful of men to haul a vessel of up to 500 tons from the river in around one hour.[4] Knight was followed by Wheeler in this regard in the following year, when a 500 ton vessel was launched from his own patent slip.[5]

A four inch to the mile map of the city of 1832 provides the earliest indications as to the physical development of the shipyards in the Brickfields area. The main concentration of activity is immediately west of Water Street where five small slipways are shown running at right angles to the foreshore. By the early 1840s a much clearer picture emerges, where the first edition of the Ordnance Survey[6] shows four slipways, two of which are patent slips, and a graving dock in George Robinson & Company's yard at Water Street. In the late 1840s Joseph Wheeler in his Lower Glanmire Road yard is known to have improvised his own ingenious drydock, which consisted of a boat-like construction 168ft long, 48ft wide and 18ft deep, which could accommodate a 2,000 ton vessel on a draught of 18ft. The entire construction was towed into a specially excavated basin within Wheeler's shipyard, into which it was bolted onto cross beams. Its 'stern' functioned as a lock which, when required, could be opened to admit a vessel for repairs.[7]

From more recent accounts of the development of Cork's shipyards (O'Mahony 1989; Bielenberg 1991), it appears that by the early 1840s there were two shipyards at Water Street, Stephen Hickson's (who appears to have superseded John Knight) and George Robinson's (**084**). According to Ernest Anderson (1984, 240), James Robinson & Co. was established around 1830, and so on the face of it both firms would appear to have been operating from Water Street contemporaneously. However, as Water Street runs at right angles to the Lower Glanmire Road obvious problems arise when one attempts to establish the physical relationship between each yard, even if we assume that these were located on either side of it with direct access to the riverfront. As far as the first edition of the Ordnance Survey (1842)[8] is concerned, there is only one dockyard occupying the eastern frontage of Water Street. However, an auction notice in a Cork newspaper of 1849[9] dealing with a dockyard at Water Street refers to a 'patent slip capable of taking two vessels of 500 tons', which can only be that built by John Knight in 1828, and later operated by Stephen Hickson (see above). The same account also refers to the yard's entrances to both Water Street and the Lower Glanmire, which was also a feature of George Robinson's yard in 1863.[10] There can, therefore, be little doubt that Robinson acquired Hickson's yard in or around 1849, and that the Water Street address of George Robinson & Company dates to this period. Furthermore, Robinson's yard must surely have been sandwiched between Hickson's and Wheeler's, for Joseph Wheeler's dockyard (**074**) was situated immediately to the east of Robinson's premises, and was ultimately absorbed by it in 1860 (O'Mahony 1989, 82).[11]

For the most part, the earliest established shipyards within the environs of the city were largely concerned with wooden sailing vessels. Joseph Wheeler's yard on the Lower Glanmire Road built at least eight ships for Simeon Hardy & Co., the largest of which was the 500 ton clipper *Mary Hardy*.[12] Repair work to wooden-hulled sailing vessels (particularly those laid up for overhaul in the port) appears to have made up the greater part of Wheeler's business (Anderson 1984, 242) before he transferred his operations to a purpose-built yard further down the river at Rushbrooke, the drydock of which was designed by Sir John Rennie (1794–1874).[13]

In 1815 the age of steamship building in Ireland was heralded by Andrew and Michael Hennessy's yard at Passage West in Cork Harbour, which was responsible for the first steam boat hull manufactured in Ireland.[14] The engine was a Boulton and Watt 12hp

side lever model, with spur wheel drive to the paddle shaft (Barry 1919, 13; Anderson 1984, 235–6). As in the case of the majority of early paddle engines, the engine of Hennessy's *City of Cork* worked on the second motion, in which spur gearing was used to gear the motion of the crankshaft either up or down to that of the paddle shaft (Guthrie 1971, 38). The Hennessy's second foray into paddle steamer manufacture in 1816 led to the first completely Irish manufactured steamship, the *Waterloo*, the engines of which were built at Thomas A. Barnes' Hive Iron Works by James Atkinson. Without detracting from the initiative which resulted in Hennessy's Irish 'first', it is worth pointing out that in the early years of steamship manufacture the shipbuilder's task was simply to leave a space for the engine amidships. The installation of the the engine and its boilers was left solely in the hands of the engine's manufacturers, who were obliged to make the best use of the space left to them (ibid., 57). For all that, the successful marriage of shipbuilder and engineer which resulted in the *Waterloo*, is still a remarkable achievement. It is also worthy of note that the first steamship launched on the Lagan, the 200 ton *Belfast* whose 70hp engines had been manufactured at Coates and Young's Lagan Foundry, did not leave the stocks until 1820 (Moss and Hume 1986, 3–4). In Dublin the first attempt to manufacture marine steam engines was at the Ringsend foundry in 1829 for the *Marchioness Wellesley* (Mullins 1863, 167).

However, despite the early advances of the Hennessy's at Passage and the expertise shown by the Hive Iron Works, city-based shipyards do not seem to have shown any alacrity in following this example. The earliest reference to a paddle steamer being built at Cork is the *Cork Screw*, which was built in Robinson's dockyard in 1835 for Coates and Lefebure.[15] The first iron screw propellor steamer to be built in Cork was launched in March 1846 at Lecky and Beale's yard, and was followed four months later by the 400 ton *Doris* built at Stephen Hickson's Water Street yard (O'Mahony 1989, 77).

The firm of Lecky and Beale was responsible for the introduction of iron shipbuilding into Cork, when in 1844 they launched the first iron-hulled vessel to be built in the port from their city shipyard. As early as 1841 the firm of R. Lecky & Co. was prepared to manufacture land and marine boilers to order,[16] although the first indication of Lecky's desire to enter into the shipbuilding trade was his overhauling of the engines of the steamship *Lee* in 1841.[17] However, by the mid-1840s Robert Lecky had gone into the shipbuilding business with Abraham Beale who in this period was the proprietor of the Monard iron works (see below), though neither appear to have had any direct experience of the shipbuilding industry. On the other hand, the technology of iron shipbuilding owed more to the skills of the iron founder than to the traditional shipwright. In any case other Quaker families in Cork, Dublin and Waterford had a long association with both successful shipping companies and shipbuilding and repairing. Indeed, the proprietors of the city's two most successful shipyards in the 1840s, Ebenezer Pike of the Cork Steamship Company, and George Robinson were also Quakers.[18] In February 1849, after 'Having just completed extensive alterations and improvement at their concerns at Penrose Quay and Alfred Street' they declared their intention to 'undertake the building of iron vessels'.[19]

Iron shipbuilding was still a relatively new technology in the Ireland of the 1840s, although there was an earlier Irish precedent for a foundry diversifying into it. In 1838 the Lagan foundry of Coates and Young of Belfast, who by this period had become the main manufacturer of marine steam engines in Ireland, built the *Countess of Caledon* for the Ulster Steam Navigation Company (Moss and Hume 1986, 5). Lecky and Beale brought English workers experienced in the manufacture of iron ships to Cork, who in turn passed their skills on to local tradesmen.[20] In 1846 the Cork dockyard of Lecky and Beale launched the 150ft long iron screw steamer, *Rattler*, the first of its type to be built in Cork. The *Rattler* had three watertight compartments and its two 50hp engines were made in Lecky and Beale's Penrose Quay Foundry.

The shipbuilding yards at Cork were the most important in the country in the early decades of the nineteenth century, and were the largest employers of skilled labour in the city's heavy engineering industries (Bielenberg 1991, 104). As far as can be seen, the physical development of these yards appears to have been a painful process from extemporised derricks and working slips adjacent to the north bank sloblands, to that of patent slips, covered work-places and on-site sawmills and foundries. Hickson's yard, for example, which was amongst the first to acquire proper facilities (see above), had entrance gates on both the Lower Glanmire Road and Water Street. It extended for a distance of 316ft from the Lower Glanmire Road to the river, and had a river frontage of 331ft. It was equipped with three building slips, large rigging and sail lofts and a mould loft.

By the early 1850s the City of Cork Steamship Company's yard at Hargrave's Quay was the city's largest shipbuilding concern. Its machine shop was equipped with industrial lathes, two planing machines, a slotting machine, a threading machine and a large vertical drill. Other tradesmen such as blacksmiths, plumbers and carpenters were also accommodated in large workshops. The industrial vista presented by the Hargrave's Quay yard, according to one contemporary account made 'the visitor forget for a moment that he is within sight of the Lee, and not on the banks of the Clyde'.[21]

A newspaper account of 1853 also provides us with a detailed account of the *modus operandi* of Pike's yard, literally from the drawing office to the machine shops. In the drawing office the essential design features of the various ships were laid out and in the adjacent mould shop, the principal components were replicated in wood by pattern makers. There was clearly no iron rolling mill in the environs of the city during this period as the yard was obliged to import the iron plates used in fabricating ship's hulls.[22]

George Robinson's yard, which appears to have absorbed Hickson's in 1849, and had certainly subsumed Wheeler's by 1860, became the city's premier shipyard. In 1859 Robinson established a steam-powered sawmill at Water Street to accommodate his timber shipbuilding operations, but this installation appears never to have worked to its full capacity.[23] By 1863 the Water Street yard could function in any weather, the sawmills, forges and furnaces all being enclosed in extensive sheds (Fig. 62). The sawmills, which were 'of greater power than is required since the alterations in the trade' were situated near the Water Street entrance. In the centre of the yard a large shed accommodated some twenty forges, a large number of furnaces, and several punching and cutting machines. The yard during this period was employing about 500 men of which 200 hundred were employed in this central fabrication shop alone. The firm also employed a number of plasterers, whose work entailed coating the iron ribs of ships with cement to prevent corrosion. Apart from about 100 timber shipbuilders who also found employment at the yard, the other trades represented included upholsterers, carvers and gilders.[24] Robinson's yard was responsible for the *Mulgrave*, the first iron barque to be built in Ireland (Anderson 1984, 241). The last ship to be launched from a city dockyard was the *Ilen*, a 280 ton steamer made for the Skibbereen and West Cork Steamship Co., which was made at Robinson's Water Street Yard.[25]

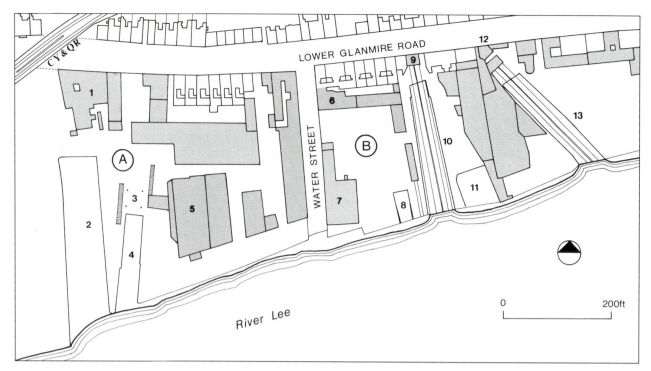

Fig. 62

Water Street dockyards in 1869.

1 Office. 2 Dock. 3 Derrick crane. 4 Dock.
5 Foundry. 6 Office. 7 Sawmill.
8 Slip. 9 Patent slip engine house.
10 Patent slip. 11 Slip. 12 Patent slip
engine house. 13 Patent slip.

Fig. 63

Wheeler's patent slipway (see fig. 62 above, no. 13).

Admiralty contracts awarded to Cork in the late 1880s and 1890s could not revive the once thriving shipbuilding industry (Cronin 1993, 733). In 1877 Cork Harbour Commissioners completed the transfer of Robinson's yard to their own control, whilst the sawmill and patent slip adjacent to its Water Street entrance was leased by the Cork Steamship Co. The Harbour Commissioners added a substantial repair shed to its frontage on the Lower Glanmire Road sometime in the late 1870s and also added a gridiron (an inclined rectangular framework of wooden beams onto which ships could be floated for repairs) at the eastern extremity of the yard near Castleview Terrace. The original patent slip of Knight's yard, which was subsequently used by Hickson, Robinson and the Cork Steamship Co., has long since been filled in. Wheeler's patent slip, however, still survives but has been extensively repaired (Fig. 63). Ebenezer Pike's yard on Hargrave's Quay was demolished during the extensions made to the Great Southern and Western Railway yards from the 1860s onwards.

ROPE-MAKING

In the eighteenth and early nineteenth centuries, sailcloth manufacture and rope-making, in the greater Cork area, were often carried out by the same manufacturer. Rope was of course an essential item for all types of shipping, from the most prosaic lighter to the Royal Navy's ships of the line. There can be little doubt that large quantities of both soft and hard fibre rope were formerly manufactured within the city and its environs. Indeed, it was claimed that there were over 200 rope-makers within the Cork Harbour area before 1800.[26]

Traditionally, the rope yarn was spun from either hard fibres such as hemp, sisal and coir, or soft fibres such as jute, European hemp or cotton. In the Cork Harbour area, however, the rope strands were generally spun from hemp and Manilla hemp. In the main, the formation of the rope involved the *laying* and *stranding* of three or four strands of spun yarn along a long (often covered) walkway or *rope-walk*. Either men or horses walked up and down the length of the rope-walk (which was generally in excess of 140 yards), intertwining the various strands of the rope or twine by hand (McCutcheon 1990, 82). From around the 1850s onwards patent ropeworks, in which many of the traditional processes became mechanised, began to appear throughout England and Scotland (Hay and Stell 1986, 86), but only one ropeworks established on similar lines came into being within the greater Cork area (see below).

A small number of rope-walks are indicated on the first edition of the Ordnance Survey map, most notably off Sunday's Well Road (a site first shown on Charles Smith's map of 1750), at Cahergal, Richmond Hill and off Blarney Lane. Not all of these, it is clear, were covered. The Douglas rope-walk, associated with Besnard's former sailcloth factory, while not expressly named as such, was clearly covered over in the early 1840s,[27] as was Denis Hanlon's rope-walk off Factory Lane on the northside of the city. Some 45 yards of Hanlon's rope-walk lay outside the municipal boundary, 140 yards of which were covered over, a feature which seems to have been singled out for special mention by Griffith's Valuation field surveyors.[28] The inference we may draw from this is that most rope-walks within the environs of the city were generally not covered over for the greater part, if not all, of their length. However, the rope-walk off Sunday's Well Road as depicted on the Ordnance Survey 1:1056 series of 1871 was by this date a covered way.[29] Many of these small rope-walks employed about ten men, and by the end of the 1880s many were being squeezed out of business by larger manufacturers like Wallis and Pollock. Three of these survived into the late 1880s and only two were in existence by the turn of the 1900s (Cronin 1993, 735–6).

The Douglas Patent Cordage Works (554)

For the greater part of the nineteenth century, the undisputed centre of the Cork rope and cordage industry was situated within the former sailcloth manufactory at Douglas. Julius Besnard continued to make rope at the Douglas factory after 1820 (Foley 1991, 14), but the Douglas factory was presumably dormant when the Ordnance surveyors visited the area in the early 1840s, although the millrace and millpond of the former flax-spinning mill, along with the adjacent covered rope-walk, are shown. The ropeworks was under the control of Bartholomew Gibbings in 1852,[30] but sometime in the early 1850s the premises was run as the 'Douglas Patent Cordage Works' by Wallis and Pollock.[31] In 1854 they were importing tar from Sweden, which was presumably used in the manufacture of their ropes, with a surplus being sold to the public at large.[32] Around the same time they were also importing European hemp directly from Archangel.[33]

By early 1858 the machinery of the ropeworks had been extensively modernised to enable the manufacture of rope from manilla hemp, presumably along the lines of contemporary Scottish ropeworks. By this period the *house machine* method was being introduced into Scotland. Trackways were now used for running wheeled bogeys or travellers, which hauled out ropes of different lengths and diameters (Hay and Stell 1986, 95). At any rate the water power was clearly being used to spin the hempen yarn which made up the strands, and in 1862 Wallis and Pollock's Patent Spinning Mill and Cordage Factory, which now employed 130 people and which was described as 'one of the most extensive in the Kingdom', had a steam engine installed. The latter event began on a tragic note. The steam engine was built by an unnamed local foundry and was intended to be connected to the firm's machinery, presumably when the available head for the waterwheel ran low. However, when the engine was being connected to the machinery its boiler exploded with tragic results, starting a fire which spread to a nearby gasometer, which presumably supplied gas lighting within the works.[34] By 1864 the company was now called the Douglas Patent Hemp Spinning Company[35] and was preparing for an ambitious changeover to flax spinning.

IRON FOUNDRIES AND ENGINEERING WORKS

In the seventeenth century, English speculators had established iron smelters and processing works throughout Ireland in areas with seemingly unlimited stands of timber, smelting a mixture of native and imported ores in charcoal-fired blast furnaces (Andrews 1956, 146; McCracken 1971, 92; Barnard 1985, 103). But an industry established on these lines could only last as long as the forests which it consumed. By 1780 there were only two charcoal-fuelled furnaces operating in Ireland, at Enniscorthy, County Wexford and Mountrath, County Laois (Young 1780, vol. 2, 325). The last operational example in County Waterford at Araglin, on the border of County Cork, ceased to function sometime in the 1750s (McCracken 1957, 128).

Eighteenth-century English technological developments in the smelting process, the most important of which involved the substitution of coal (and later coke) for charcoal as fuel, enabled blast furnaces to be transferred to the coalfields of Britain. Yet such a development could have little profitable use in Ireland where coal was, in relative terms, a scarce commodity. By the end of the eighteenth century iron-smelting and foundry work had, in many instances, become separate processes. Cast-iron was now increasingly used in specialist foundries for the manufacture of machine parts, the iron being effectively melted down again and reshaped; smelting directly from the ore was no longer necessary. By the beginning of the nineteenth century iron foundries which employed *cupola* furnaces for re-melting either pig or scrap iron, were becoming established in Ireland's larger ports and inland towns with developed communications. In the cupola furnace a mixture of pig-iron, scrap cast-iron and coke as fuel, were fed into the top of a stack-like structure made of cast-iron staves bound together with wrought iron hoops and lined internally with refractory bricks. The temperature was maintained by a blast of air from a steam-powered blowing engine, and the molten metal was drawn off through a tap hole at the base of the stack. The molten metal was often run off into greensand moulds (formed with a mixture of sand and some clay) on the foundry floor.

There were basically two types of general iron works established within and near the city in the late eighteenth and early nineteenth centuries. The first was the water-powered forge which produced a wide range of wrought ironwork: spades, shovels, and other agricultural implements along with general ironwork. Iron foundries were also established within the city for the manufacture of industrial machinery, along with prime movers such as waterwheels, water turbines and steam engines. These latter were much larger establishments, which had a much wider range of machine tools, in addition to a capacity for producing cast-iron items of all sizes.

As in all Cork City industries established during the late eighteenth and nineteenth centuries and using bulky raw materials, a quayside location was an important locational factor for many iron foundries. The main early nineteenth-century iron foundries and engineering works established within the city, such as the Hive iron works on Hanover Street and the nearby Vulcan works, the Union iron works (Lapp's Island) and the Eagle Foundry (Kyrl's Quay), were built adjacent to the quays. The establishment of new iron foundries in Cork was a direct response to the rapidly changing technological climate of the late eighteenth century, when many traditional industries were experiencing increased mechanisation. Cast-iron was beginning to replace wood in the basic components of water-powered wheels and power transmission systems, as technological change in the iron industry made cast-iron a much cheaper commodity. Other factors such as the need for greatly improved water-powered prime movers — in England because of the reduced number of available mill sites, in Ireland because of the lack of coal — also influenced the transition from wood to iron. The increased use of cast-iron framing and beams in building design and the emergence of steam-driven prime movers provided an additional stimulus to the development of foundries.

Beginning with the substitution of oak axles with cast-iron ones, and following up with cast-iron wheel rims and, ultimately, cast-iron transmission, English engineers such as John Smeaton (1724–92) revolutionised mill construction (Wilson 1957, 33; Reynolds, T.S. 1983, 289). Similarly, John Rennie successfully introduced cast-iron shafting and gearing into his Albion mill on the River Thames by Blackfriars Bridge, in 1784 (Boucher 1963, 80; Hills 1989, 72). In traditional water-powered mills the motion of the waterwheel was transmitted to the gear wheels via its wooden axle. But with the introduction of cast-iron rim gearing for waterwheels, where the principal driving wheel or segment was affixed, in sections, to the outer rim of the waterwheel or to the arms, it became possible for the diameter of the axle and the cross-sectional area of the arms to be greatly reduced. This led to the development of suspension waterwheels of lightweight, cast-iron construction with internal wrought iron suspension rods providing support for the framework of the wheel (T.S. Reynolds 1983, 292). Thomas C. Hewes of Manchester (1768–1832) is generally credited with development of the suspension wheel, and William Fairbairn (a former employee of Hewes) with its propagation and further technical development.[36]

The introduction of cast-iron frames, and later of cast-iron roof trusses, into late eighteenth-century industrial buildings, provided an additional fillip for Cork's foundries. Cast-iron also came to be used decoratively from the early decades of the nineteenth century, whilst the development of public utilities such as gas and water supply also provided outlets for Cork foundries and engineering works, although for the most part the mains were supplied by specialist English firms. The railway boom of the late 1840s also contributed to their growth, where local iron and engineering works made an important contribution to the development of the railway infrastructure. The introduction of iron shipbuilding into Cork in the 1840s added a further branch to the local heavy engineering industry, with the foundry of one shipyard even building a railway bridge for the Cork–Bandon line at Inishannon (see below). In nearly all cases the expertise required to establish the early nineteenth-century Cork foundries and engineering works was brought over from England, and the necessary skills had been established in Cork by the middle of the nineteenth century. Specialist machinery, however, continued to be imported throughout the nineteenth century. Bryan Donkin, for example, of the Fort Place works at Bermondsey, near London, supplied a Fourdrinier Brothers paper-making machine to J.B. Sullivan's paper mill near Dripsey, County Cork in 1807 (Hills 1988, 103). Indeed the same mills were visited in 1824 by George and Robert Stephenson, after which the firm of Robert Stephenson & Co. supplied a boiler and paper-making machinery to the mills (Rolt 1988, 93; Hills 1988, 175). The repertoire of local firms, however, quickly expanded to meet the demands of most mechanised industries from gunpowder mills to tanneries. A number of Cork foundries such as the Hive Iron Foundry and the King Street Iron Works were also bell foundries.

In terms of layout many of the Cork foundries were similar to their English counterparts.[37] The fabrication of large pieces and the assembly of machines required an extensive covered area in which bulky components could be lifted into position in the course of their assembly. The machine hall, as it became known, was often accessed by a wide doorway which enabled larger pieces to be dispatched from the building. Travelling cranes were also quite common in the larger engineering works, which were also equipped with smaller jib cranes. The machine hall or erecting shop was normally connected to a multistoried building which housed pattern-makers shops, finishing shops and model-makers' shops, all of which would have adjoined a foundry and forge shops. A single steam engine normally powered the furnace bellows, along the ancillary machinery such as grinders and drills, although a smaller, portable engine may also have been employed for this latter purpose.

The Hive Iron Works (285)

The Hive iron works was established on the western end of Hanover Street in 1800 by Thomas Addison Barnes, whose early output included web wire and bolting machines. Other specialist machinery manufactured by Barnes included brass wire web, and sieves for paper-making and frames for gunpowder manufacture.[38] The frames for gunpowder manufacture were presumably manufactured for the Ballincollig gunpowder mills, with which the Hive Iron Works had a long association (see below). Under Barnes tutelage the Hive foundry built the iron gates which formally graced the entrance to Cork's Mardyke Walk (Barry 1917, 15). Barnes and James Atkinson (who had worked as a machine-maker in Leeds) had manufactured flax and hemp-spinning machinery for the Besnard family's mills at Douglas (see Ch. 4) and both men formally entered a partnership in 1811. In 1813 Barnes, Atkinson and two further partners Richard Perrott (1791–1870) and Paul McSwiney extended the original Hanover Street works (Daly 1978, 176).[39]

The Hive iron works clearly paid an important role in the dissemination of new foundry and machine-making technology. Paul McSwiney founded the King Street iron works in 1816 (see below), whilst Richard Perrott set up a separate foundry on Hanover Street in 1828.[40] Indeed, Robert Stotesbury and Co.'s Eagle Foundry on Kyrl's Quay boasted in 1829 that it had John Grant 'late foreman to Messrs T.A. Barnes & Co. for the last 29 years' (i.e. since Barnes established the Hive Iron Foundry) on its staff.[41] The Hive iron works may well have been the first to manufacture steam engines within the city, and while there can be no certainty about this, the firm enjoyed the distinction of being the first in Ireland to manufacture marine steam engines. The first wholly Irish-built steamship, the *Waterloo*, built at Andrew and Michael Hennessy's yard at Passage West (see above) was fitted with engines built at the Hive iron works, under the supervision of James Atkinson. The engine appears to have been about 20hp and was in service up until 1870 (Anderson 1984, 236; O'Mahony 1986a, 18).[42]

In 1829 T.A. Barnes & Co. built a three-storey warehouse on Great George's (Washington) Street, a formal structure with elaborate pilasters and moulded parapets, facing the street front (Fig. 64). The original architect's drawing of this building which survives in the Cork Archives Institute, shows a two-storey building with a chimney at one end.[43] The chimney was presumably intended to form part of either an engine house or a small foundry, which was clearly never built. The warehouse was immediately in front of the Hive iron works, which by this period was flanked by the Vulcan foundry to the west and Perrott's foundry to the east. In 1828 Richard Perrott senior had set up on his own, building a new foundry adjoining the Hive iron works on Hanover Street with 'improved machinery' which was engaged in foundry and engineering work.[44] Perrott's Foundry appears to have later amalgamated with the Hive iron works. In 1831 Thomas Barnes' interest in the Hive Iron Foundry was advertised for sale,[45] and three years later Mrs Anne Barnes was winding up the foundry's business.[46] Finally, in 1837, the foundry was put up for sale, along with its 'steam engine, machinery lathes, forges, furnaces, blowing machines, moulding boxes, drilling machine, punching machine, cranes, loom mill...',[47] and by 1838 was clearly under the control of Richard Perrott.[48] By the late 1820s the Hive Iron Works, in addition to the manufacture of flour-bolting machines, wheat-scouring and patent separators, was also making steam boilers, both for engines and tannery-drying sheds. The amalgamated Hive Iron Works and Perrott's adjacent works occupied a long stretch of river frontage facing Wandesford's Quay, and became not only the largest engineering works in the city but one of the largest outside Belfast. In 1838 a total of twenty-eight steam engines, which collectively generated some 412hp, were at work in the city of Cork. The majority of these were manufactured by local foundries, namely Ring and Thompson's Union Iron Works on Lapp's Island, Paul McSwiney's King Street Iron Works, Edward King's Phoenix Iron Works on Smith Street and Richard Perrott's Hive Iron Works.[49] Most of these were 10–20hp engines, and were generally of the rotative beam variety, which the Hive Foundry and its principal competitors produced for factories and mills in the greater Cork area. Few technical details of these engines are available and no surviving examples have been identified. By the mid-1840s Perrott was manufacturing small portable engines of about 4hp upwards, along with stationary beam engines such as the 25hp beam engine built by the Hive iron works for Thorley's bleaching works in Upper Glanmire.[50] Perrott also fitted out Roche's flax mill at Trabolgan, County Cork, and probably also the steam engine used to power the machinery.[51] In 1859 Perrott provided a 30hp engine for Unckle's flour mill on Lancaster Quay, and in 1861 his men were entrusted with the task of erecting special counters on the Cornish engine at Cork Waterworks.[52]

The Hive foundry was probably the first within the city to manufacture water turbines, a new technology which industrialists, engaged in the flax-related industries in the Cork

Fig. 64

Hive Iron Works warehouse, Washington Street, completed in 1829 (see fig. 65 below, no. 6).

Fig. 65 BELOW

Hive Iron Foundry, plan (redrawn from Goad Insurance Plans of 1897).

1-5 Iron stores. 6 Hardware warehouse.
7 Store showrooms. 8 Foundry.
9 Cupola furnaces. 10 Forge shop.
11 Boiler house. 12 Engine house.
13 Boiler and machine shop.
14 Millwrights' 1st floor, pattern shop 2nd floor.

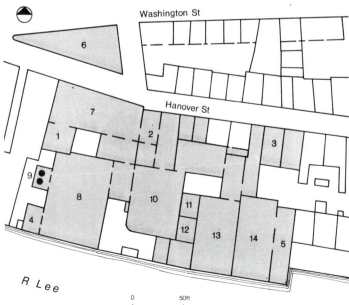

area wholeheartedly embraced (Rynne 1989b and 1989c). In 1853 there were two water turbines (probably of the Fourneyron variety) at work in County Cork, at Ballineen[53] near Bandon and at Riverstown near Cork.[54] A further turbine, of indeterminate type and make, was in the course of erection at the Woodville mills near Passage, County Cork late in 1854.[55] The first fully documented turbine manufactured by a Cork foundry, however, is the the 16hp Jonval-type turbine made by Richard Perrott for the Ballincollig gunpowder mills in 1855 (see Ch. 6), which is the first of its type known to have been manufactured in Ireland. Perrott also appears to have manufactured metal waterwheels, from perhaps the first half of the nineteenth century onwards, one of the more noteworthy examples being a 20ft diameter wheel for Robert Webb's flourmill at Quarterstown near Mallow, County Cork in 1854 (Power 1991, 5–17).[56] McSwiney's foundry is known to have manufactured a large suspension wheel for a mill near Macroom sometime before 1860 (see below), and the likelihood is that other foundries in the city such as the Hive Iron Works also made suspension waterwheels.

In 1848 Richard Perrott installed the first of his 'Registered Capstan Mills' in Cork County Prison and in the Cork Workhouse, which employed the muscle power of large numbers of the inmates to grind flour and to pump water.[57] Perrott successfully sold the idea to the Irish Poor Law Commissioners, to whom the idea of a mechanical contrivance which could perform useful work whilst simultaneously keeping up to 100 people occupied (albeit in degrading and occasionally dangerous work) had many attractions. Contemporary illustrations of Perrott's capstan mill shows a capstan with numerous radial arms, each of which was turned in a clockwise direction by at least two people. The illustration accompanying Perrott's formal submission to the Poor Law Commissioners shows forty men turning a capstan mill, which actuates two sets of large millstones through right-angled gearing, although in the Cork Workhouse it was operated by up to 150 boys or girls at any one time. Perrott appears to have supplied capstan mills to the workhouses in Midleton, County Cork and Athlone, County Westmeath, but the use of these mills was eventually abandoned by the Poor Law Commissioners in 1855 (Robins 1980, 236–7). By the late 1850s, however, Perrott had obtained a patent for his own threshing machine and was manufacturing his own corn-washing machine, whilst his business in agricultural implements and household ranges continued to expand.[58] As early as 1851, Perrott had begun to extend his manufacturing interests by building a new scrapping and plating mill just outside the city at Curraheen, near Bishopstown,[59] while by the early 1860s he had established a unit for the manufacture of steam boilers directly across the river from the Hive Iron Works on Wandesford's Quay (Measom 1866, 293). By this period the foundry and engineering works on Hanover Street appears to have reached its greatest extents. The largest building within the Hive complex was the foundry which had three cupola furnaces with blowing engines powered by a 20hp beam engine. The main forge, which had a fitting loft above it and an adjoining machine maker's shop, was situated immediately to the west of this. The foundry's engine shop was equipped with lathes, planing, drilling and finishing machinery, all of which appears to have been powered by the works' steam engine via line shafting (Fig. 65). Perrott was in the process of completing a pair of four-ton, cast-iron rollers for Ballincollig Gunpowder Mills in 1866 and was also manufacturing silk-dressing machines for export to Australia (ibid., 296). Around the same time he was fitting cast-iron stanchions for the line shafting of a flour mill at Bealick, near Macroom, County Cork.[60]

The Hive iron foundry manufactured cast-iron supporting columns, beams and trusses for many buildings within the Cork area.[61] Indeed, Perrott's warehouse on latter-day Washington Street, built in 1829, is probably one of the first within the city to employ

cast-iron supporting columns. The foundry supplied most of the cast-iron columns for St Patrick's Woollen Mills in Douglas village, built in 1882, and some impressive columns and beams for the main mashing loft of the Cork Porter Brewery in 1870 (see under 'Brewing'). Perrott was also responsible for the cast-iron framework for the steeps installed in the Nile Street maltings in the 1860s for Beamish and Crawford (see Ch. 3). Ornamental ironwork such as railings can be seen all over the city (e.g. Sunday's Well Road, Sheares Street), and includes the entrance railings for Cork City Gaol and the bollards and quayside railings manufactured for Cork Harbour Commissioners.

Many Cork foundries manufactured agricultural implements throughout the nineteenth century and by the 1840s Perrott had added lightweight ploughs and power-activated churns to his existing range.[62] It has recently been argued that the decline in tillage during the second half of the nineteenth century adversely affected the Hive and other Cork iron works (Bielenberg 1991, 97–8). This decline, it has been argued, adversely affected the demand for agricultural implements, which a number of the Cork foundries produced along with horse and steam-powered agricultural machinery.

However, while the demand for certain tools may have been on the decline, the decline in demand for Irish-made agricultural implements was offset by other developments. On the one hand, imports of foreign agricultural implements and machinery also increased. But the demand for agricultural implements such as ploughs, root cutters and harrows for use on small holdings actually increased towards the end of the nineteenth century, a development from which Irish manufacturers directly benefited (O'Neill 1984, 110). When foreign agricultural machinery was introduced into the greater Cork area it was nearly always through a Cork agency. McKenzie and Sons' Ceres Iron Works on Camden Quay, for example, became agents for Clayton and Shuttleworth's (of Lincoln) portable steam engines and threshers.[63] In 1878 McKenzie was also responsible for bringing over new butter-making machinery from Germany, part of a new range of items (which included De Laval's patent separators) which were put on show at an exhibition of new butter-making machinery held in that year.[64] Furthermore, foundries such as the Hive Iron Works were taking full advantage of the increasing use of mechanised creameries, and Perrott was actually hiring small engines to creameries along with pumps, shafting and churns. By 1884 he had already installed mechanised creamery appliances at the Munster Dairy Company's Cork works and in creameries at Tallow and Hewardstown.[65] There was, therefore, a change in emphasis in the business activities of Cork foundries such as the Hive Iron Works, which included a greater emphasis on sales and repairs, and while this may have led to a decline in overall foundry activity this was by no means as serious as more recent accounts have suggested.[66]

Amongst the last large commissions undertaken by the Hive Iron Works was the provision of large girders, gearing and thrust-bearing pedestals for the Corporation Waterworks in 1888 and in the following year a commission to provide six, six ton open wagons for the Cork and Muskerry Light Railway. As in the case of other public utilities such as gas and electricity, even though the main items of machinery and plant were supplied by specialist engineering firms in both Britain and the north of Ireland, certain items were more conveniently supplied by local foundries.

Very little of the Hive Iron Works complex survives. By the mid-1960s the furnaces had been demolished (O'Mahony 1992, 150), as were the greater part of surviving buildings in the late 1980s to enable the construction of the unemployment exchange on Hanover Street. However, the surviving buildings at the western end of Hanover Street, which are finished in brick on their north-facing elevation and stone-faced in the courtyard area to the south, date to the early years of the nineteenth century. In the later years of the foundry's operation these appear to have been used as store and showrooms, but the ground-floor level, which has impressive cast-iron support columns and an intricate tensioning beam spanning the arched entrance, would originally have housed finishing shops. In the 1890s the engine room and boiler house were positioned centrally, between the forge shop and the boiler and machine shops, although it is by no means clear whether or not the engine occupied this position throughout the entire working life of the foundry.

The Vulcan Foundry (641)

John Steele's Vulcan Foundry (the first of two foundries of that name established in the city during the nineteenth century) was established in the 1820s in the former sugar house on Lancaster Quay. The foundry began as a millwright's yard manufacturing threshing machines, waterwheels and general millwork, but later extended its activities to include steam engines.[67] By 1831 Steele appears to have been making suspension waterwheels,[68] manufacturing the iron waterwheels for the entirely rebuilt Lee mills around this time. One example of a Vulcan Foundry waterwheel, installed at a County Limerick mill in 1841, has survived *in situ* at Lyon's Flour Mill on the River Maigue, near Croom bridge, County Limerick.[69]

The Vulcan foundry on Lancaster Quay, including the four-storey former sugar house building, all of the machinery and the firm's patterns, were destroyed in a fire of 1859.[70] By 1862[71] Steele appears to have established a new foundry on Lapp's Quay (107), where it continued in use until the early 1900s.[72] Amongst the new Vulcan foundry's first important commissions was the structural ironwork for Wallis and Pollock's Donnybrook flax-spinning mill, which was completed in 1866 (see Ch. 4), and the cast-iron columns for an extension to the Green distillery which appears to have been completed around the same time. Like the small number of Cork City foundries involved in steam engine manufacture in the second half of the nineteenth century the Lapp's Quay foundry mainly supplied local flour mills. In 1874, for example, the Vulcan foundry made a pair of high-pressure engines for the Capwell Steam Flour Mill on Douglas Street.[73] By 1882, however, the foundry was put up for auction, along with its steam engine, forges, fitters' and machine shops, boiler yard, lathes, screwing, slotting, planing and drilling machines, and bending rollers and wheel cutters.[74] The Vulcan foundry was taken over by Richard Foley in 1885, and by the early 1890s had added boiler-making to its list of manufactures. In 1886 Foley supplied cast-iron segments to the Corporation Waterworks,[75] and in 1888 the foundry supplied the girders and slides for the new pumps installed in the waterworks, along with the brasses and pillow blocks needed for the new turbines.[76] Also in 1888 the foundry made a four ton plate for the press house at Ballincollig Gunpowder Mills, which was believed at that time to be the largest ever casting made in Cork.[77] Around the same time Foley was also overhauling the engines at the South Gate Brewery, St Patrick's Woollen Mills and Ballincollig Gunpowder Mills.[78]

The structural ironwork for what was to become the largest steam-powered roller mill within the greater Cork area, the Marina mills, was also undertaken by the Vulcan works. By 1897 the Vulcan foundry was run by the partnership of McClean and Park, and consisted of a foundry, machine shop and a smithy. It had two cupola furnaces and two steam engines, one 25hp the other 10hp.[79] By 1906 the foundry had been converted for use as coal stores.[80]

South facing elevation

Fig. 66

Bealick Mill, Macroom, County Cork. The cast-iron suspension wheel retained *in situ* was manufactured by Mc Swiney's King Street Iron Works sometime before 1860.

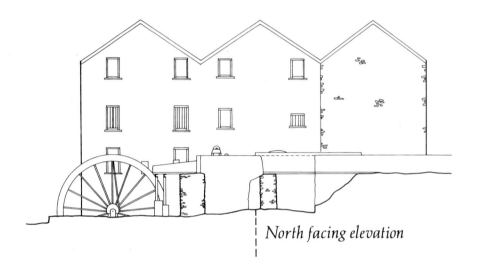

North facing elevation

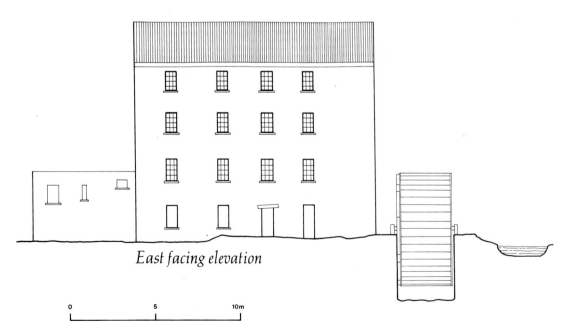

East facing elevation

0 5 10m

The King Street Iron Works (230)

This was established in 1816 by Paul McSwiney, a former partner of Barnes, Atkinson and Perrott (see above). Little is known about its early development, and the earliest-known example of its work is the structural ironwork for the multistorey grain store, built at Midleton Distillery, County Cork in 1830, the cast-iron supporting columns for which survive *in situ*. McSwiney's was one of the first foundries in the city to manufacture high-pressure steam engines, along with the only documented example of a beam engine manufactured by a Cork foundry for a Cork porter brewery. This was a 16hp beam engine installed in Lane's South Gate Brewery in or around 1860.[81]

During the railway boom years of the late 1840s and early 1850s McSwiney provided the ironwork for the roof of the City Park terminus of the Cork Blackrock and Passage Railway (in 1849), the roof of the temporary Great Southern and Western Railway terminus at Blackpool and the iron underbridge on the old Dublin Road in the Blackpool area of the city (see Ch. 7). Shortly before 1860 McSwiney made a large Fairbairn-type suspension waterwheel with ventilated buckets for a flour mill at Bealick, near Macroom, County Cork, one of only three surviving examples of its type known to have been manufactured by a Cork City foundry. The Bealick waterwheel is 6.37m in diameter and 3.26m wide and appears to have driven three pairs of stones and flour-processing machinery (Fig. 66). In the early 1860s the King Street foundry was taken over by H. and C. Smith (nephews of Paul McSwiney) under whose management a commission to manufacture supporting columns for the malt-milling loft at Beamish and Crawford's Cork Porter Brewery was carried out (see Ch. 3)[82] as well as the structural ironwork for the Millfield flax-spinning mill in 1866. By the mid-1870s the foundry was also supplying agricultural machinery.[83] In or around 1881 the King Street Iron Works was under the control of George Perrott, who in 1883 manufactured a series of massive cast-iron supporting columns for the main mashing loft of the Cork Porter Brewery (see Ch. 3). In the late nineteenth century the manufacture of spur, mitre and bevel gear wheels was considered to be one of the firm's specialities (Stratten and Stratten 1892, 162). The King Street works was also equipped with a large travelling gantry crane, which in 1829 was used in the manufacture of a large cast-iron waterwheel for a County Kildare flour mill (ibid.). By 1897 the King Street foundry operated a single cupola furnace and was under the control of Robert Merrick, and was no longer in use by the early years of the twentieth century.[84]

City of Cork Steamship Company's Foundry (082)

In the 1840s Robert J. Lecky's foundry on Penrose Quay/Alfred Street was manufacturing boilers for stationary and marine steam engines, and appears to have been the city's principal steam engine and boiler specialist, producing both condensing and high-pressure engines.[85] In the early 1850s Lecky built a 65hp engine for the Valentia slate quarries, along with the machinery driven by it (Maguire 1853, 30).[86] Lecky later formed a partnership with Abraham Beale and diversified into iron shipbuilding (see above), whilst the City of Cork Steamship Company's works actually became involved in civil engineering projects. In 1862 the City of Cork Steamship Company's foundry built a new bridge for the Cork and Bandon Railway at Inishannon, a wrought iron lattice-work structure made up of two 100ft spans resting on a masonry centre and abutment piers.[87] The same works, doubtless under stiff competition from other Cork foundries, also successfully tendered for the contract to supply three boilers for the new Corporation Waterworks in 1858 (see Ch. 8). Two of the steam engine boilers installed in the Cork Porter Brewery in the 1860s were also manufactured by the City of Cork Steamship Company's works.

The Warren's Place Iron Works (261)

Of the Cork foundries established in the second half of the nineteenth century Robert Merrick's Warren's Place Iron Works, established by Jeremiah Merrick in 1864, was clearly the most successful. Merrick was in control of the King Street iron works by the late 1890s, and his Warren's Place iron works is the only known Cork foundry to have undertaken the refurbishing of railway locomotives. In the late 1890s Merrick refurbished engine no. 4, *Blarney*, for the Cork and Muskerry Light Railway (see Ch. 7). Merrick appears to have produced most varieties of steam engines, including portable engines along with the usual complement of threshing machines, waterwheels and transmission systems manufactured by other Cork foundries (Stratten and Stratten 1892, 213). The Warren's Place foundry, however, also specialised in brewers' pumps (ibid.). In 1902 Robert Merrick won an important contract to supply three inverted triple expansion engines for the Corporation Waterworks, but later came to an agreement with the Belfast firm of Combe Barbour to manufacture the engines which were to be erected by his men (see Ch. 6). Nonetheless, that Merrick was able to confidently submit a tender for triple expansion engines which could compete with firms such as Combe Barbour provides a fair indication as to the firm's reputation. By the early years of the twentieth century Merrick had supplied all of the steelwork for Cork central GPO, many of the new turbine pumps for the Cork Corporation waterworks, a new retort house for the Cork Gas Consumers' Company works and lightship lanterns and lights for acetylene-lit buoys for the Commissioners of Irish Lights.[88]

Smaller Engineering Works

While many Cork foundries carried out a wide-ranging number of foundry and engineering activities, certain foundries tended to concentrate more on the manufacture of agricultural implements and machinery. These differed substantially from the spade mills established within the environs of the city in the late eighteenth and throughout the nineteenth century, in that they were essentially light engineering works which employed machine tools actuated by small steam engines. Typical of these would have been J. Kennedy's agricultural implement works on Hanover Street (266), which in 1875 had two drilling machines, two back-geared screw-cutting machines, three smith's hearths, a jib crane, two power or foot lathes, two drilling machines and a 6hp portable engine.[89] McKenzie and Sons Ceres iron works on Camden Quay (242), whilst acting as Cork agent's for Leffel's Patent Turbine,[90] received both national and international acclaim for its furze masticator or 'gorse mill', which was tested at the Kilburn meeting of the Royal Agricultural Society of England in the early 1880s, where it received a silver medal for being the 'only successful invention for reducing the valuable forage crop whin or gorse into a condition suitable for animal food'.[91] William McBride and Sons' foundry on Merchants Quay (426) was also a successful manufacturer and exporter of agricultural machinery. In the early decades of the twentieth century upwards of 3,000 of McBride's patent thistle cutters had been exported to England, Scotland and Wales.[92]

Other, less well-known engineering works established in the second half of the nineteenth century, such as D. Macilwraith and Sons' Rocksavage Engineering and Millwright's works on Anglesea Street specialised in smaller machine and steam engine fittings such as boiler mountings and fusible plugs.[93] However, Macilwraith also appears to have specialised in machinery for the woollen industry. A milling machine manufactured by him received an award at the Cork Industrial Exhibition of 1883.[94]

Spade mills

During the nineteenth and early twentieth centuries the small size of Irish land-holdings proved to be a serious impediment to widespread mechanisation in Irish agriculture.

Successful foundries specialising in the manufacture of agricultural machinery were established in towns and cities such as Belfast, Dublin, Cork, Wexford, Cappoquin and Coleraine. But the Irish market for agricultural machinery was a limited one. The gradual decline in tillage in favour of livestock farming in Ireland in the second half of the nineteenth century, combined with the depression of the 1870s and increased competition from imported agricultural implements and machinery, created serious economic difficulties for many Irish foundries.[95] However, in the northern and western regions of the country, particularly in areas of marginal land, the spade was an almost universal tillage implement. Indeed, in certain areas ploughs could not be used, and in these and in other regions fields were often divided into small plots to facilitate spade cultivation. Yet even in areas where ploughs could be used the availability of cheap labour tended to encourage spade cultivation (Ó Danachair 1970, 49). There was, therefore, a clear preference for spade cultivation in many areas, but for many smallholders and migrant *spailpíní* (agricultural labourers) not just any type of spade would do. Each locality often had its own set preference for a particular type of spade. The often bewildering regional variation of Irish spade types — there are in excess of 1,100 varieties and sizes of the one-sided spade alone — attests to the doggedness with which people adhered to their individual preferences (Gailey 1970, 35). Thus when water-powered spade mills became established in the eighteenth century (mostly in the northern half of the island), they were obliged to keep patterns for the different types of spade used within their intended catchment areas (Gailey 1982, 2).

There are at least nine documented examples of specialist spade and shovel mills within the greater Cork area operating, at various periods, between the closing decades of the eighteenth century and the early 1960s. By the 1830s at least five spade mills were operating within the environs of the city (Lewis 1837), the largest of which, the Monard and Coolowen iron works, was also the longest continually operated (see below). In 1888, despite the ravages of the Irish famine and the decline in tillage, there were still four spade mills working near Cork at Monard, Templemichael, Upper Glanmire and Curraheen.[96] The skills involved in traditional Irish spade and shovel making have been described elsewhere (see Gailey 1982), and it is sufficient to note here that on the island of Ireland these specialist craftsmen plied their trade in every county where spade mills were at work.

The Monard and Coolowen Iron Works (219)

The Monard works is the largest and best-preserved spade mill complex in the Ireland. It occupies a small, picturesque glacial valley on the headwaters of the Blarney River, which discharges in torrents through a series of narrow, sandstone gorges. The choice of site was clearly governed by the availability of a good head of water which was utilised by a succession of mills, each of which had its own millpond. In or around 1790 at least two water-powered forges were established on the upper reaches of the glen by a Cork Quaker merchant, Abraham Beale, along with a series of workers' dwellings and ancillary buildings. By 1819 Beale had become bankrupt, by which time he was described as a 'shovel maker' in the records of the Cork Society of Friends, who reported that '[his] failure was principally occasioned by his embarking on a business (though on the advice or consent of his near connections) and that he had not the means to carry on' (Harrison 1991, 29). Nonetheless, Beale was able to overcome his financial difficulties and to continue to operate his spade mills at Monard. By 1822 had established a Cork City premises at Half Moon Street,[97] but two years later, in 1824, he moved his retail premises to St Patrick's Quay. In this same year he was also operating a second iron works at Kilcully, near Monard, with his brother James Beale.[98] Indeed, by the mid-1840s Beale had actually diversified into shipbuilding, by entering into a partnership with the Cork

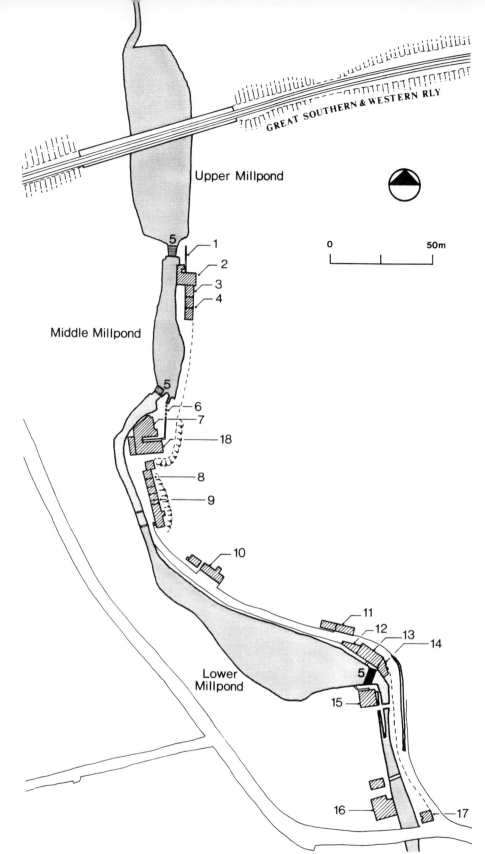

Fig. 67

Plan of Monard and Coolowen Iron Works.

1 Cast-iron feeder pipes for waterwheels of O'Hara's Mill. 2 O'Hara's Mill.
3 Forge. 4 Workers' housing. 5 Overflow dams. 6 Feeder pipe. 7 Saw mill.
8 Craftsmens' workshops. 9 and 10 Dwellings. 11 Stores. 12 Finishing shop.
13 'Logwood Mill'. 14 Store. 15 Coolowen Mill. 16 Early twentieth-century hammer forge. 17 Gate lodge. 18 'Middle Mill'.

Fig. 68 OPPOSITE ABOVE

Mechanical guillotine at Monard in 1930s (estate of Alec Day).

Fig. 69 OPPOSITE BELOW

Interior of Logwood Mill in 1930s (estate of Alec Day).

Fig. 70 ABOVE

Sectional elevation of Coolowen Mill.

1 Launder. 2 Wooden waterwheel.
3 Hammerhead. 4 Hammer beam.
5 Head bit. 6 Head stock. 7 Shuttle control. 8 Anvil. 9 Hammer fulcrum.
10 Cam wheel. 11 Cam. 12 Launder for bellows waterwheel. 13 External overshot, metal-framed waterwheel powering bellows.

Fig. 71

Hearth in use at Coolowen forge in 1930s (estate of Alec Day).

City iron-founder Robert Lecky to establish a shipyard at Cork (see above). By 1844 the Monard works was being operated by Robert Scott and Co. who appear to be responsible for the construction of the Coolowen spade mill on the east side of the lower mill, sometime before 1863, directly opposite the Logwood mill (Fig. 67).[99] In evidence to the House of Commons Select Committee on Industries in Ireland in the mid-1880s, Robert Scott and Co. claimed that there were four tilt hammers at work at Monard which, based on the layout of the site, would suggest that one was operated in the upper mill, two in the middle mill and one in the Coolowen mill.[100] This would suggest that the conversion of the former dyewood mill to spade-making post-dates this testimony. The Monard and Coolowen works was closed in 1960 after the destruction of the Patrick's Quay warehouse of Robert Scott and Co. by fire.

The water supply for the mills is ingenious. It makes the best possible use of the difficult topography of the site, the principal feature of which is a series of narrow ravines which could not be canalised, in addition to a series of steep falls between each millpond. The construction of three of the mills, 'O'Hara's', the 'Middle' mill and the 'Coolowen' mill required the preparation of rock-cut ledges, and in the case of the upper two mills elaborate water delivery systems. The fall from the upper weir to the outfall of the 'Coolowen' and 'Logwood' mills is in excess of 12m, which each of three millponds effectively divides into separate heads. Each of these was insufficient to ensure that each mill could be worked for an entire day, and when the water of the upper pond had been used up work was transferred to the next mill in succession, and thereafter to the mill immediately below it. However, despite this ingenious arrangement reduced water levels during the summer months meant that certain mills could only be worked intermittently.

The upper mill (**219:1**) was known as O'Hara's after the family of smiths associated with it (Fig. 67). Its water supply was drawn from a millpond formed on the high ground immediately north of it, which was impounded by means of a weir, and appears to have exploited what would originally have been a naturally formed cascade. The outer face of the weir consists of a series of stepped and splayed masonry plinths. The glen is traversed roughly at the middle of the millpond, by a seven-arch railway viaduct, built by William Dargan for the Great Southern and Western Railway Company in 1848, which still carries the main Cork–Dublin line.

A tall cistern, reinforced by a light metal framework, is suspended directly over the western high breastshot waterwheel. A 'shuttle' hatch at the base of this cistern regulated the flow of water onto the waterwheel, whilst a cast-iron pipe directed water into the buckets of the adjacent overshot wheel to power the furnace bellows. The sluices for the wheels could be opened by those working within the forge building by means of pivoted levers. The overshot waterwheel has an overall diameter of 3.19m, and has a cast-iron framework with 36 wooden elbow buckets, complete with sole boards, and each individual bucket is reinforced with stay rods. The driveshaft of the main waterwheel was used to power three mechanisms, a trip hammer, a grindstone and guillotine. The trip hammer has been removed and only the cast-iron brackets supporting its pivot remain.

The outfall from O'Hara's mill exits directly into the second millpond formed beneath the upper weir, via a culvert constructed beneath the forge building. The overflow weir of the Middle mill is set diagonally across the stream, immediately above a natural gorge. Two large feeder cisterns are positioned directly over the wheel-pit, the first of which serves a high breastshot waterwheel via a shuttle and an interior overshot wheel via a

Fig. 72

The remains of the former Ford Tractor
Works in 1993. (Con Brogan, Dúchas)

subsidiary pipe similar to that employed in O'Hara's mill. Each of these wheels actuated trip hammers in the forge building immediately south of the wheel-pit. A mechanical guillotine in the machine forge (Fig. 68) was also powered by the western waterwheel.

The outfall of the Middle mill is discharged into a canalised section of the Blarney River, immediately beneath the narrow cascades flowing to the east of the Middle mill. This mill-stream feeds the largest of the three Monard and Coolowen millponds, which serviced the Logwood and Coolowen spade mills. The Logwood mill, as its name suggests, was originally a water-powered woodchip crushing mill, in which the chips of tropical trees such as brazilwood and fustics would have been crushed for dyes. Sometime in the middle of the nineteenth century, however, the mill was converted for spade and shovel making. The Logwood mill has an interior wooden high breastshot waterwheel 4.24m in diameter, which is fed by a shuttle operated by a pivotted lever positioned alongside the forge hammer (Fig. 69). The wheel is of clasp arm construction, and is soled and shrouded with wood. It has two primary drive wheels, a cam wheel for actuating a trip hammer and a chain drive wheel, which drives an overhead transmission shaft suspended on the northern wall. This transmission shaft transfers the power of the waterwheel to a rotary grindstone in the north-eastern corner, and to the hearth bellows in the south-western corner of the building. A further drivewheel and transmission shaft combination transmits power from the main transmission shaft through flatbelting into the finishing shops to the north, where sanding machines and mechanical punches were operated. In the 1950s a diesel engine (since removed) was installed in an outhouse at the north-east corner of the forge building which, when operated, used the waterwheel as a giant flywheel to transmit power to all of the machinery. This is the only Monard and Coolowen spade mill which does not have a separate bellows wheel.

On the opposing bank of the millpond is the Coolowen mill, so-called because it was the only mill to erected on the Coolowen side of the glen. A splayed inlet channel is led directly from the millpond some 4m from the crest of the weir, and feeds an angled wooden launder, which delivers water, via a shuttle, onto the buckets of an interior high breastshot waterwheel. The latter is of wooden, clasp arm construction, 4.16m in overall diameter, 1.46m wide and has 30 elbow buckets. Assembly marks are also in evidence upon the clasp arms, which suggests that the wheel was manufactured elsewhere and reassembled on site. A secondary plank-built launder is led off at right angles from the main interior one, and was carried on iron brackets along the northern wall of the mill. It was continued around the north-eastern corner of the building, its purpose being to direct water onto the buckets of a cast-iron framed overshot waterwheel, which was set over the wheelpit on the eastern gable wall of the building. The waterwheel is of exactly the same size and construction as the other bellows waterwheels described above (Fig. 70).

The machinery of the Coolowen mill consists of a trip hammer and grindstone (since removed), along with a manually operated metal trimmer, which is hung on the wall near the rear end of the trip hammer. The trip hammer has survived intact, complete with its wooden beam, its sprung pivot bearing and cast-iron hammer-head. Directly alongside the trip hammer is a pivotted lever, the upper part of which (as in the Middle and Logwood mills) is slung on a cross beam slung from one of the roof trusses. The lever regulated the opening of the launder's shuttle, which a series of iron 'notches' on the lever's frame enabled to be adjusted at different heights. The exterior overshot wheel drives the forge bellows through flatbelting via overhead drivewheels; the bellows fan survives intact. The forge hearth, complete with cast-iron arches also survives on the southern wall of the building, along with a subsidiary (plating?) hearth alongside it (Fig. 71).

Tractor and Automobile Manufacture: Henry Ford and Son (451)

In 1919 Cork became the location for Henry Ford and Son's first manufacturing presence outside the United States of America. There can be little doubt that Cork had no special economic attractions for any branch of American industry, and it appears that Henry Ford's motives in locating such an important unit of production here were wholly philanthropic. Cork, it is clear, was chosen largely for social and political reasons. Henry Ford's ancestral home was near Clonakilty in County Cork and Ford himself had visited there in 1912 (Anon. 1977, 10). The raw materials needed for the mass production of tractors were non-existent, whilst the demand for tractors in Ireland was negligible (Williams 1985, 37). The only factor of production in surplus in the greater Cork area was labour.[101] The decision to locate a large tractor factory at Cork was given the full backing of the British government who passed an act of parliament to enable Ford to purchase the tractor works site at City Park (Anon. 1977, 11). For his part Henry Ford gave the British government an assurance that his company would not profit on the sale of tractors to the government. Indeed, Ford did not even charge for the use of his patents (Williams 1989, 37).

Wharves were built on the City Park side of the River Lee to accommodate the new tractor factory (Fig. 72), followed by an enormous machine shop and a mobile crane to facilitate the production of pig-iron from the factory's furnace. In 1919, the Cork plant covered over 330,000 sq ft (Anon. 1977, 14). In July 1919, the first Fordson tractor, a 22hp, four cylinder model which could work with either kerosene or paraffin, rolled off the Cork assembly line, and by the end of that year some 300 tractors were completed (Anon. 1977, 14; Williams 1985, 44).[102] However, it soon became evident that the production of the Fordson tractor was not enough to keep the Cork plant going. Cork had been intended to function as an assembly and production plant for Britain and Europe, but when tractor production reached a peak of 3,626 in 1920 the demand for tractors in First World War I Europe slumped alarmingly. It became abundantly clear that the Cork plant could not produce tractors economically, and so Ford decided that the Cork works should begin to manufacture Model T components for the new Ford plant at Manchester (Anon. 1977, 14; Williams 1985, 44). Nonetheless, in the early months of 1920 the company invested a further £327,000 on the expansion of its foundry and a machine shop, which was fitted out with new equipment, whilst the existing wharfage was also expanded. The foundation of the Irish Free State, however, brought further burdens for the Cork plant. New duties by the British government were now placed on the cost of Model T parts manufactured at Cork and exported to Manchester, the net result of which was that it was no longer viable to produce parts for the British market in Ireland (Anon. 1977, 15, 17). The future of the plant was assured, however, by its transformation into an assembly plant for Ford Model T cars for the Irish market, the production of which, at Cork, ended in 1927, by which time over 10,000 cars had been assembled (ibid., 18, 21).

In 1928 the parent company made the momentous decision to transfer the production of its tractors from its Dearborn, Michigan plant in the USA to Cork, and in the winter of 1928–9 all of the machinery of the Dearborn plant was shipped to Cork (Williams 1985, 64). Cork was now the largest tractor factory in the world, a position it held up until 1932 when Henry Ford and Son decided to shift tractor production from Cork to its plant at Dagenham in England (Anon 1977, 24; Williams 1985, 70). The Ford motor works in Cork remained one of the largest employers in the Cork region up until its closure in the early 1980s. Extensive remains of the original tractor factory, warehouses and custom-built wharfage are in evidence, most of which are now used as storage facilities.

River Lee

6 MISCELLANEOUS INDUSTRIES

Clarke's bridge

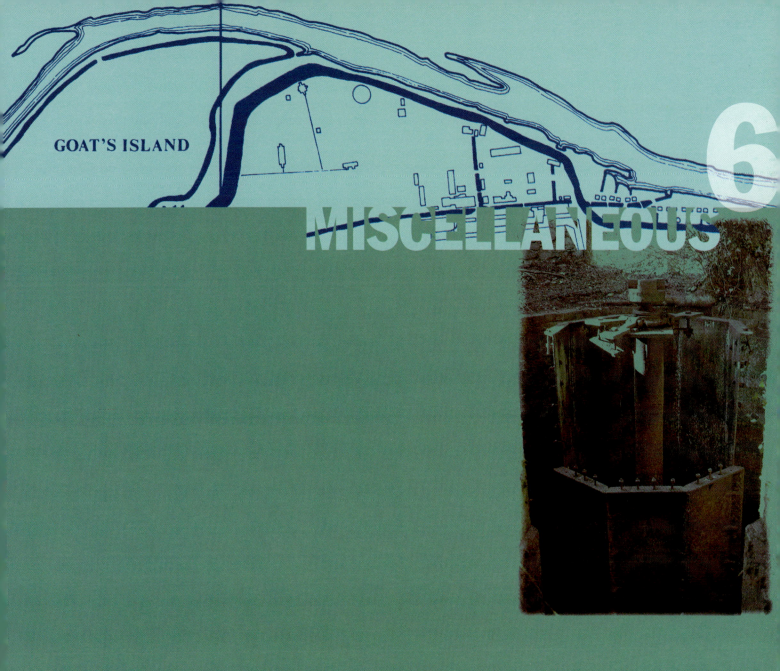

GOAT'S ISLAND

6

MISCELLANEOUS

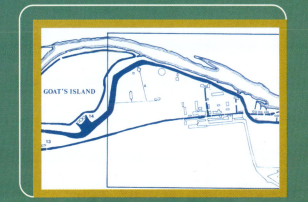

GOAT'S ISLAND

Although the Cork region is not generally associated with chemical processing industries, extensive factories producing gunpowder, superphosphates, fine chemicals and various soaps were established in Cork during the late eighteenth and nineteenth centuries, a number of which were of national importance. Tanneries were also very common in the nineteenth century, a period during which Cork was arguably the most important centre of tanning and associated leather-processing trades, such as currying, in Ireland. The present chapter will examine the industrial archaeology of these industries, along with the manufacture of footwear and glass in the city.

GUNPOWDER MANUFACTURE

Up until the establishment of the Ballincollig gunpowder mills the Irish explosives industry had been centred around Dublin. Within a relatively short period of time, however, the Ballincollig mills had become the centre of this industry. Between 1794 and 1815 the mills were the largest in Ireland and amongst the most extensive in the former United Kingdom. By 1822 gunpowder production within the environs of Dublin had effectively ceased. Moreover, in the second main period of their use, between 1833 and 1903, during which they were the only gunpowder mills in Ireland, the Ballincollig mills appears to have been second in size only to Waltham Abbey in England.

During the early part of its history, the Ballincollig gunpowder mills, along with the adjacent cavalry and artillery barracks, formed part of an enormous military-industrial complex. It is the best-preserved industrial site of its type in Europe. As with other sites of both national and international importance, such as Beamish and Crawford's Brewery and the Monard spade mills, the development of the Ballincollig gunpowder mills will be examined in detail below.

The Royal Gunpowder Mills, Ballincollig (217)

Early Developments, 1794–1804
The Ballincollig gunpowder mills were established by Charles Henry Leslie, a Cork banker and later proprietor of the River Lee porter brewery (036), and John Travers, in 1794. In that same year they acquired land near Ballincollig village, and constructed the original Inishcarra weir on the River Lee and laid out the gunpowder manufactory on the south bank (Kelleher 1992, 23).[1] Good access to the port of Cork, some six miles to the east, was a critical factor in the choice of site, as production was clearly aimed at supplying the needs of the government.[2] Nonetheless, further important criteria specific to the manufacture of gunpowder also had to be taken into consideration. In the first instance the site had to be sufficiently large and isolated to enable a notoriously hazardous series of processes to be carried out. Furthermore, as a number of these processes were mechanized, access to a water source which could be readily converted into energy was essential. In order to minimise the danger of chain-reaction type explosions, the buildings within the complex were well spaced out. This was particularly true of buildings in which gunpowder finishing processes were undertaken. In consequence, the main feeder channel within the complex (particularly in the period after 1804), had to cover a distance almost 2.5km long. The latter did, however, also facilitate the water-borne transportation of materials around the entire site. In the post-1804 period this system of hydro-power/transportation canals became one of the unique features of the site.

Leslie and Travers' manufactory occupied an area of just over 90 acres (compared to an area of over 431 acres when it came under Board of Ordnance control) situated in the eastern sector of the present complex (Fig. 73).[3] The main feeder canal ran 2km from a point immediately above the weir at Inishcarra, to its outfall into the River Lee at a point immediately east of the incorporating mills (Fig. 73). At the eastern end of the complex four millraces were drawn off from the main canal: two for the *incorporating mills* (Fig. 78, nos. 14 and 15, each with two pairs of edge-runner stones) and one each for the *composition mills* and *mixing house* and the original *corning house* (see below). The westernmost incorporating mill, which appears to have been substantially modified in the 1830s, was excavated in 1985, during which part of the foundations of Leslie's original incorporating mill came to light. The other buildings in the original Ballincollig complex included a *stove house*, a *charring* (charcoal) *house*, a *press house*, a *dusting house*, a *corning house*, and sulphur and saltpetre refineries. Accommodation for the workforce (Fig. 74), workshops and stabling were also provided. There was a lime kiln on the site, and it seems likely that the limestone quarries on the escarpment immediately south of the complex, which were later extensively used by the Board of Ordnance, were originally opened and utilised during the construction of the original complex. The only surviving features of Leslie and Travers' manufactory which can be identified with any certainty are the original hydro-power/navigation channel (running west-east through the complex), incorporating mill units 1 and 2 and the canal bridge immediately to the east of the incorporating mills.

The Manufacturing Process

Black gunpowder has three principal constituents — saltpetre (potassium nitrate), charcoal and sulphur, which were mixed in the proportions 75:15:10.[4] Saltpetre was imported into Cork from India and the sulphur from Sicily. The only locally acquired ingredient was charcoal which was provided by plantations of the appropriate woods, such as willow and alder, within the complex. The sulphur was refined in the sulphur refinery (Fig. 75a) and then ground into a fine powder under four ton limestone edge runner stones in the sulphur grinding mill, a process used in the preparation of the other ingredients prior to mixing and later during their incorporation. In the saltpetre refinery (Fig. 73, no. 8 and fig. 75a) the saltpetre was dissolved, crystallised and then allowed to cool down for a few days, before being calcined. The calcining process removed any excess moisture resulting from crystallisation, and the saltpetre was then cast into circular cakes, later removed to the saltpetre mill to be reduced to a fine powder under edge-runner stones. Softwoods such as alder, willow and hazel were used in the manufacture of charcoal, willow being preferred for blasting powder and alder for the so-called 'sporting powders' (i.e. those used in small arms ammunition such as shotgun cartridges). As in English gunpowder mills alder buckthorn (commonly referred to as dogwood, see Crocker 1986, 11), was also used at Ballincollig. In the charcoal manufacturing process the wood was cut into 2ft lengths, and then heated in sealed retorts placed in a furnace. After refining, the ingredients were taken to the mixing house, where they were weighed and mixed in their various proportions. The resulting mixture was called *green charge*, which was then transported by canal to the incorporating mills. In the period 1800–1809 Wilkes had constructed three charge houses (3, 4 and 5) along the northern bank of a newly constructed canal adjacent to the incorporating mills, and a fourth was added when the mills returned to private ownership after 1833 (see below). These are rather curious beehive-like structures with slated roofs (Fig. 76) in which the green charge was stored prior to its introduction into the incorporating mills.

By reference to Fig. 77 it will be seen that most of the buildings within the complex are concentrated around the refineries. This was a necessary precaution as the ingredients

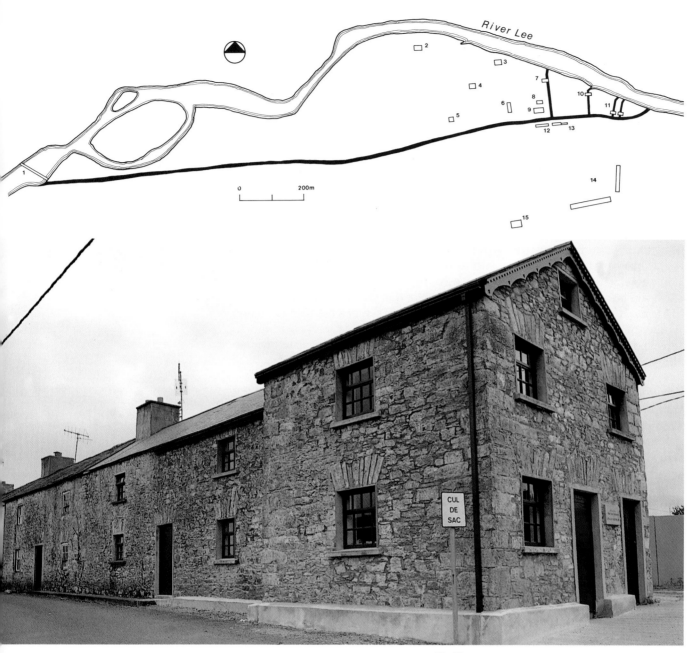

Fig. 73

Ballincollig Gunpowder Mills under Charles Henry Leslie.

1 Inishcarra weir. 2 Store. 3 Charring house. 4 Press house. 5 Dusting house. 6 Magazine. 7 Corning house. 8 Sulphur refinery. 9 Saltpetre refinery. 10 Composition mills and mixing house. 11 Incorporating mills. 12 Stables. 13 Dwelling house and workshop. 14 Foremens' houses and houses for 20 labourers. 15 Lime kiln.

Fig. 74

Workers' houses, Ballincollig Gunpowder Mills.

were not yet mixed together and were thus, relatively speaking, less volatile. But in processes which involved the finishing of the powder after its initial mixing, the plant and buildings involved had to be widely spaced apart. In the *incorporating* or *composition* mills section of the complex (Fig. 78), in which the ingredients were mechanically ground together, the double mill units were separated by substantial free-standing blast walls, which were supposed to deflect any flying debris resulting from an explosion away from the adjacent mill units (Fig. 79). The incorporating mill buildings themselves were invariably of light wooden construction, which tended to reduce the risk of injury to millworkers in the event of an explosion and to enable the mill to be recommissioned as soon as possible (Hamond 1989, 4). By the 1850s there were 24 individual incorporating mill units, which consisted of 12 double mills. In each mill four pairs of edge runner stones were driven by a single breast-fed waterwheel (Fig. 80). The incorporation process, during which the charge was kept damp, lasted between two and six hours, depending on the quality of the powder involved (Crocker 1986, 12). Lammot Du Pont, who had travelled extensively throughout Britain and Europe visiting gunpowder mills, noted that the edge runner stones at the Ballincollig mills were the largest that he had ever seen (Wilkinson 1976, 94). As in the contemporary English mills the Ballincollig incorporating mills were at work night and day, and were, according to Du Pont, largely concerned with the manufacture of blasting powder (ibid.), then in constant demand for railway construction and other civil engineering works.

After incorporation the *mill cake*, as it was then termed, was transferred by canal to the press houses in the east of the complex where the density of the cake was increased by the action of a hydraulic press to remove excess moisture. The product resulting from this was called *press cake*, which was then broken up with a large mallet to produce fragments which could be safely introduced into the *corning house*. At a later period machines with toothed rollers for granulating the press cake were introduced, and were installed in a *granulating house*. In the corning house the press cake was mechanically forced through sieves, the action of which broke the powder fragments into finer pieces. However, the corning process produced dust which tended to attract moisture to the powder if not removed. The powder was therefore, transported by canal to the *dusting house* where the dust was removed by tumbling it in gauze-covered rollers (Crocker 1986, 19).[5]

The powder was then transferred to the glazing house, where it was tumbled in a slowly rotating reel or drum, the action of which rounded the powder grains and imparted to them a slight gloss (hence 'glazing'). A small amount of graphite was also added to render the powder more resistant to moisture, and it was this which gave the powder it distinctive black appearance. In the next process the powder was removed to the *stove house*, which at Ballincollig took the form of a distinctive oval boiler house with drying houses on either side (Fig. 75b). Sealed steam pipes were led from the boiler house into the adjacent drying houses, in which the powder was carefully spread on tiered trays. The inlet pipes and valves from the boiler house still survive, and the entire structure pre-dates 1815. A large circular coal store was constructed to the east of magazine no. 1, on the site of the earlier Board of Ordnance culm yard, for the coal used in the drying process and in the distillation of the wood charcoal.

After drying, the powder was then transported to the second dusting house for a final treatment before being packed and stored in one of the two magazines. These latter were

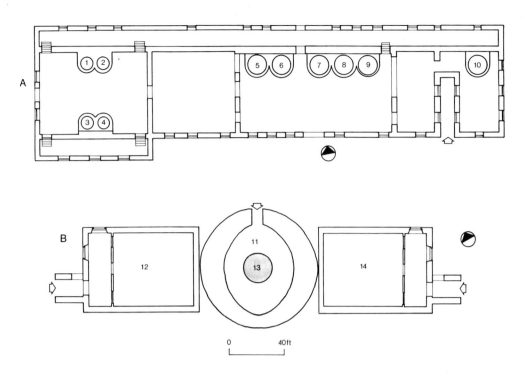

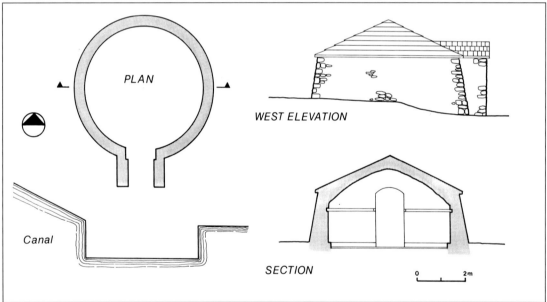

Fig. 75

(a) Saltpetre refinery, (b) stove house at
Ballincollig Gunpowder Mills in 1826
(redrawn from Royal Engineers survey dated
18th February 1826).

1–10 Boiling pans. 11 Stove house.
12 Drying house. 13 Boiler. 14 Drying
house.

Fig. 76

Charge house, Ballincollig Gunpowder Mills.

connected by a special wooden tramway. The powder was stored in wooden casks varying in size from 5 to 100lbs, and at least 50 coopers were employed on site to manufacture these.[6] Two magazines to the east of the refinery buildings were used to store the powder before its collection by customers or its transportation to the docks at Cork.

The Gunpowder Mills under the Board of Ordnance 1805–33

In the first ten years of its operation the Ballincollig manufactory had, according to an English Board of Ordnance official, become a 'highly productive and prosperous concern' (Kelleher 1992, 29).[7] Security at the mills became an ever-present concern to the British military, who were obliged to monitor their production, particularly in the aftermath of the rebellion of 1798. Indeed, government policy at the time was to seek a monopoly of gunpowder manufacture in these islands, and it was in pursuit of this goal that the Board of Ordnance bought Leslie out in 1805.[8] As Sir Henry Hardinge explained in 1828, Ballincollig 'became one of the Ordnance Stations, both as being a convenient station for the embarcation of artillery from Cork for foreign service, as well as for the protection of the mills'.[9]

In March 1805 the Board appointed its chief clerk of works for powder mills, Charles Wilkes, as superintendent of the Ballincollig mills (ibid., 32) and by the following June the Office of Ordnance at Ballincollig placed an advertisement in the Cork press looking for local 'plumbers, glaziers, painters, coopers, masons, blacksmiths, copper-smiths, founders, ironmongers, stone cutters, millwrights and bricklayers'.[10] Wilkes began by improving access to the complex from the old Killarney road to the north, by entirely rebuilding the bridge at Inishcarra with 24 arches.

Security matters were resolved once and for all by the establishment of a substantial cavalry barracks on the main Cork–Macroom road in Ballincollig village. A short distance to the west of the barracks a series of administration buildings and houses were built, which included the offices of the superintendent, the clerk of the cheque, the store keepers and the general clerks. The main range of buildings here later became Oriel Court, the residence of Sir Thomas Tobin (see below). Living accommodation was provided for 30 labourers and a foreman at Faversham Square, near the junction of the Cork–Macroom road and the Inishcarra Bridge road, and in two rows of millworkers cottages — Waltham Abbey Row and Coopers Row — at the eastern extremity of the complex. Waltham Abbey Row and Cooper's Row [11] are still extant (Fig. 74), although the workers' housing built by Leslie and Travers has long since been demolished.

The effective area of the mills, including administration buildings, a network of canals and the new cavalry barracks, was greatly expanded in the period 1806–15, and the greater part of the 431 acres involved was enclosed behind a high stone wall (Fig. 77). Limestone was quarried on the escarpment immediately north of Oriel Court, and was used extensively in the construction of the new mill buildings, the canal network and the enclosing wall. The bedstones and edge runner stones used in the various refining and composition processes (see below), which were particularly fine-grained, are also likely to have been quarried here. Two lime kilns were also erected within the complex for the manufacture of lime mortar.[12] Part of the fabric of one of these survives on the lands of Cork County Council's sewerage works at Ballincollig. All told, the Board of Ordnance invested almost £127,000 in the development of the complex and on harbour facilities for its storage and transportation in the period 1805–15 (Kelleher 1992, 34–5).[13]

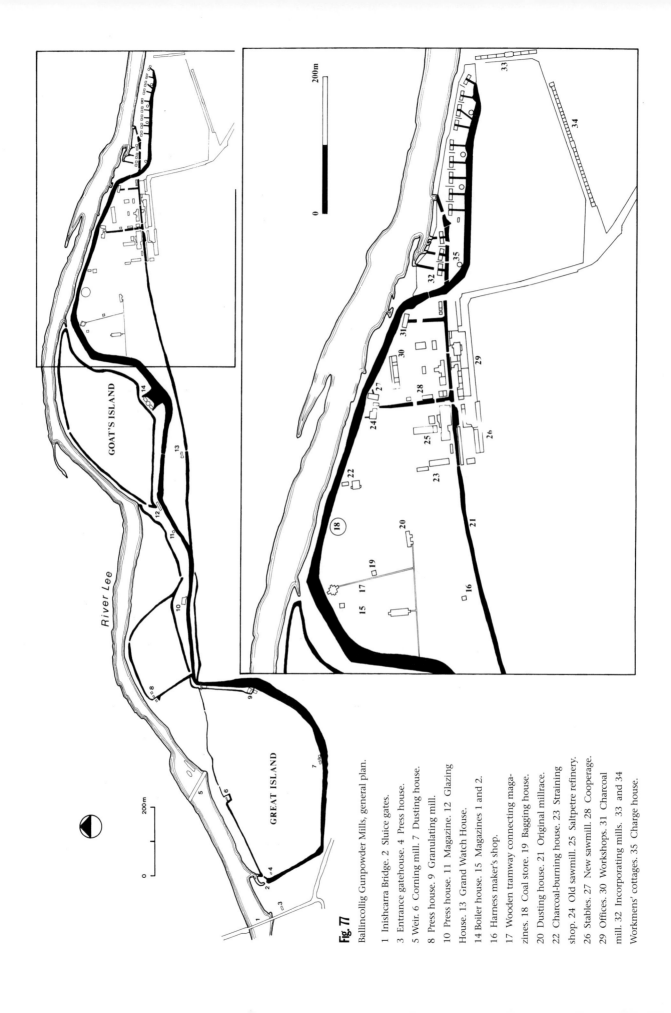

152

Fig. 77

Ballincollig Gunpowder Mills, general plan.

1 Inishcarra Bridge. 2 Sluice gates.
3 Entrance gatehouse. 4 Press house.
5 Weir. 6 Corning mill. 7 Dusting house.
8 Press house. 9 Granulating mill.
10 Press house. 11 Magazine. 12 Glazing
House. 13 Grand Watch House.
14 Boiler house. 15 Magazines 1 and 2.
16 Harness maker's shop.
17 Wooden tramway connecting magazines. 18 Coal store. 19 Bagging house.
20 Dusting house. 21 Original millrace.
22 Charcoal-burning house. 23 Straining
shop. 24 Old sawmill. 25 Saltpetre refinery.
26 Stables. 27 New sawmill. 28 Cooperage.
29 Offices. 30 Workshops. 31 Charcoal
mill. 32 Incorporating mills. 33 and 34
Workmens' cottages. 35 Charge house.

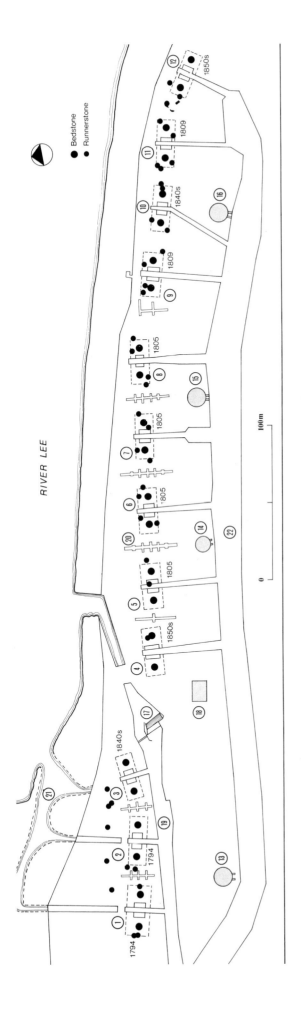

Fig. 78

Plan of incorporating mills, Ballincollig
Gunpowdermills.

1–12 Incorporating mills. 13–16 Charge
houses. 17 Overflow weir.
18 Watch house. 19 Mill canal. 20 Blast
wall. 21 Outfall channels for mills 1–3.
22 Main mill canal/navigation.

Fig. 79
Blastwall, Ballincollig Gunpowder Mills.

Fig. 80
Reconstruction of gunpowder incorporating mill at Ballincollig Gunpowder Mills, Co. Cork.

From the outset the intention of the Board of Ordnance was to greatly increase production at the mills. In order to do so the entire system of mill canals had to be extended to service a greater number of water-powered installations. The main water intake sluices for the new canal were positioned further to the west of the original canal, whilst the latter was extended to the new intake point and its original inlet from the river was blocked off. The new canal was substantially wider than that constructed by Leslie. From its intake point near Inishcarra Bridge it headed southwards past the new *press* and *dusting* houses before turning abruptly in south-easterly direction near the Inishcarra Bridge Road. It then completed a loop to take in a further set of press and dusting houses, before continuing due north passing a *proofing house* and a magazine (Fig. 77). Immediately north of the magazine a separate millrace was led off to service another set of press and dusting houses, with the main channel turning eastwards. The tailrace of the press and dusting houses was returned in a loop to the main channel. The main channel continued eastwards past a series of other installations, making a sweeping loop around the area containing the greatest concentration of buildings, which included the refineries and the craftsmens' workshops. The old canal continued in use, but the millrace drawn off it to service the original corning house was now used for a water-powered *mixing house*, and that of the former mixing house and composition mills was now used for a *charcoal mill*.[14] Leslie's original incorporating mills remained in commission, and continued to be serviced by the old canal, but the new canal cut across the latter at a point immediately east of the refineries, where it then turned eastwards to service an additional series of incorporating mills. By reference to Fig. 77 it will be seen that the large areas of land on either side of the main canal were not built upon. The latter were in fact put to good use by being planted with willow and alder.[15] Indeed, it was standard practice to plant trees around mill buildings to catch flying debris and to absorb shock waves from explosions.

Wilkes arranged the construction of four new security buildings, which included a *Grand Watch House*, situated near the centre of the complex (just north of the old canal), two small watch houses positioned on the south bank of the river Lee, near the southern extremity of Inishcarra Bridge and a *Round Tower Watch House* at the western entrance to the complex.[16] A guard house was also built to command the canal bridge near the incorporating mills. An impressive watch house (recently restored) was constructed at the complex's western entrance from the Cork–Macroom road, which has angled musket loops on its western arc. A water supply for the barracks was provided by water-driven pumps, which drew their supply from the mill canal immediately to the east of Leslie's original incorporating mills.[17]

A further twelve incorporating mill units were built between 1805 and 1809 (Hamond 1987) along with a new steam stove house, a glazing house, a fire engine house, a saw mill, a cylinder house, an extensive range of craftmens' workshops, drying houses, new saltpetre and sulphur refineries and a new gunpowder magazine. A series of three *charge houses* were also built in the incorporating mills section of the complex. Nearly all of the water-powered installations were powered by breast-fed waterwheels with an undershot action, with diameters ranging from a maximum of 21ft, in the case of the Board of Ordnance incorporating mills, to 16ft, as in the new charcoal grinding mill.[18] The vast majority of the buildings referred to above still survive in various states of dilapidation, and while these were added to and modified when the mills were returned to private ownership in the 1830s, the layout of the complex as it survives today is still essentially that designed and implemented by Charles Wilkes. Upon its closure in 1815 Ballincollig Gunpowder Mills was the largest installation of its type in Ireland, and one of the largest in these islands.

The Board of Ordnance's substantial investment in the Ballincollig manufactory was closely linked to the expanding military demand for gunpowder during the Napoleonic Wars. But in their aftermath the demand for gunpowder in the British industry as a whole slumped by almost 75%, and Ballincollig, along with a number of gunpowder mills in Britain, was closed down. Production at Ballincollig ceased sometime in 1815, and the entire complex was mothballed on the orders of the Duke of Wellington, but as the machinery within the complex could not be sold it was 'painted, oiled and taken care of'.[19] Some of the machinery appears to have been dismantled,[20] and while by 1828 the incorporating mills were described as 'much gone to decay' and the mixing house as 'in very bad order', the overall condition of the mills and plant was as good as might be expected after fifteen years of disuse.[21] In 1831 some items of plant were put up for auction,[22] and by May 1832 the machinery within the complex was said to be 'in a most dilapidated state'. [23] In July of 1832 a decision was taken to remove some of the machinery to the Waltham Abbey mills in England.[24] By this stage the weir and canal system had become so run down that it was impossible to work the water-powered pumps for the barracks' water supply.[25] In 1832 it seemed that the mills would never operate again, but by the end of the following year they had been returned to private ownership under a new and more enterprising management.

The Mills Return to Private Ownership 1833–1903

In 1833 the Board of Ordnance sold the mills to the Liverpool firm of Tobin and Horsefall for £15,000,[26] and within a short period of time work on the recommissioning of the mill canals was underway.[27] Thomas (later Sir Thomas) Tobin (1807–81), the oldest son of Thomas Tobin of Liverpool, was dispatched to County Cork to become managing director of the rejuvenated mills (King and Kinsella 1986, 21). The buildings and plant inherited by Tobin had not been operated for some 18 years, but more importantly these were designed for gunpowder manufacture in the period before 1815. Under Tobin's management the mills were transformed into one of the most up-to-date manufactories in Europe. Tobin built an additional eight incorporating mill units, four in the 1840s (Fig. 78, nos. 3 and 10) and four in the 1850s (Fig. 78, nos. 4 and 12), to supplement the operation of the pre-1815 mills (Hamond 1987, 3). The company had been in production since the summer of 1835,[28] with production gradually increasing from 7,517 casks in 1836 to 17,738 casks in 1842.[29]

The decline of the gunpowder industry was brought about by the introduction of chemically manufactured explosives such as nitrocellulose (guncotton) and nitroglycerine, and ultimately by Alfred Nobel's dynamite.[30] The so-called 'smokeless powders' which became increasingly used for small arms ammunition towards the end of the nineteenth century also eroded the traditionally strong market for 'black gunpowder'. From the second half of the nineteenth century onwards, gunpowder manufacturers found it increasingly difficult to compete with manufacturers of the 'new explosives', and were all but powerless to arrest the decline in demand for gunpowder. In its heyday the Ballincollig factory's markets included most of Ireland, the Lancashire, Yorkshire, Staffordshire and South Wales coalfields, Africa, South America and the West Indies (Kelleher 1992, 78). But after 1880 exports from Ballincollig, which had previously averaged around 30,000 barrels per annum, fell steadily, and after 1890 sales rarely rose above 13,000 barrels (Kelleher ibid., 60). In the 1880s the Ballincollig Company attempted to arrest the decline by introducing new brands, the Royal Premier (RP) and Extra Treble Strong (ETS)[31] varieties (O'Mahony 1986b, 12; Kelleher 1992, 82), but these developments could do little to prevent the substitution of black powder with smokeless powders such as cordite.

In 1889 the mills, which had for a long period manufactured powder for the African market, were refurbished for the manufacture of powder for government contracts. However, as the kegs for this powder were specially manufactured at the Royal Arsenal, the Ballincollig coopers who had formerly made kegs for the African powder were made redundant.[32] In 1898 Ballincollig formed part of an amalgamation of eight gunpowder mills (mostly English) under the management of the English firm of Curtis and Harvey, and only the onset of the Boer War seems to have prevented its immediate closure. The mills were closed for the last time in July 1903 (Kelleher 1992, 87).

The Use of Water Power at Ballincollig Gunpowder Mills 1794–1903

Water wheel							Process and machinery
Type	Diam.	Width	No. Buckets	Depth of Shrouding	HP	Section Across Inlet	
US (M)	17ft	4ft 6in	36	1ft 4in	c. 8	5ft x 3ft 5in	Mixing house and sawmill
US (M)	17ft	4ft 5in	36	1ft 4in	8	5ft x 3ft 5in	Charcoal and sulphur-grinding mill
BS with timber arms	16ft 6in	5ft	42	1ft 7in	8	7ft x 3in	Incorporating mill No. 1
BS (M)	7ft	5ft	42	1ft 3in	----	-----	Incorporating mill No. 2
BS (M)	23ft	4ft	56	1ft 4in	----	4ft x 3in	Incorporating mill No. 3
BS (M)	20ft 6in	4ft	48	1ft 4in	----	4ft x 3in	Incorporating mill No. 8

KEY US (Undershot), BS (Breastshot), M (Metal)

Table 3—Representative sample of water wheels at Ballincollig Gunpowder Mills in late 1840s. (Source: Griffith Valuation House Books (OL 5.2444)). All dimensions given in imperial as in original House Valuation Books.

In the period after 1850 up to 30 water-powered installations were at work within the Ballincollig complex, an arrangement which was unparalleled in Ireland during the nineteenth century. The variety of waterwheel types in terms of size, water-delivery and construction materials will be readily apparent from Table 3. As has been seen, most of these employed metal-framed breastshot waterwheels, but in the mid-1850s Sir Thomas Tobin introduced into the sawmill one of the earliest turbines in County Cork (Rynne 1986). This was the first of its type to be used in Ireland and the first in either Britain or Ireland to be used to power a sawmill. The turbine was manufactured by the Hive iron foundry (**285**, see Ch. 5) and installed early in 1855.[33] The following description appeared in the local Cork press in 1856.[34]

> The turbine which is employed at the Ballincollig Gunpowder Mills was constructed by Mr. Perrott [of the Hive iron works], and is of 16 horsepower. It consists of a large octagon cistern, in the centre of which is a hollow pipe, through which passes a vertical shaft. The water, as it falls through the shaft, passes into a circular disk, consisting of a number of hollow tubes or chambers curved so that the force with which the water is expelled from them causes the disk to revolve with great velocity, carrying with it the shaft which is connected

Fig. 81

Jonval water turbine, Ballincollig
Gunpowder Mills.

> with the other portions of the machinery. The fall of water is eight feet and the number of revolutions of the shaft produced per minute is 100.

The Ballincollig water turbine has survived *in situ*, and is the oldest example of any variety of turbine in either Britain or Ireland to remain so.[35] It is a downward axial flow type (Fig. 81) which appears to have been closely modelled on the design developed by the French engineer Feu Jonval in 1841. Incoming water was directed into the octagonal cistern via a wooden penstock, and onto the fixed guide vanes in the upper section of the turbine. A circular cistern would have been preferable, but a cistern of this type would have been difficult to produce with the foundry techniques then in use. Thus at Ballincollig the octagonal cistern was fabricated with eight bolted, cast-iron plates; four at the rear (2.4m high by 0.59m wide) and four at the front, each about 1.41m high to articulate with the fore end of the wooden penstock (Rynne 1989c).

The outflow from the turbine pit was clearly the most difficult engineering problem encountered by those involved in its construction. The inlet channel for the turbine was led off from the adjacent navigation canal by means of a narrow leat 7.5m long. But as the turbine had been set at over 2m below the floor level of the sawmill building in order to maximise the available head, water led away from the turbine had to make its exit beneath the actual headrace channel and could not, therefore, be re-admitted into the navigation channel. To obviate this the builders made the outfall channel a subterranean feature by constructing an arched brick conduit, which was led away from the mill building beneath both the headrace channel and the main navigation channel, to discharge directly into the River Lee.

Over 90% of the original buildings within the complex survive, in various states of preservation, and are currently the focus of a comprehensive programme of conservation by Cork County Council. To date, one of the charge houses has been entirely restored, as has a gunpowder incorporating mill, which is in working order. To facilitate the operation of this mill large sections of the canal were also repaired.

SUPERPHOSHATES AND FINE CHEMICALS

In 1856 William and Humphrey Manders Goulding purchased the Glen distillery in Blackpool in order to establish a fertiliser factory, beginning production in 1857. The Gouldings Glen Chemical Works, later W. & H. M. Goulding Ltd (**445**), covered an area of approximately eight acres.[36] Gouldings manufactured superphosphates using bones collected throughout Ireland and phosphates imported from the US and Africa. The imported bones were reduced to powder in crushing mills within the complex, prior to being dissolved in sulphuric acid. In the 1850s Gouldings imported sulphuric acid, but from 1860 onwards they installed their own sulphuric acid manufacturing plant. This originally had one lead chamber but by 1868 this had been increased to five (Anon. 1956). The acid itself was produced using sulphur extracted from imported Spanish pyrites. By 1917 some seventy kilns were operated on a twenty-four hour basis to produce around 500 tons of sulphuric acid per week. The residues resulting from this process, after the sulphur had been burnt off, was sent to England where copper was extracted from the cinders. The power requirements of the Gouldings Glen works was met by six gas and steam engines ranging from 40 to 150hp.[37] This once extensive complex was almost completely demolished in the 1970s.

In the first half of the nineteenth century, Thomas Jennings, a vinegar (and one-time bleach) manufacturer of Brown Street, Cork,[38] established the Brookefield Chemical

Works (**002**), on the Glasheen River, immediately north of the site of the former Sadleir Brother's cotton spinning mill.[39] The Brookefield Chemical Works manufactured carbonate of magnesia (in block and powder form), calcined magnesia and fluid magnesia. In 1852 the complex consisted of a chemical house, a kiln, the main factory building and a drying house. Around the same time the water power on the site, which appears to have originally powered an adjacent flour mill, had been adopted for the use of the chemical works.[40] Part of one of the walls of the limekiln still survives in the back-garden of a house on Orchard Road, near Victoria Cross.

In the early 1880s the Shandon Chemical Works (**448**) was established on the Commons Road, and by the end of the nineteenth century extended over some two acres. Harringtons Ltd (later Harrington & Goodlass Wall) were at one time the only manufacturers of 'fire red' colour in Britain and Ireland, and was the only firm in Ireland making distempers (powder-based colours painted onto plaster or chalk) and varnishes. The Shandon Chemical Works also manufactured colors and printing inks (Coakley 1919, 187). The company exported fine chemicals for analytical purposes to the universities of Oxford, Cambridge, Owen's College, Manchester and Canterbury College, New Zealand, and in the 1890s became the first Irish firm to manufacture both paint and varnish. The Great Southern and Western Railway Company bought all of its paint from Harrington's in the late nineteenth and early twentieth centuries. Harrington's was also the first Irish firm to manufacture a potato blight preventative.[41] It is the only chemical works with nineteenth-century origins within the area covered by the present survey to be still in operation, and is currently the largest manufacturer of paints in Ireland. Parts of the original complex, including a series of single-storey buildings, still survive.

SOAP FACTORIES

The growth of the textile industry within the greater Cork area brought with it an increased demand for soap for use in textile processing. With the introduction of the process developed by the French chemist, Nicholas Leblanc (1742–1806), in which common salt could be converted into soda, the manufacture of soap could now be organised on a sounder industrial footing. There were basically two varieties of soap, both of which were essentially a mixture of oils and fats with mild alkalis. The so-called hard soaps utilised soda (sodium carbonate), whilst soft soaps used potasium carbonate, i.e. potash (Cossons 1987, 206).

In Cork City during the nineteenth century the organisation of soap manufacture, for the most part, tended to betray its traditional relationship with the craft of chandlery and candle-making, where the availability of animal fat (from the city's slaughterhouses) was an important factor. The largest concentration of soap works in the city was in the Marsh area where, during the nineteenth century, up to thirty or so concerns involved in the manufacture of soap were in operation. The combined output of these soap works was quite small (Coakley 1919, 200), but in Duncan Street in the late 1860s there was one soap factory which was producing up to 60 tons of soap per week.[42] By the end of the nineteenth century, however, the largest soap works within the city was that operated by Edward Ryan and Company Ltd, established in the 1870s at Gray's Lane off Popes Quay. Ryan used tallow and caustic soda to produce his 'Keltic' brand soap.[43] Smiddy and Company's Soap Works on Watercourse Road, which was established in the 1890s, used an 80hp engine to power all of its machinery. The Watercourse Road works consisted of a soap house, which had several large boiling pans, and a cleansing room in which the ingredients were mechanically cleaned. This building contained a large vessel in which the fats were refined under high pressure. The soap was conveyed from the cleansing pans to a series of iron frames or boxes where it was allowed to stand until it hardened into large square blocks. These blocks were later cut up into individual bars of soap, which were later removed to the packing room, where the boxes used for the dispatch of the goods were made up. The eyes or waste matter resulting from the manufacturing process was a valuable source of glycerine, which was later distilled for use in the manufacture of nitroglycerine and ultimately dynamite, whilst the salt used in the process could be continually reused.[44]

TANNING

Whereas in England tanning and currying were nearly always conducted by separate firms, in Cork and throughout Ireland, both of these activities were often carried out by the same firm.[45] Indeed, the manufacture of 'uppers' and harness leather and that used for the soles of shoes were also undertaken by individual Irish firms, whilst in England these were usually produced by separate firms (Rolleston 1902, 408–9). English revenue legislation took a steady toll on Irish tanneries, the number of which, from a total of 876 licensed tanners in 1796, had fallen to 574 in 1818 and to 476 in 1823 (Barry 1920, 102–4). In 1822 Cork had 44 tanneries,[46] a figure which reached its peak in 1842 when some 48 tanneries were at work in the city (Bielenberg 1991, 82).[47] The undisputed quality of the Cork product was not enough to ensure the survival of its tanning and currying industries. Faster methods of producing lower quality but usable leather (ultimately with the use of chromic acid), led to the rapid decline of the industry in Cork. In 1853 there were only 16 tanneries within the city (Cullen 1987, 145), and by the turn of the century only four.[48] Technological stagnation within the industry, competition from cheaper American leather goods, a fall off in the quality of South American hides and the importation of ready-made boots from England also exacted a heavy toll on the industry.[49]

Tanning Processes

The manufacture of leather involves two processes; *tanning*, in which a raw skin or hide is rendered imputrescible through impregnation with tannic acid, and *currying*, in which a skilled worker finishes the leather by converting it into a useful and attractive material. Before tanning proper could begin the hides were first soaked in a *limepit*, which was filled with an alkaline liquor made out of milk of lime, the effect of which was to loosen the hairs on the skin so that the tanner could scrape them off, without damaging the grain of the leather. The hide was then removed from the pit and spread over a wooden beam, and then scraped on both sides with tanners' knives. In most cases the hide would then be returned to the limepit for a short period and then scraped again with a scudding knife. The hide was then divided into several parts — a process called *rounding* — the thickest and most prized section, the *butt*, being divided into two sections called *bends*, after which the hide was then ready for tanning (Jenkins 1973, 11; Thomson 1982, 141ff). Cork tanneries were best known for their 'satin calf' leather, and in the nineteenth century their stout butts enjoyed a wide reputation in both England and Scotland (Coakley 1919, 193).

All of the city's tanneries had at least one bark mill for grinding the vegetable matter used in mixing the tanning liquor. Native oak bark and barks imported into Cork from Algeria and Spain[50] were used in the tanning of upper and harness leather, whilst oak, cork and valonia were used for tanning sole leather. Valonia, or acorn cups from Mediterranean oaks, was imported into Cork from eastern Mediterranean locations such

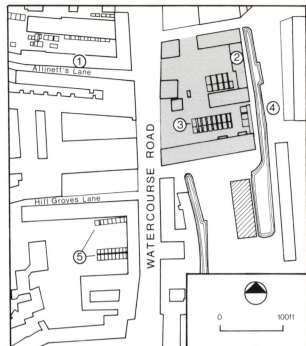

Fig. 82 ABOVE
Nineteenth-century tanneries, Watercourse
Road.

1 Drying shed. 2 Drying sheds in Dunne's
tannery. 3 Handling pits.
4 Millrace. 5 Handling pits.

Fig. 83 RIGHT
Tannery drying sheds, Allinett's Lane.

Fig. 84 OPPOSITE ABOVE
Tannery storage sheds, Corkeran's Quay.

Fig. 85 OPPOSITE BELOW
Tannery drying sheds, Watercourse Road
(Con Brogan, Dúchas).

162

as Smyrna in Turkey.[51] Cork's famous calfskins were tanned in liquor made from sumac, the shoots and leaves of a tree imported from Sicily (Rolleston 1902, 409). The bark was finely ground in bark mills under edge-runner stones, powered by horses and later by special cutting blades powered by small steam engines. The tannin in the bark was originally extracted by immersion in cold water in leaching pits, where it was left to stand for a number of weeks, but by the late 1840s most of the city's tanyards were equipped with steam boilers for boiling the water required for steam leaches, hot water now being used to draw out the tannin and thus create a tanning liquor. Steam from these boilers was also used for heating the drying lofts (see below). A number of Cork City tanneries were also equipped with steam engines which, in addition to powering bark mills, also appear to have been used for actuating pumps. Hackett's tannery on Fitton Street was reputedly the first tannery in Ireland to have a steam engine installed (O'Brien 1985, 151), whilst by 1843 the Millfield tannery was equipped with a 4hp engine.[52]

In the traditional process of vegetable tanning, each hide was progressively exposed to a succession of liquors of increasing strength in order to fix more tan. As the stronger liquors became divested of their abililty to fix tan they were pumped down the yard to the earlier stages of the process, which ensured that this process was not only continuous but more economic in terms of the materials used. The hides were first placed in a series of 8–12 pits called *suspenders*, in which they were suspended from poles laid across the top of a pit containing the weakest tanning solution, a process which ensured that absorption of the tanning liquor would be uniform when they were moved on to stronger solutions.

The hides were than transferred to *handling pits*, which contained progressively stronger tanning liquors, in which they were laid flat and moved from pit to pit, at regular intervals, being turned over in the liquor on a daily basis. Upon the satisfactory completion of this process the hides were then smoothened out before being conveyed to the *layer pits*. A layer of ground bark about 6in deep was laid on the bottom of this pit and the hide was laid flat on top of it, the hide itself being then covered with about half an inch of the same material and a second hide spread out on top of that. The pit continued to be layered in this fashion until it was almost full, whereupon a layer of tanning material about 1ft thick was spread on top of the final layer. A mixture of tanning material and cold water was then added, after which the hides were left in the pits for anything between nine and eighteen months, or longer, depending on their thickness and the quality required. When this process had been completed the hides were then rinsed and smoothened out before being removed to the drying lofts. The type of leather preferred for the soles of shoes, which needed an abrasion resistant surface, would be removed from the drying loft part way through the drying process, to be either hammered or compressed by a roller, after which it was returned to the loft (Thomson 1981, 166; 1982, 141–7).

In the *currying*, or finishing process, the leather was first dampened in a vat of warm water or weak tannin before being softened by the pummelling action of heavy mallets. The leather was then scoured on both faces with scrubbing brushes before being smoothed out. The next process, in which the currier pared down the leather to the required thickness on a near vertical curriers' beam, required great skill. Then, after further cleaning to remove loose tanning materials, the leather was partially dried, before being 'stuffed' (i.e. impregnated) with a warm dubbin made from tallow and fish oils. The skins were permeated with fat for about one week prior to being hung up in a warm room to dry, after which unwanted grease was removed (ibid., 147).

Cork City Tanneries

By far the largest concentration of tanneries (the most numerous industrial sites within the city and its environs) were located on the north side of the city, principally in the Watercourse Road/Blackpool area (Fig. 82) but also, as one might expect, on the streets and lanes leading to Cork Cattle Market (030). At least two relatively large sites were situated on the south side of the city at Fitton (Sharman Crawford) Street (213) and Hobbs Lane off Bishop Street (206), but these were clearly exceptional. The main locational considerations affecting Cork tanners and curriers were direct access to raw hides and a reliable water supply. A location on the north side of the city normally met both of these requirements, where in most cases tanneries were able to pump water from artesian wells, whilst traditionally the hides were procured from the many butchers based within the environs of the cattle market. A number of tanneries in the Blackpool area, particularly those adjacent to the Backwatercourse (Fig. 82) or the Glen stream were able to avail of running water, such as the Spring Lane (563) and Bleasby's Street tanneries (564).[53] However, for tanyards situated outside the city boundaries such as the Upper Glasheen tanyard[54] and the Millfield tannery (565),[55] direct access to running water appears to have been their principal advantage. John Rocque's map of the city in 1773 shows two tanneries to the south of the river Lee, one at Fitton Street, the other on Cove Street, though by and large south city tanyards are quite rare. Water-powered machinery appears not to have been used in Cork tanneries. Indeed, the only intimation that it may ever have done so is at the Spring Lane tannery, although the use it may have been put to is obscure. In any case most of the city's tanyards were sited in areas where the availability of waterpower appears not to have been a primary consideration, and any degree of mechanisation introduced later appears to have been met by steam power (see below).

In most cases the tannery buildings were built around a central yard, the centre of which was taken up with the various handling pits, tanning pits, leaching pits and lime pits (Fig. 82). An artesian well (either stone or wood-lined) was usually ready at hand, whilst force or double-acting pumps were generally used to pump water through a network of wooden pipes to the various pits. The tannery buildings comprised the bark stores, bark mills, the drying lofts (usually situated over the boiler house) and offices, and, if currying was undertaken by the same firm, currying sheds and beam houses. Some tanneries such as John Hackett's on Watercourse Road could have up to 106 tanning pits,[56] but generally speaking the capacity of most Cork tanneries (though by no means inconsiderable) was much smaller. Hoffman Boete & Co.'s tannery on Great Britain (Great William O'Brien) Street in 1864 is more typical of the type of combined tanning and currying installation operating in Cork during the second half of the nineteenth century. The Great Britain Street tannery specialised in the manufacture of satin calf, prepared grained and calf kid leathers, which were tanned in sumac liquor. The hides were tanned in an enormous kieve (i.e. a vat or tub), which was capable of tanning 4–5,000 dozen calfskins per year.[57] In all, the complex had six drying lofts, two of which were positioned over the boiler house and were heated by steam pipes led from it, two over the currying sheds, and one each over the kieve house and over a storeroom. There were, in addition, nine handling pits, four lime pits, two watering pits, one watering pool and two boiling leaches.[58]

At the end of the nineteenth century, the principal survivors of the contraction in the Cork industry were Treacy's tannery on Hobb's Lane, William Hegarty's tannery on Blarney Street and Dunn Bros. on Watercourse Road. In the early years of the present century Dunn Bros. tannery could handle 'several hundred Buenos Ayres [sic] ox hides every week'. The site was set on a powerful stream, with the lime pits, beam house and stores for raw hides situated on the eastern side of Watercourse Road. There the hair and

Fig. 86

The Lee Boot Company.

Fig. 87   OPPOSITE ABOVE

Cork City glasshouses.

1 Hanover Street Glassworks. 2 The
Waterloo Glasshouse Company, Wandesford
Quay. 3 The Terrace Glassworks, South
Terrace.

Fig. 88   OPPOSITE BELOW

Sketch of Hanover Street glass cone in 1838
by William Roe (Courtesy Cork Public
Museum). The bridge shown is Clarke's
bridge, completed in 1776. The building to
the left of the bridge with the oculus on its
gable is the millwrights' and pattern shop of
the Hive iron works.

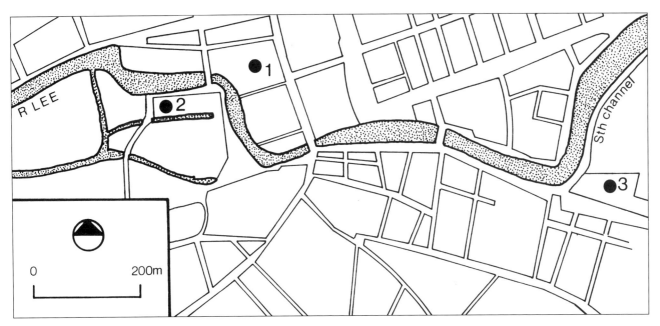

Clarke's bridge

flesh was removed from the raw hides. The Dunn Bros. still used the 'long process', and the larger part of their operation, which included the drying sheds with steam heating appliances for airing the drying lofts, were situated on the western side of Watercourse Road.[59] However, by 1888 the Dunn brothers were also manufacturing 'short process' leather and had mechanised the rolling, scraping, beating and currying processes.[60]

Despite the former prevalence of these sites, particularly on the north side of the city, the sites of only a handful have survived. Hegarty's tannery on Blarney Street (**219**) covered about 3–4 acres at the end of the nineteenth century, and manufactured monster satin calf, memel calf, levants and kip (Stratten and Stratten 1892, 192). Sections of the drying lofts of the Allinett's Lane tannery off Watercourse Road (Fig. 83), the storage sheds of the Corkeran's Quay tannery (Fig. 84) and the tannery drying sheds of Dunne's tannery on Watercourse Road (Fig. 85) survive at the time of writing.

FOOTWEAR MANUFACTURE

Towards the end of the nineteenth century a small number of important boot factories were established within the city, beginning with the Cork boot factory in Blackpool in 1882. A high degree of mechanisation clearly delineated Cork boot factories from more traditional craft-based boot and shoe-makers. In the factory-based production of boots in Cork the uppers were first cut out by highly skilled cutters and the leather pieces then sent to a machine room to be mechanically stitched together by girls. Silk thread was used for finer work but for heavy footwear such as boots, linen thread made by Barbours of Hilden, near Lisburn, was used. The pieces then received a final paring, the thread ends were trimmed and eyelet holes were punched and eyelets added, generally by younger workers. The *rough stuff* department, owing to the heavy machinery required, was generally situated on the ground floor where the soles, insoles and heel lifts were cut out with the dies of a cutting press. The soles could be attached to the piece with wooden pegs, brass rivets or with washed hempen threads. Heels were built up in pieces and, after being attached to the sole, were then levelled off. The shoes and boots were then transferred to finishers, who pared and blackened their edges before burnishing them with gas-heated hot irons.[61]

By the late 1890s there were four boot factories in the city (Murphy 1980, 34), including the Lee boot factory (**116**). Dwyer and Company began boot manufacture in Hanover Street and expanded into a new premises, the Lee Boot Manufacturing Co. Ltd at Washington Street West in 1885.[62] The main block of buildings were open plan, with wooden skylighted roofs supported on cast-iron uprights made by Merrick's foundry. The lasting and finishing rooms were enclosed within the main two-storey block with an elaborate brick frontage facing Washington Street, which intercommunicated with a three-storey block to the east (Fig. 86). The factory used mechanised lasting machinery based on an American prototype, along with stamping and splitting machinery. All of the latter was powered by a 10hp gas engine, which also ran a generator set.[63]

The almost total disappearance of the tanning industry within the Cork area by the end of the nineteenth century, was partly compensated by the relative success of the Cork footwear industry. In the period 1924–9 the Cork boot factories, whose output was largely heavy agricultural footwear, expanded their business under the aegis of the new Irish government's selective protection policies (Press 1989, 26–7). The Lee boot factory, indeed, survived until the early 1980s.

CORK CITY GLASSWORKS 1782–1841

In archaeological terms the most distinctive feature of the eighteenth- and nineteenth-century glass industry are the glassworks cones, which formerly dominated the skylines of the English and Irish towns in which glass was manufactured. Unfortunately, with the exception of the foundation of a cone at Ballycastle, County Antrim, none of the Irish examples have survived and there are, indeed, only five examples surviving in Britain.[64] The purpose of these tall truncated cones was to provide an updraught for their circular, centrally positioned furnaces, and to provide cover for the glassworkers. The furnace grate received air from an elaborate system of flues and ash tunnels which ran beneath the floor of the cone. A man called a teaser fuelled the furnace through a square stokehole. The upper section of the furnace would accommodate up to ten of the clay pots in which the glass was melted, and an aperture in the furnace wall immediately above each pot (the working hole), enabled the glassworker to extract the molten glass (Dodsworth 1984, 13; Cossons 1987, 170–71).

Particular care was exercised in the manufacture of the glass claypots, as the high temperatures to which they were exposed in the furnaces could lead to cracking, whilst the material used in their manufacture also had to be able to resist the solvent action of the molten glass (Cossons 1987, 171). The most widely used refractory clay employed in the manufacture of these pots came from the Stourbridge region of the English West Midlands. Most of the fire-clay used in Irish glasshouses (including the Cork examples) appears to have been imported from the Stourbridge area and was usually mixed in the proportions 3:1 with a powder made up of pulverised old pots called grog (Dudley Westropp 1978, 173; Dodsworth 1984, 12–13).

The sand used in the manufacture of Cork flint glass appears to have been imported from one of the principal English sources at Lynn in Norfolk, which has a low iron content, whilst that used for bottle glass may well have been drawn from the Youghal district (Dudley Westropp 1978, 169–70). Lead, saltpetre, potash and manganese, four of the five ingredients used in the manufacture of flint glass, were also imported from England (ibid., 173).[65] The ingredients of the particular type of glass to be manufactured were first weighed, and after careful mixing were calcined by partial fusion (*fritting*) in a oven, which helped to remove impurities. *Cullet* or broken glass was then added to assist the melting process, the batch of mixed ingredients being then shovelled into the pots. After fabrication the glass pieces were slowly drawn through a long gallery called a lehr or annealing arch, in which they were allowed to cool gradually (Dudley Westropp 1978, 167–8; Dodsworth 1984, 15).

The eighteenth- and early nineteenth-century Irish glass industry relied heavily on English glassworking expertise. The Cork Glass Co. recruited glassworkers from Newcastle upon Tyne (Hall 1813, vol. 1, 162), whilst the Waterloo Glass Co. (see below) employed at least one Stourbridge glassworker who had arrived in Cork via Dublin (Dudley Westropp 1978, 65). Indeed, even the buildings of the Hanover Street works appear to have been modelled closely on English glassworks (see below). In the English glass industry of the same period, ready access to cheap coal was one of the most important factors governing the location of the industry (Barker 1977, 18–19). A large glass cone could consume up to 24 tons of coal per week (Cossons 1987, 171), the quantity of which increased substantially when steam power began to be used to power glass-cutting machinery. As the Cork glasshouses had to import this from South Wales, a quayside location was essential to reduce carriage costs.[66] In consequence Cork's three glasshouse concerns were all established on sites with direct access to the south channel of the river Lee (Fig. 88).

The Cork Glasshouse Co., Hanover Street (289) 1782–1818

In 1782 two Cork brewers Richard Rowe and Atwell Hayes, in association with a maltster called Thomas Burnett established Cork's first glasshouse on the eastern side of Hanover Street.[67] In a petition of 1793 the three partners stated that they had not only modelled their works on contemporary English manufactories, but had also been at pains to employ English 'Artificers' to build their Cork glassworks, which comprised two glasshouses, one for bottle and window (crown) glass, and one for plate and flint glass (Dudley Westropp 1978, 115; Warren 1981, 53).

Bottle glass was manufactured with cheap, easily obtainable materials, and could be made with locally acquired sand. As has been seen above, the sand used in Cork bottle glass was probably shipped from Youghal, whilst the other ingredients used in its manufacture — soap maker's waste, lime, rock salt (or even ground bricks) — could be cheaply and conveniently acquired. Most bottles made with these raw materials tend to have a greenish hue owing to the iron content of the sand, whereas that used in the manufacture of flint glass (where colour was more important) had a low iron content. The Hanover Street glassworks, in 1793,[68] was also making 'black bottles', in which the iron content of the sand produced a blackish green colour, which rendered the glass almost opaque (Dudley Westropp 1978, 175).

Flint glass was manufactured by all of the Cork glasshouses, mostly in the form of quality tableware. Silica sand with a very low iron content was employed in its manufacture, along with lead oxide, potash (or pearlash), saltpetre and manganese.[69] Flint or lead glasses (English Crystal) have a high refractive index, and are admirably suited both to hand manufacture and secondary working by cutters and engravers (Dudley Westropp 1978, 175; Cossons 1987, 171).

Window or crown glass was formed by blowing, heating and rolling the molten glass on a polished metal surface. The globe of molten glass formed by these actions was ultimately spun around on the end of an iron rod, which threw the molten glass out centrifugally to form a flat disc. Plate glass, on the other hand, which was made by casting molten glass, was generally made of much finer ingredients than those employed in window glass. It was normally made thicker than window glass in order that it could be ground and polished. Most plate glass was generally silvered for use as mirrors, although it was sometimes used for coach windows (Barker 1977, 12, 23–5). Apart from the Cork Glasshouse Company's announcement of its intention to manufacture window and plate glass, there is little direct evidence that the various Cork glasshouses made anything other than flint and bottle glass. However, the company's announcement in 1793 that they were now prepared to take in other partners help begin production at their 'crown and bottle work', and the subsequent entry of a further partner into the firm in 1793, would suggest that crown glass was eventually manufactured at their works.[70] In any case it seems quite probable that window glass for local use was manufactured by some, if not all, of the Cork glasshouses.

The original partners of the Hanover Street glassworks refer to their successful efforts to erect two glasshouses at Hanover Street in 1792, from which it can be reasonably inferred that two glass cones were in position by this date. However, only one glasshouse cone is shown on Daniel Murphy's map of the city of 1789, as is the case on Beauford's map of 1801. Indeed, there are at least two early panoramic views of the city which would suggest that there was only one glasshouse cone built at Hanover Street by 1807. Only one glasshouse cone appears in a late eighteenth/early nineteenth-century panorama of the city, which shows a view of the city from the Sunday's Well area.[71] A panorama by Calvert of 1807 which also shows a single glassworks cone at Hanover Street, as seen from the Boreenamanna Road area on the south side of the city, certainly seems to bear this out.[72] On present evidence, therefore, it would appear that only one glassworking cone was constructed on this site. The Cork Glasshouse Company invested in a steam engine in 1813 for driving glass-cutting machinery (Bielenberg 1991, 86). The quality of its products was second only to those of Waterford in the same period, but by 1818 the company was forced to sell the concern and thereafter glass production ceased (Dudley Westropp 1978, 121; Warren 1981, 54).

An early large-scale plan of the Cork Porter Brewery of 1839[73] shows a segment of a glass cone which was by then the brewery's property. By December 1863 the entire Hanover Street glassworks site was in control of Beamish and Crawford's brewery — the glassworks cone appears on a map of the brewery completed in that year marked as a coal store.[74] From the map it is clear that the cone had a maximum external diameter of approximately 54ft at the base. The most interesting feature that can be gleaned from the ground plan are the six recesses indicated at the base. There can be little doubt that these represent arcading in which the glass-blowers worked. These were a common feature of early Irish and English glassworks cones, and there was at least one other Irish example at Ballycastle, which was built in 1755 and demolished in the 1870s. Indeed, the illustration of a glassworks cone shown in Diderot's *Encyclopaedia* of 1772, with its nozzle-like extension at the top of the cone and its arcading at the base, is not unlike the Hanover Street example.[75] The Hanover Street glassworks cone was described by Alfred Barnard, who visited the Cork Porter Brewery in the late 1880s as:

> a conical brick building, upwards of 80ft high, its walls covered with rock plants and creepers almost to the top, which give it a picturesque appearance. It is 45ft in diameter at its base, but only 16ft at the top, forming quite a conspicuous object from the main road and neighbourhood. (Fig. 88) (Barnard 1890, vol.1 353).

The cone is clearly shown in a photograph taken sometime before its demolition in 1915 and provides a clear view of the cone from Beamish and Crawford's Cork Porter Brewery coal yard looking westwards towards Crosses Green Quay, with Harte's sawmills in the background.

The Waterloo Glasshouse Co., Wandesford Quay (570) 1815–35

A number of the skilled glassworkers from the defunct Hanover Street glassworks were given employment in a new glasshouse established by Daniel Foley on Wandesford Quay in 1815 (Dudley Westropp 1978, 121; MacCleod 1978, 62). During the twenty-year period in which the Waterloo glassworks was in existence, it manufactured flint and bottle glass, and was later engaged in the manufacture of engraved and cut wares. From 1829 onwards improvements in the annealing process made it possible for them to advertise their ability to manufacture glass which was 'hot-water proof'.[76] The removal of excise duties on Irish glass in 1825, however, along with a general erosion of its markets led to its closure in 1835. An auction notice for the works, which appeared in a local newspaper of the same year,[77] lists 'ten excellent [glass] pots' amongst the glassworks equipment, along with fireproof clay (presumably used in the manufacture of such pots), bricks, coal, sand and cullet. The works was also equipped with a steam engine which was used to actuate glass-cutting equipment.[78] The site does not feature on any of the early nineteenth-century maps of the city and is not shown on the first edition of the Ordnance Survey of the city for 1842, whilst the glasshouse cone of the Hanover Street works clearly is. As far as can be seen the site of the Waterloo glassworks

was on Wandesford Quay near Clarke's bridge, an area currently occupied by a business centre.

The Terrace Glassworks (090) 1811–41

Edward and Richard Ronayne's glassworks on South Terrace was the last to operate in Cork. The Terrace glassworks appears to have made only flint glass. In 1838 the original Ronayne brothers partnership was dissolved and the control of the operation passed to Edward Ronayne who managed to stay in business up until 1841. The South Terrace works was equipped with a steam engine capable of actuating forty glass-cutting wheels and was also equipped with its own clay mill. What appears to be a glasshouse cone at South Terrace is shown on the first edition of the Ordnance Survey, but the site was certainly redeveloped by the 1890s. However, the remains of the glasshouse furnace came to light in the 1950s and were apparently concreted over.

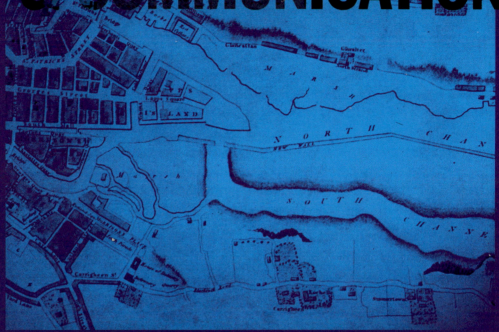

In County Cork the lack of navigable waterways led to the development of a sophisticated road network. The development of this network continued apace during the eighteenth and nineteenth centuries, with special attention being paid to the development of the so-called 'Butter Roads'. These latter facilitated the transport of salted butter from many of the Munster counties to the Cork Butter Market at Shandon. However, the absence of suitable water transport within the county was keenly felt. As early as 1715 formal proposals were made to create river navigations between Youghal and Newmarket (via the Blackwater), Cork and Limerick (via the Martin, Clyda, Blackwater, Awbeg and Maigue), Cork and Macroom (via the Lee) and Kinsale and Dunmanway (via the Bandon).[1] But at the end of the eighteenth century there were only two canal networks in Cork — within Ballincollig Gunpowder Mills and a short unfinished section between Mallow and Lombardstown. Thus within Ireland's largest county the transportation of goods by inland waterways was negligible, and until the development of an extensive railway network in the county almost all of the goods, transported to and from the hinterland of the port of Cork, were carried by road. However, in the early years of the present century only one of the county's railways had a direct link into the national railway network. But most remarkable of all, access for larger vessels between the upper and lower reaches of Cork harbour was restricted up until the 1870s, until such time as the main shipping lane had been deepened.

ROADS

By the second half of the eighteenth century the stature of Cork as a port had led to the creation of an extensive road network, the undisputed focal point of which was the city of Cork. For the most part, a county-based administrative system responsible for the general upkeep of roads and bridges peculiar to Ireland, was is no small way responsible for the relatively high quality of Irish roads. However, in County Cork and, indeed, in most other Irish counties, there were four principal ways in which both intra- and inter-county roads were constructed and maintained from the second half of the eighteenth century onwards: (1) *By Grand Jury presentment*, (2) *by turnpike trust*, (3) *by the Irish Board of Public Works*, and (4) *by the Irish Post Office*.[2] Each of these will now be considered in relation to the roads in the survey area.

The Cork Grand Jury: Road Construction and Repair by Presentment

From Arthur Young's observations of 1780 onwards English travellers in Ireland in the late eighteenth century and the early nineteenth century were almost unanimous in their praise of the quality of Irish roads *vis à vis* those of contemporary England (Nolan 1974, 8–10; McCutcheon 1980, 44, n. 13). However, these roads were more attuned to the needs of small-wheeled vehicles carrying light loads, and were not likely to have been worn out by heavy goods traffic (Ó Gráda 1994, 154).

In the main, the credit for this development lies with the Irish Grand Juries. An Act of 1634 empowered Justices of the Assize and of Peace to levy direct taxes for the repair and construction of roads, causeways, toghers and bridges which were 'broken or decayed', works which by 1710 were already being undertaken by presentment (Nolan 1974, 2; McCutcheon 1980, 2). Under the presentment system a formal application was made for funding and, after consideration, a presentment was made that a sum of money be raised and allocated (Meghan 1959; Crossman 1994). In 1739 the so-called Grand Juries, the precursors of latter-day County Councils, became empowered to 'facilitate the laying out of roads in straight lines from market town to market town' and were now enabled to buy land for this purpose. An Act of 1777–8 further enabled the Grand Jury to grant contracts for the repair of roads, by which time the repair and general maintenance of most of the county roads had become its complete responsibility. In this way Irish Grand Juries became responsible for the bulk of the roads constructed in the eighteenth and nineteenth centuries.[3] The Grand Jury system of road management had no real analogue in Britain, and its origin and structure owed much to social and economic conditions peculiar to Ireland. First and foremost, it was an instrument of the wealthy protestant ascendancy, and its actions, for the most part, reflected their interests. Most contemporary commentators complained about their financial mismanagement and, indeed, their priorities with regard to road construction were by no means always intended to benefit the entire population. Up until the 1760s Grand Juries showed a marked preference for laying out 'geometrical' roads, which were laid in straight lines without proper reference to the difficulty of the terrain they happened to traverse. Many roads of this type tended to have steep gradients unsuited to wheeled vehicles and became impassable on certain stretches during the winter months. Furthermore, it is all too obvious that many roads paid for by presentment were constructed solely for the convenience of wealthy landowners, and there are many instances where presentment roads were deliberately planned to converge upon or avoid (as the case may be) a 'big house' (Nolan 1974, 11–12; d'Alton 1980, 4). Nevertheless, despite the idiosyncrasies of Grand Jury roads and the questionable utility of some of them, the system was efficient enough to ensure that the quality of Irish roads by the early nineteenth century greatly exceeded those of contemporary Britain.

In 1780 Arthur Young wrote that 'By Act of Parliament all presentment roads must be 21 feet wide, at least, from fence to fence and 14 feet of it formed with stone and gravel' (Young 1780, vol. 2, 66; McCutcheon 1980, 4). According to Carr, writing in 1806, presentment roads were normally formed by

> throwing up a foundation of earth in the middle, from the outsides, by placing a layer of limestone on this, broken to about the size of an egg, by scattering earth on the stones to make them bind and by throwing over the whole a coat of gravel when it can be had. (Carr 1806, 211; Nolan 1974, 11)

Compared to the roads built by Griffith in parts of Munster in the period 1822–36 (see below) the surfacing of presentment roads may have often left much to be desired. Nonetheless, the general lightness of the wheeled traffic using them was such that they fared tolerably well during the winter months, whilst many appear to have been able to dry out quickly after wet spells (McCracken 1973, 53–5).

The Cork Grand Jury

The extent of the Cork Grand Jury's activity within and near the city by the closing decade of the nineteenth century is revealed by the accounts of the Spring Assizes of 1793 at which presentments were made for the repair of 5.96 miles of feeder roads to Cork at a cost of £656. The roads for which presentments were passed included the road from Passage to Cork, from Cork to Kinsale, from Cork to Curraheen Mills, from Cork to Fivemilebridge, the Kilcully Road on the northern outskirts of the city leading to Mallow, the Watercourse Road, the road from Cork to Bandon, Cork to Carrigaline, Cork to Youghal, the Strand Road (latterly the Lower Glanmire Road), the road from Cork to Macroom and the road from Cork to Blarney.[4]

At the close of the eighteenth century the main business of the Cork Grand Jury was directly related to road construction and repair (Fig. 89a) (Nolan 1974, 6–8). In 1810 the Spring Assizes gave its approval for the construction of a mail-coach road from Cork to

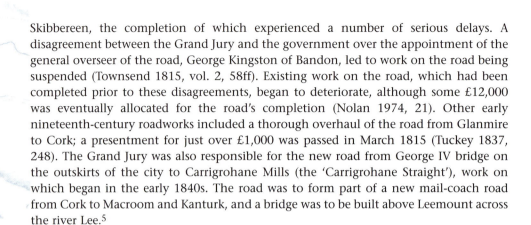

Skibbereen, the completion of which experienced a number of serious delays. A disagreement between the Grand Jury and the government over the appointment of the general overseer of the road, George Kingston of Bandon, led to work on the road being suspended (Townsend 1815, vol. 2, 58ff). Existing work on the road, which had been completed prior to these disagreements, began to deteriorate, although some £12,000 was eventually allocated for the road's completion (Nolan 1974, 21). Other early nineteenth-century roadworks included a thorough overhaul of the road from Glanmire to Cork; a presentment for just over £1,000 was passed in March 1815 (Tuckey 1837, 248). The Grand Jury was also responsible for the new road from George IV bridge on the outskirts of the city to Carrigrohane Mills (the 'Carrigrohane Straight'), work on which began in the early 1840s. The road was to form part of a new mail-coach road from Cork to Macroom and Kanturk, and a bridge was to be built above Leemount across the river Lee.[5]

The Cork Grand Jury was extremely active in the early nineteenth century. The Scottish-born County Cork magnate, John Anderson (1742–1820) regularly attended as a member of the Cork Grand Jury which enabled him 'to promote the improvements so much wanted' and to obtain

> 'presentments for the widening and repairing of many roads, and also of making new lines where they were found necessary. The road from Cork to Kinsale, and also the one from Cork through Bandon to Skibbereen and to Bantry were very bad, and were made almost entirely new. The one from Cork to Limerick via Mallow, had been proverbially bad during the memory of the oldest inhabitants of the county, and was also made entirely new. The one from Cork to Limerick by Fermoy, Castle Oliver and Bruff, was, in many instances, altered and greatly improved; though I did not individually undertake the execution of these latter works, yet I have the satisfaction to believe, it is universally admitted, that I was chiefly and actively instrumental in bringing forward these valuable improvements, and many others which have escaped my memory.' (Brunicardi 1987, 30)

The Grand Jury's responsibility for the county road network increased steadily throughout the nineteenth century. In 1834 it had some 1,599 miles of road within the East Riding of the county under contract and this increased to 2,300 miles by 1844.[6] The Grand Jury was also responsible for the erection of mile-posts (Fig. 89c), when new roads were constructed (Nolan 1974, 42–3), and as in the case of the section of the new mail coach road from Cork to Dublin between Glanmire village and the turnpike at Annasilly, for the erection of fences.[7] In 1854 all 85 miles of road within the county previously under the jurisdiction of the Board of Works became the responsibility of the Grand Jury, along with all of the county's turnpike roads and piers[8] and by the 1870s the maintenance and construction of roads and bridges had become the Cork Grand Jury's single most important function (ibid., 179).

The administration and monitoring of the civil engineering works associated with the city and county's road network in this, Ireland's largest county, was a formidable undertaking. In 1817 all Irish Grand Juries were legally obliged to have any works conducted by presentment certified by engineers, a measure calculated to prevent waste of public funds. This legal obligation eventually led to the creation of County Surveyors who were to fulfill this monitoring function on a full-time basis. As early as 1823, for Quarter Session purposes, the county was divided into East and West Ridings and in 1834 the Lord Lieutenant appointed Patrick Leahy as County Surveyor for the East Riding and the city of Cork. Leahy's son Edmund was rather injudiciously appointed as surveyor for the West Riding. As their subsequent actions confirmed, both men proved only too willing to court controversy, and appear to have neglected their Grand Jury-related work at the expense of private contracts.[9] In 1846 the Sligo engineer John Benson (1812–74), who was to make an enormous contribution to the infrastructural development of the city, was appointed County Surveyor for the East Riding, and a Cork City engineer, William A. Treacy, as surveyor for the West Riding.[10] Benson and Treacy's appointments correspond with the period of Famine relief works which included such schemes as a new road from Cork to Kinsale. Work on the latter had commenced in 1844, and was completed as a relief work during the famine period (Mulcahy 1966, 47; Nolan 1974, 108). By around 1860, however, there were complaints about the general state of the roads in the county. The County Surveyors pointed out that cut-throat competition amongst road contractors had led to low and irresponsible tendering, and that as a direct consequence of this many road repairs were poorly executed.[11] Under the conditions of the Local Government Act of 1899 the responsibilities of the Cork Grand Jury were transferred to the newly constituted County Council. The cess was replaced by rates which were, up until very recently, struck on a yearly basis by Irish County Councils.

Roads Built by Turnpike Trusts: 1731–1857

Turnpike roads, which had been in existence in England since 1663, were not introduced into Ireland until 1729. Essentially, turnpike roads were a product of local initiative. Local interest groups raised the necessary finance to obtain an Act of Parliament which invested powers in named trustees to erect gates and toll houses (*turnpikes*) with which to collect tolls. The latter were collected from most road users, save pedestrians and local farmers who had to use the road on a daily basis, and were to be used for the upkeep of the road. As we have seen in the previous section, the Irish Grand Jury system of road construction and repair saw to it that there was no shortage of good, toll-free roads in Ireland by the end of the eighteenth century which ultimately led to a decline in the volume of traffic using the turnpike roads (Andrews 1964, 26). By Arthur Young's time these were a key target for the criticism of English visitors to Ireland (McCutcheon 1980, 6). However, the fortunes of many Irish turnpikes improved substantially in the first half of the nineteenth century when the condition of many of them began to compare favourably to that of the presentment roads. By 1837 it is clear that many were accommodating high traffic densities.[12] Nonetheless, the existence of so many good toll-free roads and the advent of the railways brought a terminal decline in the fortunes of the Irish turnpike roads, the extent of which had fallen from approximately 1,500 miles in 1820 to 300 in 1856 (Andrews, 1964, 23–6; McCutcheon 1980, 9).

In 1731 *An Act for repairing the road leading from the city of Cork to the brook which bounds the counties of Cork and Tipperary near the foot of Kilworth Mountain* provided the city and county with its first turnpike road.[13] The road 'leading from the town of Newcastle in the County of Limerick to the City of Limerick and from thence to the City of Cork' also became the responsibility of a turnpike trust in the same year.[14] The development of further turnpikes serving the city, however, was somewhat slower. In 1747 the roads leading from 'the City of Corke through Millstreet to Shannah Mill in the County of Kerry and from Shannah Mill to Killarney' became turnpiked, although in this instance the responsibilities normally delegated to turnpike trustees became vested in an

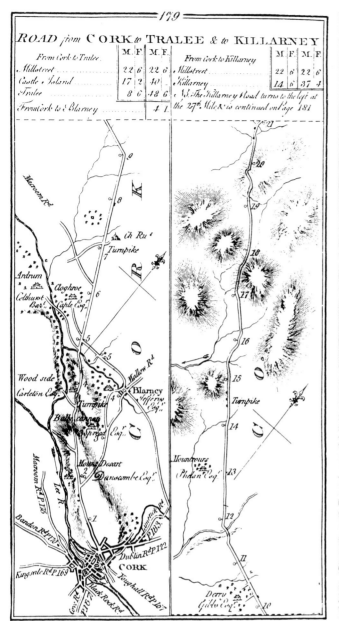

Fig. 89 (a) ABOVE LEFT

Cork City roads, Taylor and Skinner 1778.

Fig. 89 (b) ABOVE RIGHT

Extract from Grand Jury map of County Cork, by Neville Bath, 1811, showing main Cork City roads (Courtesy, Cork Public Museum).

Fig. 89 (c) OPPOSITE

Cast-iron milepost on Western Road, for coach road to Skibbereen, cast in 1829 by Hive Iron Works. A second cast-iron milepost survives near Wilton roundabout.

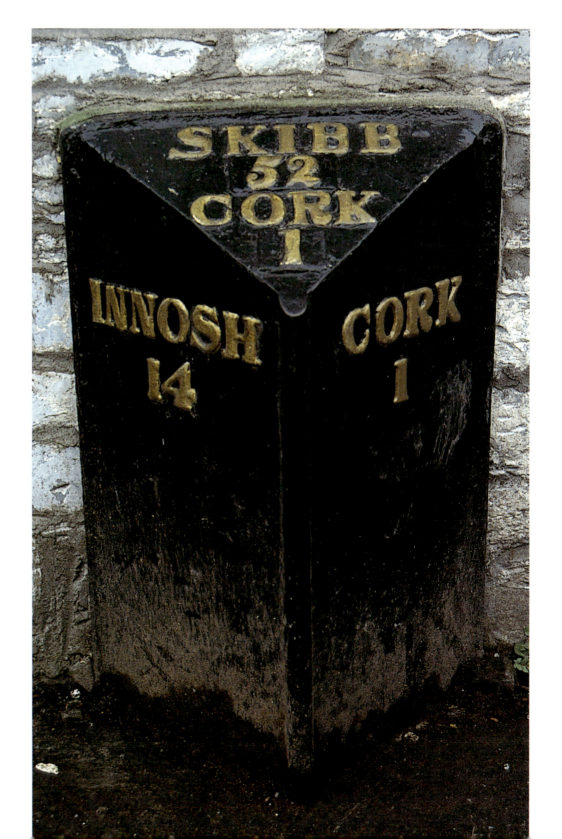

undertaker.[15] The turnpike's undertaker, John Murphy, became embroiled with the corporation of Cork over the right to levy tolls on the road at the Cork City end. In January 1749 Murphy petitioned the Irish Parliament to be enabled to bring the turnpike of the Kerry road to the mile house in the north liberties of the city (Caulfield 1876, 656). The subsequent parliamentary approval of this went against the wishes of Cork Corporation, who were indignant that their hitherto exclusive privilege to levy tolls on traffic moving within the county and city of Cork was now directly challenged. In 1765 the road from Kanturk in County Cork to Fair Lane in the north liberties of the city of Cork also became a turnpike administered by an undertaker, but appears not to have been opened for traffic until 1768 (Fig. 89a).[16]

In the wake of the legislation of 1783, which established an independent Irish post office, mail-coach services were established to serve the principal Irish towns, beginning with the Cork–Dublin line in 1789 (McCracken 1973, 53; McCutcheon 1980, 8). The tolls paid by mail-coaches using turnpikes were a welcome and often lucrative source of income for the turnpike trusts, and the early decades of the nineteenth century saw an upturn in their fortunes. However, the turnpike roads from Cork to Cashel, which received just over £1,100 in tolls p.a. from the Post Office Mails in the early 1830s, and the Cork to Kilworth Mountain turnpike, controlled by Robert Briscoe of Fermoy, which received around £867 p.a.,[17] were exceptional by contemporary Cork standards. The trustees of the Cork–Limerick turnpike, by way of contrast, chose to waive all tolls on Post Office mails and, like the overwhelming majority of Cork turnpike roads, was unprofitable (see below).[18]

The parliamentary Select Committee on Turnpike Roads of 1831–2 classified existing Irish turnpike roads under two headings — those under the management of trustees, responsible for a total of 631 miles of road — and those vested by acts of parliament in named individuals for unexpired terms (119 miles). The 34 miles of turnpike road from Cork to Kilworth Mountain, which had 65 trustees but whose profits were shared equally between Robert Briscoe and John Anderson of Fermoy (and by Briscoe alone after Anderson's death in 1820), was of the latter type. It was also the only profitable turnpike serving the city of Cork, with an average income of £2,462 in the period 1829–30, of which an average of around £1000 p.a. was spent on repairs in the years 1829–31.[19] The road comprised three divisions, the 'southern division' of which lies within the survey area. This division commenced at the bottom of Dublin Hill, on the northern outskirts of the city, and terminated at the turnpike gate at the southern end of Watergrass Hill, roughly midway between Cork and Fermoy. The turnpike at the Cork end was erected at the junction of the Ballyhooly turnpike (which opened in 1834)[20] and the Dublin road. The materials used in the construction of the road were described as 'broken lime and brownstone [sandstone]'. The average distance between the dumps of stone used for repairs to the road was one and a half miles.[21] A speed rate of 7½ English miles per hour was possible between Clonmel and Cork, whilst the road itself over Kilworth Mountain was described as having a smooth surface although it was not very well fenced.[22]

The other turnpike roads leading from Cork to Limerick and Cork to Tralee were administered by conventional turnpike trusts. The Cork to Limerick via Mallow turnpike road, which had 31 trustees, was in good condition by the early 1830s. Some £2,157 was expended on its upkeep in 1830, and although all of the tolls collected on it were spent on the road, this was said to 'have hardly been adequate to keep the road in repair'. Indeed, the tolls collected on the road in 1830 amounted to only £1,799.[23] The road itself was constructed with limestone, brownstone and limestone gravel.[24] The sixty miles of turnpike road between Cork and Tralee, which was administered by no less than

173 trustees, on the other hand, was built with 'pounded stone' and surfaced with gravel of the 'best description sometimes'.[25]

Roads financed by the Irish Board of Public Works

In the wake of the Whiteboy Insurrection of 1821 Richard Griffith (1784–1878) was dispatched to survey the Munster counties most affected by the disturbances, and to undertake essential public works as a form of relief. Public funds were to be expended on these and other works under the aegis of the Board of Public Works. As late as the early 1820s inter-county link roads between Cork, Kerry and Limerick were non-existent in many border areas, whilst the existing roads linking these areas with the port of Cork followed unnecessarily indirect routes (Ó Luing 1975, 94). The roads which were to be constructed by Griffith provided improved arteries of commerce between the principal towns of Kerry and Limerick and the port of Cork, whilst Griffith himself was anxious that the route taken by Kerry farmers to convey their butter to the Cork Butter Market should be as direct as possible (ibid., 102).[26] Between 1822 and 1836 Griffith was responsible for the construction of some 243 miles of road in counties Cork, Kerry, Tipperary and Limerick (O'Keeffe 1980, 62). In 1829 a new road between Newmarket and Listowel was completed, which accomplished the not inconsiderable feat of reducing the journey between Listowel and Cork from 102 to 66 miles (Ó Luing 1976, 95). A further road between Glenfesk and Macroom reduced the routes between Cork and Kenmare and Cork and Killarney. The road distance from Cork to Kenmare was now 57 statute miles (it was formerly 88 statute miles). Some seven and a half miles were now taken off the previous Cork to Killarney route, whilst before the completion of the new road the journey from Cork took two days. The journey time after 1827 was approximately seven hours (ibid., 98).

For the most part, the design of Griffith's roads fell in with those of principal British road engineers of his day. When conditions allowed, the main roads were generally 32ft wide between fences, with cross, back and guard drains provided where appropriate.[27] The main difference between Griffith's specifications and those of Thomas Telford (1757–1834) and John Loudon MacAdam (1756–1836), however, was Griffith's insistence on the addition of a layer of either clay or loam immediately above the road's pavement. Both Telford and MacAdam expressly advised against this, simply because the pavement could be more easily damaged by ground water and frost (O'Keeffe 1980, 69).

Roads financed by the Irish Post Office

Under an Act of 1805 both turnpike and presentment roads in Ireland used by Post Office mails had now to meet a series of new standards designed to improve their general upkeep. Under the provisions of this act some 2,068 miles of road throughout Ireland were surveyed and planned between 1805 and 1826. All such roads now had to be at least 42ft wide between fences and have a gradient of less than 1 in 35 (Andrews 1964; O'Keeffe 1980, 60). While it is clear that the Cork Grand Jury footed most of the bill for improvements to the Cork–Skibbereen road, it is by no means clear, however, the extent to which these various stipulations (if at all) affected the mail-coach routes running from Cork after 1805, such as Cork to Tralee and Limerick to Cork via Mallow. Certainly the contract between John Anderson, George Bell and Alexander Taylor to carry the Royal Mail between Dublin and Cork involved an enormous outlay, for while they were paid an agreed rate per mile for carrying the mail, and the Irish Post Office undertook to take care of the various turnpike tolls incurred, the contractors had to maintain the roads at their own expense (Brunicardi 1987, 24). The section of the Cork–Dublin Road from the city of Cork to the county bounds at Glenduff, for example, was a cause of major anxiety to John Anderson, who in 1814 complained that the road was at one time 'in a state which required the immediate expenditure of a large sum of money'. Furthermore:

> Considerable alterations and deviations from the old line of road were necessary. A heavy debt, bearing interest, was due upon it, which the contractor undertook the payment of. The materials for forming the new lines and for keeping the road in repair were, for the greater part of its extent, very indifferent, limestone and gravel not being in the neighbourhood. (Brunicardi 1987, 31–2)

Nonetheless, significant improvements were made to the important Cork–Dublin route, with an extra coach running to Cork via Cashel. In the early years of the mail-coaches, the unsuitability of the coach roads meant that speeds of only four miles per hour were possible, but with the improvement of many of the major routes speeds of seven miles per hour were possible by the 1830s (Reynolds, M. 1983, 45). However, the existence of what were effectively mail-coach monopolies, such as those operated by John Anderson, may well have stymied the long-term development of the post-road system in Ireland (ibid., 46).

Coach and Car Transportation *c.* 1750–1850

For the greater part of the eighteenth century, travel in Ireland, particularly by the gentry and commercial travellers, was conducted on horseback (McCutcheon 1980, 16). Wheeled transport, however, became much more common as the century wore on. Before the advent of both stage- and mail-coach services in 1789, most wheeled transport used within the city and county comprised either the post-chaise or the jaunting-car, both of which would have been available for hire.[28] But while both of these were used for long-distance travel in the era before the stagecoach, their principal disadvantage was that there were few hostelries on the main routes and a scarcity of fresh posthorses (ibid., 17). This general lack of infrastructure for 'staged' travel necessitated enormous cash outlays by early mail contractors. John Anderson found that in addition to the actual investment in coaching stock, accessories and roads, and in order 'to counteract the illiberal combination of the innkeepers against the measure, and provide proper accommodation for those who might travel on our coaches'

> it was absolutely necessary, in various instances, to build and otherwise provide hotels, and place in them proper persons for the accommodation of the public. The cash advances required for those different purposes, amounted at one period to about forty thousand pounds, and required between twelve and thirteen years of the prime of my life, with a degree of patience and perseverance which seldom meet, before I derived one guinea of profit for all the risks I had run, and all the exertions I had made. (Brunicardi 1987, 30)

In July 1789 (see above) the first Post Office mail-coach ran between Dublin and Cork (McCracken 1973, 53 ; Brunicardi 1987, 26), the citizens of Cork being 'respectfully informed' in the local Cork press that:

> the Royal Mail coach sets out for Dublin every evening at 6 o'clock. Fare for two inside passengers, two guineas to Dublin, and 14 shillings, 1 penny to Clonmel. 14lb luggage included extra weight to Dublin at two and a half pence per pound. Small parcels at one shilling one penny each to and short of Clonmel and two shillings, two pence beyond that place. All goods beyond the value of £5 to be entered and paid for accordingly. Outside passengers half price.[29]

By 1810 there were two coaches serving Dublin, the Dublin stagecoach and the Royal Mail, which now left Patrick Street for Dublin four hours later at 10pm, taking over 31 hours to reach Dublin.[30] In the late eighteenth century and early nineteenth century the Dublin mail-coach left the city via North Gate Bridge and through Blackpool to reach the Dublin turnpike.[31] A Limerick mail-coach and a Limerick day-coach (both 12-hour journeys via Fermoy and Mallow respectively) were also in service, as was a mail-coach service to Waterford via Youghal. There was also a diligence service (a form of public coach) to Kinsale and the Passage 'Stage', the latter costing 2s 2d inside and 1s 8d outside.[32] From 1811 onwards there was a mail-coach to Tralee[33] and from 1812 onwards a new coach service between Cork and Passage (Tuckey 1837, 242; O'Mahony 1986a, 9–10).[34] By 1824, in addition to the above services, there was also a diligence service to Mallow and Macroom and a Fermoy day-coach.[35] Bianconi's car service was also extended to Cork by 1821, linking the city to a network of towns which included Clonmel, Limerick, Waterford, New Ross, Enniscorthy and Wexford (O'Neill 1973, 85).[36]

ROAD BRIDGES

According to Arthur Young who visited Cork in 1776, the city, with its multiple water frontages resembled a 'dutch town',[37] an impression no doubt reinforced by the presence of Dutch-style town houses on the city's quaysides. From the earliest times the single most important factor affecting the physical development of the city of Cork has been the division of the river Lee into a number of divergent channels. The subsequent expansion of the city beyond its medieval town walls was at the expense of the intervening islands and marshes, the reclamation of which, by the beginning of the nineteenth century, had left just the two main channels of the river Lee. From the second half of the eighteenth century onwards, the expansion of the city required new bridges over these, which would not only ease communication with expanded areas of settlement but relieve the pressure on existing bridges. But by the early 1760s bridge development within the city appears not to have been in step with its expansion. Up until 1791, indeed, there was only one bridge spanning the north channel (see below). However, the most surprising aspect about the relatively slow pace of bridge development within the city is that it effectively limited access to and from its immediate hinterland. The general scarcity of bridges spanning the main channels of the river Lee was a throwback to the city's former role as a walled citadel, a role which it could no longer be expected to fulfil after the siege of 1690. A full seventy years afterwards, however, access to the city by road was still limited to the North and South Gate Bridges (Fig. 90a).

Bridge Development *c.* 1750–1800

In 1750 no less than three bridges spanned the open channel, latterly occupied by Patrick Street and Grand Parade, linking the north and south channels of the Lee (Fig. 90a). Two bridges connected Tuckey's Quay, on the south side of the present-day Grand Parade, with the opposing quayside — Daunt's Bridge (**572**) and Tuckey's Bridge (**573**). The channel spanned by them made an almost right-angled turn down what is now Patrick Street, where a drawbridge (**571**) at its north-eastern extremity enabled access for vessels from the north channel to Cabwell's Quay on the north side of the latter-day Patrick Street and to the Long Quay and Hoar's Quay on its south side (Fig. 90).[38] As early as 1698 a stone bridge linking Tuckey's Quay with Dunscombe's Marsh to the east was built 'so high and broad that any lighter may pass through laden at Spring tide'. It also had a drawbridge 16ft in the clear (O'Keeffe and Simington 1991, 224). This latter

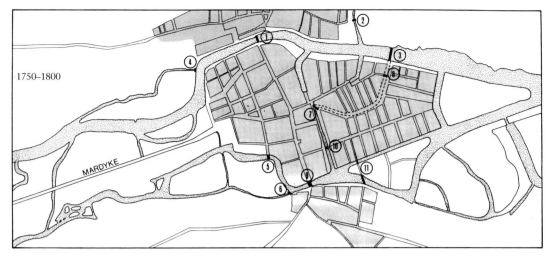

1750–1800

MARDYKE

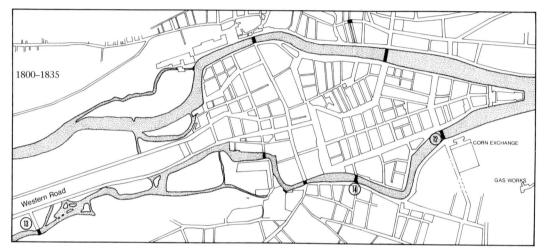

1800–1835

Western Road

CORN EXCHANGE

GAS WORKS

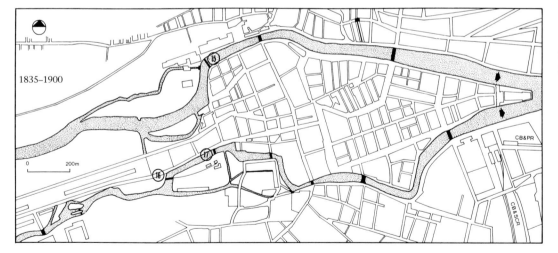

1835–1900

0   200m

CB&PR

CB&SCR

Fig. 90

Bridge development in Cork City:

(a) ABOVE

1750–1800; 1 North Gate Bridge.
2 Punch's Bridge.
3 St Patrick's Bridge.
4 O'Reilly's Bridge.
5 Clarke's Bridge. 6 Proby's Bridge.
7 Daunt's Bridge.
8 Drawbridge. 9 South Gate Bridge.
10 Tuckey's Bridge. 11 Red Abbey
Marsh Bridge.

(b) CENTRE

1800–1835; 12 Anglesea Bridge.
13 Gaol Bridge.
14 Parliament Bridge.

(c) BELOW

1835–1900; 15 St Vincent's Bridge.
16 Cork and Muskerry Light Railway
Bridge. 17 Bridge to Cork and
Muskerry Light Railway terminus on
Bishop's Marsh.

appears to be Daunt's Bridge, as the only other bridge on Tuckey's Quay was a stone bridge built by Francis Tuckey in 1705, to connect it with George's Street. However, as the corporation required that Tuckey's bridge 'be made as high and as broad as the bridge to the Marsh' (i.e. Dunscombe's or Daunt's bridge), it is abundantly clear that the corporation was intent on keeping this channel navigable at all times (ibid.). Such considerations are unlikely to have applied to the smaller bridges spanning the lesser channels within the city, such as the 'wooden bridge' built by Alderman Crone in 1728 on Dunscombe's Marsh, the 'little bridge' on Hammond's Marsh and St Peter's Church Bridge, although the 'large bridge' connecting Hammond's and Pike's Marshes may well have facilitated shipping. Many of the smaller bridges are likely to have consisted of simple wooden decks carried on trestles.

As late as 1761 there were only two bridges spanning the north and south channels of the river Lee; the North Bridge (078) and the South Bridge (081), both of which occupied former fortified river crossing points into the walled city (O'Sullivan 1937, 205).[39] In the early years of the eighteenth century the corporation decided to replace these with stone bridges, beginning with the North Gate Bridge in or around 1712 (O'Keeffe and Simington 1991, 224). During the excavation for the south abutment of its nineteenth-century replacement in 1863 (see below) workers came across 'very inferior masonry' from which 'large masses of oak' were removed, in order that the foundations of the new bridge could be underpinned.[40] This timber was possibly that used in construction of the abutments for the early eighteenth-century bridge (ibid.) or in an even earlier one. The North Bridge which had five arches and four piers, is shown in an illustration by Nathaniel Grogan of about 1796 (Fig. 91).

In 1713 the precarious condition of the South Bridge prompted the corporation to enter into a contract with a mason called Thomas Chatterton and a stonecutter called John Coltsman 'to build the same by the great, to wit, £300 and the old wooden bridge, the Corporation finding what cramps may be thought fit, and to allow them to use what centres may be convenient with the boards for the same, also to give them the tarass left of the North Bridge' (ibid., 224–5). The substance called tarass which, as this account implies, was employed in the construction of both the North and South Bridges, was a form of hydraulic mortar imported from Holland consisting of ground basaltic rock mixed with lime (ibid., 225). South Gate Bridge and Quoile Bridge in County Down have the oldest surviving three-centred arches in Ireland, a style which was widely adopted when bridge spans increased to reduce road gradients. The South Gate Bridge has two, 4ft 5in wide river piers with cutwaters, and three, three-centred arches, the northern and southern side arches of which have 21ft and 23ft spans respectively (Figs. 92 and 93). The bridge's centre arch has a span of 26ft (ibid.). The limestone used in the construction of the bridge was probably quarried locally. As far as can be seen, the west-facing or upriver section of the bridge is the original section of the bridge built by Coltsman in 1713 (Hill 1943, 97), the downriver section (designed by Alexander Deane in 1824) being added later (Brunicardi 1985, 11).

The problem of restricted access to the city for traffic from the west of the county was addressed by the corporation in 1761, after it had been petitioned the previous year 'for liberty to build a stone bridge over the south river from Pelican's corner to Sullivan's Quay'. The bridge was to be at least 20ft in the clear, with provision for a lift bridge (O'Keeffe and Simington 1991, 225). An act of 1761 sanctioned the construction of a 'Stone Bridge from the Quay opposite Princes Street in the city of Cork to Lavitt's Island, and a stone Bridge from thence to the Red Abbey Marsh, with a Drawbridge'.[41] The Princes Street bridge (579) is shown on Joseph Connor's map of 1774, where by this time

Fig. 91

North Gate Bridge by Nathaniel Grogan,
1796 (Courtesy Crawford Art Gallery).

Fig. 92 OPPOSITE ABOVE

South Gate Bridge by John Fitzgerald, 1797
(Courtesy Crawford Art Gallery).

Fig. 93 OPPOSITE CENTRE

South Gate Bridge. The earliest section of
this bridge dates to 1713, the downriver section was added by Alexander Deane in 1824.

Fig. 94 OPPOSITE BELOW

Clarke's Bridge, completed in 1776 (cf. fig.
88).

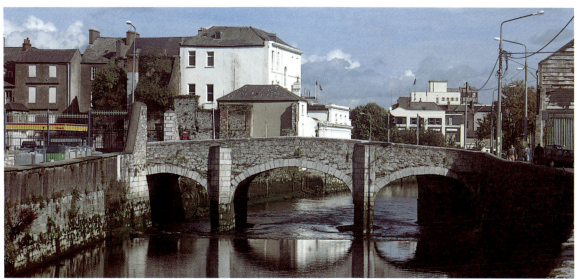

189

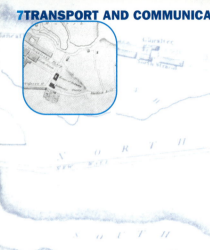

there was a second bridge (**580**) downstream from it, linking the South Mall, then an open channel, with Lavitt's Island. The stone bridge to Red Abbey Marsh, which was completed in 1764, can be none other than the forerunner of the later Parliament Bridge (see below).[42] Up until its construction, traffic on the roads from Macroom, Bandon, Kinsale, Cobh and Blackrock, which entered the city to the south of the River Lee,[43] converged upon the South Bridge. In 1776 'Wandesford's' or Clarke's Bridge (**453**), the construction of which was supervised by a master builder called Samuel Hobbs (Tuckey 1837, 174), was built over the south channel to connect Wandesford's Quay and Clarke's Marsh with the city.[44] Clarke's Bridge is the only surviving eighteenth-century bridge within the city whose building stone, including its voussoirs, is predominantly local red sandstone (Fig. 94). It had one of the longest spans of any Irish, single-span, segmental-arch bridge built during the eighteenth century, and may well have used as its model the Pontypridd Bridge built on the river Taft in Wales by William Edwards (1719–89) in the 1750s (Cossons 1987, 245; O'Keeffe and Simington 1991, 226).

The provision of additional bridges on the north channel, was somewhat slower, though by 1773 'Alderman Reilly's Bridge', which linked Reilly's Marsh with the North Mall, was in position.[45] However, the increased volume of traffic entering the city from the north side necessitated at least one further crossing point on the north channel in the early 1780s. Up until this time ferries had accommodated those wishing to cross the north channel downstream of the North Bridge, and this interest group and traders in the Blarney Lane and Mallow Lane (Shandon Street) areas had stymied earlier attempts to provide a bridge (O'Sullivan 1937, 206). Indeed, even after the construction of the first St Patrick's Bridge (see below) north channel ferries continued to be important. In March 1815 a Grand Jury presentment of £33 11s was passed for rebuilding the ferry slip at the end of 'the little road leading from the Mardyke to the Sunday's Well, then in a ruinous state, and for fixing therein twenty nine and a half feet of hammered lime or brownstone steps at 1s 8d per foot, and for building 24 perches of mason's work, to be contained on quay walls on the east and west sides of the said slip at 7s 6d per perch' (Caulfield 1876, 248). In 1816 the Court of D'Oyer Hundred proposed that the ferry between Lapp's Island and the New Wall, part of the Navigation Wall (see below) be let for £25 pounds a year, a proposal which was abandoned (ibid., 250), whilst in 1830 the corporation leased the ferries plying between Merchants Quay and the north bank, and the Navigation Wall and the north bank.[46] River ferries were obviously still seen as an important means of river communication, an importance which appears to have only been slightly diminished by the addition of a second north channel bridge. Provisions were made, however, to compensate ferrymen (O'Sullivan 1937, 206).

The corporation finally received parliamentary sanction to begin work on a new bridge connecting New Street (Patrick Street) with the north bank of the river in 1786. The overall cost of the bridge, some £13,000, was to be met through the imposition of tolls and a corporation advance of £1,000, the bridge becoming toll-free in 1812. A design by the Cork architect Michael Shanahan, who also acted as contractor, was chosen, which included a portcullis to enable shipping to proceed to the quays upstream from the bridge.[47] In July 1788 the foundation stone was laid, but in January of the following year during a disastrous flood, a brig broke its mooring upstream from the bridge at the Sand Quay and collided with the bridge causing extensive damage. In September 1789 the keystone of the last arch was laid and in 1791 the bridge was finally completed.[48] A late eighteenth-century illustration of the bridge, which had three segmental arches, shows the portcullis in action, with a ship being towed through by two rowing boats. By all accounts this was both an inconvenience and danger to shipping, and it was condemned by the Court of D'Oyer Hundred in 1812, but as navigation upstream of the bridge was still considered important the Grand Jury made a presentment of £200 to have it replaced with a new one, and a further presentment of £40 for sheathing it in iron was made at the Spring Assizes of 1815.[49] In 1824, after the payment of compensation to store owners to the west of the bridge, the portcullis was finally removed by the Wide Streets Commissioners.[50]

Bridge Development 1800–1900

In the early years of the nineteenth century a single-arch limestone bridge, designed by William Hargrave, was built on the site of an earlier bridge constructed between Red Abbey Marsh and Lavitt's Island (see above). The earlier bridge was in poor condition and its replacement, the present Parliament Bridge, which has a span of 65½ft, was opened in 1806 (O'Callaghan 1991, 39). As in the case of the South Gate Bridge, Parliament Bridge was constructed with neatly cut limestone blocks (Fig. 95), although in this instance the bridge parapet, as in the original Patrick's Bridge, is finished with a sculptured stone balustrade.[51]

Up until 1820 traffic approaching the city from the south-west was channelled onto two main routes, the Bandon Road and the Macroom Road. In that year the George IV Bridge (097), which crossed the south channel (Lewis 1837, vol. 1, 410), was opened to accommodate traffic which was to enter or leave the city via a new western route terminating at the western end of Great George's Street (Washington Street), which was completed by the Deanes in 1825. The 'Western Road' was completed between 1825 and 1831 and cost £7,649.[52] George IV (latterly O'Neill-Crowley) bridge has three segmental arches and was built by the brothers James and George Richard Pain. In 1888 the raising of the Waterworks weir by the corporation necessitated the deepening of the reaches of the south channel above George IV Bridge.[53]

As late as 1830 the only upstream method of crossing the north channel to Sunday's Well was by ferry, which had been refurbished in 1815 by Grand Jury presentment (see above). Wellington Bridge (041), designed by Richard Griffith, and built by the Pain brothers in 1830 (ibid.), was intended to improve cross-river communications and allow more direct access for agricultural produce from the west of the county and Kerry to the city's northside. Wellington Bridge (Fig. 96) is constructed with cut limestone, and has three arches; two side arches of 45ft span and a centre arch of 50ft: the bridge piers were sunk in caissons (ibid.).

That same year a further bridge designed by Richard Griffiths, Anglesea Bridge (079), was under construction. Provision for the construction of this bridge was made under *An Act for the establishment of Markets for the sale of Corn and other articles in the City of Cork*,[54] and it was built to provide more direct access from the city to the new Cornmarket, which opened in 1833, on Sleigh's Marsh or latter-day Anglesea Street. The work was supervised by Alexander Nimmo and contracted out to Sir Thomas Deane (Lewis 1837, vol. 1, 410, 413; O'Callaghan 1991, 42–4). Anglesea Bridge, which was replaced in the 1880s (see below), had two semi-elliptical arches of 44ft span and an 11ft rise, with a 32ft span cast-iron bascule (i.e. lifting) bridge in the centre.[55] In 1835 a 50ft single-span bridge (Gaol Bridge, 457) was built across the south channel immediately in front of the portico of the county gaol, to provide the latter with direct access to the Western Road (completed in 1831) via a raised causeway across the intervening marsh (Lewis 1837, vol. 1, 410–11).[56] The bridge (Fig. 97) was designed by Marc Isambard Brunel (1769–1849) who had visited Cork in the early 1830s.[57]

In November 1853 Cork witnessed one of the most spectacular bridge failures in

Fig. 95 OPPOSITE ABOVE
Parliament Bridge, 1806.

Fig. 96 OPPOSITE BELOW
Wellington Bridge, designed by Richard Griffiths and built by the Pain brothers in 1830. (Con Brogan, Dúchas)

Fig. 97 ABOVE
Gaol Bridge, designed by Marc Isambard Brunel and completed in 1835.

Fig. 98 CENTRE
St Patrick's Bridge, designed by Sir John Benson and completed in 1861.

Fig. 99 BELOW
St. Vincent's Bridge, completed in 1878.

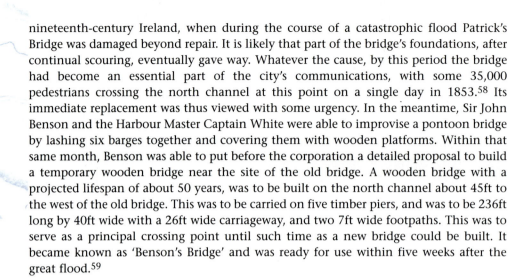

nineteenth-century Ireland, when during the course of a catastrophic flood Patrick's Bridge was damaged beyond repair. It is likely that part of the bridge's foundations, after continual scouring, eventually gave way. Whatever the cause, by this period the bridge had become an essential part of the city's communications, with some 35,000 pedestrians crossing the north channel at this point on a single day in 1853.[58] Its immediate replacement was thus viewed with some urgency. In the meantime, Sir John Benson and the Harbour Master Captain White were able to improvise a pontoon bridge by lashing six barges together and covering them with wooden platforms. Within that same month, Benson was able to put before the corporation a detailed proposal to build a temporary wooden bridge near the site of the old bridge. A wooden bridge with a projected lifespan of about 50 years, was to be built on the north channel about 45ft to the west of the old bridge. This was to be carried on five timber piers, and was to be 236ft long by 40ft wide with a 26ft wide carriageway, and two 7ft wide footpaths. This was to serve as a principal crossing point until such time as a new bridge could be built. It became known as 'Benson's Bridge' and was ready for use within five weeks after the great flood.[59]

It took some five years to decide what type of bridge would replace the old Patrick's Bridge. In 1855 a petition to replace it with a swivel bridge to facilitate navigation to the west of it was put before the corporation,[60] but although the corporation received parliamentary sanction for the replacement of both Patrick's Bridge and North Gate Bridge in 1856,[61] as late as 1858 there were still public meetings as to whether the new bridges should be iron or stone.[62] In the event, Benson was compelled to draw up three designs, for a swivel bridge, an iron bridge and a stone bridge with three arches.[63] The third option was eventually adopted on Benson's recommendation, and early in 1858 the corporation gave notice of its desire to receive tenders for the work involved.[64]

As early as 1857 work had begun on the removal of the old bridge,[65] along with its foundations and all of the debris which had fallen from it during the flood of 1853. Divers were employed to tie lifting chains around the larger stones on the river bed, which were removed downstream to the New Wall for re-dressing, and ultimately for reuse in the new bridge where possible. The river dredgers acquired by the Harbour Commissioners in the 1850s (see below) were used to excavate the foundations of the new bridge. [66] Upon its completion in 1861 Patrick's Bridge (Fig. 98) had three semi-elliptical arches, with a centre span of 60ft and two side arches with 54ft spans, with an ascent of 1:50, compared to 1:20 for the bridge it replaced. As originally built, its 40ft wide carriageway was surfaced with welsh block-paving, whilst the flagging on its footpath was chiselled granite from Deegan's Quarry at Bagnelstown, County Carlow.[67]

In 1831 the corporation widened and repaired the North Gate Bridge and provided it with cast-iron footpaths (Lewis 1837, vol. 1, 410). As has been seen above, the Cork Bridge and Waterworks Act of 1856 enabled the corporation to proceed with its replacement. In 1858 a temporary wooden bridge was fabricated in a yard in White Street, and later was assembled on a harbour barge positioned on the north channel. The barge was then manoeuvred into position in a half-hour operation directed by Sir John Benson, the extremities of the bridge coming to rest on the opposing banks as the level of the tide fell; the barge being floated away once the bridge was in position. The temporary bridge performed two necessary tasks, to allow continued access from North Main Street to Shandon Street and to carry water and gas services (O'Sullivan 1975a). As late as September 1862 there were still doubts as to whether an iron or a stone bridge should replace the existing early eighteenth-century bridge, but by the end of the month the corporation eventually opted for a cast-iron design.[68]

The bridge, which was fabricated by the Liverpool firm of Rankin and Company and designed by John Benson, called for a cast-iron arch 106ft in the clear. The arch consisted of eight cast-iron ribs, each fabricated in six sections 2ft 6in deep and 2in thick. Work on the bridge abutments commenced in April 1863, and by the following November five of the cast-iron arch ribs had been put in place by Rankin and Co. The roadway was carried upon cast-iron plates. The plates were, in turn, covered by asphalt and surfaced with concrete. Benson provided the new bridge with a incline of 1:20 (the old bridge had an incline of 1:7) and a roadway 24ft wide with two 8ft wide footpaths. The new bridge, which was built over an 11-month period under the supervision of Jerome J. Collins, was opened on St Patrick's Day 1864.[69] It was replaced by the present Griffith's Bridge in 1961.

In May 1859 a new timber footbridge connecting Patrick's Quay to Merchants Quay was nearing completion. Upon the completion of the new Patrick's Bridge, the timber footbridge was to be removed to the bottom of Wise's Hill to connect Sunday's Well with Grenville Place.[70] This was duly carried out in 1862, where the bridge remained in commission up until its replacement by St Vincent's Bridge in 1878.[71] St Vincent's Bridge (**581**), provision for which was made under the Cork Improvements Act of 1875,[72] is a steel lattice girder structure supported on two pairs of cylindrical, concrete-filled caissons, each reinforced with steel scissor braces (Fig. 99). Its decking consists of bolted steel plates covered with concrete, which originally may have been set on a asphalt base.

Under the Cork Improvements Act of 1875, Cork Corporation received parliamentary sanction to replace Anglesea Bridge, built in the early 1830s (see above) which, by the early 1870s, was likely to prove inadequate to the task of carrying a substantially increased volume of traffic. The bridge had 'recently exhibited indications of subsiding and becoming insecure, and was now also insufficient for traffic, which had greatly increased'.[73] The two railway termini alone on the south bank of the Lee (see below) carried almost three quarters of a million passengers à year, and the old Anglesea Bridge provided the only direct access to the city centre for passengers on the Cork Blackrock and Passage Railway, the Cork Bandon and South Coast Railway and the Cork Macroom Direct Railway. The corporation, under the terms of the new Act, was empowered to borrow some £25,000 with which to provide a temporary bridge whilst the proposed new bridge, projected cost £20,000, was under construction (O'Callaghan 1991, 48). In 1876 the corporation sought tenders for the bridge's design,[74] but by February of the following the year the question of whether the new structure was to be either a swing or a drawbridge had still not been decided upon.[75] A design for a swing bridge by a London engineer, T. Claxton Fiddler, was eventually chosen in 1877, with Claxton Fiddler being appointed as engineer in charge in March 1879 (O'Sullivan 1975b).

By September 1879 the temporary wooden bridge situated about 120ft to the west of Anglesea Bridge had been completed but work on the new, permanent bridge proceeded much less expeditiously. The contractor Alexander Rooney experienced serious delays in the delivery of the bridge's iron components, the manufacture of which had been sub-contracted to an English firm, the Stockton Forge Company (ibid.). Under the terms of the 1875 enabling act the corporation had until the beginning of August 1881 to complete the construction of the new bridge and in order to meet this deadline they decided to withdraw the contract from Rooney.[76] Shortly after Rooney's removal in February 1881 a new contractor, John Delaney, had begun work on the excavation of the cylinders under the bridge's north abutment, with his men working under electric lights powered by a portable generator, in order to complete the work by August 1st.[77] Delaney,

Fig. 100

The Navigation Wall, shown as 'New Wall',
centre of map (Beauford's map of Cork, 1801).

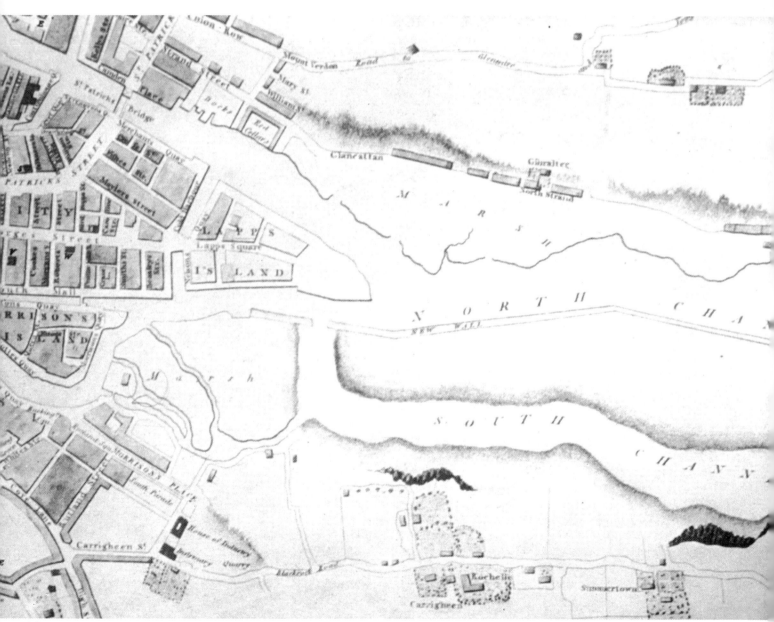

196

however, experienced similar difficulties with the Stockton Forge Company and the corporation found itself forced to acquire a further act of parliament which made provision for additional time to complete the bridge.[78] By June of 1881 the corporation was preparing to remove the temporary bridge[79] but by early November 1882 the opening of the bridge was delayed owing to a legal dispute between the Harbour Commissioners and the corporation.[80] The bridge was finally opened on November 11th 1882, the final cost amounting to £28,000, well in excess of the £16,350 which had originally been budgeted.[81]

THE PHYSICAL DEVELOPMENT OF THE UPPER HARBOUR

The many natural advantages that Cork harbour offered to international shipping from the earliest times, were largely confined to its lower regions for the greater part of the eighteenth and nineteenth centuries. The location of the city and the approaches to it along the river from Passage were entirely unsuited to the types of overseas vessels in use during the eighteenth century, whilst from the second half of the eighteenth century up until the second half of the nineteenth century berthing facilities for overseas vessels at the city's quaysides were entirely inadequate. The main channel of the river Lee from Passage to the city was only 3ft deep in many places, and vessels of over 80 tons could only reach the city quays safely on the spring tides. In consequence, as late as the early 1870s large vessels were obliged to tranship at least part of their cargoes to lighters at Passage West. Another remarkable feature, given the size and relative importance of the port of Cork, is that it was never provided with basins or enclosed docks, which would enable larger vessels to unload irrespective of the tides. In the 1870s the problem was partially solved by the provision of deep water berths, and subsequently by extending the available wharfage downstream. In most other Irish ports, however, enclosed docks had been constructed by the second half of the nineteenth century (Marmion 1855).

The first real attempts to improve the upper harbour for shipping before the establishment of the Harbour Commissioners in 1813, were made in the 1760s, when work began on the construction of a 'navigation' or 'tracking' wall. The north and south channels of the river Lee currently converge to the east of Custom House Quay, but in the eighteenth century the south channel at this point was separated from the north channel by a large marsh. The 'Navigation Wall', as it became known, was intended to regularise the current in the north channel of the river by directing the flow of the south channel into it at a point nearer to the city quays, and to enable ships facing contrary winds to be pulled by horses up to the city quays (Coakley 1919, 84; O'Sullivan 1937, 209). As late as 1800, a gap was left in the wall at its western extremity to enable smaller vessels access to the original course of the south channel (Fig. 100) a feature no longer in existence in 1832.[82]

A parliamentary committee report of 1769 indicates that the improvements made in the early 1760s enabled vessels of between 300 and 350 tons to reach the city quaysides on the spring tides, and that it was now possible for vessels of 100 tons to do so at all times (O'Sullivan 1837, 210; McCarthy 1949, 18). By this period the Navigation Wall extended over 800 yards eastwards, and the committee recommended that it be extended further for a distance of 1,160 yards to 'Lotagh Beg', and that a long section of the main channel be deepened. Further grants were made available in the period 1773–84 to enable these works to be completed, and a report of 1783 suggests that by this period some 1,529 yards of tracking wall (the 'New Wall') had been completed (McCarthy 1949, 19). However, in the period between 1794 and the establishment of the Harbour

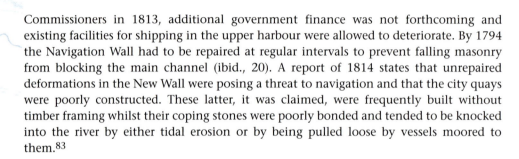

Commissioners in 1813, additional government finance was not forthcoming and existing facilities for shipping in the upper harbour were allowed to deteriorate. By 1794 the Navigation Wall had to be repaired at regular intervals to prevent falling masonry from blocking the main channel (ibid., 20). A report of 1814 states that unrepaired deformations in the New Wall were posing a threat to navigation and that the city quays were poorly constructed. These latter, it was claimed, were frequently built without timber framing whilst their coping stones were poorly bonded and tended to be knocked into the river by either tidal erosion or by being pulled loose by vessels moored to them.[83]

In 1815 the Scottish engineer, Alexander Nimmo (1783–1832),[84] reported that the city's rubblestone quays were poorly founded, being constructed on the strand at high water level, and that no ship drawing more than 15ft of water could safely sail upstream beyond Passage (McCarthy 1949, 18). Nimmo also expressed doubts about the benefits of the Navigation Wall, a view which later commentators (see below) also shared (ibid., 38).[85] Before 1813 the city's quaysides appear to have been developed piecemeal, with individuals being allowed to enlarge them at their own expense after obtaining liberty to do so from the corporation. In September 1753, for example, Horatio Townsend and John Hughes were allowed to add to the Coal Quay near their houses, whilst in January 1754 a certain widow Gossart, her sons and a Mrs Francis Carleton were given liberty to enlarge the quayside near their house 'by taking in some ground from the channel leading to Daunt's Bridge' (Caulfield 1876, 674, 677). The corporation also appears to have taken responsibility for the repair and enlargement of sections of the city's quaysides as was the case with Batchelor's Quay in 1767 (ibid., 818). Indeed, alterations to the city's quays appears also to have been carried out by Grand Jury presentment. At the Spring Assizes of 1793, for example, presentments were made for repairs to Sullivan's Quay, for 39,060 cu ft of material for the filling in of the Potato Quay and for repairs to the quay wall at Strand Road.[86] In March 1815, a presentment of £11 11s was passed for the infilling and levelling of Warren's Quay (or Lapp's Island Dock, latterly Parnell Place) with 231 yards of 'earth and rubbish' at 1s a yard (ibid., 248). Many Cork quaysides bear the names of the merchants responsible for their development, e.g. Penrose Quay, originally built between 1800 and 1808 (Read 1980, 91–2), Lapp's Quay named after John Lapp and Anderson's Quay named after the Scottish magnate John Anderson.

The newly established Harbour Commissioners also considered the maintenance and repair of the city's quay walls to be within its remit, and in the period 1820–33 it undertook a large-scale programme of quay repairs. During this period repairs were undertaken on Charlotte Quay, Morrison's Island, Camden Quay, French's Quay, Grenville Quay and Merchants Quay. In addition up to 50ft of George's Quay was embanked and repaired, whilst a new quay wall constructed on the north side of Lapp's Island was extended by 370ft. Furthermore, a series of buoys and beacons were positioned in the main channel (McCarthy 1949, 45–7). According to Lewis (1837, vol. 1, 415) the Harbour Commissioners spent some £34,389 from Harbour dues on the development of new city quays between 1827 and 1834.

The shoals in the main channel, however, which prevented larger ships from proceeding beyond Horsehead, proved to be a much more serious problem for the Harbour Commissioners than the repair of the quay walls. As late as 1820 navigation between the Powder Quay near Blackrock and Queen's Quay proved difficult even for steamers (McCarthy 1949, 50). The only practical solution, and one which the Commissioners wholeheartedly adopted when finance was available, was to dredge the main channel, but despite their best efforts dredging operations proceeded slowly. Although the dredging of the channel began in earnest in 1822 it was still not safe for larger vessels to proceed to the city quaysides until 1874 (see below). Manual dredging by private contract commenced in 1822 on the shoal near Tivoli and in 1826 the Commissioners purchased a 12hp dredger, which was followed by a second, 20hp dredger in 1839 at a cost of £1,850 (Marmion 1855, 528; O'Mahony 1986a, 12). By 1837 the New Wall had been extended for a distance of some 3,000ft by which time it was possible for vessels drawing up to 16ft of water to proceed directly to the city quays on the high spring tides (McCarthy 1949, 48). Dredging operations continued apace and by 1843 vessels drawing up to 18ft could now reach Cork on the spring tides.[87] As early as 1830 a telegraph system, which employed signal stations at Roche's Point and Blackrock Castle, enabled the arrival of ships in the lower harbour to be signalled to Cork.[88]

Despite these improvements the condition of the upper harbour was still in a sorry state, being entirely inadequate for the principal types of ocean-going vessel then in use. The Tidal Harbours Commissioners' Report of March 30th 1846 stated that:

> Complaints are made that banks at the foot of the quays cause great risk to the fine steamers which ply between the City and Cove; that seven weirs cross the River Lee within one and a half miles of Cork, and impede the upward flow of the tide; that a wall [i.e. the Navigation Wall] has been built for 1,500 yards in a doubtful direction, to guide the set of the current, and is now left in an unfinished state; that the silt dredged up from the channel is laid at the back of this wall and washed down again into the river by every high tide. (Coakley 1919, 84)

According to an Admiralty inquiry into Cork docks and harbour improvements in 1850 there were 26,359ft of quay walls at Cork, of which some 5,047ft were on the north channel and 6,370ft on the south. The latter had cut limestone foundations which were set 2–4ft below the low water of the ordinary spring tides. By this period the Navigation Wall was 7,000ft long, with cut stone foundations laid 2ft below the low water level of the ordinary spring tides, 3,300ft of which was built with dry rubblestone (McCarthy 1949, 49–50). In the period 1813–50 the Harbour Commissioners had spent £23,000 on dredging operations and £250,000 on improvements to the city's quaysides, some 10,800ft of which had been built with cut limestone to the east of the city's bridges since 1821.[89]

The lack of proper deep water berths at Cork added substantially to the cost of importing goods into the city. In 1849 the sixty-seven ships which were obliged to tranship their cargoes at Passage, incurred extra costs totalling £2,274, which in most cases averaged around two guineas per lighter-load carried from Passage to the city (McCarthy 1949, 55; O'Mahony 1986a, 21). Indeed, where ship's masters where concerned this situation was generally not simply a matter of choice, for in many cases even those who may not have baulked at bringing heavily laden vessels up to Cork were often contractually bound to discharge all or at least part of their cargoes in deep water. In the event, most captains did not relish the prospect of letting their vessels lie aground at the city quaysides (O'Mahony 1986a, 21). However, while the Great Southern and Western Railway Company was to obtain government sanction to construct a floating dock on a four-acre site at Penrose's Quay in 1850, the Harbour Commissioners' attempts to acquire parliamentary approval for their proposed improvements to Cork berthage facilities did not bear any fruit until the 1870s.

In the early 1850s the 'Lee' dredger which was specially designed for work on the river

Lee by Robert Lecky's Cork shipyard, at a cost of £5,600, began work on the channel between Blackrock and the city, the aim of which was to produce a 10ft deep channel at low water from Passage to Cork. The dredge stuff was brought ashore behind the Navigation Wall to form what eventually became the Marina embankment (McCarthy 1949, 76). Between 1850 and 1859 buoys and lights were added to the channel, which included new lights at Dunkettle and in Lough Mahon, in addition to that already in place at Blackrock Castle, and for the first time it could be said that the channel was adequately marked (McCarthy 1949, 76; Coakley 1919, 85). The generally poor foundations of the city's quay walls meant that deep dredging in their immediate vicinity could not be undertaken until such time as they were underpinned. Thus in 1855 toe-piling of the city quay walls was commenced to facilitate dredging to a depth of 8ft below the lowest tides. The commissioners acquired a 24 ton, Nasmyth type steam driven pile driver from a Liverpool firm which began work on the Custom House Quay in 1857. The engine, which cost £1,565, developed 16hp and had a 35cwt hammer head, could be moved by means of locomotive wheels. It was used to pile over 8,000ft of the city quays with up to 8,000 piles of memel timber. The individual piles were shoed with iron and were driven to a depth of about 21ft.[90]

A second dredger (no. 2) was acquired in 1857 for work along the city's quaysides, and in 1865 six, 120 ton barges were purchased to remove dredge stuff, most of which was used to fill in slobland near the city (Coakley 1919, 85; McCarthy 1949, 77). The use of hopper barges for dredging on the river Clyde also aroused the interest of the commissioners, who in 1865 sent their mechanical engineer to assess its usefulness for the ongoing dredging operation in the upper harbour.[91] In the hopper float or barge, the barge was equipped with bottom-opening doors. When the vessel had been filled by the dredger, it could be towed out to sea where, by opening the bottom doors, the load could emptied in a location where it could be washed away by tidal currents (Gilligan 1988, 131). The obvious advantages of this system were not lost on the commissioners, and as a direct result of this four steam hopper barges were built by Robinson's shipyard at Cork for dredging operations on the river Lee between 1867 and 1871 (Coakley 1919, 85). By 1865, a channel, 8ft deep at low water, had been dredged, but with the use of two existing dredgers ('Lee' and no. 2) and the four new hopper barges from 1867 onwards, the depth of the cut was increased to 11ft by May 1872 (Coakley 1919, 85; McCarthy 1949, 77–8).

In the 1870s a number of important steps were taken towards the modernisation of the city quays. Hitherto, many seagoing vessels had been unable to discharge afloat at the city quaysides, but in 1874 timber jetties were built at Victoria Quay, whilst dredging to a depth of 20ft near these berths enabled vessels of 18ft draught to be accommodated without resting on the bottom. By 1875 some 1000ft of deep-water berthage was available at Victoria Quay, which was later extended by 100ft (Coakley 1919, 85; McCarthy 1949, 78). The Cork Harbour Act of 1875 had sanctioned the deepening of the berthage at Victoria Quay and a further Act of 1877 allowed work to proceed on the deepening of the berthage on the north bank of the channel. Construction work on a south bank deep-water quay began in 1877 and on a similar facility on the north bank in 1878, both of which were opened for shipping in 1884. The north deep-water quay had a depth of 20ft at low water of the spring tides and extended for a distance of 1,421 yards, whilst the southern deep-water quay was 3ft deeper and was 650ft long (Coakley 1919, 86; McCarthy 1949, 78–9).

Further work on the deepening of the river channel leading to Cork ran concurrently with that concerned with providing deep water berthage. A series of banks in the channel continued to restrict access to the city quaysides at low water, and so work began on facilitating full access to the city for all vessels. In the period 1876–7 the commissioners purchased a Wingate dredger (which was built in Glasgow) and two additional steam hoppers, the total cost of which was £37,460. These latter, along with the 'Lee' dredger and three of the existing hopper barges, commenced work on producing a 14ft deep, 250ft wide channel from Horse Head to Cork, which was completed in 1882.[92] However, the overall cost of these works effectively precluded further large-scale projects until 1894, up until which the commissioners had to confine their efforts to repairing the Marina embankment, rebuilding Charlotte's Quay and the construction of a new wharf at Penrose Quay (McCarthy 1949, 80).

In the first half of 1894 the commissioners contracted out work on the addition over 1,200ft of timber wharfage to St Patrick's Quay and Penrose Quay, which was to have 13ft of water alongside. These works were completed in 1896. In the period after 1903 the extent of the city's deep-water berthage was extended up the quaysides on the north and south channels, and the Custom House Quay was reconstructed to facilitate dredging to a depth of 22ft feet alongside it. In addition greenheart wharves were erected on the north channel as far as Parnell Place, and up as far as the Cork, Bandon and South Coast Railway on the south channel.

In 1895 the commissioners had made the important decision of deepening the channel from Horse Head to Cork to 16ft at low water of the ordinary tides, and to widen the channel in certain areas to 350ft. The following year the contract for providing the dredging plant was awarded to Fleming and Ferguson of Paisley, which consisted of the 'Lough Mahon Dredger' at a cost of £16,550, and two screw steam hopper barges of 1,200 tons. The channel cut by this machinery was designed to improve the channel's natural scour in such a way as to minimise the need for further dredging operations; the necessary works were completed in 1904 (Coakley 1919, 86; McCarthy 1949, 81).

The vast majority of the 9km of stone quay walls on the south channel were erected by the Harbour Commissioners in the early nineteenth century (Fig. 101). The latter are mainly bonded rubble masonry walls, faced with cut limestone blocks around 0.6m thick. As far as can be seen, most of the limestone used in their construction was shipped up river from quarries at Little Island and Rostellan (Lewis 1837, vol. 1, 415). These walls are, in the main, around 5m high and are founded roughly at the low water of the spring tides. As was seen above, toe-piling was added to the base of these walls from 1855 onwards to enable the area alongside them to be deeply dredged. The piles are typically greenheart and occasionally memel pine, cut into 30cm square, 5.5m lengths (Langford and Mulherin 1982, 3). The reconstruction of Charlotte's Quay in the late 1880s (see above) involved the laying of mass concrete foundations behind timber sheet piling, which had a cutstone-faced rubble masonry wall with coping stones laid on top of it. Indeed, the majority of the quay walls built on the north channel in the second half of the nineteenth century were similarly constructed (ibid., 4). The Marina river wall (the former New Wall), by way of contrast, which is over 2.3km long, was built with bonded rubble masonry. The western half of the latter is faced with large rectangular cut stone, whilst the eastern half is faced with smaller randomly sized cut stones. The Navigation Wall averages 4.5m in height and 2m in overall thickness (ibid.).

CORK CITY RAILWAYS

No less than five county-based rail networks and one national rail link had established

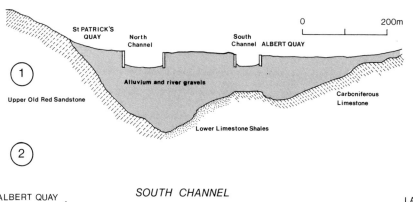

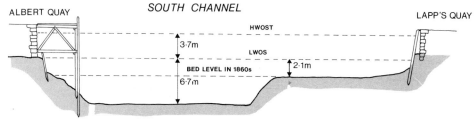

Fig. 101

Sections through city quaysides (after Langford and Mulherin 1982).

Fig. 102 OPPOSITE ABOVE

Standard and Narrow Gauge lines in survey area;

Standard gauge: Great Southern and Western Railway (GS and WR), Cork, Bandon and South Coast Railway (CB and SCR), Cork and Macroom Direct Railway (C and MDR), Cork, Blackrock and Passage Railway (CB and PR) (1850-1900), Cork, Youghal and Queenstown Railway (CY and QR).

Narrow gauge: Cork and Muskerry Light Railway (C and MLR), Cork, Blackrock and Passage Railway (CB and PR) (1900–1932).

Fig. 103 OPPOSITE BELOW

Cork, Blackrock and Passage and Cork, Youghal and Queenstown line routes in Cork Harbour area.

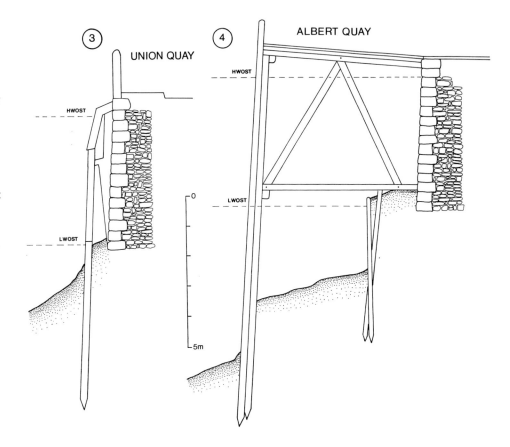

202

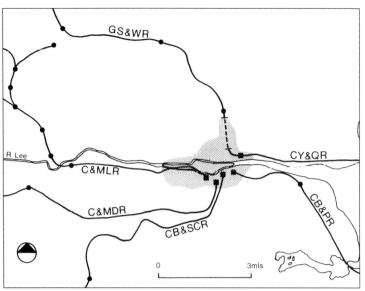

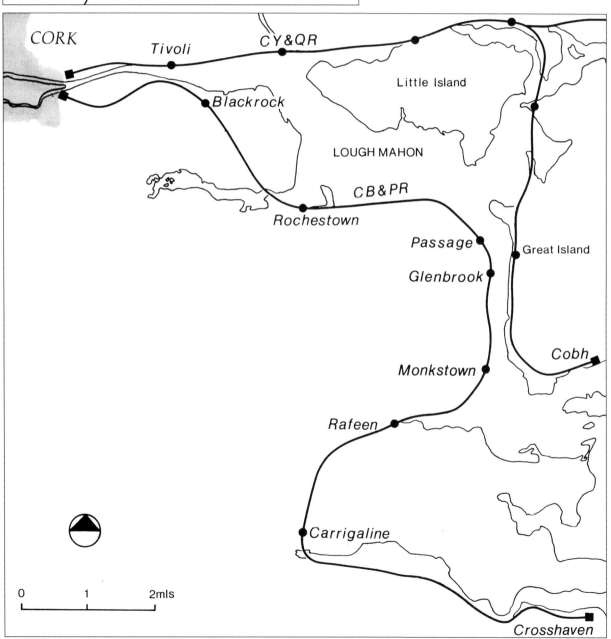

termini within the city of Cork by the end of the nineteenth century (Fig. 102). The national rail link and three of the county lines were built to the Irish standard gauge of 5ft 3in, with two county lines built to the Irish narrow gauge of 3ft[93] one of which had in fact converted from standard to narrow gauge early in the twentieth century (see below).[94] Four of the Cork City railway termini were established to the south of the river Lee, but despite the proximity of some stations it was not until the early twentieth century that any attempt was made to provide a cross-city link between a county line and the national rail network (see below).

Many of the Cork railway companies sought quayside locations for their termini and a few of the early companies, such as the Cork and Bandon, Cork, Blackrock and Passage and Great Southern and Western, built stations with direct access to the city quaysides. However, while Penrose Quay and the Custom House Quay experienced the considerable advantages of feeder lines, the only industrial units within the city to benefit from such a provision were, much later, the Marina mills and the Ford tractor works. Indeed, long-established institutions such as the Cork Cattle and Butter Markets, on the north side of the city, would surely have benefited considerably from direct access to rail heads.

Standard Gauge Lines

The Cork, Blackrock and Passage Railway 1850–1900

By 1836, two years after Ireland's first railway, the Dublin and Kingstown, was officially opened, the route of a proposed railway, linking Cork and Passage (an important outport in Cork's lower harbour) via Lakelands and Ballinure on the Mahon peninsula, had been surveyed. By September of 1836 the engineer of the Dublin and Kingstown line, Charles Vignoles (1793–1874),[95] had already deliberated upon the eventual route, whilst preparatory works had commenced at the Cork end. In 1837 the Passage Railway Bill was steered through parliament, but by the end of 1838 the project had been effectively shelved. However, the scheme was resurrected in various forms in the mid-1840s when no less than three separate railway sanctions were sought for a Cork and Passage railway, two of which eventually amalgamated to form the Cork, Blackrock and Passage Railway Company (CB & PR) in 1846 (O'Mahony 1986a, 76–7). The enabling legislation was passed in 1846 and in September of that year the company's engineer Sir John Macneill (1793–1880)[96] was involved in survey work (ibid., 78).

Patrick Moore[97] of Dublin won the contract for the first six miles of the line between Cork and Horse Head with a tender of £38,000, and work finally began in June 1847 (ibid., 78). Land acquisition along the route proved to be a costly enterprise, as the company hoped to double up the line at a later stage; to this end it was considered expedient to ensure that sufficient land was acquired during the early stages of development to facilitate later expansion. The net result of this was that the total cost of the line was about £21,000 per mile.[98]

A low embankment at the city end of the line, which carried the railway over the Monerea marshes, had almost been completed by May 1847, whilst over 91,000 cubic yards of material removed from a deep cutting at Dundanion had been used to form 350 yards of the Blackrock embankment (O'Mahony 1986a, 79). For the most part the gradients on the line were minimal, the line itself reaching its summit immediately south of Blackrock station where it was 21ft above Cork City. The original standard gauge track had 84lbs per yard cast-iron bridge rails, which were completely replaced with steel rails in 1890 (Creedon 1992, 44). William Dargan (1799–1867), Ireland's most successful nineteenth-century railway contractor, was engaged to complete the final section of the line between Toureen Strand and the steam packet quay at Passage (Jenkins 1993, 10; Creedon 1992, 13). The entire length of track between Cork and Passage (Fig. 103) was in position by April 1850, and within two months the line was opened for passenger traffic (O'Mahony 1986a, 79).

The CB & PR's original city terminus was located at Victoria Road ('City Park' **067.12**) and was a two-storey stone structure, with a three-span corrugated-iron roof made up of a large centre span and two side spans. These latter were supported on cast-iron columns manufactured by the King Street Iron Works (**230**), and covered the station platforms and four tracks — an area 290 x 90ft in extent (Creedon 1985, 15). As early as 1849, before the line had even been completed, the local press was already pointing to the obvious disadvantages of the Victoria Road location, namely that the terminus was half a mile from Patrick Street and, more importantly, that it would interfere with any future dock development in the Monerea Marshes.[99] Indeed, the section of the line near the station occupied a considerable area of river frontage which the Harbour Board and Cork Corporation became increasingly anxious to acquire.

Practical measures addressing the problem of diverting the line away from the riverfront were formally proposed in the *Cork Improvement Act* of 1868 and in a further amending act of 1872 (Creedon 1985, 18; O'Mahony 1986a, 81). The proposal involved a one and a half mile diversion from the metal overbridge on the Marina, which was to lead the line away from the riverfront along the Monerea marshes to a new terminus west of the City Park station at Albert Road.[100] The cost of this diversion was to be borne by Cork Corporation.[101] The necessary works were completed by 1873 when the CB & PR's new Cork terminus at Albert Street (**067.1**), designed by Sir John Benson, was officially opened. A siding was provided for Hall's Mills on Victoria Quay, the general area of which became a large roller milling complex with the construction of Furlong's Marina Mills (**072**) in 1896 (see Ch. 3). The original Victoria Road terminus, after some rebuilding, eventually became part of this complex and was used as a flour mill up until its demolition in the 1930s (Creedon 1985, 19). Both the original turntable and the water tank from Victoria Road were installed in the new terminus at Albert Road (ibid., 18).

During its standard gauge period (i.e. 1849–1900) the CB & PR employed three 2-2-2 [102] well tank engines made by Sharp Brothers of Manchester, which were bought in the period 1849–50 for £1,500 (O'Mahony 1986a, 79).[103] The three engines and some 15 passenger carriages were found to be sufficient for the railway's volume of traffic before the conversion of the line to narrow gauge (see below).

The CB & PR also operated a loss-bearing fleet of river steamers, which it ran in direct competition to the River Steamer Company (RSC), a conflict which affected its early financial development. Beginning with a single river steamer (the *Queenstown*) in 1851, the railway company was operating four steamers by 1854, in the early stages of a battle for passengers with the RSC which only ended by agreement in 1860. The railway company was granted permission to expand its fleet of harbour steamers in 1881, although the company's profits from the river steamers only bore some fruit when the service was extended to Aghada. The steamers departed from Patrick's Bridge to take in a route which included Passage, Glenbrook, Monkstown, Ringaskiddy, Haulbowline, Queenstown and Aghada, or an alternate route which included Spike Island, Curraghbinny and Aghada (O'Mahony 1986a, 80–82; Creedon 1992, 136–7; Jenkins 1993, 20–23, 55).

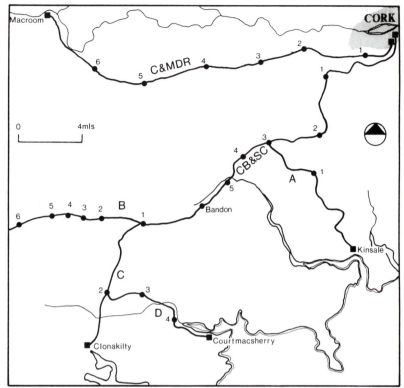

Fig. 104

Cork and Macroom Direct Railway and Cork, Bandon and South Coast Railway routes.

Cork and Macroom Direct Railway:
1 Bishopstown. 2 Ballincollig. 3 Kilumney.
4 Kilcrea. 5 Crookstown Road.
6 Dooniskey.

Cork, Bandon and South Coast Railway:
1 Waterfall. 2 Ballinhassig.
3 Crossbarry (Kinsale Junction). 4 Brinny (Brinny and Upton).
5 Inishannon.

A CB & SCR Kinsale Extension (1863):
1 Ballymartle.

B CB & SCR (West Cork Line):
1 Clonakilty Junction. 2 Desert.
3 Enniskeane.
4 Ballineen and Enniskeane. 5 Ballineen.
6 Manch Platform.

C 2 Ballinascarty.

D Timoleague and Courtmacsherry Extension: 3 Skeaf Bridge.
4 Timoleague.

Fig. 105

Cork, Bandon and South Coast Railway terminus, Albert Quay.

The Cork, Bandon and South Coast Railway, 1849–1961 (Fig. 104)

The idea of a west Cork railway was first proposed by Charles Vignoles in the Railway Commissioners' report of 1837–8, but it was not until 1843 when the County Surveyor for the West Riding, Edmund Leahy, and a local solicitor, J.C. Bernard, began to promote a railway link between Cork and Bandon, that any purposeful steps were made towards achieving this goal. A provisional 'Bandon and Cork Railway' Committee was set up in 1844, which appointed Vignoles as consulting engineer to survey and deliberate upon the route proposed by the acting engineers Edmund Leahy and his father Patrick. The enabling legislation was passed through parliament in July 1845 and by the winter of 1845 work had begun on the Bandon–Ballinhassig section of the line (Shepherd 1984a, 209; Creedon 1986, 5–6). However, in July 1846 the company took the rather drastic step of sacking Edmund Leahy, who had ordered rails which the company deemed unsuitable (Shepherd 1984a, 209–10).

Charles Nixon, who had worked under I.K. Brunel (1806–59), was appointed consulting engineer and was assisted by a young Cork engineer called Joseph Philip Ronayne (1822–76).[104] Nixon decided that the timber members of the planned viaduct at Chetwynd be replaced with cast-iron, and that tunnels should be bored at Gogginshill and Kilpatrick instead of the deep cuttings proposed by his predecessor Leahy (ibid., 210). The line's original twenty mile route had been divided into six lengths, each of which was let out to a number of different contractors. But in 1849 financial difficulties appear to have influenced the company's decision to open the Bandon–Ballinhassig section of the line as soon as it was completed: the first trains ran between Bandon and Ballinhassig in June 1849 (Shepherd 1984a, 210; Creedon 1986, 13).

In September 1849 a tender of £87,000 for the Ballinhassig–Cork section of the line was accepted from the London contractors Sir Charles Fox and John Henderson and Company, on the understanding that it should be completed by the end of 1850. The contract included what was to become for a short period the longest railway tunnel in Ireland at Gogginshill[105] near Ballinhassig, the impressive Chetwynd viaduct, the short tunnel bridge under the Old Blackrock Road (066.3) near the Albert Quay terminus (066.1), and some 21 cuttings, 19 embankments and 15 road bridges (Shepherd 1984a, 210; Creedon 1986, 14). As far as the immediate environs of the city were concerned, the greatest problem encountered by the contractors appears to have been the Ballyphehane embankment. The greater part of the latter, which was 28ft high and described an arc from Ballycurreen to a point immediately south of what was later to become Macroom junction (066.6), traversed the flood plain of the Tramore River. In the early years of the line, the track crossed the Tramore river on a wooden bridge which was eventually replaced by a stone culvert (Creedon 1986, 14).

The immediate south city approach to the terminus at Albert Quay required a relatively deep cutting through limestone bedrock, with the line cutting across no less than three south-eastern approach roads into the city. Wooden overbridges originally spanned the cutting at Evergreen (066.5, South Douglas Road) and Quarry Road (066.4, High Street), which were later rebuilt in stone (ibid., 18). These, together with the short tunnel bridge at the Old Blackrock Road (066.3), were demolished during the construction of the present south city link road. After an unsavoury disagreement involving payment with the contractors Fox, Henderson and Co., which actually led to violence early in August of 1851, the entire stretch of line between Cork and Bandon was opened to the public on the 6th December 1851.[106]

The CB & SCR's Cork terminus at Albert Quay, completed in 1851 (Fig. 105), is the oldest surviving railway terminus in the city. The main station building facing Albert Quay is a two-storey structure built with ashlar limestone, and in its original configuration the station building and the track leading into it formed a figure 'Y'. The station was flanked on the east by an engine shed and by a repair shop on the west, with sidings running off at right angles into the corporation's stone yard and into the Corn Market (ibid., 22). There were three passenger platforms, two of which were 390ft long, and a carriage storage road (Shepherd 1984b, 292). In 1869 a new 170 yard long goods siding was added to Albert Quay, and by 1875 a further siding had been laid for carriage repairs. Further improvements made to the Cork terminus and the line within the immediate environs of the city between 1875 and 1879 included a new goods store at Albert Quay and the replacement of the timber viaducts over the Tramore river and at Frankfield Road with cast-iron and stone structures (Shepherd 1984b, 292; Creedon 1986, 35–9). One of the most curious features about the Albert Quay station is that despite its importance it never had locomotive sheds, the engines either being left under the road bridge built at Hibernian Road (**066.2**) in 1911 to replace a level crossing, or out in the open. Indeed, even the unprepossessing Western Road terminus of the Cork and Muskerry Light Railway was provided with locomotive sheds (see below). In later years feeder lines for the roller milling complex on Victoria Quay and the Ford tractor works on the Marina were provided, while in 1912 the Cork City Railway linked Albert Quay with the Great Southern and Western Railway's Cork terminus at Glanmire Road (see below).

The first locomotives used on the line were two 0-2-2 engines, built by W.B. Adams of the Fairfield Works, Bow, London in 1849, and these originally worked on the Bandon–Ballinhassig section. They were reputedly given the Irish names *Sighe Gaoithe* and *Rith Teineadh*. Both engines were withdrawn in 1867 and were sold the following year (Shepherd 1984b, 290; Creedon 1986, 63). In the period 1849–51 two 2-2-2 tender engines — no. 3 (*Fag an Beallach*), delivered in 1849, and no. 4 (which arrived shortly before the completion of the Ballinhassig–Cork section of the line in 1851) — were supplied by the Vulcan foundry of Newton-le-Willows.[107] Between 1852 and 1894 a further 25 engines were acquired by the company, and some five engines were also acquired second-hand. The latter included two 0-6-0 side tank engines by Sharpe, Stewart and Co. from the Lough Swilly Railway (Creedon 1986, 65–6; Patterson 1988, 144) and three Bury engines from the Great Southern and Western Railway (Creedon 1986, 65). In 1900 the CB & SCR bought two 0-6-2 saddle tanks from the Baldwin Locomotive Co. of Philadelphia: these were the only American-built locomotives to run on an Irish railway (Casserley 1974, 115; Creedon 1989, 137). In all, some 20 of the company's engines became part of the Great Southern Railway's rolling stock after the CB & SCR amalgamated with it in 1925. Only five were still at work in 1950 (Creedon 1989, 141).

Between 1851 and 1893 the mileage of the west Cork line was extended from 20 to 94. Beginning with the Kinsale branch line, which was opened in 1863, the west Cork network was extended to Dunmanway in 1866, to Skibbereen (the Ilen Valley Railway) in 1877, Bantry in 1881, Clonakilty in 1886, Timoleague and Courtmacsherry in 1890 and Bantry Bay in 1892. The last extension of the line was to Baltimore in 1893 (Shepherd 1984a and b; Creedon 1986). In 1888 the nominally independent Cork and Bandon Railway, the Cork and Kinsale Junction Railway and the West Cork Railway became amalgamated as the Cork, Bandon and South Coast Railway (Casserley 1974, 111). The CB & SCR was one of the last city and county lines to close, the last passenger services running in 1961. In 1979 the track bed was widened for the construction of the south city link road which now occupies the line's original route as far as the former Macroom junction in Ballyphehane.

The Great Southern and Western Railway

Construction work on the Great Southern and Western Railway (GS & WR) network, which was to effectively link the capital to the southern provinces, began in 1845. The network eventually covered some 1,500 miles, making the GS & WR, Ireland's largest railway company. In 1846 William Dargan was awarded the contract for the 78 mile Thurles–Cork section of the line, which within three years had reached the northern outskirts of Cork (Murray and McNeill 1976, 17–18). The stretch from Mallow to Cork traversed some quite difficult country which required a series of high embankments, and three impressive stone viaducts over the Blackwater at Mallow, at Monard and at Kilnap near Cork. The Kilnap viaduct (**069.12**) has eight masonry arches, each with a 42½ft span (Fig. 106) (Barry 1985), and carries the line over the deep gorge formerly occupied by Shaw's flour mills. However, the railway's approach to the city quaysides required that a long tunnel be bored through a high sandstone ridge, a feat of engineering to which Dargan and Sir John Macneill proved more than equal, but which was to take almost seven years to complete. Thus, as an interim measure to accommodate Dublin–Cork services, a temporary terminus was erected at Kilbarry (**069.7**) which became known as Blackpool (Murray and McNeill 1976, 18; Creedon 1985, 7).

The Blackpool terminus, a timber structure with a slate roof,[108] was opened in October 1849, but was destroyed in a fire of March 1850. It was rebuilt soon afterwards but this time with a cast-iron roof supported by iron pillars, fabricated at McSwiney's King Street Iron Works (**230**), who also appear to have made the iron underbridge at the old Dublin Road.[109] The temporary terminus had a four track double-ended engine shed, to which a forge, repair shop and a series of further sidings were later added (Creedon 1985, 9).

Meanwhile work proceeded on the tunnel to the terminus at Penrose Quay. Work on this had already begun as early as 1847 on the four ventilation shafts, each of which had two headings. Two shafts were sunk on either side of what is now Assumption Road, one in Barrackton and the southernmost shaft at Bellvue Park (Fig. 107). Macneill and Dargan were assisted by Joseph Ronayne and by William R. le Fanu, le Fanu superintending the work in 1852. The work was slow and not without fatal accidents.[110] By the end of 1848 day and night shifts could only advance some three and half feet per week, and at the southern heading only 70 yards had been bored, whilst the Barrackton shaft (at 207ft the deepest of the four) had only progressed 105ft (McGrath 1955). However, in March 1850 Sir John Macneill could report to the GS & WR board that about one third of the tunnel had been completed, by which stage the viaducts between Mallow and Cork (with the exception of some additional rock cutting at Rathpeacon to enable a second line to be laid) had also been finished. The approaches to the tunnel from the Blackpool terminus were also nearing completion, and the bridges over the Old Dublin Road and Spring Lane were in position.[111] The section of the Strand Road (now the Lower Glanmire Road) also appears to have been curved inwards towards the portal of the railway tunnel to obviate the need for a level crossing (Read 1980, 94). Finally on July 19th 1854 the tunnel headings (which were laid in a straight line) met, forming what was then Ireland's longest railway tunnel which, with the overbridge at the Penrose Quay end, was 1,355 yards long (Creedon 1985, 24).[112] The lattice girder bridge at the southern entrance to the tunnel was built by McSwiney's King Street Iron Works, who also provided the roof girders for the Penrose Quay station goods store (ibid.).

Although the railway tunnel was open in 1855 the passenger building and train shed at Penrose Quay were not completed until July of 1856 (ibid., 27). Penrose Quay station (**069.1**) was Cork's largest and most architecturally elaborate railway station. It was designed by Sir John Benson who provided it with a colonnade of twenty Doric

Fig. 106 ABOVE
Great Southern and Western Railway viaduct at Kilnap in 1849 (contemporary water-colour by R. L. Stopford, courtesy Crawford Art Gallery).

Fig. 107 LEFT
Air shaft of Cork tunnel.

Fig. 108 OPPOSITE ABOVE
Glanmire Road terminus, completed in 1893. (Con Brogan, Dúchas)

Fig. 109 OPPOSITE CENTRE
Goods shed (right), Penrose Quay Station, 1855.

Fig. 110 OPPOSITE BELOW
Engine no. 36. A 2-2-2T engine built by Bury, Curtis and Kennedy of Liverpool in 1847 for GS and WR, on display at Kent Station, Cork.

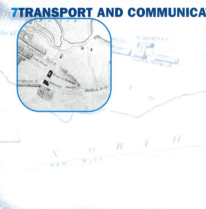

columns which formed a covered way 200ft wide in the centre. The roof over the passenger platform was constructed with cast-iron components, supplied by Robert Mallet's Victoria Foundry in Dublin, and wood with a 62ft clear span.[113] As the site occupied by the station was slob, substantial piling was involved, the foundations consisting of six hundred beech piles over 24ft long, over which concrete was laid.[114] In 1866 the Cork, Youghal and Queenstown Railway, whose trains ran into Summerhill Station, immediately north of Penrose Quay (see below), became part of the GS & WR network. A viaduct was constructed across Hargreave's Quay to the east of the Penrose Quay terminus to facilitate a link line for traffic between the Cork, Youghal and Queenstown Railway (CY & QR) and the GS & WR.[115] In the 1870s a series of further improvements were made to the Penrose Quay station, beginning in 1870 with the construction of a carriage and wagon repair depot. A turntable, originating from the GS & WR main depot at Inchicore, was installed at the northern entrance to the latter, near the entrance to the railway tunnel. The company also sought and obtained parliamentary sanction in 1874 to widen the tunnel mouth at the Penrose Quay entrance to the railway tunnel. In the same period the Lower Glanmire Road viaduct was also widened (ibid., 28).

Towards the end of the nineteenth century it became necessary to replace the original Penrose Quay terminus with a larger station facing the Lower Glanmire Road, which could also accommodate the CY & QR traffic. The slobland adjacent to Penrose Quay was reclaimed by 1890, and building work on the new terminus (Glanmire Road, **069.2**) (Fig. 108) began early in 1891 (ibid., 55).[116] The final cost of the station was £60,000, which included the cost of the new bridge at Water Street,[117] and when it opened in February 1893 CY & QR traffic terminated at the new station, the Summerhill station thenceforth being closed for passenger traffic. Intercommunication between the two main platforms, then as now, was facilitated by a subway, and originally some six platforms were in regular use. The roof of the station's engine shed was acquired second- hand from the Glasgow and South Western Railway in the 1890s (ibid., 55). The original Penrose Quay station was later used as a cattle depot and its doric colonnade was demolished in the period 1895–6 (ibid., 29). A small number of its associated buildings have survived, which include the former station manager's house near Penrose Quay and the shell of the former goods shed adjacent to the Cork tunnel entrance (Fig. 109).

In the foyer of the present Glanmire Road (Kent) station, one of the original 2-2-2T engines (no. 36) made for the GS & WR in 1847 by Bury Curtis and Kennedy of Liverpool, is on open display. It has 6ft driving wheels and an overall weight of 22 tons and 19cwt, and had covered over 350,000 miles when it was withdrawn from service in 1875 (Murray and McNeill 1976, 142; Middlemass 1981, 15). The engine is displayed upon original GS & WR 92lb per yard cast-iron rails (Fig. 110).

The Cork, Youghal and Queenstown Railway

The rail link between Cork and Youghal, which was built between 1854 and 1862 was originally intended to be the southern half of a proposed line between Waterford and Cork.[118] However, while the Cork–Waterford link never materialised, lines between Waterford and Tramore and between Cork and Youghal were eventually completed by independent companies. The Cork–Youghal line received parliamentary sanction in 1854, with approval for a branch line to the important transatlantic port of Queenstown (Cobh) being obtained in 1855. Initially the contract for the first section of the line between Midleton and Dunkettle (Fig. 103) was awarded to Moores of Dublin, who eventually declined and were replaced by R.T. Carlisle of Canterbury. In the event, the railway company, evidently disappointed by the line's slow progress, decided to finish the work itself. Their endeavours were successful and the line was opened between Midleton and Dunkettle in November 1859, three years after work on it had commenced (Murray and McNeill 1976, 37).

Dunkettle is approximately two miles from the Cork and Youghal company's intended terminus at King (MacCurtain) Street, and as a temporary measure Cork-bound passengers continued their journey in horse-drawn omnibuses.[119] In May of 1860 the line was completed to Youghal, whilst at the Cork end the line had been completed as far as Tivoli (**065.13**) in September of the same year. By October of 1860 a temporary line on which wagons were towed by horses had been extended as far as the area above the portal of the GS & WR tunnel. It was not until December 1861 that the first locomotive-driven carriages left Cork for Youghal, from what the Cork and Youghal Company had originally intended to be its goods station at Summerhill (**065.1**).[120] The layout of the Summerhill terminus, which was seriously restricted by its location on a rock-cut ledge above the Lower Glanmire Road, could accommodate only two tracks, and was provided with a simple station house, a goods shed and single passenger and goods platforms (Creedon 1985, 32). Upon leaving Cork the line ran parallel with the Glanmire Road as far as Tivoli where the road crossed over it, with access to a number of the more important residences on the north side of the line being facilitated by three ornate cast-iron footbridges (**065.9**, **065.10**, and **065.11**) supported on substantial brick columns (Fig. 111).

In March 1862 the Queenstown branch line was opened[121] and the railway company should now have been in a position to reap the benefit of the passenger and goods traffic servicing transatlantic liners. It was, instead, dogged by financial troubles which forced its directors to sell the line to the GS & WR in 1865 for £310,000 (Murray and McNeill 1976, 38–9). From 1868 onwards a direct link with the CY & Q line was available via a connection at Grattan Hill Junction, and a lattice girder bridge which spanned the former Hargreave's Quay to enable access into Penrose Quay station from the east. Nonetheless, the first direct passenger trains from Queenstown to Dublin Kingsbridge did not avail of this arrangement, which required new signalling equipment, until 1873, whilst American mail trains did not take the direct route between both stations until 1877 (Creedon 1986, 40).

Prior to its incorporation with the GS & WR network the Cork and Youghal company had operated ten locomotives. All of these had been built by Neilson and Co. of Glasgow between 1859 and 1862. Some twenty wagons and a directors' coach built by Long and Co. of Youghal, and eight coaches by Ashbury's of Manchester, were amongst the final tally of CY & QR rolling stock later acquired by the GS &WR (Murray and McNeill 1976, 40).

Summerhill station was closed to passenger traffic when the Glanmire Road station opened in 1893, and thereafter Youghal and Queenstown-bound trains were run from the platforms at the eastern end of the new station. The present Cork–Cobh line is currently the only suburban line run from the latter-day Kent station. In February 1963 regular passenger services from Cork to Youghal were discontinued, except for excursion services during the holiday season, although up to quite recent times goods trains were operated on a regular basis. However, in 1992 Iarnród Éireann began to remove the rails on certain sections of the Cork–Youghal line.

The Cork and Macroom Direct Railway 1866–1953

The Cork and Macroom Direct Railway Company (C & MDR) was incorporated in 1861,

Fig. 111 LEFT

Cast-iron footbridges on Lower Glanmire Road, Cork, Youghal and Queenstown Railway, completed *c.* 1860.

Fig. 112 BELOW

Capwell terminus of Cork and Macroom Direct Railway, completed in 1879.

Fig. 113 OPPOSITE ABOVE

Cork City Railway Co. route in Cork City.

1 Great Southern and Western line terminus, Glanmire Road (Kent Station). 2 Custom House. 3 Marina Mills. 4 Cork, Bandon and South Coast terminus, Albert Quay. 5 Cork, Blackrock and Passage Railway terminus, Albert Road.

Fig. 114 OPPOSITE BELOW

Clontarf Bridge, opened in 1912.

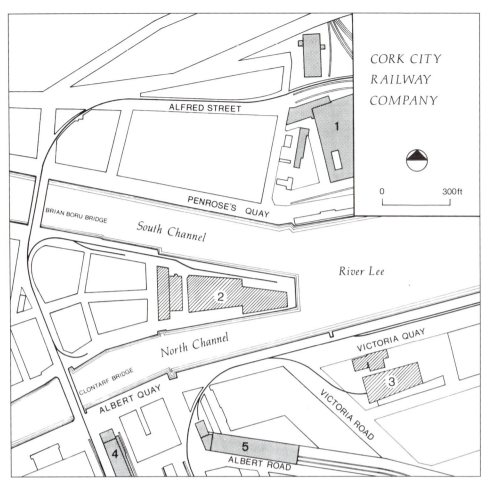

CORK CITY RAILWAY COMPANY

0   300ft

ALFRED STREET

1

PENROSE'S QUAY

BRIAN BORU BRIDGE

South Channel

River Lee

2

North Channel

CLONTARF BRIDGE

ALBERT QUAY

VICTORIA QUAY

3

VICTORIA ROAD

4

5

ALBERT ROAD

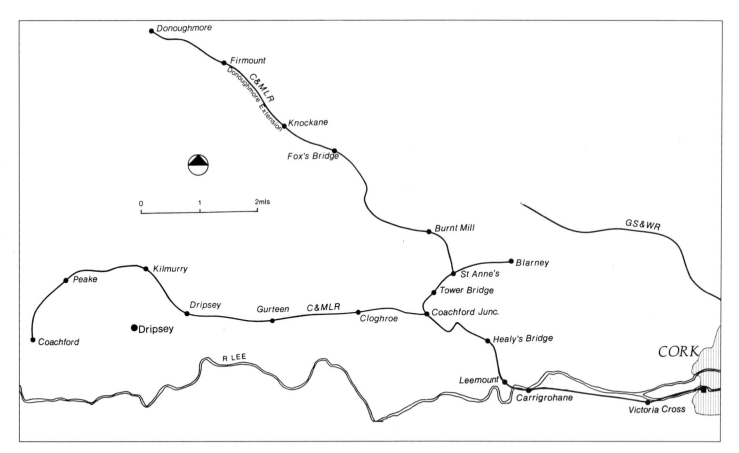

Fig. 115 ABOVE
Cork and Muskerry Light Railway route.

Fig. 116
C & MLR engine on Western Road in the early years of this century (Courtesy *Cork Examiner*).

under the Chairmanship of Sir John Arnott. Joseph Ronayne who, as has already been seen, had acquired vast experience of Cork railways by this period, was awarded the contract for the line, and Sir John Benson, who had proposed a route for the line in 1856, became the line's engineer. The first eight miles of the route, the Cork–Grange division, was purchased in 1863, where a foundation of logs was laid beneath the permanent way traversing a marshy section of land near Wilton (Creedon 1960, 5–7). There were five stations along the line's 24½ mile route, on which the company spent some £6,000 per mile of permanent way (Middlemass 1981, 43).

From the opening of the C & MDR in May 1866 to 1879 the Company's trains ran into Albert Quay station under a working arrangement with the CB & SCR company.[122] However, the leasing arrangements and the CB & SCR company's preferential treatment for its own services were not to the C & MDR company's liking, and in the 1870s the company decided to build its own, independent city terminus. In 1877 the company obtained parliamentary approval for a ¾ mile extension from the Cork–Macroom line's junction with the west Cork line at Ballyphehane to the site of the proposed C & MDR terminus at Capwell (**071.1**, Fig. 112). The new terminus was opened for traffic in September 1879, the cost of the works being upwards of £28,000 (Middlemass 1981, 43; Creedon 1985, 49).

Capwell station had two passenger platforms, an engine shed and a repair depot: a new train shed built on steel pillars with a galvanised roof was erected in 1897. The company, on cost grounds, also chose to use draught horses for shunting wagons and carriages within the station's precincts. In the aftermath of the C & MDR's amalgamation with the GSR in 1925 the Capwell terminus was closed and Macroom-bound trains once again ran from the west Cork line's terminus at Albert Quay. The station buildings were acquired by the Irish Omnibus Company in 1929, and eventually came into the possession of CIE (Córas Iompair Éireann) to be used as a bus depot (Creedon 1985, 49–52). The engine shed and the former engine repair shop were demolished in 1962, although the main brick, two-storey office buildings facing Windmill Road still survive (Fig. 112).

In the period 1866–1925 the C & MDR ran only six locomotives between Cork and Macroom, five of which, along with 27 coaches and 117 wagons, became part of the GSR's rolling stock in 1925. Three of the engines were 2-4-0Ts built by Dubs and Co. of Glasgow, two of which were purchased in 1865 for the opening of the line (Middlemass 1981, 44; Creedon 1960, 20).

The Cork City Railway 1912–76

Throughout the entire nineteenth century the CB & SCR and the C & MDR were the only lines within the environs of the city to have any physical link. As was seen above this link was severed in 1879, but despite the proximity of the Albert Quay and Albert Street stations, it was never possible for a train from Passage to travel as far as Bandon or beyond via a rail link between the CB & PR and the CB & SCR. But most surprisingly of all none of the Cork county lines were connected to the national rail network.

As early as 1888 the Allport Commission recommended a cross-city rail link between the Penrose Quay and Albert Quay stations as a means of increasing market opportunities for produce from west Cork. Yet despite the obvious advantages of creating such a link it did not become a reality until the early twentieth century, and even when it did the emphasis was clearly on goods rather than passenger traffic. The largest single investor in the consortium formed to finance the construction of the rail link was the Great Western Company of England, the other contributors being the CB & SCR and the Cork

Fig. 117 OPPOSITE ABOVE
Albert Street Station, second terminus of Cork, Blackrock and Passage Railway, designed by Sir John Benson and opened in 1873. (Con Brogan, Dúchas)

Fig. 118 OPPOSITE BELOW
Cork, Blackrock and Passage Railway bridges at Dundanion, completed in 1848. (Con Brogan, Dúchas)

Fig. 119 LEFT
Rochestown Viaduct, Cork, Blackrock and Passage Railway.

Fig. 120 BELOW
Cork City tramways (after McGrath 1981).

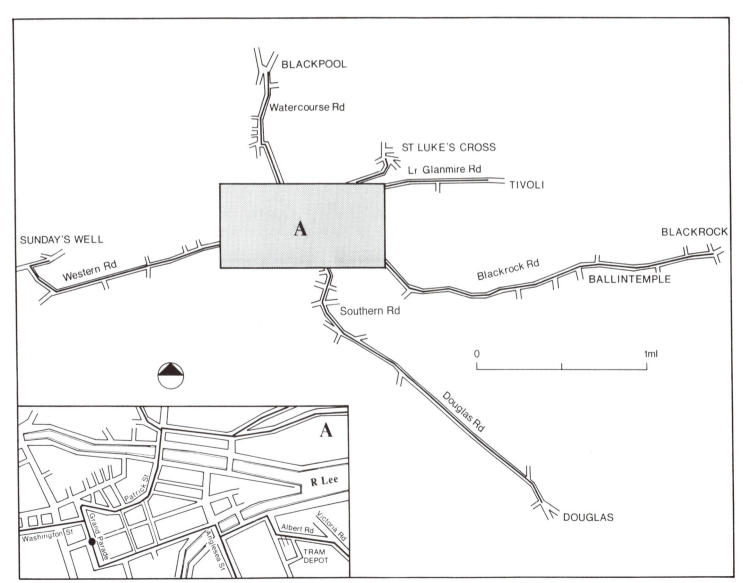

Harbour Commissioners, with the shortfall being met by a government grant (Middlemass 1981, 47).

The main engineering problem facing builders of the three-quarter mile rail link was the provision of movable bridges across the north and south channels of the river Lee (Fig. 113). At an early stage the use of swivel bridges was considered to be too impractical, and instead bridges with central lifting spans operating on the Scherzer 'Rolling Lift Bridge' principle, in which the lifting span was raised by an electrically powered counterbalance, were eventually adopted. The lifting mechanism was first used to effect on the Chicago River Bridge, the Cork bridges Brian Boru (on the north channel, 237ft long) and Clontarf (on the south channel, 197ft long, fig. 114), each with lifting spans of 62ft, being supplied by the Cleveland Bridge and Engineering Company. Work on the lift bridges began in 1909, the lifting spans being built in their upright position. The components of the lifting mechanism, electrically driven by current received from the Albert Road power station (see Ch. 8), was supplied by Crompton and Company of Chelmesford and Stevens and Sons of Glasgow and London. The Clontarf lift bridge could be raised in three and a half minutes. The line was opened on January 1st 1912, and all of the goods traffic was operated by the GS & WR although this declined considerably with the closure of the CB & SCR by CIE in 1961. Both of the lifting bridges were lifted on a regular basis up until the war years, but by 1950 Clontarf bridge was barely used. The last trains to use the cross-city link ran in September 1976 and in 1980 their control cabins and lifting machinery were removed (McGrath 1950, 1976 and 1980; Creedon 1989, 25–6).

Narrow Gauge Lines

The Cork and Muskerry Light Railway 1887–1934

Popularly known as the 'Muskerry Tram', the Cork and Muskerry Light Railway (C & MLR) was the city's first line built to the Irish narrow gauge of 3ft. The creation of this and other cheaply constructed light railways throughout rural Ireland was made possible by the *Tramways and Public Expenses (Ireland) Act* of 1883. The act enabled tramway companies to obtain part or all of the finance to construct a line, the principal beneficiaries in the greater Cork area being the C & MLR and the Schull and Skibbereen line (Prideaux 1981, 6). Tourism provided the impetus for the Cork and Muskerry scheme, the line providing a link between the city and Blarney Castle then, as now, one of the main visitor attractions in the Cork area. Work on the 8½ mile stretch between Cork and Blarney began early in 1887, the contract being awarded to the Irish railway contractor, Robert Worthington (Jenkins 1993, 10–11). The Cork–Blarney section of the line was opened in 1887, with further sections being opened as far as Coachford in the following year and to Donoughmore in 1893 (Fig. 115) (ibid., 14–16).

The Cork terminus of the line was located at Bishop's Marsh, one of the last remaining islands of the River Lee's two main channels, and crossed the south channel via a small bridge leading to Western Road. For its first four miles the line acted to all intents and purposes as a tramway, before continuing across country as a normal railway. The upper face of the line on Western Road was laid flush with the roadway (Fig. 116), and was set some 3ft in from the footpath on the left-hand side, whilst the line itself was single after emerging from the Bishop's Marsh terminus (ibid., 39). From 1898 onwards, the rolling stock of the C & MLR and the electric trams running from the city to Sunday's Well ran side by side on Western Road, a circumstance unique to Cork. The Bishop's Marsh terminus was clearly the most architecturally undistinguished station building within the city. It was provided with a long platform (on the northern side of the line) with a single-storey structure covered by a corrugated iron roof serving as the station building. A further structure was added to eastern end of the platform in the period 1898–9. The corrugated iron engine and carriage sheds spanned three tracks, the locomotive sheds being provided with swing doors, with ridge ventilators and smoke hoods on their roofs. The adjacent water tank was supported on an open timber framework with scissor braces. A turntable was provided at the very end of the line (ibid., 39).

In the period 1887–1934 the C & MLR ran some nine locomotives beginning with three 2-4-0 side-tank engines. The Falcon Engine and Car Company of Loughborough provided two coaches, four 3rd class carriages and twenty-two wagons (ibid., 11). Perrott's Hive Iron Foundry also won an order in 1889 for six, six ton open wagons (ibid., 15), whilst Robert Merrick's foundry on Warren (Parnell) Place also won a contract to renew the C & MLR's engine No. 4, *Blarney*, in the 1890s (ibid., 16). All of the company's engines were four-coupled, and while the company's first three engines were 2-4-0Ts, most of the locomotives which ran on the line were 4-4-0Ts. However, there were also two 0-4-4Ts which were among a small number of engines of this type ever to run on an Irish narrow-gauge line.[123]

The C & MLR, like its counterpart the CB & PR (see below), was amongst the first victims of the motor omnibus in the Cork area. The Southern Motorways omnibus company was operating buses on the Western Road in the 1920s, and by the early 1930s motor vehicles had already taken away most of the passenger traffic. In December 1934 the Great Southern Railway Company closed the line for the last time. Few vestiges of the line survive within the survey area. Indeed, there are no surviving traces of the Bishop's Marsh terminus site (now occupied by Jury's Hotel), whilst only the piers of the bridge spanning the south channel of the Lee to the west of Jury's Hotel survive *in situ*.

The Cork, Blackrock and Passage Railway 1900–1931

Between 1897 and 1900 the Cork, Blackrock and Passage Railway (CB & PR) underwent a remarkable transformation, during which Cork's oldest standard gauge line became Ireland's last narrow gauge line to be constructed.[124] In 1896 an act of Parliament was obtained to extend the line, which the railway company's directors hoped would ultimately extend as far as Crosshaven. John Best of Leith, Scotland was awarded the contract for the regauging of the line, for just over £82,000, and the necessary works began in 1897. The section between Cork and Blackrock was laid as a double track (Fig. 103), which was to remain the only example of double track, narrow gauge line in Ireland. In 1899 four 2-4-2Ts were built for the new narrow gauge line by Nielson, Reid and Company of Glasgow, which ran for the first time out of Albert Street station in October 1900 (Fayle 1970, 106; McGrath 1974, 212; Creedon 1992, 31–3).

The CB & PR was closed in 1932, again because motor transport had seriously eroded its passenger base. The Albert Street Station (Fig. 117) now forms part of the Cork Metal Company's works but is still recognisably a railway station. Industrial development in the City Park area has destroyed nearly all traces of the line but the section between Blackrock and Rochestown, which includes a number of the original nineteenth-century under bridges (Fig. 118), has recently been reused as a pedestrian walkway. The original line crossed the Douglas estuary on a steel viaduct (Fig. 119) which now forms part of the pedestrian walkway between Blackrock and Rochestown.

TRAMWAYS

Horse Tramways

In the early 1860s a horse drawn tramway network for the city of Cork was proposed by George Francis Train, who surveyed a route which was intended to link the existing four railway termini, whilst catering for ordinary passengers travelling within the city en route.[125] However, work on the Cork City horse tramway did not begin until 1871, when a total length of track of just under two miles at the Irish standard gauge of 5ft 3in was laid in the city's streets at a cost of £10,000 (McGrath 1981, 20). The line actually followed the route proposed in the 1860s by Train, but its failure to service the suburbs was to prove to be its downfall. The new line opened in September 1872, operating with six tramcars built by Starbuck and Company of Birkenhead, each of which was drawn by two horses (ibid., 20–21). That same year horse trams were also in service in both Dublin and Belfast (Kilroy 1996). In the event, the horse tram network in Cork did not survive beyond its first three years of operation, and proved to be costly failure. By 1876 the trackway was in the process of being torn up by Cork Corporation.

Electric Tramways 1898–1931

The network of electric tramways which operated within the city and its main suburbs in the period 1898–1931, was the product of an arrangement made between Cork Corporation and the Cork Electric Lighting and Tramway Company. Under this arrangement the company not only operated a network of electric tramways within the city, but also provided electricity from its own independently run electricity generating station for public lighting and domestic use. The tramway company (which had close links to the British Thomson-Houston Company), ran three cross-city routes: Blackpool–Douglas, Summerhill–Sunday's Well and Tivoli–Blackrock, a total length of just under ten miles (Fig. 120) (McGrath 1981, 29–31). The permanent way was laid at a gauge of 2ft 11½ in, an interesting compromise which allowed the flanged wheels of conventional narrow gauge rolling stock to run on tram rails, although none of the narrow gauge lines operating out of the city are known to have availed of this facility (ibid., 39–40).[126]

Between 1898 and 1931 the tramway company operated some thirty-five tramcars from its depot adjoining the Albert Road electricity-generating station, all of which were manufactured by the Brush Electrical Company of Loughborough, each equipped with two British Thomson Houston 27hp electric motors. The eventual demise of the tramway system in Cork was brought about three main factors: the rise of motor transport, the nationalisation of the electricity supply in the Irish Free State and the humble bicycle. The Cork trams were badly hit by the growth of motor omnibus services within the Cork area[127] and, like the local narrow gauge railways, did not survive beyond the 1930s (ibid., 99). Both the original tramway depot and the electricity-generating station still survive on Albert Road, the depot retaining the only surviving sections of the tram line. The Albert Road power station now houses the Cork Sculpture Factory.

8 UTILITY INDUSTRIES

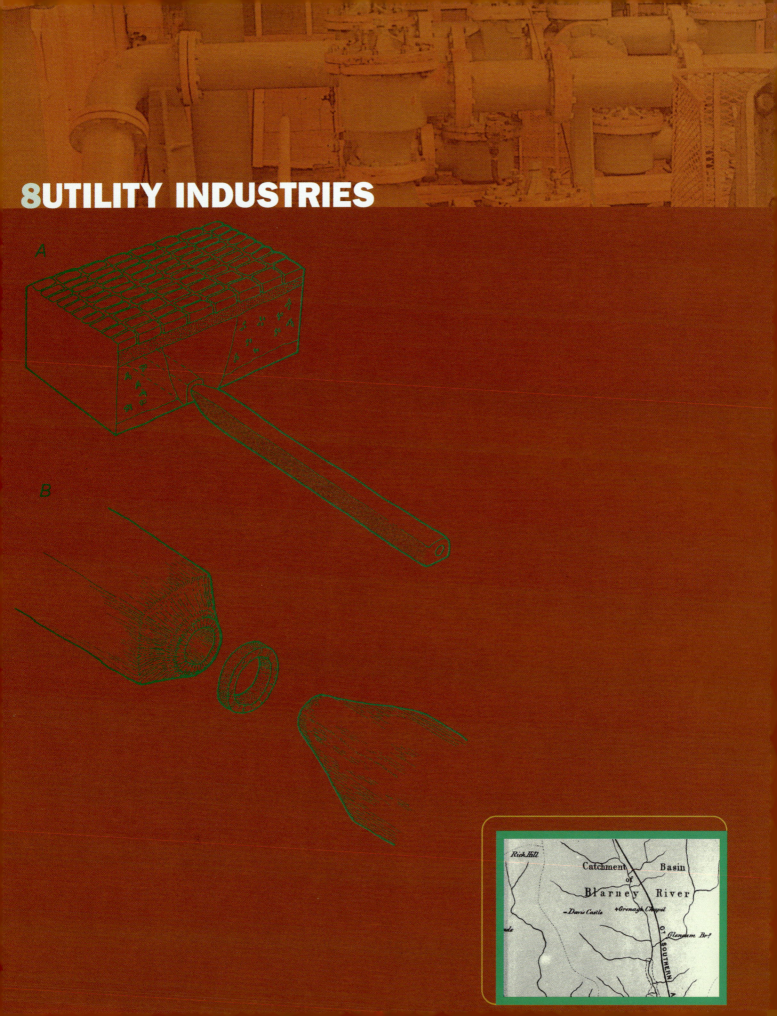

A

B

Catchment Basin
of
Blarney River

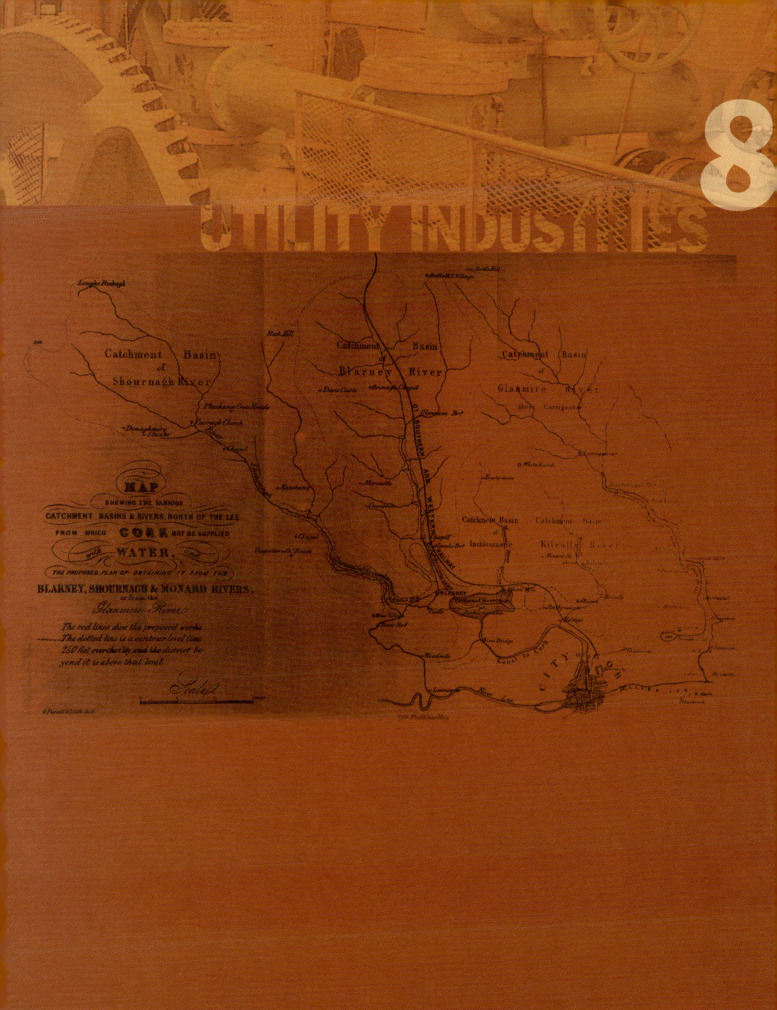

MAP

SHEWING THE VARIOUS

CATCHMENT BASINS & RIVERS, NORTH OF THE LEE

FROM WHICH CORK MAY BE SUPPLIED

with WATER, and

THE PROPOSED PLAN OF OBTAINING IT FROM THE

BLARNEY, SHOURNAGH & MONARD RIVERS,

or from the

Glanmire River

The red lines shew the proposed works.
The dotted line is a contour level line
250 feet over the City, and the district beyond it is above that level

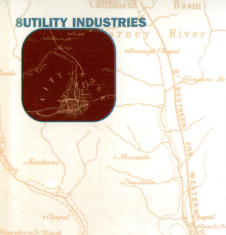

Utility industries provided important services such as water and later, gas and electricity, directly to the consumer. The directness of this consumer-producer relationship required intricate planning. Networks of piping or cable, storage reservoirs and transformer stations had to be established throughout the city. Furthermore, more than most other industries, those providing important public utilities were obliged to keep pace with technological change as their customer base continually increased. The networks required for their operation also had to cater for daily peaks in demand, and as long-term demand for water, gas and electricity could nearly always be expected to increase (both for industrial and domestic customers) susbtantial investment in expanding capacity was essential.

The provision of a regular water supply for the city, from the middle of the nineteenth century onwards, required an enormous capital outlay, most of which came directly in the form of loans to Cork Corporation from Westminster. The cost of maintaining and continually expanding the city's water supply was a formidable burden for the city authorities. Gas and electricity supply, on the other hand, remained largely in private hands during the early stages of their development. Nonetheless, privately owned public utilities were also obliged to expand their services as demand increased.

WATER SUPPLY: THE DEVELOPMENT OF CORK CORPORATION WATERWORKS

The earliest attempts to regularise the city's water supply were made in the fourteenth century, when a charter of 1303 effectively renewed a murage grant of 1294, the purpose of which was to both maintain the city walls and provide the city with water (O'Sullivan 1937, 43). Little is known about subsequent efforts to establish a municipal water supply up until the second half of the eighteenth century, but it is likely that for most purposes the consistency of supply appears to have been a matter of individual initiative. Until the development of more sophisticated distribution networks water-supply networks operated with wooden water mains serving cisterns and public fountains. The eighteenth-century water supply of Cork was operated on similar lines, but artesian wells sunk within the precincts of the walled city required no great depth, owing to the low-lying situation of the city and the relatively high level of the water table. It seems likely, however, that owing to their relatively shallow depth many of these wells would have been prone to pollution. In certain quarters their utility was preferred to that of piped water, particularly for those whose water requirements were modest, or who were unable or disinclined to pay for piped water. Indeed, it is doubtful if the eighteenth-century piped water supply could meet the existing demand, particularly during the summer months when the level of the river would have disabled the water-powered pumps at the city's waterworks.

The Early Waterworks *c.* 1762–1863

Two eighteenth-century, stone-lined wells have recently been investigated at Grattan Street[1] and near Smith Street (Cleary 1985), the former sited within the precincts of the walled city. Either of these could conceivably post-date the establishment of the Pipe Water Company in 1762 (see below), and similar wells are likely to have been situated throughout the low-lying areas of the city. The well adjacent to Smith Street is of especial interest because it is depicted on John Rocque's map of 1773, and because the remains of a two- or possibly three-piece wooden double acting pump were recovered from the site. The lower pump block was 2.7m long and had a 0.13m bore which was plugged at its lower extremity, whilst some 20cm from the base four water intake holes had been executed (ibid., 122). The upper cylinder, which could have been an intermediate pump block or a piston chamber, was connected to the lower block by means of a crude spigot joint, which was reinforced with a wrought iron collar. Its mode of manufacture is similar to those which have survived up to recent times, although the variety of wood preferred for these was larch (O'Sullivan 1969) — the Smith Street pump blocks were of elm. Both varieties of wood were extremely resistant to rot, but as we shall see below larch was the variety used for the city's early water mains. The pump mechanism of the Smith Street example is also similar to more recent examples, in which the water was raised upwards through the piston chamber, to be ejected through a spout at right-angles to the pump lever (ibid.). Some 25 pumps were erected throughout the city on the orders of the corporation in 1814 (Windele 1843, 106; Cleary 1985, 124), and it is possible that the Smith Street pump may have come into existence at this time. However, 'pump block makers' are listed in the late eighteenth- and early nineteenth-century city trade and street directories, and it is equally possible that their products were bought by private well owners.

By the second half of the eighteenth century the demand for water for both domestic and industrial purposes appears to have increased to the extent that firm action was considered necessary by the civic authorities. In 1761 the common council of Cork was empowered by an Act to provide the means by which the city could be supplied with water.[2] The provisions made in the Act may well have been a proposal, but if it was intended as a remedial measure its enactment was certainly unsuccessful. A further Act of 1762 amended its provisions and empowered the Mayor, Sheriffs and the Communalty of Cork to raise the necessary finance by issuing shares and establishing a Pipe Water Company.[3] Water rates were set at a yearly rate of two guineas per household, while those for industrial enterprises were arranged by agreement (O'Sullivan 1937, 143). By 1762 the architect/engineer Davis Ducart (who is better known for his tub boat canal) had completed a set of plans for the proposed waterworks (Caulfield 1876, 751–2). In 1768, after a period of six years, during which time the Pipe Water Company had presumably raised the necessary cash, a Cork iron founder called Nicholas Fitton was appointed to carry out the installation of the pumping plant (ibid., 827).

The location of the pumping works — well outside the city precincts on the north bank of the northern channel — was probably determined by four factors. The river Lee was the obvious source of supply, but in order to ensure that this was regular and uncontaminated, it was necessary to extract water at a point upstream from the city and beyond the tidal reaches of the river. A second important consideration is likely to have been the siting of storage reservoirs. The eventual choice of the site is likely to have been determined by proximity to an area where such a reservoir could be constructed at an elevation that would enable the water pumped into it to be distributed to all of the areas of the city served by the network. A further contributory factor appears to have been the location of an existing salmon weir owned by the Duke of Devonshire, which could have (and seems likely to have) been readily adapted to meet the water-power requirements of the pumping plant.

The first open reservoir, called the 'city basin' (O'Kelly 1970, 128), was built on the adjacent hillside, at a height of c. 60ft OD, into which untreated river water was pumped. Its capacity is not known, but it appears that one of the expectations of its builders was that it could, to some extent, serve as a settling tank for turbid water. A second reservoir was built alongside this in 1774 (Caulfield 1876, 895), but its lack of elevation restricted the number of areas within the city that could supply, whilst the reservoir itself was only

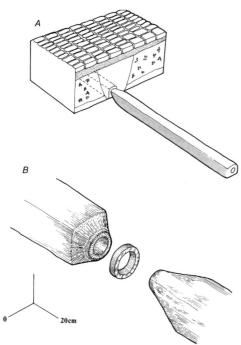

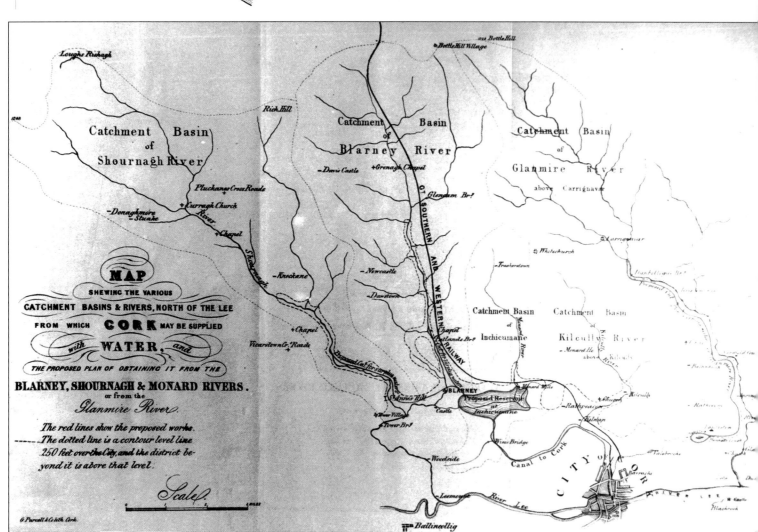

A

B

0   20cm

Fig. 121   LEFT

Eighteenth-century wooden water main,
South Terrace, Cork City.

(a) Water main relative to street level. (b)
Detail of spigot joint and iron collar.

Fig. 122   BELOW

Ronayne's scheme of 1854 for providing
municipal water supply for Cork City.
(Courtesy, Cork City Library)

about 5ft deep.[4] Indeed, as late as 1844 the Pipe Water Company was supplying only 800 of the city's 10,000 households.[5] The present turbine house occupies the site of the original pumping works, the foundation stone of which (bearing the inscription 'Cork Pipe Water Company Established 1768', along with the municipal crest) has been incorporated into this structure. A French visitor to the city in 1790 observed that water was conveyed from the city basin in wooden conduits along the north bank of the river, a service which cost a guinea per year (Ní Chinnéide 1973, 3).

In 1970 an 18m section of the Pipe Water Company's original wooden water mains was exposed during roadworks on South Terrace (O'Kelly 1970). Two complete sections, 5.6 and 5.7m, adze-dressed externally to a roughly square section of 25cm, were investigated *in situ* (ibid., 125–6). The pipe joints were turned and bored into crude spigots, with the tapered extremity of one pipe being forced into the end of another, with wrought iron straps fitted onto the collars to reinforce the joint (Fig. 121). Each of the pipes was of larch, and had been bored from both ends to a thickness of 9cm (ibid., 126). The South Terrace pipes, which exhibited no side tappings, provide a valuable insight into the arrangement of the city water supply, before its re-organisation in the second half of the nineteenth century. The material used in their construction was unsuited to bearing substantial internal pressures, and up until the introduction of cast-iron mains these were generally used to feed cisterns and fountains (ibid., 127). Further examples have also been noted (but not recorded) at Rutland Street and Patrick Street sometime before 1970 (ibid.).

In the early years of the nineteenth century the corporation investigated various schemes for supplying the expanding city with a regular supply of water.[6] However, by the mid-1840s the ability of the Pipe Water Company to supply the expanding needs of the city had become a matter of concern, and the corporation commissioned Thomas Wicksteed, the engineer of the East London waterworks and one of the most important water engineers of his day, to report on the city of Cork's existing services in 1842 and 1843. Wicksteed recommended against bringing water over great distances for the supply of the city, on grounds of the expense involved in acquiring the sites of mills which used the adjacent rivers and streams. He also recommended that the corporation should take over the responsibility of supplying the city from the Pipe Water Company and up-date its existing works.[7] Little appears to have resulted from Wicksteed's report, although the Pipe Water Company, apparently of its own volition, erected a new cut-stone weir across the river Lee near its works in 1844.[8]

In 1845 the idea of tapping the waters of the river Shournagh to the north of the city was resurrected, independently, by William Gillespie, a Cork architect and the Scottish engineer Robert Thom (1774–1847). Gillespie proposed that Thomas Wicksteed's plan be replaced by one in which water from the river Shournagh would be conveyed to the city in an aqueduct, and then directed into reservoirs sited immediately above the city.[9] Thom, on the other hand, proposed that a large reservoir capable of holding a month's supply of water for the city be constructed at Ruby's bridge, and that the river Shournagh be used to fill it. Some 13 miles of aqueduct would be required to convey water from this collecting reservoir to a proposed distributing basin, situated above the existing Pipe Water Company's works.[10] Thom's scheme for supplying Greenock in Scotland with both a town water supply and water power for industry, completed in 1827, was in many ways a pioneering one. He was also an early advocate of maintaining continuous

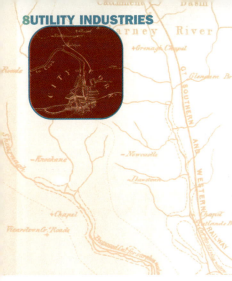

pressure in water mains, in order that fire-fighting services in urban areas be properly supplied by municipal waterworks (Binnie 1981, 9). The principal advantage of Thom's scheme over that proposed by Wicksteed was its cost — £19,000 as opposed to £58,200.[11] Nonetheless, the corporation clearly appears to have favoured Wicksteed's proposal, for in 1846 he was asked by the Pipe Water trustees to prepare plans for the extension of their works, some of which, including the installation of a new waterwheel and pumps were actually carried out.[12] When completed, the modernised Pipe Water Company's works, as proposed by Wicksteed, was to have new settling reservoirs on its riverside from which two waterwheels of 62½hp each and a steam engine of 80–90hp would pump water to distribution reservoirs (Ronayne 1854, 4). Wicksteed's scheme, which also involved the purchase of 75 shares of the Pipe Water Company, was adopted by the corporation.

In 1854, Joseph Ronayne took the extraordinary step of publishing an alternative scheme modelled, it would seem, on that pioneered by Robert Thom at Greenock. Ronayne advocated the use of gathering reservoirs which would provide the city of Cork with both a supply of town water and with an extra source of hydro-power. He proposed that the Blarney, Shournagh and Monard Rivers be collected in a large reservoir constructed in the valley of Inchicumane (Fig. 122), and led from the latter via an open canal into a distribution reservoir in the vicinity of the North Monastery at Blackpool. Ronayne estimated that an additional 3–6,000hp would be available to factories and mills within the city (Ronayne 1854, 13). Sir John Benson, however, while acknowledging the ingenuity of Ronayne's scheme, objected to it on the grounds that as the water would be led from the main collection reservoir in an open canal, it would have to do so slowly so as to avoid the erosion of its sides. This, he argued, would lead to its turbidity and would lessen its utility for human consumption: all further consideration of Ronayne's pioneering scheme disappears from the official sources thereafter.[13]

If the city of Cork was to have a municipal water supply which could adequately provide for the increasing demands of its households and industries, a series of wide-ranging improvements would have to be made. But it was not until 1852, with the Cork City Improvement Act, that the corporation could attempt to do so.[14] In 1854 Benson was instructed by the Pipe Water Company to make a survey of its works.[15] A further Improvement Act of 1856[16] enabled the corporation to purchase the remaining 75 shares in the Pipe Water Company for £13,875 and empowered it to levy a 'Public Water Rate' of 3d in the pound and a 'Domestic Water Rate', which was not to exceed 1s in every pound (Delany 1911, 30). However, the outright purchase of the Pipe Water Company's works brought with it the responsibility of upgrading and expanding its capacity. In 1855 the total daily supply of the city was estimated at 1.72 million gallons (ibid.), which is probably too high, considering that in 1867, the entirely modernised corporation pumping station which, while it had not met all expectations (see below), was pumping slightly more than 1.2 million gallons per day.[17] But even if the demand in 1855 had approached the 1.7 million gallon figure, it is highly unlikely that the plant installed before 1858 could have come anywhere near meeting it. Thus in 1856–7 the corporation obtained the sanction of the Treasury to acquire a loan of £20,000 to upgrade the waterworks (ibid.).

By February of 1857 Benson's plan for the new waterworks, based on Wicksteed's revised plan of 1846, had been submitted to 'several eminent engineers in London',[18] whilst by May of the same year tenders had been issued for the construction of the new waterwork's reservoirs.[19] The corporation used imported cast-iron mains to replace the original wooden pipes, the first of which were shipped to Cork in 1857.[20]   The pipe-laying process was an ongoing one which continued apace throughout 1858 and 1859, with the pipes from the new corporation waterworks finally reaching the military barracks on the Old Youghal Road in February of 1859.[21]   What was to become the low-level reservoir was already under construction. This reservoir covered around one acre and, in accordance with Benson's specifications, was to be 15ft deep and be capable of holding up to four million gallons. A 10ft thick rubble masonry wall divided it into two almost equal sections, which allowed one section to be drained and cleaned when necessary whilst enabling the other section to remain in commission.[22]

By June of 1857, 100 navvies were employed in the excavation of this reservoir, the earth from which was used to form an embankment.[23] Cut stone blocks from Foynes, County Limerick, were used in the construction of the reservoir basin,[24] which was lined with local slob brick and 2–3,000 Belvelly bricks.[25]   The new low-level reservoir had a capacity of 3.5 million gallons, with a top water level of 196ft OD,[26] and supplied the low-lying areas of the city. A second, high-level reservoir, with a capacity of 0.75 million gallons and a top water level of 386ft OD, designed to supply the higher districts of the city, was constructed on the adjacent Prayer Hill in 1860.[27]   The design and execution of these reservoirs, however, was later to be subjected to severe criticism, which was to lead to the eventual censure of John Benson.

A 90hp Cornish beam engine, costing £2,875,[28] was ordered from the MacAdam Brothers' Soho foundry in Belfast, the installation of which began in April 1858,[29] the engine itself entering commission in August of that year.[30]   The Cornish engine was designed to lift two million gallons per day to the lower reservoir, and had three boilers supplied by the Cork Steamship Company's foundry. MacAdam Bros. also supplied two Fourneyron turbines, which were 7½ ft in diameter internally and 10½ ft externally for £2,100. The turbines powered two double-acting pumps with 11in plungers, and operated in conjunction with a 20ft diameter low breastshot waterwheel, which powered three, 12in diameter single acting horizontal pumps.[31] This is the earliest recorded instance of the use of reaction turbines to pump a municipal water supply in either Britain or Ireland, whilst the Cornish engine is also the first example known to have been used in Ireland in association with a municipal water supply.

In September of 1858 the first signs of future operational problems began to emerge when the new Cornish engine was working only intermittently, [32] the engine itself only becoming fully operational again in October of that year.[33]   But far worse, from Benson's point of view, were the reports that the low level reservoir was leaking early in 1860.[34] By the summer of 1860 there was already serious disquiet within the corporation council chamber with regard to the effectiveness of the recently commissioned water pumping station. Thomas Hawksley (1807–93), one of Britain's most respected waterworks engineers, who was by his own account responsible for the design and erection of around 150 waterworks (Binnie 1981, 156), was retained as a consultant by the Pipe Water committee.[35] His initial report to the committee appears to have caused grave concern, mainly because of the extra expense involved in his proposals and in particular his suggestion that a settling reservoir be constructed.[36]   By February of 1861 the Cornish engine was becoming the subject of long deliberations about its performance which, according to contemporary accounts, was not what the corporation had been led to expect. The engine was consuming some 27,300lbs of coal in a 144 hour working week, and had been consuming more than this in 1860.[37]   A lengthy dispute arose between the corporation and the engine's manufacturer, MacAdam Bros. of Belfast, which was only settled in 1862.[38]   In order to assess the mounting criticism of the new

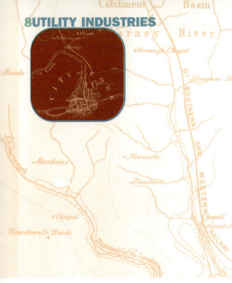

pumping works, the Pipe Water committee commissioned Hawksley to report on the operation of the works in 1861.[39]

The performance and design of the Cornish engine was sharply criticised by Hawksley. 'This engine', he wrote, was 'exceedingly imperfect both in design and workmanship. The action is irregular, noisy and uncomfortable in the extreme, and the wear and tear, as evidenced by the loose and worn condition of the working parts is very great'.[40] He was also generally unimpressed by the design and performance of the water turbines, his only favourable comment being reserved for the breastshot iron waterwheel which, in his opinion, was 'well designed'. Hawksley also pointed out that the leakages in the reservoir were simply a consequence of the failure to use sufficient puddled clay, the most common and practical means of sealing dams, water channels and reservoirs, although he was, nonetheless, reasonably sympathetic to Benson's rationale in not doing so.[41] In a report dated 2 July 1861, William Crowe, a Dublin builder found that puddled clay had been substituted with a paving of brick and concrete. This was only 8in thick in places and on the sloped sides of the reservoir no concrete had been used at all. In his opinion, the absence of a proper foundation for the sloped sides was the principal factor causing leakages.[42] In June of 1861 Benson was called to account for all of the problems, real and imagined, associated with the new waterworks[43] and in July of the same year the council passed a motion for Benson to discontinue all private commissions or to resign from his post as city engineer. Benson agreed to this but did not admit to any acts of negligence on his part,[44] and there can be little doubt that he provided a welcome scapegoat for the Pipe Water Committee.

In retrospect all of the misgivings about the performance of the water turbines and the Cornish engine appear to have been premature. The Cork Corporation waterwork's employment of turbines instead of more traditional waterwheels or steam engines appears to have been viewed with suspicion by Hawksley, and his assessment of their performance relative to other water-powered prime movers would not have been shared by many of his contemporaries. James and Robert MacAdam played an important role in the introduction of Fourneyron-type turbines in Ireland, producing their first turbine to specifications outlined by the Armagh millwright, William Cullen, in 1850 (McCutcheon 1980, 261). Indeed, one of the MacAdam turbines remained in commission until the turn of the twentieth century (see below). The complaints about the Cornish engine also appear not to bear close scrutiny. The 'Cornish cycle' was not dissimilar to Watt's single-acting principle, in which the steam acted on top of the piston, but in Cornish engines the steam was used expansively, which enabled greater economy of running costs (Crowley 1986, 22). The introduction of rotative engines by no means entirely replaced older designs of reciprocating-type beam engine, particularly where water-pumping operations were involved. Thus while the waterworks engine may well have been inefficient, its design would not have been considered inappropriate for its allotted task.

It should be borne in mind that Benson, in installing a Cornish engine in Cork waterworks, was simply acting on the advice of Thomas Wicksteed, one of the most respected engineers of his day. Furthermore, Hawksley's ideas on the ideal mode of town water supply were quite different from those of Thomas Wicksteed, and it is highly likely that Hawksley, who had a formidable reputation as an expert witness (Binnie 1981, 130–36) had little difficulty in convincing the corporation. There also appears to have been little local understanding of Cornish engines and, indeed, only one Cork iron foundry submitted a tender for the waterwork's engine in 1857,[45] and this at a time when a number of Cork City iron works were of national importance (see Ch. 5).

References to Cornish engines in the contemporary Cork press are extremely rare[46] whilst the Cornish engines used in the west Cork copper mines from the 1820s onwards were imported from foundries based in important mining districts in Cornwall and South Wales (Williams 1991). In the event the MacAdams' Cornish engine outlived its harshest critics and continued in use until its replacement in 1906 (see below).

Further Developments 1863–1900

From the early 1860s onwards the corporation's Pipe Water committee (later the waterworks committee) endeavoured, often in the face of contradictory engineering advice and infighting between corporation engineers, to ensure that all measures were taken to cater for the city's increasing demand for water. Sir John Benson was obliged to

	Lower reservoir in million gallons pumped	Upper reservoir in million gallons pumped
Waterpower		
North turbine	180	25
South turbine	240	
Waterwheel	150	42
Steampower		
Rotative engines	460	------
Cornish engine	109	------

Table 4 — Water pumped to upper and lower level reservoirs by Cork Corporation Waterworks in 1867. (Source: Cork Corporation Waterworks Committee Report 1866–7).

give up his private practice and devote his attention to these and other matters. In 1863 two 40hp rotative beam engines by Boulton and Watt were installed to supplement a 35hp breastshot waterwheel, two water turbines (total 110hp) and the 90hp Cornish engine.[47] All of the steam plant pumped water to the lower reservoir, and the waterwheel and turbines pumped to both the latter and the high-level reservoir. [48]

From Table 4 it is clear that a total of 637 million gallons was pumped using water power alone in 1867 and that for the lower reservoir at least this was almost matched by that pumped by the steam-powered plant. As none of the steam plant pumped to the upper reservoir, we must assume that during the summer months when water levels in the river Lee were low, there was still enough to provide a sufficient head for the water-powered plant to pump to the upper reservoir. In 1867 the pumping works raised a total of 1,206 million gallons to the upper and lower reservoirs, all of which was supplied to the city.[49] This figure was in excess of that of 1866, but various contingencies relating to ongoing repairs to the existing plant in 1868, and particularly low water levels in the river, highlighted the need for auxiliary steam plant. The waterworks committee recommended that a new steam engine of 38 nominal horse power be acquired for this purpose in July 1868.[50] The preferred type of engine was to be of the horizontal expansion condensing type, which was 'extensively used in America as an auxiliary to other engines and at the Crystal Palace for all purposes'.[51] By this period horizontal engines, which had the advantage of greater compactness, were already beginning to replace older varieties of beam engine (Hills 1989, 191), and the contract was awarded to Platt & Co. of London who submitted the lowest tender of £2,985.[52] The engine, after some delay in constructing its housing, was installed late in 1869.[53]

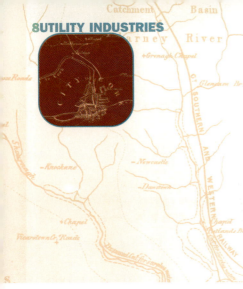

In the 1870s the first measures to filter water drawn from the river and to scientifically monitor the wastage of water were introduced. Two English engineers were invited to advise on the condition of the waterworks: Thomas Hawksley in 1873 and George Stevenson in 1875 (Delaney 1911, 30). As late as 1884, B.A. Burrell, the city analyst, could report that the water of the river Lee above the waterwork's weir was 'a soft water of good quality, and quite free from any sewerage or other injurious matter'.[54] However, when the river was in flood the water tended to become turbid, and in Stevenson's first report of 1876 he recommended that a filter tunnel be constructed at the waterworks (ibid.). This recommendation was duly accepted by the waterworks committee, but its implementation was to become a focus of often bitter acrimony amongst those responsible for the improvement and maintenance of the city's water supply. In his second report of 1878 Stevenson recommended that a system of metering water usage be adopted, in view of the considerable wastage of water in the city (ibid., 31). Acting upon Stevenson's recommendations, and those of the resident engineer at the waterworks, the corporation borrowed almost £29,000 for the proposed improvements under the Public Health Act (ibid.). In March 1879, John Frederick La Trobe Bateman (1810–89), president of the Institution of Civil Engineers, visited the waterworks at the invitation of the corporation.[55] Bateman, like his contemporaries Wicksteed and Hawksley, was one of the most important and influential waterworks engineers of the nineteenth century (Binnie 1981, 157) and in his final report to the corporation he concluded that three million gals per day was 'more than abundant for all the purposes of Cork':[56] clearly the consumption of water within the city was much too high in relation to actual consumer needs, and strong measures were necessary to counteract wastage. However, another of Bateman's recommendations (which had earlier been proposed by Stevenson in October 1876), was that the turbines currently at work 'be replaced by waterwheels of about the same power as that now existing' [57] — a proposal which was ridiculed by the resident waterworks engineer, James O'Toole, in 1880.[58]

The filtration tunnel and pure water basin were the first attempts to supply the city with filtered water, and before their construction water was drawn directly from the river without any treatment. Work on the filter tunnel and pure water basin began in March 1879 and was 'practically completed' by December 1879.[59] This was a circular tunnel which ran parallel to the bank of the river, in which a process termed natural filtration took place. Its first 100 yards had a series of perforated, glazed earthenware pipes 2ft in diameter, carefully buried in a layer of sand. The remaining section of the filtration gallery was constructed with unmortared bricks, around which were laid layers of sand and gravel which served as filters. Every 100 yards the filtration tunnel was intersected by a series of wells 12ft deep and 20ft in diameter, designed to increase water flow and to trap deposits filtered through the tunnel.[60] Filtered water from the tunnel was then directed to the pure water basin, a circular reservoir 45ft in diameter capable of holding 309,176 gallons.[61]

The suction pipes from the various water and steam-powered plant were to draw directly from the pure water basin, and the first attempt to do so by connecting the turbine pumps was made in December 1879.[62] However, the resident engineer reported in January 1880 that the yield from the tunnel and the pure water basin was insufficient for the pumps to be connected to it, and that Stevenson's estimate of the expected yield was erroneous.[63] Stevenson would not accept that there had been 'a mistake about the yield of the tunnel', and so began a protracted argument about the alleged utility of the filter tunnel which occasioned no less than 60 sittings of the waterworks committee (Delaney 1911, 31). The completed work cost over £7,500 [64] and the members of the waterworks committee, angered by its alleged lack of success, decided to commission two independent authorities Mathias O'Keefe, and Prof. Alex Jack of Queen's College Cork, to investigate the yield of the tunnel.[65] Stevenson queried the results of O'Keefe's and Jack's examination of the relevant works in a letter dated 24 January 1880, [66] which brought a further response from O'Keefe and Prof. Jack early in 1881.[67] The most telling pronouncement on the utility of the tunnel, however, had already been made by resident engineer James O'Toole in August 1880. For according to O'Toole, not only was the filter tunnel 'unable to yield the quantity of water required to supply the city' but it was further, in his opinion, 'positively dangerous to work it'. [68] The matter was not finally resolved until 1883 when the filter tunnel was enlarged to supply the needs of the city.[69] A flood in the river early in January of 1884 enabled its yield to be tested, and the pumps of the turbines, the two beam engines and the horizontal engine were connected to the pure water basin. The results of the test confirmed that its yield was in the region of 5 million gals. per day, [70] and that its yield, at least in times of flood, would now be sufficient to supply the city. It was not without satisfaction that the committee could report in April 1885 that the filter tunnel 'which for so long...lay comparatively worthless, is now a practical success'.[71]

In 1884 the waterworks committee decided to install a Green's Patent economiser for four of the existing boilers. Edward Green & Company of Manchester agreed to fit one of their economisers at the pumping station, complete with 128 heating pipes, 'improved scrapers' (which continually cleaned the economiser tubes), and gearing blow-off and safety valves for £235 10s.[72] James O'Toole doubted the maker's claim for a 23% saving — his estimate was 10% , subsequently confirmed as 12% — but even at this the economiser would pay for itself in four years.[73]

The virtual 24-hour operation of the pumping plant occasioned heavy wear and tear, and the increasing costs incurred in overhauling it became prohibitive. In a special report, by James O'Toole, on the remaining working life of the existing machinery read in May 1885, it emerged that the continued use of the various pumping engines would involve a considerable outlay. Furthermore, even if the pumping engines were entirely reconditioned, only the working life of the existing turbines could be extended into the twentieth century.[74] The replacement of the existing plant would have to be undertaken gradually, and it appears that this was a primary consideration for O'Toole when he suggested that two additional turbines be acquired. In April 1886 the committee agreed in principal to adopt O'Toole's revised proposal to replace the existing turbine sets for four new ones, and to increase the head at the weir by raising it by 2–3ft.[75] The breastshot waterwheel retained in John Benson's original plan for the waterworks of the late 1850s, required regular maintenance and the costs incurred in doing so were becoming prohibitive.

From the maintenance accounts recorded in the waterworks committee minute books, it is evident that over £500 had been spent on periodically reconditioning the waterwheel in the period 1867–86. This latter circumstance prompted O'Toole's proposal that it should be replaced by the two new water turbines.[76] However, once the scheme to raise the height of the waterworks weir began to be executed, the committee found itself threatened with legal action by those who felt their traditional water rights were under threat. Cork Distilleries Co. Ltd felt that 'any diminution in the water of the north channel would be a serious loss' in the operation of its North Mall distillery, [77] at which a water-powered malt mill was at work, whilst Edward Hall of St Dominick's Mills on the south channel gave notice that he would hold the corporation liable for any infringement of his water rights.[78]

The city and resident engineers recommended that the arrangement of the new machinery be varied by extending the existing turbine house, and installing two of the new turbines in the new section. The original wheelhouse was to be removed and the other pair of new turbines were to be installed in the north bay of the existing turbine house, with the existing turbines to be left untouched.[79] The new turbines were to be erected in a new, custom-built turbine house which was completed in 1888 (Fig. 123). An order was placed with the American firm of Stout, Mills & Temple of Ohio, who agreed to furnish two of their 60in 'New American Turbines', one right hand and one left hand, for $3,666. The latter were to be tested with a guarantee of 76–78% efficiency.[80] Each turbine was duly tested at the testing flume of the Holyoke Water Power Company between May and June of 1888,[81] at which efficiencies as high as 77.2% were recorded, whilst the combined power of both turbines was 370hp.[82] Additional ironwork for the turbine mountings was supplied by Cork firms. The Vulcan Iron Works provided the girders and slides for the pumps, the Hive Iron Works supplied the larger girders and the gearing, along with pedestals for the thrust bearings of the turbine shafts. Four large pedestals for the main transmission shafts and a series of 24in straight branch and curved pipes were manufactured at the City of Cork Iron Works. Two of the larger girders were believed to be the 'largest castings ever made in Cork'.[83] In April 1889, the waterwheel was about to removed,[84] but in July an offer of £8 for same from a Mr Cornelius Casey of Bandon Road was accepted by the committee.[85] The building stone of its wheelhouse was, in addition, used in the construction of some of the new buildings.[86]

The installation of the new turbines required not only that the existing weir be raised, but also that the bed of the south channel of the Lee be deepened at, and slightly above, George IV Bridge (now O'Neill-Crowley Bridge). The deepening of this channel necessitated the lowering of the bridge's invert arch, a U-shaped masonry channel which had been built into the river bed immediately beneath the central arch to counteract scouring. This was completed in October 1888.[87] The weir itself, which was in need of major repairs after a flood of January 1887, was entirely reconstituted to facilitate the new works. The new weir was 393ft long (110ft longer than the original weir) and had been raised some 14in above the level of its predecessor. Over 2,000 cubic yards of concrete had been used in its construction, and the total cost of its erection was around £1,136. The original angle of the weir was also altered, whilst the headrace channel which led from it was deepened.[88]

The turbines arrived in Cork in 1888 and were at work by February of 1890.[89] At the latter date the new turbines were put to work with six pumps, three each to the high- and low-level reservoirs. Both of the turbines were at work 24 hours a day, and their performance was in O'Toole's opinion 'not only equal to what was expected of them but somewhat better'.[90] The water supply to the city could now be maintained without using the steam plant right up until the summer months, whilst coal consumption in the six months from July to December 1890 was reduced from 1,760 to 770 tons.[91] As has been seen above, the updating of the waterwork's water-powered pumping plant, as suggested by James O'Toole, was to involve the replacement of both the north and south turbines. In January 1895, O'Toole recommended to the committee that the north turbine (installed in 1858, see above), should be replaced by two new ones, the estimated cost of all the works involved being £4,000.[92] The old turbine had at this stage been 36 years at work, and its headage requirements were twice that needed to operate two modern turbines.[93] In April 1895 a tender to supply two 54in 'New American Turbines' for £475 was accepted from W.H. Shaw of Kilnap, a decision which was no doubt influenced by the excellent performance of those installed in 1890 along with the availability of spare parts.[94] However, while the turbines appear to have been delivered before the end of 1895, a series of protracted delays which the city engineer attributed to certain components being 'ordered piecemeal' saw to it that the turbines were not in operation until the end of 1901.[95]

The Early Twentieth Century 1901–28

In a report delayed until 1902 the then city engineer, Henry A. Cutler, informed the waterworks committee of the existing state of the pumping machinery plant. Cutler pointed out that the Cornish engine boilers were 'unfit for further use', and were being 'worked at risk'. As far as Cutler was concerned the matter was so grave that the time had arrived for him to 'report fully on the matter' (Ryan and Davey 1902, 17). Cutler provided tables showing the performance of both the water- and steam-powered plant which, while they provide us with a valuable insight into the capacity of the pumping plant at the turn of the century, could have brought little consolation to the waterworks committee.

By comparing Tables 4 and 5 it will be seen that in the period 1867–1901 the daily requirements of the city had expanded considerably. Yet while new plant had been installed to meet increased demand, increasingly unreliable plant — some of which had been in commission for almost half a century — was likely to cause future problems. Thus in 1902 J.H. Ryan, president of the Institution of Civil Engineers of Ireland, and Henry Davey, a mechanical engineer, were asked by the waterworks committee to conduct an investigation into the condition of the pumping station. One of their primary tasks was to attempt to adjudicate on the radically opposite views of Cutler and O'Toole in regard to the efficiency of the filter tunnel, but they were also instructed to make a full examination of the pumping station itself (Ryan and Davey 1902, 9). O'Toole contended that 'the filter scheme is not able to supply the City in a proper manner' and that unless Cutler's suction pipe arrangement to it were modified the existing plant

	Water pumped to lower reservoir in gals./day	Water pumped to upper reservoir in gals./day
Waterpower		
South turbines	1,123,632	--------
North turbines	1,367,568	578,448
New turbines (est.)	2,736,000	---------
Steampower		
Horizontal engine	1,645,656	529,584
East beam engine	1,332,024	---------
West beam engine	1,332,024	---------
Cornish engine	1,661,472	---------

Table 5—Cork Corporation Waterworks daily pumping capacity in 1901. (Source: Ryan and Davey, 1902).

would be 'seriously injured' (ibid., 11). The filter scheme from Cutler's point of view had 'turned out even more successful than I dared to hope' (ibid., 12). Cutler's account of the success of the scheme was the exact opposite of that put forward by O'Toole, but with it came the clear inference that O'Toole's opposition to it amounted to both disobedience to a superior and worse, professional negligence.[96]

In their final report, which appeared in April 1902, Ryan and Davey could draw no firm conclusions as to the ability of the filter tunnel to supply the city, but they did,

Fig. 123 OPPOSITE ABOVE

Turbine House, Cork Corporation Waterworks. (Con Brogan, Dúchas)

Fig. 124 OPPOSITE CENTRE

General view, Cork Corporation Waterworks.

Fig. 125 OPPOSITE BELOW

Beam engine house, Cork Corporation Waterworks.

Fig. 126 RIGHT

Stack, Cork Corporation Waterworks. (Con Brogan, Dúchas)

nonetheless, effectively vindicate Cutler. In 1900 Cutler had extended the filter tunnel (Delaney 1911, 32), and to improve the draw of the pumps from the pure water basin he arranged for all the suction pipes, led to this from the individual pumping engines, to be connected to a single 24in pipe. When Ryan and Cutler visited the waterworks they found that the turbine pumps, the three throw pumps of the beam engines and the horizontal engine were all arranged in this fashion. The pumps of the Cornish engine drew water directly from the river (Ryan and Davey 1902, 4). In their opinion this arrangement 'as a tentative measure...was justifiable' and in the circumstances 'the only alternative Mr Cutler had at his disposal' (ibid., 7). They also noted, however, that all of the steam plant was 'of an obsolete and antiquated description, and from long wear and tear is in a very bad condition, requiring constant and careful attention to keep it in a working order' (ibid., 5). In concluding their report they further observed that the existing arrangements for supplying the city with water were 'not only unsatisfactory, but critical' (ibid., 7), and thus effectively endorsed the opinion provided by Cutler in the report first presented by him in 1901.

The basic thrust of Cutler's argument was this: as the water-powered plant could not be relied upon to supply the city's needs in the summer months, the maintenance of the supply during this period relied heavily on the operation of the steam plant. The fuel consumption of the latter, however, was far too high. For whereas more modern steam engines required only 1.5–2.5lbs of coal per hour, the waterworks engines needed 5.27–7.2lbs (ibid., 18). Such a low level of performance could no longer be justified, and so Cutler proposed to replace the Cornish engine with three triple expansion engines, and to retain the existing beam engines and the horizontal engine as a stand-by. Two of the new engines were to pump 2 million gals. per day to the low-level reservoir, and the third was to pump 0.5 million gals. per day to the high-level reservoir. The new engines were also to be fitted with Lancashire boilers (equipped with superheaters and economisers) and a new engine house was to be built on the site of the old Cornish engine (ibid., 19). The total cost of works, including the suction and delivery pipes, was estimated at £12,000 (ibid.).

The waterworks committee wasted no time in acting on Cutler's advice, and by September of 1902 it was already receiving tenders for the new pumping engines.[97] A Cork iron founder, Robert Merrick (see Ch. 5), made arrangements with Combe Barbour of Belfast to provide him with the necessary engines which he would install using local labour. Merrick himself had tendered for the manufacture of the engines, and the committee's desire that a local manufacturer receive the commission had initially swung their final decision in his favour. However, Merrick found it expedient for Combe Barbour to build the engines and for his own foundry to produce the iron for the associated works, a proposal which satisfied the aspirations of the corporation. The waterworks committee accepted Merrick's proposal and allowed him to increase his original tender by £500.[98] However, the finance involved in the new scheme was not finally approved until 1903 (Delaney 1911, 32), and it was not until mid-1904 that the two large engines were under construction at Combe Barbour's Belfast works.[99] The engines were completed by 1905 but as late as April 1906 only one of the low-level engines had been installed, whilst that of the second was underway.[100] By August all of the work had almost been completed, yet it was not until February of 1907 that the old plant was finally shut down, and the new steam plant became fully operational.[101]

Early in the twentieth century demand was threatening to outpace the capacity of the earlier filtration arrangements, and the long-suffering committee, as always, was obliged to keep in step with such developments. In 1900 Cutler recommended that the filter tunnel be extended, which was subsequently carried out (Delaney 1910, 103), whilst an auxiliary filter tunnel was constructed at a cost £350 in 1908 (ibid., 18). The consumption of water rapidly exceeded the available yield of the tunnel, and a second extension to it was completed in 1906 at a cost of £450 (Delaney 1911, 32). By this time, however, their was no further room available on the waterworks property to allow further expansion (Delaney 1910, 103). Gross consumption for all of the city's needs in 1910 was 5 million gallons per day, the demand for general domestic use in the city alone being in excess of three million gallons (Delaney 1911, 16). Nonetheless, the filter tunnel was able to cater for the demand of the city up until 1928, by which time four rapid gravity and sand filters had been added to the system. A fifth water turbine was added in 1916 while in the years 1912–16 all of the turbine sets were reconditioned (Fitzgerald 1984), and between 1912 and 1920 their reciprocating pumps were rebuilt. The castings were manufactured at Robert Merrick's foundry from a design by the then resident engineer, whilst the final machining and installation was carried out by waterworks fitters (ibid., 15).

The Surviving Pumping Station Plant

Cork Corporation Waterworks is the best-preserved Victorian water pumping station in Ireland (Fig. 124). Most of the surviving buildings date to the second half of the nineteenth century and to the early years of the present century — these include the beam engine house of 1863 (Fig. 125), the main stack, 1858, (Fig. 126) and the turbine house of 1888. The turbine shafts drive a flywheel through a large bevel gear (Fig. 127) which in turn powers a reciprocating pump; four of those connected to individual turbine sets are twin double acting, the other is single double acting. There are three low lift pumps, each of which are twin double acting, which are able to pump *c*. 495,000 gals. per day against a static head of 239ft to the low-level reservoir, operating at 18rpm. The remaining two pumps lift *c*. 990,000 gals. per day against a static head of 383ft to the high-level reservoir. The five sets of turbine pumps all extract their supply from the original pure water basin, although the supply is no longer entirely dependent upon the filter tunnel (Fitzgerald 1984). The high- and low-level reservoirs were phased out in the mid-1980s, but remarkably, the turbines continued to perform the function for which they were originally installed, and it was only in 1938 that the steam plant was initially decommissioned after the installation of electrically powered centrifugal pumps.

The three inverted triple expansion engines built by Combe Barbour in 1905, and installed between 1905 and 1907, however, are the most striking features of the surviving plant (Fig. 128). In the early 1980s the Institute of Mechanical Engineers of Ireland supervised a superb restoration of the surviving steam plant, although unfortunately (even though there are no plans to raise steam) the engine house is not open for public inspection. In triple expansion engines the steam passes, successively, through a high- pressure cylinder, an intermediate-pressure cylinder and then into a low-pressure cylinder to act upon a low-pressure piston to initiate the cycle. The two large engines (Fig. 128) each have a Corliss valve gear, whilst the individual steam valves are also fitted with Combe Barbour's own patent trip gear. The trip gear on the high-pressure cylinder was controlled by a fly-ball type governor, whilst those of the intermediate- and low-pressure cylinders are equipped with hand-operated cut-off gears. The individual flywheels are 12ft in diameter. In the basement of the engine house are positioned the ram pumps driven by the individual units of steam plant, and these are actuated through slide rods from the engine crossheads (Cooper 1986, 52; Bowie 1980, 86–8). Two surface condensers, which utilised the delivery mains as a cooling medium, are situated at the rear of the engine house (Cooper 1986, 52). To the north of the engine house is a boiler

Fig. 127

Driving gear and connecting rod for pump set, Cork Corporation Waterworks. (Con Brogan, Dúchas)

Fig. 128 **OPPOSITE ABOVE**

Triple expansion engine (1906) by Combe Barbour of Belfast, Cork Waterworks. (Con Brogan, Dúchas)

Fig. 129 **OPPOSITE CENTRE**

Lancashire boilers by Victor Coates of Belfast installed in Cork Waterworks in 1904. (Con Brogan, Dúchas)

Fig. 130 **OPPOSITE BELOW**

Green's Economiser, Cork Waterworks.

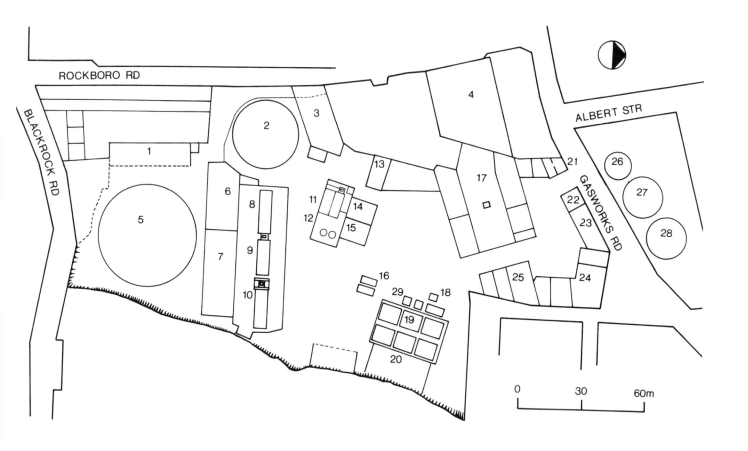

ROCKBORO RD

BLACKROCK RD

ALBERT STR

GASWORKS RD

0   30   60m

Fig. 131 ABOVE
Cork Gasworks.

1 Sulphate of ammonia plant. 2 Gasholder
No. 3. 3 Coalstore No. 5. 4 Coalstore no. 1.
5 Gasholder No. 4. 6 Coalstore No. 6.
7 Coalstore No. 7. 8 Retorts (5 settings, 40
retorts). 9 Retorts (6 settings, 40 retorts).
10 Retorts (5 settings, 40 retorts). 11 Boiler
house. 12 Engine house. 13 Power house.
14 Meter house. 15 Exhauster house.
16 Weighbridge. 17 Tar plant. 18 Livesey
washer. 19 Purifiers. 20 Oxide shed.
21 Gatelodge. 22 Office. 23 Office, stores
and paintshop. 24 General stores.
25 Machine shop. 26 Tar tank.
27 Gasholder No.1. 28 Gasholder No. 2.
29 Scrubbers.

Fig. 132 LEFT
Meter and Exhauster houses, Cork
Gasworks. (Con Brogan, Dúchas)

244

house with two Lancashire boilers built by Victor Coates of Belfast in 1904 (Fig. 129) which are fitted with a 72-tube Green's Economiser with superheaters (Fig. 130). During the Second World War the steam plant was recommissioned to obviate an over reliance on oil-powered generators of the electric pumping plant, and continued to be used for short periods afterwards.

GAS

The development of the Cork gas industry is historically important for two reasons. Firstly because the first recorded instance of coal gas in Ireland for domestic use occurred here, and secondly because a consortium of local consumers managed to successfully wrest a monopoly of the supply of gas within the city from a London company. The net result of this commerial battle between the London and Cork companies was that for a short period in the 1850s two independent gasworks were operating side by side on the former Monerea Marsh. For the greater part of the nineteenth century the gasworks at Cork, first under the control of the United Gas Co. and later under the Cork Gas Consumers Co., supplied coal gas for both industrial and domestic needs, and for public lighting. Larger industrial units, however, especially those operating outside the pipe networks such as the textile mills at Douglas and at Millfield, operated their own gas plants for heating and lighting purposes. Other large industries such as Murphy's Brewery, and institutions such as Queen's College (UCC) which lay well within the main pipe network, found it more cost-effective to operate their own gas plant.

Gas Manufacture

Coal gas was manufactured in a process called *carbonisation*, which involved the distillation of bituminous coal with a low ash content in a refractory vessel called a *retort*, and the cleaning of the gas to extract important by-products such as tar and ammonia. The retorts were D-sectioned tubes which were originally made with cast-iron, and later with refractory clay (after 1853) and, from the 1920s onwards, with silica. Early retorts were heated from a furnace set immediately beneath them, in an arrangement called a *direct fire setting*. However, as most of the coke manufactured in the retorts was needed to stoke the furnace only a small proportion of it was available for sale. A new gas producer furnace invented by Siemens in 1861, largely overcame this problem, and was in turn superseded by the Klonne recuperator after 1885, when even more efficient coke-firing could be achieved (Wilson 1974, 35). The coal was heated in the retorts at temperatures in excess of 1000 degrees centigrade, the effect of which was to drive off the gas and other substances, some of which were later collected and sold (see below).

The crude gas was conducted through a series of cast-iron pipes set in a metal box known as a *condenser*, in which the gas was cooled. As the gas began to cool the tar began to condense, and was then led to an underground storage tank. A series of rotary pumps called *exhausters*, actuated by a steam engine, were employed to move the gas from the retorts to the condenser, through the remaining cleaning processes (called purification) which removed tar, ammonia and hydrogen sulphide, and finally to the gasholder for distribution (ibid., 37–8). The spent iron oxide was often sold to manufacturers of sulphuric acid or, indeed, used as a weed killer, which in Ireland was called *meather* (Wilson 1974, 39; O'Sullivan 1987, 18).

The gas was stored in gasholders (or gasometers in general parlance), large composite bells manufactured with rolled iron plates. The lower part of the bell rested upon a

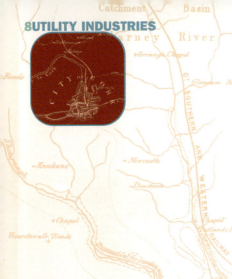

water-filled tank, the water acting as a seal preventing gas from seeping out. The admission of gas into the bell caused it to rise upwards, and the addition of telescoped sections to the bell from 1824 onwards, which rose and sank telescopically, allowed larger quantities of gas to be stored.

Early Town Gas Manufacture in Cork (Figs. 131 and 132)

In February 1816 a Cork newspaper reported that a 'Gas apparatus fitted up by Mr James O'Brien of Tuckey Street draws every night a crowded assembly of the citizens to witness its effects'.[102] O'Brien was using gas to illuminate his shop and its associated workshops, in what is clearly the earliest recorded instance of a private gas supply in Ireland. No further details of O'Brien's system are known, even though its novelty value at this time is evident, nor are there any indications as to the impetus behind this development. In the event, it was not until almost a decade later that the first steps were made to provide Cork with a town gas supply. In 1825 the Wide-Street Commissioners entered into an arrangement with the United Gas Company of London to provide the city with gas lighting between the hours of sunset and sunrise, with each gas lamp to provide light equivalent to that of twelve mould tallow candles (Windele 1843, 108). The United Gas Company's network served the city between 1826 and 1859, until its amalgamation with the adjacent Cork Gas Consumers Company works. Surprisingly little is known about the early physical development of the United Gas Company's works on Monerea Marsh. Early nineteenth-century maps of the city show the early gasworks as a range of small buildings in outline, but without anything which would resemble a gasholder.[103] The choice of site, a low-lying area taking advantage of the gas's tendency to rise, with direct access to water transportation for receiving bulk cargoes of coal, accords well with what is known about contemporary English works. As far as can be seen there are few indications that the safety of the works created any real anxiety for the municipal authorities, and the only accident of note in the early years of the United Gas Company's works involved an incident in 1827, when the iron hoops around a large water tank at the works, with a capacity of 180,000 gallons, are reported to have given way.[104] The capacity of this tank would suggest that this was an above-ground gasholder.

However, by the mid-1850s local interest groups began to mount a strong and ultimately successful challenge to the monopoly exercised by the United General Gas Co. of London. John Francis Maguire (1815–72), proprietor of the *Cork Examiner* and a staunch advocate of economic nationalism, was the main prime mover in the campaign to curb the influence of the UGC in Cork. In September 1856 Maguire and his associates formally incorporated a rival Cork gas company — the Cork Gas Consumers' Company (CGCC) — which acquired a three-acre site for its own proposed gasworks adjacent to the UGC works at Albert Road (O'Sullivan 1992, 48). Work began on the new gasworks in January 1857.[105] By March the new company's engineer, George Anderson[106] reported that the work in hand required lime for building and the gas purification process, and advised that a lime kiln costing £60 would ensure a steady supply.[107] Pipelaying began in earnest in June 1857 when 280yds of pipe (in 9ft lengths) were laid on the first day. By September service pipes were being connected.[108] The pipes were supplied by the English firm of Cochrane & Co. of the Woodside Works, near Dudley in Staffordshire. By September of 1857 the new pipes — each of which was given three coatings of lead paint — were being supplied at a rate of 3,500yds per week, which eventually replaced a total of 36 miles of service pipes and 43 miles of mains which the UGC had laid for its customers in 1826 (ibid., 48).

Richard Rolt Brash supervised the covering in of the engine house and purifying house, which was completed in June of 1857. Finch and Heath of Chepstow provided an iron roof for the retort house, whilst the Newcastle firms of Ormond & Co. and Stephenson & Co. supplied the fire bricks used in the construction of the works. Some of the main fittings were produced by the local firm of James Reidy & Co.[109] but the 100ft diameter gasholder was supplied by an English firm. The CGCC began to manufacture gas at its new works on 22 December, 1857, by which time over 700 service pipes had been laid with some 230 gasmeters in service. The companies and institutions which agreed to use the new source of town gas included the Corn and Butter Exchanges, the main city-based banks and the Cork, Blackrock & Passage Railway Co.[110] The main subscriber to the new scheme, however, was Cork Corporation, who accepted the new gas company's tender to provide a gas supplying for its public lighting, whilst J.F. Maguire led a campaign to have the required 516 street lamps manufactured locally (ibid., 48).

By March of 1858 the new works was capable of producing up to 1,415,000 cubic metres of gas p.a., which by this stage of its development was distributed through about 35 miles of mains.[111] In September of the same year a further bench of retorts was being erected, and the demand for its product was such that in the period 1858–60 the number of gas meters installed by the company increased from 1,370 to 3,244.[112] The increased demand, already in evidence in 1858, necessitated the construction of a new gasholder in 1860, capable of holding an additional 160,000 cubic metres of gas.[113] Two years later a new telescopic gasholder was in use.[114] Indeed, the rise of the Cork Gas Consumers Co. was marked by the rapid decline of the United Gas Company in Cork, whose works was purchased by the CGCC as early as 1859 for the sum of £25,700.[115] Further expansion continued apace, and by 1867 a new gasholder, 156ft in diameter, and described as 'the largest which has yet been made in this country', had been erected.[116] The opening of a tar factory, on Little Island in the upper harbour, in 1875 provided a lucrative outlet for the CGCC's main by-product — tar.[117] Tar distillation led to the manufacture of products such as creosote and pitch. By the early decades of the twentieth century the retorts at Cork gasworks were charged mechanically, and by 1919 the company had 11,180 consumers (Coakley 1919, 51).

In the early years of the present century the Cork gas company faced an increasingly hostile commercial environment. Increased duties on imported goods necessary for its operation and an independent Irish government which was anxious to reap the rewards of its hydro-electric scheme on the river Shannon at Adnacrusha near Limerick, militated against the future development of many Irish gas companies. In 1898 street lighting in Cork had been converted to electricity, a utility which was to become the Cork gas company's principal rival. Although domestic customers were initially reluctant to have electricity installed, the gas company began to slowly lose customers. Government policy on the development of electricity, after the formation of the ESB (see below) and the national implications of a direct supply from Ardnacrusha after 1929 for Cork City and the county towns (see below) proved to be heavy burdens. With the advent of natural gas from the Kinsale field in the early 1980s, the Cork gasworks was finally closed and it now serves as a depot for Bord Gáis.

Surviving Buildings
The amalgamation of the UGC and the CGCC brought about a rationalisation of the two formerly separate plants, the UGC section being transformed into stores and workshops. By the late 1860s the layout of the site (with the exception of the sulphate of ammonia plant) had almost reached its greatest extents. The original gatehouse dates to c. 1826 and is a formal gatelodge, designed to command and accentuate the original entrance. It is built of local limestone and may well have originally accommodated a gatekeeper.

Fig .133

Coal stores, Cork Gasworks.

Fig. 134

Albert Road generating station, completed in
1898.

Only the larger gasworks in Ireland would have had such structures, and on present evidence this is the earliest surviving example of its type in Ireland. Immediately to the east of the gatelodge is a two-storey administrative block, with a frontage facing Gasworks Road. The details of the doorway and its ashlar surround indicate that this building would have been contemporary with the gatelodge (i.e. mid-1820s). These buildings are clearly shown on the first edition of the Ordnance Survey of 1842, and belong to the earliest phase of construction. The United Gas Company is known to have slightly expanded its works in the mid-1850s, shortly before the rival Cork Consumers' Company opened its own plant immediately behind it. It is possible that some of the surviving ancillary buildings conjoined to the original offices and workshops on Gasworks Road, which now defined the eastern extent of the entrance courtyard, date to this period.

In the period *c.* 1859–65 a new range of buildings were constructed in the north-east quadrant of the site. These buildings originally served as stores, workshops and offices, and are currently used mostly as office accommodation. The existing windows and doorways are clearly more recent additions but the roof profiles and general layout have remained unaltered, as the building elevations to the courtyard clearly indicate. The original exhauster and meter houses of the Cork Gas Consumers' works of 1857 survive within the centre of the existing site, where they currently serve as workshops. Both have been extensively modified within the present century with the addition of new roofs and new window frames. The exhauster house, the eastern building of this block, is a rare survival. It would have originally housed a table top and later, perhaps, a small compound horizontal engine, to work the exhauster. The height of the building could also be an indication that a larger vertical, direct drive engine was installed towards the end of the nineteenth century to power additional plant. Extra motive power would certainly have been needed to power the conveyors when vertical retorts were introduced. At any rate two Lancashire boilers were in use by the mid-1920s, along with a third boiler (probably a Babcock and Wilcox watertube design). This could be an indication that triple expansion engines may well have been in use by this period, although the additional ability to raise steam may well have been used for processes which did not involve motive power, such as preventing ice accumulating on the seals of the gasholders. The meter house accommodated the station meter, which monitored gas production. In the 1850s the meter would have been a cast-iron drum about 4ft in diameter, which was half filled with water. The passage of gas through the drum rotated a compartmented tin drum which, in turn, actuated a series of graduated dials. In Irish and English gasworks the meter house was normally as separate building, and so the surviving example within the Cork works is unusual. The original coal store of the Cork Gas Consumers' Co. survives near the southern boundary of the site. Its roof profile has been entirely modified in more recent times. However, on present evidence its design in terms of other Irish examples is unique to Cork.

ELECTRICITY SUPPLY

The beginnings of electricity supply in Ireland date to the 1880s, when the Dublin Electric Light Company powered seventeen arc lamps in Kildare Street, Dawson Street and Stephen's Green with current from its generating station in Schoolhouse Lane.[118] The first recorded instances of the use of electricity for lighting in Cork resulted from local initiative. In 1881, for example, the contractor John Delaney had used electric lights, powered by a portable generator, in the construction of the bridge completed in

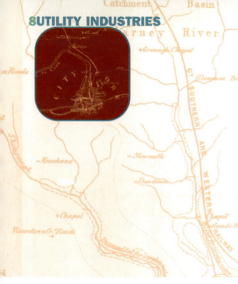

1882 to replace Anglesea Bridge. At Morrough's woollen mill near Douglas, the mill's 250hp engine was also used to power a generator set for lighting in 1890.[119] By far the most ambitious early scheme for electricity supply, however, was that carried out by Murphy's Brewery, sometime before 1892. The brewery had installed a Parsons steam turbine with two sets of accumulators, which provided enough current to electrically light the entire Lady's Well complex (Stratten and Stratten 1892, 145).[120] The Parsons steam turbine was developed by Sir Charles Parsons (1854–1931), the sixth son of William the third Earl of Rosse, of Birr Castle, County Offaly.[121] In Parsons design steam was used to set a turbine in motion rather than exert pressure on a piston as in a conventional steam engine. Parson's model, which like all steam turbines ran at high speeds, was ideally suited to electricity generation, and was available in a non-condensing form by 1891 (Hills 1989, 286–7), although it is not known whether or not the Lady's Well Brewery example was of this type. This is the earliest recorded use of a Parsons steam turbine in the Cork area and is clearly one of the earliest recorded instances of such a turbine in Ireland. The Murphy's Brewery electricity generating installation marks a significant departure from more conventional practice, in that high-speed steam engines were normally used in Ireland's larger early power stations. Indeed, the first steam turbine used in the Albert Road power station at Cork was not installed until 1917 (see below).

During the mid-1890s Cork Corporation made its first serious attempts to provide a system of public lighting for Cork City when, in 1895, it employed T.W. Smith of the Manchester firm of Calvert and Company as its consulting engineer. Smith was to report to the corporation on the feasibility of lighting the city using electricity and eventually proposed that two schemes be undertaken — the public lighting of the main streets (projected cost of installation c. £8,000) and a scheme for providing all of the city's main power needs (including lighting and power for domestic and industrial use) with a projected cost of £20,000.[122] In 1896 the corporation obtained a provisional order for an electricity supply both for a series of electric tramways and for public lighting, and appointed the firm of Kincaid, Waller and Manville as its consulting engineers.[123] The corporation was to arrange for a private company to provide the city with a network of electric tramways and public lighting. This was a common practice throughout Britain where small power stations often supplied current for tramways and public lighting (Cossons 1987, 228).

In August 1896 the corporation had issued tenders for suitable companies to provide these services.[124] By September of 1898 the fifteen miles of cable which had been laid in the city was being charged by the three dynamos installed at Albert Road.[125] The recently formed Cork Electric Tramways and Lighting Company Ltd. built its electricity-generating station — a twin-gabled brick structure (Fig. 134) 100ft long — at Albert Road.[126] Its chimney was a self-supporting steel structure 130ft high. The station's generating plant was powered by three McIntosh and Seymour, side-crank tandem compound condensing engines, which were fitted with expansion governors and separate exhaust valves on both their high- and low-pressure cylinders. The engines were serviced by three Babcock and Wilcox boilers, a type of boiler whose main advantages were that it had good circulation of water whilst occupying a relatively small floor area. Such boilers were commonly used in power stations of the period, and were also employed in the Fleet Street power station in Dublin (Hills 1989, 221; O'Flanagan 1992, 42). In many contemporary generating stations power transmission was normally by means of a belt drive from the engine to the generator. This was certainly the case at Dublin's Fleet Street Power Station, opened in 1892 (Manning and McDowell 1984, 9), and in the majority of the English generating stations. But at Albert Road the engine crankshafts were directly coupled to six-pole, 200kW compound wound generators, which yielded 500 volts at 135rpm. A direct current (DC), three-wire cable system with 460 volts between the outers and the mains, was used for lighting distribution, most of the insulated cables were sheathed in lead. Some twenty miles of cable had been laid by the end of 1898.[127]

The output of the Albert Road station increased rapidly in the early decades of the twentieth century. In 1900 the station was producing 1.8 million units of electricity a year, which had increased to 4.9 million by 1916, by which time the existing generating plant required replacement. By 1919 the original side-crank compound engines had been replaced by three Belliss and Morcom vertical triple expansion engines, which were direct coupled to two DC generators, two Allis and Chalmers horizontal compound steam engines direct coupled to DC generators and a separate Belliss and Morcom engine coupled to a 6,600 volt alternator (Coakley 1919, 81–2). The engines produced by Belliss and Morcom of Birmingham were entirely enclosed with forced lubrication, and were ideally suited to powering small generators (Hills 1989, 219). In 1917 a 1,500kW geared Curtis steam turbine was also installed at the Albert Road station, which was coupled to a DC generator manufactured by the British Thompson Houston Company of Rugby.[128]

After its establishment in 1927, the Electricity Supply Board (ESB), moved rapidly to acquire all of the Irish electricity supply companies which remained in private hands. In 1929 the Cork Electricity Supply Co., which was then in control of the Albert Street generating station, was acquired by the ESB. Thereafter, and up to the establishment of the Marina station in the 1940s, Cork was supplied via a 110kV cable from the Ardnacrusha hydro-electric plant, which commenced operations in October of 1929. Most of the county towns such as Charleville, Mallow, Fermoy, Youghal and Dunmanway were also supplied directly from the Ardnacrusha scheme, via a 38kV cable, from 1929.

NOTES

ABBREVIATIONS

BPP   British Parliamentary Papers
CAI   Cork Archives Institute
CPM   Cork Public Museum
HC   House of Commons
ICJ   Irish Commons Journals
IDC   Irish Distillers Collection
Pf.   Portfolio
Ph.   Parish
PRO   Public Record Office
RIA   Royal Irish Academy
TCD   Trinity College Dublin
WO   War Office

CC   *The Cork Constitution or The Cork Advertiser* 1825–73; *The Cork Constitution* 1873–1922
CE   *The Cork Examiner*
CJ   *The Corke Journal*
CMC   *The Cork Mercantile Chronicle*
CMI   *The Cork Morning Intelligencer*
CS   *The Cork Sun*
HCh   *The Hibernian Chronicle*
MA   *The Cork Evening Herald or Munster Advertiser*
NCEP   *The New Cork Evening Post*
SR   *The Southern Reporter and Cork Commercial Courier*

1 The Economic Development of Cork 1750–1930

1. This figure does not include the engine originally installed in Isaac Morgan's flour mill in Cork, which was later sold to a Dublin distiller Nicholas Roe in 1811 (see 'Grain Milling' Ch. 3). The fourth pre-1812 example was a 24hp rotative beam engine installed in Stein, Brown & Company's Distillery in Limerick, B & W Pf. 411, Birmingham Central Library.

2 Extractive Industries

1. In modern times there is only one recorded instance of a copper smelter in Ireland at Arklow, Co. Wicklow run by Whaley and Co. from about 1768 to around the close of the eighteenth century. The smelting works appears to have been closed owing to the difficulty of landing coal at Arklow during the winter months. As with all Irish copper ores, the copper from the Wicklow mines was thereafter exported to Wales; see Fraser 1801, 18; Cole 1922, 34–5.
2. For the development of the Cork copper mines see O'Mahony 1987, Cowman and Reilly 1988, Williams 1991 and O'Brien 1994b.
3. CJ, 23 April 1754.
4. *Commission of enquiry into the resources and industries of Ireland. Memoir on the coalfields of Ireland.* Stationery Office, Dublin 1921, 2 vols.
5. CE, 4 November 1882.
6. This is not to say that any of the pits on the Kanturk coalfield were never extensively worked. Recent borings have shown that the Dromagh shaft was mined to at least at least 210ft; see Coughlan and O'Reilly, 1992.
7. CJ, 16 August 1759; CC, 5 May 1828. Charles Smith noted in 1750 that the culm from Dromagh was suitable for malting, unlike that raised from other parts of the North Cork Coalfields which was only considered suitable for lime-burning (see Smith 1750, vol. 1, 294 and vol. 2, 375). Further collieries were established at Coolclogh near Kanturk and Coolbane, County Cork (NCEP, 23 January 1769, 26 March 1769) and by the early 1800s collieries were also at work at Duarigle (NCEP, 19 May 1803) and Gooleegeely near Kanturk (ibid., 6 April 1807).
8. CC, 22 February 1831.
9. See Bielenberg 1991, 52, 57 and 66; also BPP, 1871, LXII, 10; 1911, LXXXVI, 407–39.
10. Cork marble is so called because of its capacity to take a good polish like Kilkenny 'marble'.
11. *Report from the select committee on industries (Ireland)*, HC, 1884–5 (288), ix, 77. The individual blocks of stone were polished by the firm of Sibthorpe and Son of Dublin.
12. An example of one of the 'Blackrock diamonds' survives in the collections of Cork Public Museum.
13 This is an inference: a local newspaper account (CMC, 5 November 1810) describes a catastrophic explosion in the Brandy Lane area of the city in which twenty-two people were killed. The cause of the explosion was gunpowder stolen from Ballincollig Gunpowder Mills which a local worker was illegally supplying to local quarries.
14. The name Beaumount is taken from the adjacent Beaumount House and Park.
15. Printed list of presentments made at Spring Assizes of 1793, Cork Public Museum (CPM) 1952:146.
16. See Seamus Murphy's memoir *Stone Mad* (1966, repr. 1986) on the stonecutters of Cork City during the 1930s.

17. CE, 8 March 1858; CC, 6 March 1858.
18. CE, 14 February 1842.
19. Lime produced from William Carroll's quarries was singled out for special mention in *Report from the select committee on industries (Ireland)*, HC, 1884–5 (288), ix, 449.
20. The 'marble and limestone quarries' at Carrigacrump were producing 'headstones...flagstones, stone rollers, caps for piers...' in 1857; CC, 13 January, 1857.
21. 1 June 1858.
22. The 'Quarry' as it was known to generations of University College Cork students, scene of many violent intra-college rugby encounters, was filled in during the late 1970s. The site is now occupied by the Boole library.
23. CC, 28 June 1832.
24. See Guy's *Directory* of 1893.
25. E.g. CC, 18 March 1843, Roman cement and plaster of Paris works in Maylor Street.
26. MA, 20 September 1840.
27. CC, 2 January 1840.
28. *Southern Industry*, January 1889.
29. Letter from J.J. O'Connor to *Cork Examiner*, 5 June 1848. According to Marmion (1855, 537) 3,670 bags and barrels of salt were imported into Cork in 1853. Some 6,597 tons were imported in 1861, increasing slightly to 6,621 tons in 1871 (McCarthy 1949, 103).
30. Between Pope's Quay and the Ferry Slip a salt-boiling house was at work in 1769, CEP, 16 March 1769, whilst Maurice Hennessy was operating a salt and lime works on Dunscombes' Marsh around the same time (ibid., 10 April 1769). For early north city works see Lucas' *Directory* 1787, David Hennessey, Mallow Lane (p. 145) and David Sherrard, Blackpool (p. 152); Hennessey's works appears to have been taken over by John Shinkwin sometime before 1803 (CMC, 9 May 1803). The Blackpool works may have been that at Clarence Street advertised in the local press in 1833 (**583**) (see CC, 21 May 1833).
31. CE, 12 January 1849.
32. CC, 2 January 1840.
33. CC, 15 May 1854. Daly also seems to have owned the Watercourse Road/Gerald Griffin Street Salt and Lime Works; see Slater's *Directory*, 1856 and CC, 4 June 1864.
34. CE, 12 March 1851. According to this notice the site had been built six years previously (i.e. *c.* 1845) and its quarry had an 'abundance' of stone and flags.
35. HCh, 26 March 1801; CC, 2 March 1830, 26 October 1839; Slater's *Directory*, 1856.
36. Cork Archives Institute (CAI), U18, Beamish and Crawford Collection. See also ground plan of Beamish and Crawford's porter brewery by O.E. Edwards, dated December 1863, which also shows the works; U18, box 2 T.26.
37. HCh, 7 January 1802.
38. CC, 5 January 1843; CE, 4 January 1843. Mark Collins was the father of the Cork-born arctic explorer Jerome Collins, who also supervised the construction of North Gate Bridge in 1863–4 (see Ch. 7).
39. HCh, 26 March 1801.
40. Valuation Office, OL, 5.2499, St Anne's, Shandon.
41. HCh, 7 January 1802.
42. CC, 27 November 1847, 15 February 1848.
43. *Cork County Eagle*, 20 July 1901; CS, 24 October 1903. Spillane was also buying salt from Cheshire, the cost of transportation from England being less than that from Carrickfergus.
44. CS, 24 October 1903.
45. This act attempted to regularise brick sizes to 9 ½ x 4 ½ x 2 ¼, see Craig 1983, 177–8.
46. The vaulted corridors of Cork City Gaol, for example, which were built in 1824, appear to have been built with local slob brick. Generally speaking such bricks in eighteenth-century contexts are only exposed in industrial buildings built with rubble stone, when the brick is used to decorate window or door opes.
47. Geo. III, C 38, XV–XVI; O'Sullivan 1937, 199; Cadogan 1988.
48. The Waterford Penroses are perhaps better known for their involvement in the glass industry of that city (see Dudley Westropp 1978, 69ff and Dunlevy 1989).
49. CC, 12 February 1828.
50. According to Foley (1991, 34) the brick used in some of the windows on the south elevation of South Monastery Schools at Douglas Street, Cork, which was completed in 1827, was manufactured on the Douglas brickfields.
51. CE, 24 May 1858.
52. Ibid., 14 February 1842.
53. Ibid., 6 September 1852, 27 February 1854.
54. Youghal brick was used in the construction of the vaults of the five Martello towers, built by the Office of Ordnance around Cork harbour between 1813 and 1815. The bricks, costing 'Fifty nine shillings per thousand' were brought by sea to Spike Island and to the individual Martello tower sites around the harbour (Office of Ordnance Ireland, Letter Book 1813–15, NLI Ms. 5195, f. 41, 15 November 1813, f. 52, 29 December 1813). I am indebted to Mr Paul Kerrigan for this reference. Some two million Youghal bricks were used in the construction of the roof of the Great Southern and Western Railway tunnel, which was built between 1847 and 1855 (Kinahan 1889, 372). The main enclosing walls of Wallis and Pollock's flax-spinning mill at Douglas, built in 1866, were built with Youghal brick externally faced with Ballinphellic brick.
55. Geo. III, C38, XV–XVI; O'Sullivan 1937, 199; Cadogan 1988.
56. The reservoirs of Cork Corporation, built in 1858, were lined with 'old Cork brick' with the exception of 2–3,000 Belvelly bricks (see CE, 1 February 1861). William Moore, a Dublin builder, reported that the retaining wall of one of the reservoirs was constructed

with 'bad or unburnt bricks', a clear reference to locally manufactured slob bricks. See CE, 5 July 1851.

57. CC, 4 June 1864; *Irish Builder*, vol. XLII, no. 1014, 1,080–81.
58. The site which in 1844 consisted of two potteries controlled by Sarah Byres and Joseph Leahy (see Aldwell's *Directory* of 1844–5), is shown on the OS 1:1056 series (1871), 74/43.
59. Wm. Restrick & Co., Knapp's Square, (see Pigot's *Directory* of 1824). This pottery appears to have been controlled by Mrs E. Osmond in 1871, and manufactured domestic brownware, bricks and ceramic pipes (see *City of Cork Directory*, 1871).
60. This was Powell & Sons of Merchants Quay (see Henry and Coghlan's *Directory* of 1867).
61. CS, 26 September 1903.
62. As note 61, see also Ayto 1987, 19–24 for a description of English clay pipe making.
63. As note 61.

3 Food-processing Industries

1. The type of malt generally preferred by porter brewers and distillers was that which had been dried for a long period of time.
2. In 1848 most of the buildings of Cowperthwaite's Brewery were idle, although some malt continued to be made here (Valuation Office, OL, Ph, 5.2554, St Nicholas Ph.). They continued to function as a maltings until the early 1920s (see Goad Insurance Plans, revised to 1926, (10, 57)), and as barm brewers up until the turn of the century (see *Guy's Directory of Munster*, Cork 1893).
3. Beamish and Crawford acquired Noblet Johnson's interest in this malthouse in 1792, and eventually bought the premises outright in November 1800. CAI, U18, *Beamish and Crawford—Book containing their title to the premises belonging to the Cork Porter Brewery 1837*, p. 1.
4. *Ground plan and sections of Morrison's Island Malthouse*, by W.C. Ryder; ink and colour wash drawing at scale of 10ft to 1in; CAI, U18, T26, Box 1.
5. *Part plan and section of Morrison's Island Malthouse*, by W.C. Ryder, 26 June 1866; ink and colour wash on paper at scale of 4ft to 1in; CAI, U18.
6. Undated (probably mid-1860s) ink and colour wash drawing on paper at scale of 4ft to 1in; CAI, U18.
7. On 5 March 1753, the malthouse was transferred by Samuel Hoare to Benjamin Sullivan; Beamish and Crawford purchased all of these premises from Charles Henry Leslie on 1 February 1813. CAI, U18, *Beamish and Crawford— Book containing their title to the premises belonging to the Cork Porter Brewery 1837*, p. 4.
8. CAI, U18, T27, Box 1. *Map of premises belonging to Beamish and Crawford*. Ink and colour wash, scale 20ft to 1in; undated (probably mid 1860s).
9. As note 4 above.
10. This malthouse had been erected on the site of the former Corporation fish market. CAI, U18, *Beamish and Crawford — Book containing their title to the premises belonging to the Cork Porter Brewery 1837*, p. 2.
11. Ink drawing, scale 10ft to 1in, CAI, U18, T27, Box 1.
12. The malthouse was in existence by 1770 and in 1771 it was leased to Atwell Hayes, who later established a large flour mill on the site of the present Lee Mills (**036:1**) in 1787 (see 'Grain milling' section). Beamish and Crawford acquired the interest in these premises in 1823. The Francis Street malthouse and stores, described as a 'brewhouse' in 1743, were leased by Beamish and Crawford in 1799. CAI, U18, *Beamish and Crawford —— Book containing their title to the premises belonging to the Cork Porter Brewery 1837*, pp. 3, 12.
13. Bielenberg (1991, 56) gives the impression that the Lee mills with their 'fifteen pairs of millstones' were somehow involved in the malting operation at Nile Street, which was patently not the case. The latter were clearly leased as flour mills for most of the nineteenth century, before their conversion to malting floors around the turn of the nineteenth century (see 'Grain milling' section).
14. CAI, U18, T26, Box 2.
15. *Plan and section of steep of No. 3 Malthouse belonging to Beamish and Crawford*. Ink and colour wash on paper, scale 4ft to 1in, 1866; CAI, U18, T26, Box 1.
16. *Sections showing elevations of steeps etc., No. 3 Malthouse, Lee Mills*. Ink and colour wash on paper, scale 4ft to 1in; CAI, U18, T26, Box 1.
17. *Ground plan of the Lee mills and Stores property of Messrs Beamish and Crawford*, by W.C. Ryder, March 29th, 1866; CAI, U18.
18. CAI, U18, T26, Box 2. Series of working drawings numbered 16 to 27 dated 1903, showing ground plans of malthouses nos. 1 and 2 at a scale of 8ft to 1in, and sections on N/S and E/W axes (Drawings 22 and 23).
19. CAI, U18, Unbound drawings.
20. CAI, U18, T26, Box 1.
21. The Mary Street malthouses of Andrew Drinan were up for auction in 1845 (CC, 4 January 1845), and may well have been controlled by Lane's Brewery by this period.
22. Brewery-controlled and independent maltings are dealt with under 'Malting'.
23. e.g. CC, 27 October 1837, Samuel Abbott's Brewery at Fitton Street lets the grains of its brewery for one year.
24. A sketch of the brewery complex from the west drawn by T. Crofton-Croker in 1831 has been reproduced by Holland 1917, 203–4.
25. Goad Insurance Plans (GIP), Cork, 71, 1897.
26. Ibid., 71, 1906 revision.
27. CAI, U18, T27, Box 1.
28. SR, 29 May 1819. As early as 1793 the brewery was advertising for mill horses, see NCEP, 16 June 1793.
29. Andy Bielenberg (1991, 57) suggests that these were replaced by two steam engines *c.* 1819, which can be documented by 1837 and they are shown on a large-scale survey of the brewery of 1839. Apart from the fact that the date-stone on the early engine house clearly indicates that the first steam engine used in the brewery was installed in 1818, there are two large-scale surveys of

the brewery which on present evidence must date to the period after 1802 and before 1837, which indicate that a combination of horse whims and a steam engine were in use after 1818. The first of these pre-1837 plans shows the same extents of the brewery as in 1802, with a steam engine shown in the position of a later example at the north-west corner of the site. The two horse whims are shown in the same position as on the second plan, but in different positions to those shown on Aher's plan of 1802. In the later plan they are clearly shown to actuate pumps whereas on Aher's plan two of the horse whims are used to work the malt-milling machinery, CAI, U18.

30. CAI, U18.
31. CAI, U18, T27, Box 1.
32. As note 31, pre-1837 survey of brewery.
33. As note 31, annotation to survey drawing.
34. CAI, U18, T27, Box 1. Both of these plans are large-scale surveys showing, respectively, a ground plan and plan of the 'upper storey' at the same scale. The ground plan shows two beam engines (each of 20hp, Stark 1850, 78–9), the earliest one in the north-west corner of the complex with two boilers (probably of the wagon type), and the second, later engine facing Allen's Lane. The latter is shown with a single boiler, and this engine, like the earlier model, is likely to have been single-acting. There were four cleansing cellars, four coolers and four coppers, the coppers being roughly in the same positions as the late nineteenth-century examples which have survived *in situ*.
35. It is too often assumed that all of this work was carried out in 1865. However, the extensive collection of engineers' and architects' drawings in the Cork Archives Institute make it abundantly clear that many alterations were made in the period 1865–8.
36. CAI, U18.
37. An elevation and plan of these are shown in a drawing at a scale of 4ft to 1in by W.C. Ryder, dated 4 January, 1873, CAI, U18, T25. According to Alfred Barnard (1890, vol.1, 355) the brewery's power requirements were augmented by the acquisition of a pair of horizontal condensing engines (35 and 45hp), one of which may have replaced the brewery's earliest beam engine.
38. These are shown in part profile in a section of the main brewery buildings dating to around 1863, CAI, U18.
39. See advertisements in Barnard 1887.
40. Portfolio of drawings dated June 1884, by I. Adams, showing setting of copper no. 3, CAI, U18, T26, Box 2.
41. CAI, U18, T26, Box 2.
42. The roller mill units, which are in excellent condition, bear the name plates 'Magnetic Apparatus Schaeffers Patent, H. Stopes & Co. 24 Southwark Street London'. This machinery was still in working order in the mid-1970s, pers. comm. Mr George Ellis, Chief Engineer, Beamish and Crawford.
43. As note 39.
44. CAI, U18, *Beamish and Crawford — Book containing their title to the premises belonging to the Cork Porter Brewery establishment 1837*, p. 5, 9 March 1799, John Carelton and William Cowley to Charles Henry Leslie. John Carr, writing in the early 1800s lists the River Lee Porter Brewery amongst the four main porter breweries in the city (Carr 1806, 415).
45. CAI, U18, T27, Box 1.
46. SR, 19 March 1833. I am grateful to Mr Tim Cadogan of Cork County Library for this reference.
47. On 1 February 1813, as note 44.
48. CE, 8 January 1851.
49. Ibid., 8 January 1858.
50. CC, 16 October 1860; see also CE, 27 August, 1860 and 25 March 1861.
51. CC, 28 November 1861.
52. Ibid., 1 May 1876.
53. E.B. McGuire (1973, 375) notes that a small distillery with a 208 gallon still, owned by Samuel Newsom, was in operation in the North Abbey by 1782, and suggests the Wise brothers 'may have acquired this since their distillery is said to have been built on the site of a friary'. However, while they did come to own the former Franciscan Abbey mill, the North Mall distillery was not built on the site of the medieval abbey. Indeed the area known as the North Abbey is further east of the present North Mall distillery, adjacent to Newsom's Quay (which is clearly named after Samuel Newsom) near the North Gate Bridge. Alfred Barnard (1887, 405) in his account of the North Mall distillery, states that it was built on the site of the 'Old Dominican Friary called the Abbey of St Mary of the Isle'. Barnard, however, was clearly misinformed: the Dominican abbey of St Mary's of the Isle was situated on an island near the south channel of the Lee, immediately north of the present St Finbarr's cathedral.
54. SR, 21 March 1833. I am indebted to Mr Tim Cadogan, Cork County Library for drawing this reference to my attention.
55. *Portions of the River Lee*, dated 26 August 1863; ink and colour wash drawing on paper, CAI, U18.
56. The site of Wise's malt mill and its millrace is clearly shown on John Rocque's map of 1773 as the 'Abbey Mill'. The distillery's title to the 'St Francis Abbey Mill' derived from a lease made to William and Thomas Wise by the Earl of Cork dated 26 March 1804; SR, 18 March 1833. I am indebted to Mr Tim Cadogan for this reference.
57. SR, 18 March, 1833.
58. Boulton and Watt archive, Pf. 405; Boulton and Watt Letter Book, July 1807– September 1808, 22 August 1880, Birmingham Central Library.
59. Valuation Office, OL, 5.2584, St Peter's.
60. One of Rowan's single cylinder horizontal engines, equipped with cam-operated drop valves is on display in the main engineering hall of the Ulster Museum.
61. NCEP, 6 January 1784; Bielenberg 1991, 61.
62. See CC, 18 August 1831.
63. Lease of mills at Kilnap, William Furlong to Morgan Coldwell, 10 August 1790, CAI, Sunbeam Wolsey Collection, Box 505.
64. CC, 2 August 1831; also 9 January and 5 August 1834. Coldwell apparently spent £20,000 on it before going bankrupt in 1815; *Cork Advertiser*, 20 April 1815; Bielenberg 1991, 150, n. 4.

65. The distillery was bought by James Daly of the John Street distillery, who leased parts of the Millfield premises, separately, to Frederick Lyons and to Thomas Dawson (a miller and flour factor) in July 1836. Dawson's lease included a provision that he should not use any of the premises as a distillery. *Lease of part of the concerns called the Millfield Distillery, Jas. Daly to Thos Dawson*, 21 July 1836; *Lease of part of the concerns called the Millfield Distillery, Jas. Daly to Frederick Lyons*, 29 July 1836; CAI, Sunbeam Wolsey Collection, Box 505.

66. A Saintmarc still was at work in Belfast in 1834, see McGuire 1973, 39, n. 26. The auction notice for the Millfield distillery (CC, 2 August 1831) lists a 'new patent still capable of making 180,000 gallons in season' amongst the distillery's equipment which, as the distillery closed in 1831, can only be the Saintmarc still listed in the buildings and plant inventory of the distillery on the map accompanying the lease of 1836, CAI, Sunbeam Wolsey Collection, Box 505, copy of map accompanying lease of part of Millfield Distillery made on 21 July 1836 (see note 65 above). This map appears to be a copy (dated 6 August 1836 and signed Thomas Holt, Surveyor, Rutland Street, Cork) of a survey of the distillery made by Sir Thomas Deane. Thomas Holt is perhaps best known for his *Map of Cork*, printed in 1832. See also auction notices in CC, 2 August 1831, 9 January and 5 August 1834.

67. CAI, Sunbeam Wolsey Collection, Box 505, copy of map accompanying lease of part of Millfield Distillery made on 21 July 1836 (see note 65 above).

68. Assignment of lands of Kilnap by Y. Dawson to the Cork Spinning and Weaving Company Ltd, 20 May 1862, CAI, Sunbeam Wolsey Collection, Box 505.

69. E.B. McGuire (1973, 355), followed by Andy Bielenberg (1991, 61), confuses this site with the distillery established at Kilnap (also called the Glen distillery) in the 1880s. The Dodges Glen distillery ('Callaghan's Distillery'), along with its associated malt and meal mills, is clearly shown in the valley of the Glen River on a map of 1832 showing the city boundaries; *Instructions given by the Chief Secretary of Ireland with reference to the cities and boroughs sending representatives to Parliament*, 1832. The site is also shown as the 'Glen Distillery' on the 1st ed. OS (Sheet 74) for Cork City of 1842.

70. CMC, 9 May 1803.

71. Ibid., 3 June 1804.

72. Ibid., 26 June 1805.

73. The distillery's malt mills had been sold off to John Perrott by at least 1848 (see OL, 5.0393). The distillery complex was put up for auction in 1856; CC, 8 March 1856.

74. Valuation Office, OL, House Book 5.0393; CC, 8 March 1856.

75. CC, 21 November 1846.

76. Valuation Office, OL, House Book 5.0393. By 1856 these mills appear to have been entirely given over to flour and meal production, see 'Grain milling'.

77. CC, 8 March 1856.

78. Ibid., 7 January 1834.

79. In 1828 Ring's distillery was the smallest at work within the city, accounting for less than 1% of the city's output; *Accounts relating to Distilling from malt and raw corn* HC, 1828, 217, xviii, Bielenberg 1991, 64, tab.1. The distillery of M. Ring & Co., Blackpool was to let in 1831; CC, 9 July 1831; 10 January 1834. An auction notice of 1834 (CC, 20 February 1834) refers to the 'Blackpool Distillery and Mill' which was capable of manufacturing 600 puncheons of spirits annually. Later in 1834 it was advertised for sale as a 'distillery in good working order' with a waterwheel, a 'plentiful supply of water', a corn store, a kiln and a cooperage, all of which had been built 'within the last six years' (i.e. *c.* 1828) (CC, 7 November 1834). The only other distillery mills in the Blackpool area were those controlled by the Green distillery at Wherland's Lane and the Watercourse distillery on the Back Watercourse Road. The distillery does not feature in any of the city trade directories.

80. O'Keefe 1974, 58 gives the foundation date as 1783. An auction notice of 1801 (HCh, 19 January 1801) states that the distillery had been built for four years i.e. in 1796; the site was certainly in existence in 1797, *Cork Gazette and General Advertiser*, 4 March 1797. This site should not be confused with Ring's Blackpool Distillery, which is listed as a separate entity in 1828 (see note 79 above).

81. HCh, 19 January 1801; see also 9 March 1801 which advertises malt shovels and other items for sale at Allan and Corcoran's Blackpoole Distillery.

82. CC, 3 September 1844. Its capacity was calculated at 300,000 gallons (1,363,800 litres) p.a.

83. CC, 6 February 1836. According to McGuire (1973, 377) the distillery was acquired by James Kiernan in 1835, and upon his death in December 1844 was put up for auction on instructions in his will. However, the auction notice for the distillery appears in CC, 3 September 1844.

84. The Green distillery's malt stores and kilns, along with a corn mill and kiln (which may have originally functioned as a malt mill) were situated at Wherland's Lane, where they are listed as the property of George Waters in the Griffith Valuation of 1851, Parish of St Anne's, Shandon, 248. The mills at Wherland's Lane associated with the distillery were called 'Water's Mills', but should not be confused with that associated with the Watercourse distillery. George Waters & Co. were in control of the Green distillery from July 1850 onwards (McGuire 1973, 377), and had brought it back into full production within a matter of months; CC, 12 October 1850.

85. By 1848 these mills appear to have been entirely given over to the grinding of oats, Valuation House Book OL 5.2582, see under 'Grain milling'.

86. See CC, 25 September 1851 in which three of the Green distillery's small copper boilers ('suitable for a small brewery') are advertised for sale and CC, 29 November 1851: 'George Waters & Co. have adapted their works to the production of whiskey the old fire still solely...'

87. 1st ed. OS 25-inch, Cork sheet 74/6, 1899.

88. CAI, Irish Distillers Collection (IDC), Hewitt's Copy Letterbook, 1789–1802. Hewitt to Cave, 1 August 1793. In the event 'a hard rock appeared which disputed every inch' and the builders were forced to bring in quarry men to free the foundations.

89. Ibid., 2 November 1793, Hewitt to Harrison of Liverpool; Bielenberg 1991, 72.

90. CAI, IDC, Copy Letterbook 1794–1802, Hewitt, Teulon and Blunt to Chief Commissioners to His Majesty's Revenue, 24 September 1794; Bielenberg 1991, 72.
91. CAI, IDC, Copy Letterbook 1794–1802, Hewitt to Edgar Curtis of Bristol, 22 June 1796 and 24 August 1797; Bielenberg 1991, 72.
92. Valuation Office, OL, 5.2499, St Anne's, Shandon. The surveyors also noted that it was necessary to pump water up to the cisterns.
93. CAI, Hewitt Copy Letter book 1808–15, Hewitt to Morton, 19 May 1810; Bielenberg 1991, 73.
94. CMC, 21 June 1811. This mill had two waterwheels and operated three drying kilns, and is shown on Joseph Connor's map of the city dated 1774.
95. CC, 30 January 1830. This was part of the bankrupt estate of George Carr, and according to the auction notice the sawmilling machinery had been 'lately erected'.
96. Valuation Office, OL, 5.2499, St Anne's, Shandon. The mill had been bought from Morgan and White for 2,000 guineas.
97. CAI, Hewitt Copy Letter Book 1808–15, Hewitt to Boulton and Watt, 17 December 1810, 1 March 1811, 16 December 1812; Bielenberg 1991, 73; Boulton and Watt archive, Birmingham Central Library, Pf. 442; see also Boulton and Watt Letter Book, March 1811–July 1812, 34.
98. Henry Maudslay (1771–1831) is best known for his screw-cutting lathe, amongst other important contributions to the development of machine tools (see Rolt 1986, 90–98). The firm of Maudslay, Sons & Field was founded in 1810 and was one of the most important English engineering firms of the nineteenth century (Rolt 1980, 31; 1986, 97). Maudslay was also responsible for the side lever engines of I.K. Brunel's *Great Western* which crossed the Atlantic in April 1838 (Hills 1989, 144).
99. CAI, Hewitt's Copy Letter Book 1829–34, Hewitt to Maudslay, Sons and Field, 3 August 1823; Bielenberg 1991, 75.
100. Auction notice CC, 6 February 1836.
101. Bielenberg 1991, 74–5; CC, 6 February 1836.
102. *Accounts relating to distilling from malt and raw corn*; HC,1828 (217), xviii.
103. CAI, Map at scale of 60ft to 1in accompanying auction of property of Rev. William Bleasby on 7th May 1861 by Landed Estates Court, Ireland. The OS 5ft to 1 mile survey of the city of 1869 shows the circular objects shown on the 1861 map as 'wash tubs'.
104. CC, 17 October 1865.
105. Boulton and Watt Letter Book, 1793–1803. Boulton and Watt to Thomas Walker, 16, Birmingham Central Library.
106. Boulton and Watt archive, Pf. 359, sketch of Walker's Distillery accompanying letter from Alex Johnston to Boulton and Watt dated 20 February 1805.
107. Boulton and Watt archive, Pf. 359; see also Wakefield's *Account of Ireland*, 1812, 51, n. 32; Dickson 1977, 609–10.
108. CC, 25 November 1831.
109. Ibid., 24 June 1843.
110. According to McGuire the distillery was established in John Street in 1807. However, the distillery does not feature in any of the pre-1820 street directories, and Daly is first mentioned as a rectifier in Blarney Lane in the *Commercial Directory for Ireland and Scotland for the years 1820–1821–1822*. Pigot's *Directory* of 1824 also lists Daly and Murray of Blarney Lane as 'rectifiers only'.
111. Waters originally ran a rectifying distillery in Paul Street (see *Commercial Directory of Ireland, Scotland...etc.*) and later came to control the Green Distillery, St Finn-Barre's Brewery (see under 'Brewing') and the Riverstown Distillery (see McGuire 1973, 377).
112. As note 65.
113. CE, 14 August 1850.
114. McGuire (1973) and Bielenberg (1991) have confused this site with Callaghan's Distillery at Dodges Glen; see note 69.
115. CAI, U229/115/1, High Court of Ireland Chancery Division auction notice for Glen Distillery.
116. As note 115.
117. CC, 10 March 1829.
118. Ibid., 31 August 1830.
119. Ibid., 19 September 1845.
120. Ibid., 16 November 1830. By 1835 this appears to have become the property of Abraham Beale (ibid., 30 August 1835), the Quaker merchant who established the Monard Iron Works in the 1790s.
121. CC, 29 and 30 September 1845.
122. Ibid., 9 August 1834. This appears to have been that owned by Thomas Dunscombe, the quayside of which could accommodate vessels of up to 300 tons; see CC, 20 May 1829.
123. Goad Insurance Plans, Cork, 71, 1906 revision.
124. CC, 10 November 1849.
125. Ibid., 14 February 1848.
126. CAI, U18, *Beamish and Crawford — Book containing their title to the premises belonging to the Cork Porter Brewery 1837*, p. 4.
127. See CC, 19 February 1831, which advertises French burr stones imported by Reuben Harvey & Sons from Havre de Grace; also 25 September 1834 which reports that William Harvey was about to land 'A prime parcel of French burr stones' at Charlotte's (Father Matthew) Quay. In 1845 Thomas McKenzie of Camden Quay was the agent for Hughes and Sons millstone makers of London; CC, 1 June 1845. Andy Bielenberg's assertion (1991, 43) that 'Most of the millstones used were imported' can only be said to hold for grinding stones. The vast majority of shelling stones used in the processing of oats and Indian corn, as the Valuation House Books clearly indicate, were made from Irish sandstone.
128. According to Charles Smith, Samuel Pike of Cork had a 'curious' bolting mill (Smith 1750, vol.1, 167; Cullen 1977, 10).
129. NCEP, 26 May 1796.
130. See also CC, 6 November 1849, where second-hand mill machinery made by Key and Hilton of Liverpool is advertised for sale.
131. CC, 15 August 1833.
132. Ibid., 20 February 1855.
133. In all likelihood the origins of this mill go back to the period period 1177–82, when a mill site was granted to St Thomas' Abbey Dublin 'between the city of Cork and Dungarvan' (Bradley and Halpin 1993, 28). The mill presumably derives its name from

William Droup who was granted a mill site here in around 1348 (ibid.). The *Pacata Hibernia* map of *c*.1585–1601 shows a possible mill building on the channel dividing the north and south islands of the city, whilst the Hardiman Map (TCD, No. 46) clearly shows a mill with a vertical undershot waterwheel on this channel. The site is referred to in a number of seventeenth-century sources (see Caulfield 1876, 32, 115–16; Simington 1942, 410), the most interesting of which relates to the siege of Cork in 1690. During the siege Dean Davies (through whose Gillabbey lands Droop's millstream ran) 'took care to have the course of Droop's millstream turned' (Ó Murchadha 1990, 9, 17, n. 17) in order to deny the use of the mill to the defenders. In the eighteenth century the mill was known locally as the Fishamble Lane mill and as 'Ben Deebles Mill' in the nineteenth century (MacCarthy 1983, 116 n. 2), but as late as 1780 there is at least one reference to the site as Droop's Mill (Bradley and Halpin 1993, 28). Indeed, the site was still known by this name as late as 1876 (see CC, 9 September 1876).

134. CAI, U18, *Beamish and Crawford —Book containing their title to the premises belonging to the Cork Porter Brewery 1837*. On 20 March 1712, Water Gate (Fenn's) Marsh was leased by Ebenezer Pike to Joseph Fenn, Sugar Maker.

135. CJ, 11 February 1754. In this account a man called Henry Whitcroft was found drowned in the 'mill dam near Fishamble Lane'.

136. Printed list of presentments made at Spring Assizes for City and County of Cork, 1793, CPM 1952:146.

137. RIA, Ms. 'Southwell Papers', 753–6; Bradley and Halpin 1993, 28.

138. Valuation Office, OL, 5.2571 St Peter's .

139. As note 138.

140. CAI, *City of Cork general system of drainage*, July 1866, by John Benson and Robert Walker, City Engineers. 'The tail race of the Fishamble Lane mill runs nearly through the centre of the city from Nile Street to Merchants Quay and acts as a main sewer for a large portion of the district, the outfall is into the north channel at St Patrick's bridge and the effluvia arising therefrom is most offensive and therefore a great nuisance to the inhabitants in the locality and persons going on board and leaving the river steam boats.'

141. SR, 19 March 1833. I am indebted to Mr Tim Cadogan of Cork County Library for drawing my attention to this reference. The use of the term 'tide mill' in this context denotes a water-powered mill whose daily operation was interrupted by the tide. The term itself, in modern usage, is generally only applied to mills whose millponds exploit tidal changes, whereas the Abbey Mill and St Dominick's Mills (which are similarly described) both utilised freshwater supplies.

142. *Pacata Hibernia* 1585–1601; Hardiman Collection, TCD, no. 46.

143. Valuation Office, OL, 5.2553, Ph. St Nicholas.

144. As note 143.

145. The events surrounding this were revealed in a court action (CC, 17 October 1865) concerning a claim for damages against the Corporation Waterworks, who according to the the owners of St Dominick's Mills reduced the level of water in the south channel of the Lee. According to the owners this had resulted in the mills becoming 'considerably reduced in value'. In the event, the court ruled against the Corporation and, it seems, not without proper justification. The Griffith Valuation Housebook for the area, collated in 1849, observed that 'The supply of water except for two or three months of a dry summer is good' (Valuation Office, OL, 5.2553, Ph. St Nicholas).

146. The mills were the property of the Fitton family, who obtained a lease of the mills for 999 years from a Mr Lucey in 1753. In 1848 the mills were let for £70 p.a. to a Mrs O'Keeffe, who let the premises to Thomas Merrick for £100; see CC, 17 October 1865.

147. OS 1:1056 map (5ft to 1 mile), 1869, 74/65.

148. ICJ, IX, app. CLXXXIX (1771–2). In the year 1772 the mills at Glasheen were owned by Denis Forrest and James Raynes. St John's Mills also availed of these bounties (ibid., app. CCCXCVI).

149. See HCh, 18 February 1803, 'Flour mills at Crosses Green formerly called Clarke's Mills'.

150. Bielenberg 1991, 101; CC, 10 April 1829. Rennie was one of the first millwrights to use cast-iron shafting and gearing, see Ch. 5.

151. MA, 22 June 1839.

152. An undated ink and wash drawing of these mills (scale 20ft to 1in) shows a small weir and what appears to be a narrow millpond on the Proby's Quay side of the mill buildings. CAI, U18.

153. Valuation Office, OL, 5.2553, Ph. St Nicholas.

154. SR, 19 March 1833; CAI, U18 *Beamish and Crawford — Book containing their title to the premises belonging to the Cork Porter Brewery establishment 1837*, p. 5. The site is shown on Daniel Murphy's map of 1789 as 'Hayes' Mills'. According to Tuckey (1837, 196) on 27 July 1787, after a severe flood, 'The works on the marsh near the Mardyke, then in progress for a grist mill, were carried off'.

155. SR, 19 March 1833.

156. HCh, 9 May 1803.

157. As note 154. Mill tolls normally involved a percentage of the grain brought to the mill by an independent party for grinding.

158. CAI, U18, *Beamish and Crawford —Book containing their title to the premises belonging to the Cork Porter Brewery 1837*. When Hayes's mills were advertised for sale in 1821 it was claimed that they 'possessed an abundant supply of water at all times'. So much so, indeed, that during the particularly dry summer of 1819 'over 1500 bags of wheat were manufactured...when nearly all of the mills contiguous to the city were at a stand' (CMI, 13 March 1821). In 1821 Hayes's interest was sold to Daniel Lane & Co. for £700 and in July 1825 passed on to George Crawford, Beamish and Crawford acquiring complete control in 1842. In 1846 the Lee mills appear to have been leased to the House of Baring who were agents for the government (CC, 31 January 1846).

159. Valuation Office, OL, 5.2571, St Peter's.

160. SR, 21 March 1833.

161. See CC, 11 April 1835 which states that the machinery concerned was 'not more than three months in use'. Peele, Williams and Peele supplied a steam engine to Midleton Distillery in 1835, Bowie 1975, 211; Bielenberg 1991, 101.

162. Valuation Office, OL, 5.2516, St Finn-barre's.

163. There is an unfinished pencil sketch in the Beamish and Crawford collection relating to the Lee maltings (see under 'Malting') which shows a frontal elevation of a metal waterwheel assembly. The waterwheel itself has compass arms and power transmission from it is through bevel gearing (CAI, U18).

164. CC, 20 February 1847.
165. Jackson also controlled St John's Steam Mills on John Street and had granaries in Smith Street and Beasly Street with storage for 30,000 barrels of grain; CC, 3 August 1877.
166. CC, 20 April 1881.
167. CJ, 17 February 1755.
168. See John Rocque's Map of Cork of 1774. A lease dated 16 April 1756 (CAI, Sunbeam Wolsey Collection, Box 505) from John Rye to Moses Newsom involving 'part of Kilnapp', refers to 7 acres and two roods (English statute acres) 'bounding on the West with the meadow formerly called Dodge's Meadow on the South with *Waters Mill land* on the east' (my italics). The lands concerned included the River Bride in the Millfield area, just outside the city boundary and well to the north of the site of Water's Mills which is currently occupied by the remains of the Watercourse distillery's former malt mill (**059**). This reference to Water's Mill land clearly refers to the Wherland's Lane Mills (see under 'Distilling') which were also called 'Water's Mills' (see HCh, 19 January 1801; CC, 23 July 1853) and should not be confused with the Water's Mills to the south of Watercourse Distillery. Furthermore, a survey of the Millfield distillery lands dated December 1862, refers to the tailstream from its associated flour mills as 'Waters Mill stream' (CAI, Sunbeam Wolsey Collection Box 505). The Water's Mills later associated with the Watercourse distillery were also known as 'Archdeacon's Mills', see CC, 20 September 1834.
169. CMC, 21 June 1811. The mill was dismantled in the 1830s by the Watercourse distillery, see under 'Distilling'.
170. *A map of part of the lands of Kilnap and Kilbarry...belonging to Mr Wm. Furlong...* (*c.* 1790). See also *Lease of lands of Kilnapp, John Rye to Thos. Furlong*, 18 March 1752 (which includes lease of 'mills, mill streams, mill dams... watercourses'), *Lease of part of Kilnapp, John Rye to Moses Newcom*, 16 April 1756; CAI, Sunbeam Wolsey Collection, Box 505.
171. Lyon's Mill was grinding Indian corn in 1847; CC, 20 May 1847.
172. Valuation Office, OL, 5.0392, St Anne's, Shandon, Td. Kilnap.
173. CC, 24 March 1859.
174. As note 172.
175. CC, 23 February 1828. In an oral submission to the Pipe Water Committee of Cork Corporation in 1845 Thom stated that 'There is 3,000,000 cubic feet of water per minute brought into Shaw's watermill which I constructed' (see CC, 30 September 1845). Shaw's Mill appears to have succeeded an earlier mill on the same site, which is shown on Neville Bath's county survey of 1811 for the Cork Grand Jury.
176. CC, 9 January 1861.
177. Ibid., 21 November 1846 and 26 May 1849.
178. Valuation Office, OL, 5.0393, Td. Ballyvollane.
179. CC, 8 March, 30 September 1856. Each mill had two pairs of stones, one French burr the other 'Irish', which by 1850 could grind up to 400 barrels of wheat per day.
180. CC, 16 January 1861. In 1861 the Glen Distillery mills were controlled by W. & H.M. Goulding, who had bought the former Glen Distillery site in 1858 (see Ch. 6 'Superphosphates and fine chemicals').
181. Valuation Office, OL, 5.0393, Tds. Ballyvollane and Cahergal.
182. These mills were also known as the 'mills of Glounaspike', *Instructions given by the Chief Secretary of Ireland with reference to the cities and boroughs sending representatives to Parliament*, 1832.
183. CE, 13 December 1850. Two pairs of stones, one French burr the other 'Irish', which by 1850 could grind up to 400 barrels of wheat per day.
184. Valuation Office, OL, 5.0393, Td. Cahergal; CC, 15 February 1855.
185. SR, 23 October 1824. I am indebted to Mr Tim Cadogan, Cork County Library for this reference.
186. Boulton and Watt Collection, Birmingham City Libraries, Pf. 217. According to Bowie (1978, 173) this was the only sun and planet gear engine by Boulton and Watt to have been supplied to Ireland. Strictly speaking, however, this is not true as a sun and planet engine, originally used in the construction of locks on the Birmingham Canal, came into the possession of the Dublin Canal Company in 1792; Boulton and Watt Collection Pf. 567.
187. CMC, 19 November 1802. My thanks to Mr C.J. F. MacCarthy for important biographical details of Isaac Morgan's family and to Mr Colman O'Mahony for using his unrivalled knowledge of nineteenth-century Cork newspapers to locate contemporary details of Isaac Morgan's mill. Morgan eventually received some £5,000 by way of compensation from the Dublin Insurance Company, see HCh, 21 March 1804.
188. As note 186 above. For details of Nicholas Roe's distillery see McGuire 1973, 338–9.
189. Valuation Office, OL, 5.2554, St Nicholas.
190. CC, 18 May 1844; Valuation Office, OL, 5.2554, St Nicholas.
191. CC, 18 May 1844.
192. Ibid., 2 May 1876.
193. Ibid., 9 September 1876.
194. CC, 11 October 1865.
195. Valuation Office, OL, 5.0392; Plan of Millfield Distillery near Cork, copy of map accompanying lease made to Thomas Dawson, 21 July 1836, CAI, Sunbeam Wolsey Collection Box 505.
196. CC, 24 March 1859; CAI, Sunbeam Wolsey Collection: *Map of Millfield and the lands of Kilnap*, surveyed by Alex Jack; CE, December 1862.
197. CC, 14 August 1858; CE, 6 September 1858, 17 June 1859.
198. CC, 9 January and 18 December 1861.
199. CC, 24 March 1862. 'McNaughted' beam engines operated on a principle developed by William McNaught of Glasgow in 1845, whereby the engine was compounded by the addition of a high-pressure cylinder to the crank side of the engine, between its centre and the connecting rod: see Hills 1989, 157–9.

200. CC, 25 March 1876.
201. Ibid., 3 August 1877, 20 April 1881.
202. Ibid., 9 September 1876.
203. *Southern Industry*, new series, no. 6, September, 1889.
204. Goad Insurance Plans, Cork 1897.
205. As note 204.
206. *Irish Builder*, 15 December 1890.
207. As note 206. The Carrigacrump Quarries also provided stone for the engine beds of Wallis and Pollock's flax mill at Douglas (see under 'Linen', Ch. 4).
208. James Petrie had begun to build engines at his Rochdale works in 1819 and in 1844 patented his own cut off gear (see Hills 1989, 175).
209. As note 206 above.
210. Goad Insurance Plans, Cork 1897, 1906.

4 Textile Industries

1. CC, 11 November 1863.
2. Indenture of part of lands at Poullacurry, Glanmire, Co. Cork in possession of William Irwin Solicitors, Cork. My thanks to Mr Richard Irwin for bringing this document to my attention.
3. For the economic rationale behind the plantation strategy which led to the establishment of important flax-growing areas outside Ulster see Crawford 1988.
4. CC, 18 January 1853.
5. Ibid., 20 January 1853.
6. Ibid., 13 December 1850.
7. Ibid., 20 November 1853.
8. *Agricultural census of Ireland* 1860. Return of mills in Ireland constructed for scutching flax, Smyth 1988, 246.
9. CC, 11th November 1863.
10. CE, 23 October 1867.
11. CC, 27 February 1864.
12. Ibid., 7 October 1864.
13. Ibid., 21 December 1865.
14. Ibid., 7 October 1864.
15. Ibid., 14 October 1865.
16. Ibid., 29 September 1866.
17. Ibid., 23 October 1867.
18. Ibid., 7 October 1864.
19. CE, 17 October 1867. The mills were sold in November 1871 for £19,000, see ibid., 9 November 1871.
20. Guy's *Directory* 1875–6.
21. CC, 22 October 1881.
22. CE, 22 June 1883.
23. *Report from the select committee on industries* (Ireland) HC, 1884–5 (288) ix, 630.
24. CC, 2 January 1891. I am indebted to Mr C.J.F. MacCarthy for this reference. See also ibid., 25 September 1917.
25. Ibid., 25 September 1917.
26. CE, 18 October 1871.
27. CC, 2 January 1891.
28. Ibid., 2 January 1891.
29. Ibid., 2 January 1891.
30. CE, 12 October 1870.
31. CC, 2 January 1891.
32. As note 31.
33. CC, 29 September 1866. In the first period of the mill's use some 12,168 spindles were operated; see CE, 18 October 1870. Combe Barbour were the most important textile machine makers during the nineteenth century, see *Industries of Ireland*, Part 1, 1891, 95 and Lindsay 1971.
34. CC, 2 January 1891.
35. Ibid., 2 January 1891.
36. Ibid., 2 January 1891.
37. Ibid., 20 November 1863.
38. I am indebted to Mr C.J.F. MacCarthy for important biographical details about Brash. Brash was also a member of the Munster Flax Improvement Society, see CC, 21 December 1864.
39. CC, 28 January 1867; *Irish Builder*, 1 March 1867.
40. As note 39.
41. As note 39.
42. As note 39.
43. As note 39.
43. As note 39.

44. CE, 15 April 1886.
45. Robert Stephenson, *The inquiry into the state of progress into the linen manufacture of Ireland*, Dublin 1757, 182–3; Foley 1991, 12.
46. Besnard's efforts appear to follow a brief lull in activity at the factory which in March 1801 was available for lease, HCh, 9 March 1801.
47. CC, 4 March 1841. In 1771 a sailcoth factory and its bleachyard were advertised for sale in the Cork press (NCEP, 18 July 1771), which seems to have been the Cahergal factory.
48. CE, 13 December 1850, 14 February 1855.
49. For a detailed description of the processes involved in the manufacture of woollen and worsted cloth see Aspin 1987 and Giles and Goodall 1992. The Bantry and Dripsey mills are described, respectively, in the *Cork Sun*, 2 May and 16 May 1903.
50. *The Corke Journal* , 17 February 1755; Collins 1958, 100.
51. Bransfield spun yarn and manufactured flannel and blankets, *Cork Total Abstainer*, 17 April 1841 (copy in Cork County Library). The mill was 'situated at the cross of the Bandon and Ballincollig Roads', CE, 30 August 1841, and appears to have been originally run as a carding and spinning mill by the Biggs brothers; MA, 11 May 1839.
52. CE, 5 January 1883.
53. Ibid., 27 June 1883.
54. CS, 30 May 1903.
55. CC, 7 April 1883.
56. CE, 21 January 1885.
57. Ibid., 19 October 1889.
58. CC, 18 October 1890.
59. CS, 27 June 1903.
60. CC, 25 September 1917.
61. CE, 2 May 1933.
62. *Report of John Arbuthnot to the Trustees of the Linen Board* (1783, 44–6), (O'Sullivan 1937, 192; Dickson 1977, 104; Bielenberg 1991, 22).
63. CE, 30 August 1841.
64. CC, 27 June 1871; Cronin 1993, 739.

5 Shipbuilding and Associated Industries, Iron Foundries and Engineering Works

1. See Lucas' *Directory* of 1787, which lists William Harrington, Edward Allen & Son and William Owen as independent shipbuilders in the Leitrim area on the north side of the city.
2. Wooden shipbuilding was by no means a capital intensive enterprise in the late eighteenth and early nineteenth centuries, when the workshops involved were no bigger than those utilised by other trades. R. Morton's shipyard in Dublin, which included his own house, was set out in 1812 at a cost of £5,000; see Pollard and Robertson 1979, 71.
3. O'Mahony 1989, 74, see also *Commercial Directory for Ireland, Scotland... for years 1820, 1821, 1822.*
4. CC, 1 January 1829; O'Mahony 1989, n. 77, p. 75.
5. CC, 5 November 1829; O'Mahony 1989, n. 77, p. 75.
6. OS 6-inch, Cork 74, 1842.
7. CE, 18 September 1848; O'Mahony 1989, n. 77, p. 78.
8. CC, 5 January 1825.
9. CC, 2 October 1849.
10. Ibid., 16 July 1863.
11. cf. Anderson 1984, 242 'Wheeler's dockyard...was situated on the north side of the river, just below Hickson's Dockyard and Pike's Iron Ship Yard'. Pike's yard was a good distance to the west of Water Street at Hargrave's Quay.
12. For further details of the ships built at Cork City dockyards the reader is referred to W.J. Barry's three papers (1895a etc.); Anderson 1984 and Bielenberg 1991. The best recent account is by Colman O'Mahony.
13. CE, 3 October 1855; O'Mahony 1989, 82. The John Rennie concerned is the son of the famous Scottish engineer, John Rennie (1761–1821).
14. SR, 3 June 1815.
15. According to Anderson (1984, 240) Robinson did not build a further steamer until 1848, when he launched his first iron-hulled screw steamer *Gannet* for the Cork Steamship Co. However, the *Gannet* was in fact built at the Cork Steam Company's own yard at Hargrave's Qy, and was designed by James Cassidy, the company's foreman shipwright; see CE, 3 July 1848.
16. CE, 12 November 1841.
17. *Cork Total Abstainer*, 17 April 1841.
18. Anthony George Robinson is likely to have been a Quaker of American extraction, and appears to have learnt the shipbuilding trade there; see Harrison 1991, 38, who provides a well-documented account of Cork's Quaker families and their business connections.
19. CE, 9 February 1849.
20. The main centres of English iron shipbuilding during this period was the London dockyards at Millwall and Lambeth, where again it was iron founders such as William Fairbairn and Maudslay Sons and Field who diversified into shipbuilding.
21. CE, 8 October 1852.
22. CE, 24 April 1853; O'Mahony 1989, 80.
23. CC, 14 July 1849.

24. CE, 16 July 1863; O'Mahony 1989, 84.
25. Anderson 1984, 242, who is followed by Bielenberg 1991, 112, states that Robinson's yard built its last ship in 1869, although Colman O'Mahony (1989, 85) has conclusively demonstrated that this did not take place until 1872.
26. CMC, 8 July 1833; O'Mahony 1986a, 5.
27. OS 6-inch, Cork 86, 1842.
28. Valuation Office, OL, 5.2499A, St Anne's, Shandon; OL, 5.2500, Td. Farranferris, St Anne's, Shandon.
29. OS 1:1056 (5ft to one mile), Cork 74/54, 1871.
30. Griffith Valuation 1852, Td. Castletreasure, Ph. Carrigaline.
31. CC, 7 February 1857.
32. Ibid., 2 January 1854.
33. Ibid., 29 March 1854.
34. CE, 26 May 1862.
35. CC, 5 January 1864.
36. The suspension waterwheel which survives *in situ* at Midleton Distillery, Co. Cork was built by William Fairbairn's Manchester works in 1852.
37. For a description of the main features of nineteenth-century foundries see Hay and Stell 1986, 115–16.
38. HCh, 10 November 1800.
39. See also *Cork Advertiser*, 15 July 1813. A foundation stone, with a distinctive beehive motif, and dated 1811 is currently housed in Cork Public Museum, whilst two similar stones dated 1810 and 1813 are mounted (although not in their original positions) on the south-facing walls of the surviving Hive Iron Works buildings.
40. CC, 6 March 1828 'Richard Perrott has retired from the Hive Iron Foundry to the Iron Stores and Foundry Warehouse adjoining'.
41. CC, 10 February 1829.
42. According to Barry (1919, 15) the *Waterloo* was converted into a lighter in 1850 and her engines taken out and sold to a Bandon manufacturer.
43. This drawing was done on behalf of Thomas Barnes' widow, Anne, in 1828. Barnes died in 1816 and thereafter Anne Barnes appears to have run the Hive Iron Works on her own behalf. See also CC, 13 February 1830.
44. CC, 6 March and 10 June 1828.
45. Ibid., 19 February 1831.
46. CC, 27 March 1834. In August of 1834 Thomas Barnes' estate was transferred to William Henry Barnes; CC, 23 August 1834.
47. CC, 31 August 1837.
48. CC, 29 May, 1838.
49. *Second report of the commissioners appointed to consider and recommend a general system of railways for Ireland*, HC, 1837–8 (145) xxxv, 449: vol. 4, Appendix B, No. 17.
50. CC, 23 August 1845.
51. CE, 20 April 1853; see also Maguire 1853, 375–6.
52. CC, 19 February 1861.
53. Ibid., 20 November 1853.
54. Ibid., 15 May 1856.
55. Ibid., 7 December 1854.
56. Only three of the waterwheels at Ballincollig Gunpowder Mills, and a handful of those in the city, appear to have been made entirely of cast-iron by the late 1840s. Indeed, the existence of all-metal waterwheels as in the case of Thomas Dawson's at Kilnap, a 30ft (9.14m) diameter, 30hp example was considered by the valuation surveyors to be worthy of comment (Valuation Office, OL, 5.0393, St Anne's, Shandon).
57. CE, 6 December 1848 and 8 June 1849. As early as 1835 the County Gaol was ready to receive proposals for 'erecting and completing machinery, to be connected with a tread mill', CMC, 27 April 1835.
58. CE, 26 January 1857.
59. CC, 23 October 1851.
60. The suspension wheel of the Bealick mill was built by Paul McSwiney's King Street iron works, sometime before 1860. As the transmission shafting built by Perrott for this mill appears to be contemporary with this waterwheel, it seems likely that it dates to before 1860.
61. See Bielenberg 1991. Iron-framed structures, which became the norm for most multistorey industrial buildings during the nineteenth century, required large amounts of cast-iron.
62. CE, 8 August 1845.
63. Ibid., 18 March 1876.
64. Ibid., 21 July 1878.
65. Ibid., 9 April 1886. McKenzie and Sons were also fitting out creameries around the same time, CE, 20 February 1886.
66. Many Cork foundries also sold second-hand waterwheels, steam engines and machinery.
67. CC, 5 February 1829.
68. Ibid., 25 July 1835.
69. Mr Plunkett Hayes, Croom Mills.
70. CC, 25 June 1859.
71. Ibid., 21 February 1862.
72. Henry and Coghlan's *Directory* for 1863.
73. CC, 25 March 1876.
74. Ibid., 28 October 1882.

75. CAI, Cork Corporation Waterworks Committee minute book, 1885–8, 27 June 1886.
76. CAI, Cork Corporation Waterworks Committee minute book, 1885–8, 27 February 1886.
77. *Southern Industry*, December 1888.
78. Ibid., June 1889.
79. Goad Insurance Plans, Cork, 1897.
80. Ibid., 1906.
81. While this is the only documented example of a Cork-made beam engine being employed in a local brewery one suspects that many of the early nineteenth-century beam engines used in Cork breweries were manufactured locally.
82. See Henry and Coghlan's *Directory* for 1863.
83. CC, 29 March 1879.
84. Goad Insurance Plans, Cork, 1897 and 1906.
85. CC, 19 May 1840.
86. Lecky took over the management of the Valentia quarries in the early 1850s, see Ó Cléirigh 1992, 65.
87. CC, 25 October 1862.
88. Ibid., 25 September 1917.
89. Ibid., 1 March 1875. The works was again put up for auction in 1880 (ibid., 6 April 1880).
90. Ibid., 31 March 1876.
91. *Cork Industrial Exhibition Report 1883* (Cork, 1886), 369.
92. CC, 10 July 1918.
93. Ibid., 30 September 1875.
94. *Cork Industrial Exhibition Report 1883* (Cork, 1886), 365.
95. *Report from the select committee on industries (Ireland): with proceedings, evidence appendix and index*, Parliamentary Papers *1884–5* (288) ix, L. sess.1 xii, Appendix 26.
96. *Southern Industry*, no. 6, vol. 1, June 1888, p. 6.
97. *Commercial Directory of Ireland, Scotland... for the years 1820–1821–1822*, p. 174.
98. SR, 26 June 1824.
99. Aldwell's *Directory* of 1844–5, p. 26. Henry and Coghlan's Cork *Directory* of 1863, p. 71 provides the earliest reference to spade making at Coolowen that I have been able to locate.
100. *Report from the select committee on industries (Ireland): with proceedings, evidence appendix and index*, Parliamentary Papers, 1884–5 (288) ix, L. sess.1 xii, Appendix 26, 828.
101. When he later reflected, in 1926, on the Ford Motor Company's presence in Ireland Henry Ford noted that 'Cork has for many years been a city of casual labour and extreme poverty. There are breweries and distilling but no real industry', see Anon. 1977, 12.
102. The first tractor to be produced in Cork was later presented to the contemporary English prime minister, David Lloyd George, and was apparently used on his farm in Wales (see Williams 1985, 44). For the technical development of the Ford and Fordson tractors, and of these and other early tractors see Williams 1985 and 1991.

6 Miscellaneous Industries

1. The Gunpowder Act of 1795 implies that the Ballincollig manufactory was in existence before that date. Presumably the original canal system operated without the additional head provided by the weir. In its early years the Ballincollig mills traded as Leslie, Travers and Co., Royal Irish Gunpowder Mills (see Kelleher 1992, 28).
2. In a letter of September 1801 the Company deposed that it had been established with its 'principle objective being the supply of His Majesty's Government'. Letter accompanying *An account of the quantity of gunpowder sold by Leslie, Travers and Company, August 1800 to August 1801*.
3. *Plan of the Royal Gunpowder Mills Ballincollig*; 28 February, 1806 Wilkes, Superintendent, PRO London, MPH 206 L BP/1342.
4. The account of the manufacture of gunpowder which follows is largely based on a description published in the *Cork Constitution* of 15 May 1856.
5. This process is not described in the *Cork Constitution* account (see above n. 4), but there were two dusting houses within the complex which were clearly used for this purpose. Serious accidents associated with the dusting process occurred in 1859 and 1861; see O'Mahony 1986b who documents these and other serious explosions associated with the mills during their 200-year history.
6. According to Lammot Du Pont, 55 coopers were employed at Ballincollig in 1858 (see Wilkinson 1976, 94). Curiously, very few coopers appear to have been employed at Ballincollig when it was controlled by the Board of Ordnance, PRO London, WO/54 517, (see Corcoran and Murphy 1986).
7. The importance and extent of Leslie's business by this period is highlighted by his ability to obtain permission to build a magazine near the government-controlled magazine in the Phoenix Park. Leslie's customers included the Hibernian Copper Mines in County Wicklow and the captains of yeomanry in different parts of Munster. A small amount of gunpowder was also shipped to Liverpool for the 'African trade', but the Board of Ordnance was Leslie's most important customer (Kelleher 1992, 28).
8. Leslie was by this time sole proprietor of the mills, having bought out Travers interest in the lands in 1804. The mills were sold by Leslie for £30,000 and an annual rent of £11,275; Kelleher 1992, 29. Some 91 acres were leased under the agreement from 31 December 1804 onwards; PRO London, WO/44 102.
9. CC, 7 July 1828.
10. CMC, 24 June and 1 July 1805.
11. Waltham Abbey was the main Board of Ordnance controlled gunpowder mills in England. The name Cooper's Row presumably reflects the principal occupation of its inhabitants, coopering being an important trade within the mills throughout the nineteenth

century.
12. PRO London, WO/44 102.
13. These included the magazine on Rocky Island (£15,292), and a crane and other equipment at Ordnance or King's Quay ('Gunpowder Quay') at Blackrock; see Kelleher 1992, 34–5.
14. PRO London; *Sketch of ordnance land and buildings at Ballincollig*, dated 26 February 1828.
15. As note 14. All of the intervening islands within the complex to the north of the old canal along with an area to the south-east of it are shown as planted.
16. As note 14.
17. A scheme for a piped water supply to the barracks is shown on a drawing dated 8 February 1837 involving a 'three throw crank forcing pump worked by a pinion wheel connected with the pit and water wheels'. The waterwheel in the accompanying illustration is a breastshot waterwheel with an inclined sluice. This system was to work in conjunction with a horse wheel, which was to serve as a back-up when the water in the channel was insufficient to turn the wheel. PRO London, WO /44 102.
18. PRO London, WO 44/643 1066.
19. CC, 7 July 1828.
20. Ibid., 5 July 1828.
21. *Report on the present state and appropriation of the ordnance buildings at Ballincollig called for by Lt. General Myers letter December 11th 1827. Engineer Office Cork, 18th February 1828.* PRO London, WO 44/643.
22. CC, 22 November 1831.
23. Office of Ordnance, Dublin, 30 May 1832; PRO London, WO/44 102.
24. CC, 4 July 1832.
25. CC, 5 July 1828.
26. CMC, 25 October 1833; PRO London, WO/44 102.
27. CMC, 16 April 1834.
28. Ibid., 5 June 1835.
29. CE, 11 October 1843.
30. For a detailed and authoritative account of these developments see Earl, 1978.
31. The treble strong classification had to stand comparison with the grades of gunpowder made by the English firms of Curtis and Harvey and Pigou and Wilkes, who more or less set the standard for the types of 'sporting powders' used in Britain (see Earl 1978, 50).
32. *Southern Industry*, April 1889.
33. CE, 23 April 1855; I am indebted to Mr Tim Cadogan of the Cork County library for kindly drawing my attention to this reference.
34. CC, 15 May 1856, quoted *in extenso* in Rynne 1989c.
35. A Fourneyron-type turbine by MacAdam's of Belfast, recently discovered at Green's mill in Cavan, probably dates to around the same period.
36. CC, 6 April 1861. Goulding's opened a Dublin plant in 1868, see *Irish Times*, 26 January 1869 and Daly 1985, 39, and one at Grace Dieu, Waterford (1878, closed in 1898) see Anon. 1956. I am grateful to Mr Eric Peard former Works Manager of Gouldings, Cork for general information on the development of Goulding's and for the loan of a rare copy of the company's history.
37. CC, 25 September 1917; Coakley 1919, 83–5.
38. See Holden's *Directory* (1805–7) and Aldwell's *Directory* for 1844–5. As early as 1801 an 'Oil and Vitriol manufactory' was in operation at Glasheen (see HCh, 6 April 1801 and 25 August 1802), although thus far no clear link can be established between this and Jennings' later chemical works.
39. OS 6-inch, Cork 74, 1842.
40. Valuation Office, OL, 5.0395, St Finn-barre's.
41. CS, 6 June 1903.
42. CC, 20 July 1867. This appears to have been Olden's soap factory, see *Southern Industry*, October 1888.
43. CS, 18 July 1903.
44. Ibid., 19 September 1903.
45. e.g. James Dwyer & Co. Hodder's Lane, Hegarty Bros. of Blarney Street; see Slater's *Directory* of 1856, 251. In Wales, from the mid-nineteenth century onwards tanning and currying were carried out on the same premises, see Jenkins 1973, 4.
46. *Fourth report on revenue in Ireland*, HC, 1822 (606) xiii, App. 58, 343–5; Bielenberg 1991, 81.
47. See also Lewis 1837, vol. 1, 417 and Cullen 1987, 145. According to Coakley (1919, 193) there were 60 tanneries in the city in 1845.
48. See OS 25-inch, 1st ed. 1899.
49. *Southern Industry*, September 1888.
50. According to Stratten and Stratten (1892, 183), James L. Lyons of Cork, Leather, Bark and Valonia Merchants (who had been in business since the eighteenth century), imported bark from Algeria and Spain.
51. See CC, 23 September 1834.
52. Ibid., 13 May 1833. A further, unspecified, early nineteenth-century Cork tannery also had a steam engine; see CC, 14 December 1844.
53. In 1828 the Spring Lane tanyard boasted the 'rare advantage of a constant supply of water... sufficient to command a waterwheel for seven or eight months of the year equal to eight horsepower', CC, 22 July 1828, which was presumably drawn from the adjacent Glen River. In the same year the Bleasby's Street tannery is said to have had a supply of 'running water'; ibid., 18 September.
54. The Glasheen tanyard was supplied by the adjacent Glasheen River; CC, 22 August 1837.
55. The Millfield tannery was supplied by the millrace of the adjacent Millfield Distillery (**096**); CC, 13 May 1843.

56. Valuation Housebook, OL, 5.2499, St Anne's, Shandon.
57. Tanning was also done in tubs in Thomas Kennedy's Watercourse Road tanyard; Valuation Housebook, OL, 5.2499, St Anne's, Shandon.
58. CC, 5 January 1864, 2 March 1867, 23 June 1883.
59. CS, 18 April 1903.
60. *Southern Industry*, December 1888.
61. Ibid., September 1888.
62. CS, 25 April 1903; *Cork County Eagle*, 20 July 1901.
63. CS, 25 April 1903.
64. These are at Catcliff near Sheffield (the oldest surviving example in Europe), Lemington near Newcastle upon Tyne, Wordesley (Stourbridge) Worcestershire, Bristol and Alloa in Scotland (Dodsworth 1984, 12; Hay and Stell 1986, 174; Cossons 1987, 171–2).
65. Saltpetre, the principal constituent of gunpowder, was also being imported into Cork from 1793 onwards for the Ballincollig gunpowder mills, and it is likely that at least up to 1815 (when the Ballincollig mills were temporarily closed down) that the Cork glasshouses used the same supplier.
66. The coke cinders raked from the city's glass furnaces were later sold to maltsters, smiths and lime burners; see Bielenberg 1991, 85.
67. Dudley Westropp 1978, 153; Warren 1981, 53. Burnett and Rowe took a lease on the premises in July 1776, with Hayes, the third partner, acquiring the lease of a nearby premises at a later date; see MacCarthy 1985, 197.
68. HCh, 6 May 1793; Dudley Westropp 1978, 115.
69. Potash and pearl ash were being imported into Cork as early as 1795, see *Cork Gazette and General Advertiser*, 14 February 1795.
70. NCEP, 30 August 1792.
71. Print in Cork Public Museum collections.
72. See McCarthy 1985, 197.
73. Lithograph by Unkles of Cork, dated 1839, at scale of 20ft to 1in; CAI, U18, Beamish and Crawford collection.
74. See McCarthy 1985, 197. The brewery was, by this period, using the glasshouse's former slip to unload coal for its steam engines and its coppers, via a wooden tramway (see under 'Brewing'). The brewery installed its first steam engine in an engine house immediately adjacent to this slip in the year the glasshouse was closed down (i.e. 1818), and one wonders if both events were related. It is not beyond the bounds of possibility that the brewery bought the glasshouse premises upon its closure and began to use its coal storage facilities for its own use.
75. Hay and Stell 1986, 175, illustrate a similar cone, dated to 1825, at the Alloa Glassworks, Clamannanshire.
76. CC, 27 June 1829; Dudley Westropp 1978, 122. This advertisement clearly states that improvements to the annealing process were applied.
77. CC, 21 July 1835; Dudley Westropp 1978, 125.
78. Dudley Westropp 1978, 125. The National Museum of Ireland has an iron glass-cutting wheel from an unspecified Cork glasshouse which was donated by Dudley Westropp; ibid., 160.

7 Transport and Communications

1. Geo. I, C12.
2. See McCutcheon 1980, 1–13 for the best available summary on the means by which Irish, and in particular, Ulster roads, were constructed and repaired. These roads also brought about an improvement in the conditions of agriculture in north-western County Cork (Donnelly 1975, 28–9).
3. For a detailed treatment of the origins and development of the Cork Grand Jury see Nolan 1974, 8–16.
4. Printed list of presentments made at Spring Assizes of 1793, Cork Public Museum 1952:146.
5. The 1st edition of the OS (1842) clearly indicates that work on this road was already underway by 1841; see also CC, 10 June 1843.
6. CC, 16 March 1844.
7. Ibid., 10 June 1843.
8. Ibid., 29 July 1854. *The Report of the Commissioner appointed to enquire into the Turnpike Trusts, Ireland*, HC 1856 (2110) xix, 617; recommended all of the Irish turnpike trusts be dissolved and their responsibilities transferred to the County Surveyors (see McCutcheon 1980, 9).
9. Leahy senior, who had acted as architect to the Ecclesiastical Commissioners in the period 1835–6, was by no means averse to enhancing his income by other means. He was eventually dismissed on grounds of fraud after being accused of passing questionable road repairs. Edmund Leahy's involvement with railway development in Cork was carried on to the detriment of his duties as County Surveyor, although his employers chose to turn a blind eye to this activity as railway development was considered to be in everybody's interest (see Nolan 1974, 93–5). Leahy junior eventually ran foul of the Cork and Bandon Railway Company, who dismissed him in 1846.
10. CC, 11 April 1846.
11. CC, 14 January, 1 May 1860; Nolan 1974, 183.
12. See *Report of the Commissioners of Inland Revenue*, HC 1829 (353) xii, 536 and *Report of select committee on turnpike roads in Ireland*, HC 1831–2 (645) xvii, 399; McCutcheon 1980, 8.
13. Geo. II, C20, IV, 55, 61; O'Sullivan 1937, 212.
14. Geo. II, C22, I–XVII; O'Sullivan 1937, 212.
15. Geo. II, C13, IV, 344, 567; O'Sullivan 1937, 213.
16. Geo. III, C13; Tuckey 1837, 152; O'Sullivan 1937, 213.
17. *Report of select committee on turnpike roads in Ireland*, HC, 1831–2 (645) XVII, 397, Appendix, xliv, 641.
18. As note 17, Appendix, lii, 30. The Cork–Kinsale and Cork–Skibbereen coach lines also did not receive tolls from mail coaches (ibid.,

641).

19. As note 17.
20. CC, 9 October 1834.
21. As note 17.
22. As note 17, p. 88.
23. As note 17, p. 641.
24. As note 17, lii, 30.
25. As note 17, lvi.
26. The returns from the Cork weigh house obtained by Griffith indicated that some 30,000 firkins of butter worth £52,000 were conveyed annually from North Kerry to the Cork Butter Market; see *Report on the roads made at the public expense in the southern district of Ireland*, HC 1831, XII, no. 119, 7; Ó Luing 1975, 102.
27. *Report on the roads made at the public expense in the southern district of Ireland*, HC 1831, XII, no. 119, 7; see also Ó Luing 1976, 104–5.
28. For a description of the types of vehicle used in Cork during the early 1840s see Mr and Mrs Hall's *Ireland* (1841, vol. 1, 64–6).
29. HCh, 9 July 1789, reproduced by Brunicardi 1987, 18.
30. West's Cork *Directory*, 1809–10; McCracken 1973, 59.
31. See Taylor and Skinner 1778, 122. By 1832 the main route to Dublin from Cork was via Glanmire; see Richard Holt's *Map* of 1832.
32. West's Cork *Directory*, 1809–10.
33. As note 32.
34. According to Holt's *Directory* of 1837, in 1810 'but one diligence ran between Cork and Passage which carried four persons, and which was rarely filled. At present there are 300 gingles licensed, of which, perhaps, two thirds run between Cork and Passage, each of which holds four persons. Some of them make three to four trips, daily, besides a day car, which holds six passengers'. The same account estimated that some 420,000 passengers travelled between Cork and Passage each year.
35. Pigot's *Directory*, 1824.
36. Charles Bianconi (1786–1875) was an expatriate Italian who established an almost nationwide horse-drawn car service in Ireland. His *Bians* or open-topped cars were driven by two horses and could travel at speeds of 8–9 mph. At the close of 1825 Bianconi's cars were covering about 1,170 miles every day (Bianconi and Watson 1962, 67).
37. Young 1780, vol. 1, 332.
38. See *A plan of the City of Cork as in the year 1750*, in Smith's *History*, and Joseph Connor's map of 1774. In 1771 the drawbridge was described as 'old and out of repair' (Tuckey 1837, 159) and in 1787 the mayor 'gave directions that the old drawbridge be taken down, and the timber of it sold by auction, as it was in a dangerous condition, and had become comparatively useless, by a great part of Patrick Street having been arched over' (ibid., 196).
39. A description of the city of *c.* 1741 states that 'the Entrance [sic] into it [is] by two stately fine Bridges of hewnstone, upon which are two noble large Gaols, all built of hewnstone... these Gaols are built on Arches wide enough for two coaches to pass in a breast', Dickson 1971, 154.
40. CC, 18 November 1863.
41. ICJ VII, 168, 171–2; O'Sullivan 1937, 205–6.
42. According to Hill (1943, 97), the Red Abbey Marsh bridge was the work of Samuel Hobbs who later built Clarke's Bridge (see above).
43. See Taylor and Skinner 1778, 179.
44. O'Keeffe and Simington's recent claim (1991, 226), based on the notion that Clarke's Bridge was built in 1766, and had the longest span in Ireland up until construction of the Lismore Bridge by Thomas Ivory in 1775, cannot be sustained, simply because the Cork City bridge was not built until 1776 (see Tuckey 1837, 174). Needless to say, Clarke's Bridge is not shown on Joseph Connor's map of 1774.
45. See John Rocque's *Map* of 1773 and Connor's *Map* of 1774.
46. CC, 21 February 1830. Tenders for the repair of the Penrose Quay ferry slip were sought in 1850; ibid., 10 August 1850.
47. Shanahan and General Charles Vallancey were responsible for the construction of Fort Westmorland on Spike Island in Cork Harbour, which was completed in 1806 (see Brunicardi 1982, 39). For an account of Shanahan's work elsewhere in Ireland, particularly for the Earl Bishop Frederick Augustus Hervey in the diocese of Derry, see Craig 1983.
48. HCh, 1 October 1789; Tuckey 1837, 202; Windele 1843, 30; CE, 12 December 1861; O'Sullivan 1937, 206; O'Callaghan 1991, 24–7. According to one unnamed correspondent in the *Cork Examiner* of 17 April 1857, the bridge was designed by Shanahan's wife, and the damage caused to the bridge in the floods of 1789 revealed that loose, unbonded rubble had been used in its construction, which led to the dismissal of Shanahan.
49. Tuckey 1837, 242, 248; CE, 12 December 1861. The extent to which the Cork Grand Jury was involved in bridge construction and repair prior to the modification of St Patrick's bridge is somewhat obscure, although it is clear that the Watercourse Road bridge was repaired by presentment in 1793. Printed list of presentments made at Spring Assizes of 1793, Cork Public Museum 1952:146.
50. Lewis 1837, vol. 1, 410; CE, 12 December 1861; O'Sullivan 1975b; O'Callaghan 1991, 29.
51. By the early 1990s Parliament Bridge was carrying up to 15,000 vehicles per day and in 1992 was strengthened by Cork Corporation, during which all of the spandrel material was removed down to the barrel of the arch. The barrel of the arch was then reinforced by the installation of a 30cm concrete saddle, see CE, 22 December 1992.
52. *Public Works Ireland*, HC, 1831, XVII, 18.
53. CAI Waterworks Committee minute books 1885–8, 29 October 1888, 85; 1888–91, 20 February 1890, 147.
54. Geo. IV, CXXXIX.
55. *Report on the roads made at the public expense in the southern district of Ireland*, HC 1831, XII, no. 119, XII, 61.
56. Up until quite recently the remains of this causeway could be detected in a sharp fall in ground level from the road to gardens on the western side of it.

57. Marc Isambard Brunel was the father of Isambard Kingdom Brunel who also visited Cork in the late 1840s. The enquiry for Gaol Bridge came from the County Engineer, Richard Beamish, which led to Brunel's visit to Cork in 1833 (see Clement's 1970, 204). Beamish later became Marc Brunel's biographer.
58. CE, 3 October 1855.
59. CC, 19 November 1853; O'Sullivan 1975a.
60. CC, 3 May 1855.
61. Ibid., 5 June 1856.
62. CE, 3 May 1858.
63. Ibid., 1 October 1860.
64. CE, 6 January 1858; CC, 23 January 1858. The projected cost of the bridge was estimated at £16,000, see CC, 25 January 1859. The contract was originally awarded to a Mr Enright of Dublin for £11,642 (CC, 9 April 1859), who later found that he had underestimated the cost by over £2,000 (ibid., 9 June 1859). The contract was later awarded to Joshua Hargrave who submitted a tender of £14,500. An original copy of Enright's contract with Cork Corporation, which includes detailed schedules of the work involved forms part of the collections of Cork Public Museum (CPM, 1955:42).
65. CE, 3 April 1857.
66. CC, 31 October 1860; CE, 1 October 1860.
67. CC, 31 October 1860, 13 December 1861; CE, 1 October 1860, 12 December 1861.
68. CC, 29 and 30 September 1862.
69. CC, 18 November 1863; CE, 18 March 1864.
70. CE, 25 May 1859. As early as 1804 a new bridge linking the North Mall with Grenville Place was proposed and estimates for its construction sought; see HCh, 2 January and 9 March 1804. The timber footbridge set in position in 1862 is shown on the OS 1:1056 series of 1869–71, Sh. 74/44.
71. CC, 24 January 1862. In a recent account (O'Callaghan 1991, 56) it has been claimed that the temporary replacement for the North Gate Bridge was floated into position at the base of Wise's Hill. It is quite clear from the contemporary Cork press, however, that this was not the case (see above). In more recent accounts conflicting dates have been given for the opening of the existing St Vincent's Bridge. O'Callaghan (ibid., 58) states that it was opened in 1875, an assertion which is presumably based on the plaque on the south side of the bridge, which simply states that the bridge was built in 1875. This, however, is clearly a later feature as the Corporation did not even begin to seek tenders for this bridge until 1877 (see CC, 7 April 1877), and in point of fact, St Vincent's Bridge was not opened until May 1878 (O'Sullivan 1975a).
72. 38 and 39 Vict. C. CIX.
73. As note 72.
74. CC, 8 July 1876.
75. Ibid., 7 February 1877.
76. Ibid., 11 February 1881. The Vice Chancellor granted an injunction to the Corporation to have Rooney give up immediate possession of the bridge.
77. Ibid., 15 February 1881.
78. 44 and 45 Vict. C. CCIV.
79. CC, 22 June 1881.
80. CC, 7 November 1882. These arguments continued the following year; see ibid., 31 March 1883.
81. Ibid., 7 November 1882.
82. See Joseph Connor's map of 1774 and William Beauford's map of 1801. On Thomas Holt's map of 1832 the gap in the navigation wall is not shown.
83. *The Report of the sub committee to examine the state of the quays and river at Cork*, dated 15 October 1814; see McCarthy 1949, 38.
84. Nimmo's engineering career in Ireland involved a large number of harbour surveys; see Marshall 1978, 164–5.
85. Nimmo did, however, propose that a docks be constructed at the west end of the New Wall, see G.M. 1917, 172.
86. Printed list of presentments made at Spring Assizes of 1793, Cork Public Museum 1952:146.
87. CC, 11 November 1843; a lot of the channel dredge was sold by the Commissioners as ballast at one shilling per ton; O'Mahony 1986a, 12.
88. CC, 17 June 1830; O'Mahony 1986a, 12.
89. CE, 8 February and 11 February 1850; O'Mahony 1986a, 21.
90. CC, 11 August 1857.
91. For the development of steam dredgers on the River Clyde see Skempton 1975.
92. None of the existing secondary sources agree on the date when this work was completed. Coakley (1919, 85) gives 1884, McCarthy (1949, 79), 1883, but there can be little doubt that the deepening of the channel to 14ft was, as Colman O'Mahony (1986a, 27) has documented, completed by the end of 1882 (see CE, 11 December 1882).
93. The only other European region where this gauge was adopted is the Isle of Man. In England narrow gauge lines (generally defined as those less than 1m in width) were never more than 2ft 6in and even as narrow as 10 ¼ in.
94. The Gauges (Ireland) Act of 1846 established the Irish Standard Gauge at 5ft 3in (Middlemass 1981, 6), making it the only European region to do so, although it was also adopted in South Australia and Brazil. The contemporary English standard gauge of 4ft 8 ½ in had earlier been adopted by the Dublin and Kingstown line which opened in 1834 (Murray 1981), and later by the Belfast tramways (Waller and Waller 1992, 15).
95. In August 1825 the brothers George and John Rennie, the sons of the renowned Scottish engineer John Rennie (1761–1821), appointed the young Wexford-born engineer Charles Blacker Vignoles to survey the route of the Liverpool and Manchester Railway. Vignoles was to become engineer for the western end of the line until a disagreement with George Stephenson led to his resignation in 1826 (see Rolt 1988, 114–15). He went on to engineer the English Midland Counties Railway and to design the flat-

bottomed, 'I'-sectioned rails which bear his name. Vignoles was also a good friend of I.K. Brunel (1806–59) and eventually became President of the Institution of Civil Engineers. In an Irish context he has the distinction of engineering Ireland's first railway, the Dublin and Kingstown Railway.

96. Macneill's railway career began in Scotland, where he worked on the Slamannan line during the late 1830s, the Wishaw and Coltness railway (1838) and the Newhaven line in 1840 (Robertson 1983, 196–7). He had also, like his contemporary William Dargan, worked under Thomas Telford (1757–1834) the famous English road engineer. Macneill became one of the leading 'railway mania' engineers in Ireland, and had already achieved acclaim for his work on the Dublin and Drogheda railway completed in 1844, and was knighted for it. He was also responsible for surveying many of the northern railway routes (see McCutcheon 1980) and for laying out the Great Southern and Western Railway.

97. Moore later collaborated with Macneill on the Belfast and County Down Railway, of which Macneill was appointed chief engineer in 1855 (McCutcheon 1980, 142). Moore died in Cork on 1 July 1864 (O'Mahony 1986a, 191).

98. Newham's account has recently been updated by Stanley Jenkins (1993).

99. CE, 26 October 1849.

100. This metal footbridge was known locally as the 'Crinoline Bridge', reputedly because of the propensity of women's garments of that name to become caught in its spiral steps.

101. For John Benson's proposals see CC, 8 October 1867. Benson had in fact addressed the problem of moving the railway as early as 1849–50, when he carried out a survey.

102. The designation of railway locomotive types 2-2-2, 2-4-0T etc. is based on the wheel arrangements of individual engines. This system was developed by Frederic M. White (1865–1941), a New York Central Railroad official. In White's system the wheel arrangement is seen on the engine with its fore end facing to the left of the observer. An engine with wheels arranged thus oOo is designated 2-2-2, oOO as 2-4-0, OO as 0-4-0 etc.; the O being the driving wheels. In the designation 2-4-0T, the T indicates that it is a tank engine, i.e. where the locomotive's fuel and water are carried on its own frame; ST indicates saddle tanks.

103. Sharp Brothers supplied a number of similar locomotives to the English Midland Railway in the period 1848–9 (see Stretton 1896, 103).

104. Joseph Ronayne was the son of Edmund Ronayne of the Terrace glassworks (see Ch. 6.). His earliest railway engineering experience was acquired in the office of John Macneill (see n. 96 above), working first on Irish arterial lines and then on the Cork and Bandon line. Between 1854 and 1859 he worked in California superintending the hydraulic works during which the waters of the Sierra Nevada were diverted for the use of the Californian goldfields. Ronayne became a railway contractor upon his return to Ireland, and was responsible for the construction of the Queenstown branch of the Cork–Youghal line and for the Cork and Macroom railway. Shortly before his death he won the contract for the South Tipperary railway. In 1872 he succeeded John Francis Maguire as MP for Cork, a seat which he held until his death in 1876 (See CC, 8 May 1876; Dictionary of Nat. Biogr., vol. xvii, 1917, 204). For details of Ronayne's scheme for providing the city of Cork with water see Ch. 8). My thanks to Dr Charles O'Sullivan for discussing Ronayne's career with me and for providing important references.

105. The construction of the GS & WR tunnel at Cork had begun in 1847, and was to become the longest railway tunnel in Ireland upon its completion in 1855.

106. The railway company was actively pursued by both Fox, Henderson and Co. and the Public Works Loans Commissioners (who had advanced £35,000) for payment. The Commissioners finally agreed to be paid back in instalments, whilst I.K. Brunel was called in to arbitrate between the railway company and its contractors (see Shepherd 1984a, 210).

107. The firm of Charles Tayleur, Junior and Co., of the Hey foundry near Warrington, resulted from the need of George and Robert Stephenson to expand their existing capacity to manufacture locomotives (hitherto based on their small works at Newcastle). The firm of Tayleur and Co. became better known as the Vulcan foundry, which began by manufacturing locomotives of the Stephenson's Planet class (See Rolt 1988, 187).

108. CC, 18 October 1849.

109. Ibid., 14 March 1850.

110. Ibid., 14 March 1850.

111. Ibid., 21 March 1850.

112. The roof of the tunnel was lined with an estimated two million Youghal bricks, see CC, 3 January 1855.

113. Mallet also fabricated iron roofs for the stations at Belfast, Portadown and Armagh, along with the impressive cast-iron roof covering the platforms at Kingsbridge (Heuston) Station, the Dublin terminus of the GS & WR (see Cox 1982, 88).

114. The Dublin Builder, 1st July 1860.

115. See O'Donovan 1984, for a rare photograph of the Hargreaves Quay viaduct (which preceded the present nearby viaduct over Water Street), and the note by Walter McGrath accompanying it, which explains that the government of the period wanted to transport troops directly from Cobh to the Curragh without changing trains at Penrose Quay.

116. See also Irish Builder, April 1891, 73.

117. CC, 1 February 1893.

118. An east coast line linking Dublin, Wicklow, Wexford, Waterford and Cork was originally promoted by interests representing the English Great Western Railway, under the overall engineering control of I.K. Brunel; see Rolt 1980, 196. Brunel's assistant, O.E. Edwardes, became engineer for the Cork–Youghal line; see Creedon 1986, 30.

119. Similar measures were adopted by the GS & WR between 1849 and 1855 when the Cork tunnel was under construction.

120. The intended site for the line's Cork terminus was on the corner of Patrick's Hill and MacCurtain Street, a proposal which the company was later forced to abandon; see Creedon 1986, 30.

121. The contract for this section of the line was awarded to Joseph Ronayne, and its opening was delayed for six months by a dispute with the admiralty over the viaducts carrying the line to Great Island; see Murray and McNeill 1976, 38).

122. Over 80,000 passengers were carried by the line during the first six months of 1867, despite Fenian disturbances; see CE, 2 September 1867.

123. According to Jenkins (1992, 65) these were the only 0-4-4 tanks to run on the Irish narrow gauge. However, at least one engine of this type was run on the Castlederg and Victoria Bridge line, see Whitehouse and Snell 1984, 141.
124. The CB & PR was one of three Irish standard gauge lines to convert to narrow gauge, the others being the Lough Swilly railway (in 1885, see Patterson 1988) and the Finn Valley railway which formed part of the Donegal system (Prideaux 1981, 6).
125. CE, 10 May 1861.
126. The Dublin electric tramways networks operated with gauges ranging from 5ft 3in to 3ft 6in , whilst the Belfast network was the only one in Ireland to adopt the British standard gauge of 4ft 8 ½ in (see Waller and Waller 1992, 15, 60–61).
127. For a memoir of Southern Motorways, see Swanton 1992.

8 Utility Industries

1. Anne-Marie Lennon pers. comm.
2. Geo. III, C19, II et seq.; see Caulfield 1876, 751–2.
3. O'Sullivan 1937, 143; George III, C24, X. Additional amendments were made under 17 and 18 George III, C38, sections XVII, XVIII; 26 George III, C28, LIII et seq. See also Caulfield 1876, 765.
4. CE, 15 June 1857.
5. Ibid., 11 January 1844.
6. As early as 1805 a Mr Lynch reported to the corporation on supplying the city with a constant supply of water by diverting the River Shournagh at Healy's Bridge, a proposal which was to surface in various forms during the first half of the nineteenth century. Lynch provided sections and surveys of his proposed scheme for the corporation in 1816, but his scheme was apparently abandoned. In 1826 a Mr Meredith was employed by the corporation to prepare a section from a point above the Pouladuff cross roads of the Pouladuff stream, and to investigate the means by which this source could be used for the supply of the city. Meredith proposed that the water be conveyed to the city in a 9in square brick aqueduct and by pipe to a reservoir near the Evergreen area of the city. It appears that this scheme was not proceeded with, although according to Sir John Benson there was some evidence to suggest that a reservoir was built at Pouladuff. See CE, 11 January 1844.
7. As note 5.
8. CC, 18 May 1844.
9. Ibid., 5 June 1845.
10. Ibid., 30 September 1845.
11. Ibid., 2 October 1845.
12. CE, 23 January 1857.
13. As note 12.
14. 15th and 16th Victoria, see O'Kelly 1970, 127.
15. CE, 22 December 1854.
16. 29th and 30th Victoria.
17. CAI, Cork Corporation Committee minute book 1867–74, Pipe Water Committee, 6 December 1867.
18. CC, 21 February 1857.
19. Ibid., 5 May 1857.
20. These were supplied by Eddington and Co. of Glasgow CE, 4 May 1857; CC, 14 May 1857.
21. For the progress of pipe-laying within the city during 1858–9 see CE, 8 November, 13 December 1858; 7 February, 16 April, 2 September 1859.
22. CC, 14 May 1857.
23. CC, 16 June 1857.
24. Ibid., 12 June 1858.
25. Ibid., 2 February 1860; CE, 1 February, 5 July 1861.
26. CAI Reports relating to the water supply of Cork City, Cork. 1906, p. 9.
27. As note 26.
28. CE, 9 April 1861
29. CC, 17 April 1858.
30. Ibid., 11 August 1858.
31. CE, 1 February, 3 June 1861.
32. CC, 11 September 1858.
33. Ibid., 9 October 1858.
34. Ibid., 9 February 1860.
35. Hawksley built pumping stations for the Nottingham Waterworks Company and for at least 18 other towns throughout England (see Binnie 1981, 131–2). However, after his work on the Liverpool waterworks he tended to concentrate on constant supplies i.e. water supply systems based on forming reservoirs through the construction of dams. His other noteworthy contribution to Irish water engineering was the Wexford waterworks (Binnie 1981, 149).
36. CC, 1 July 1860. Benson was in London negotiating the purchase of an additional pumping engine.
37. CE, 11 February 1860.
38. A pending lawsuit between the corporation and MacAdam Bros. for the money withheld by the corporation, and owed to the manufacturers, was avoided when the matter was settled by arbitration. Two consultant engineers McClean and J.F. La Trobe Bateman ruled that the corporation was to pay MacAdam brothers £800; CE, 8 February 1862.
39. CE, 31 May 1861.

40. CE, 31 May 1861. The waterworks engine was a source of great derision for contemporaries, the *Cork Examiner*, for its part, calling it a 'great blot' (3 June 1861). Gibson (1861, vol. 2, 311) appears to have been voicing popular opinion when he remarked that 'Judging from the fearful thumping of the engine, I suspect it will soon work itself out, or beat itself down. It consumes more coals than the corporation had reason to expect'.
41. CE, 31 May 1861.
42. Ibid., 5 July 1861.
43. Ibid., 17 June 1861.
44. Ibid., 9 July 1861.
45. Ibid., 11 February 1861.
46. See CC, 23 August 1845.
47. CC, 21 July 1863; CE, 28 August 1863; CAI, Cork Corporation Committee minute book 1867–74), Pipe Water Committee, 4 September 1868; CAI Corporation Waterworks and Fire Brigade minute book 1879–85, p. 290, 25 May 1885.
48. CAI Cork Corporation minute book 1867–74, Pipe Water Committee, 6 December 1867.
49. CAI, Cork Corporation Committees minute book 1867–74, Pipe Water Committee, 4 September 1868.
50. As note 49, p. 58.
51. As note 49, p. 62, 4 September 1868.
52. As note 49, p. 71, 10 October 1868.
53. Note 49, p. 81–2, 31 October 1869.
54. CAI, Cork Corporation Waterworks and Fire Brigade Committee minute book, 1879–85, Report of Waterworks Committee for Quarter ended 31 March 1884: Analyst's Report Jan 15 1884, p. 224.
55. As note 54, p. 3. Bateman originally worked for William Fairbairn, conducting surveys on his behalf, and eventually became his son-in-law. Bateman's other commissions undertaken in Ireland include the river Bann reservoir, Vartry reservoir for Dublin Corporation, and the Dublin Harbour Board's proposal to construct a quay wall on the river Liffey. He was also appointed engineer by the Lords' Commissioners to report on the flooding of the river Shannon (see Russell 1980–81 and Binnie 1981).
56. As note 54, p. 10.
57. As note 54, p. 5.
58. As note 54, p. 96, Resident Engineer's Report, 16 November 1880.
59. As note 54, p. 3, 50–51, 30 December 1879.
60. CAI, *Reports relating to the water supply of Cork*, Cork. 1906, 7–8.
61. Ibid., p. 8.
62. As note 54, p. 52, 6 January 1880.
63. As note 54, p. 55, 20 January 1880.
64. As note 54, p. 56, letter from Stevenson read at waterworks committee meeting, 27 January 1880.
65. As note 54, p. 60–61, 2 March 1880.
66. As note 54, p. 97½ (sic).
67. As note 54, p. 103, letter dated 24 January 1881.
68. As note 54, p. 80, Resident Engineer's Report, 19 August 1880.
69. As note 54, p. 193–4, Waterworks Committee Report, 20 September 1883.
70. As note 54, p. 212, Resident Engineer's Report, 7 January 1884.
71. As note 54, p. 280–81, 9 April 1885.
72. As note 54, p. 246–9, 29 and 30 September 1884, 13 October 1884.
73. As note 54, p. 250, Resident Engineer's Report, 8 September 1884.
74. CAI, Cork Corporation Waterworks and Fire Brigade Committee minute book, 1879–85, 289–91, 25 May 1885.
75. As note 74, 1886–91, 47, 8 April 1886.
76. As note 74, p. 92, 27 July 1886.
77. As note 74, p. 170, 27 May 1887.
78. As note 74, p. 275, 21 May 1888. St Dominick's Mills had been involved in a legal action against the corporation over the waterwork's weir in 1865, whilst Benjamin Deebles also claimed compensation for the damage done to his Fishamble Lane Mill (Droop's Mill) by the waterworks in 1860. George Waters, proprietor of St Finn-Barre's Brewery also complained to the Corporation about the lack of water in the south channel of the river Lee resulting from the erection of the turbines (see Ch. 3).
79. As note 74, p. 113, 26 October 1886.
80. As note 74, p. 146, 9 March 1887.
81. As note 74, p. 275, 27 May 1888, 283, 6 June 1888.
82. CAI, Cork Corporation Waterworks and Fire Brigade Committee minute book 1888–91, Resident Engineer's Report, 26 February 1889, 149.
83. As note 82, p. 85, Waterworks Committee Report, 30 September 1888.
84. As note 82, p. 82, 20 April 1889.
85. As note 82, p. 95, 3 July 1889.
86. As note 82, p. 148, 26 February 1890, Report on Proceedings for year 1889.
87. As note 82, p. 85, 29 October 1888.
88. As note 82, p. 147–8 Report on proceedings for year 1889, Appendix, City Engineer's Report dated 29 January 1890, 149.
89. As note 82, p. 149, Resident Engineer's Report.
90. As note 82, p. 268, Resident Engineer's Yearly Report for 1890.
91. As note 90.
92. CAI, Cork Corporation Waterworks and Fire Brigade Committee minute book 1888–91, 124, 23 January 1895.

93. CAI, Waterworks Resident Engineer's report book, 1893–1900, 106–7, 20 January 1895.
94. CAI, Cork Corporation Waterworks and Fire Brigade Committee minute book 1891–3, 142.
95. CAI, Waterworks Committee minute book, 1899–1903, City Engineer's Weekly Report, 19 June 1901. This was a rejoinder to an earlier report by O'Toole (ibid., 183, 29 May 1901), and the inference is that O'Toole, as Resident Engineer, was clearly to blame for the delay.
96. O'Toole was eventually forced to resign in 1903, see CAI, Waterworks Committee minute book, 1903–1906, 27, 10 June 1903.
97. CAI, Waterworks Committee minute book, 1899–1903, 346, 24 September 1902.
98. As note 97, p. 351, 8 October 1902.
99. CAI, Cork Corporation Waterworks and Fire Brigade Committee minute book, 1903–6, 152, 16 July 1904.
100. CAI, Cork Corporation Waterworks and Fire Brigade Committee minute book, 1906–10, 8, 18 April 1906.
101. As note 100, p. 120, 5 March 1907.
102. CMI, 24 February 1816; Tuckey 1837, 250; O'Sullivan 1987, 75.
103. See Thomas Holt's *Plan of the city and suburbs of Cork* (1832) and map accompanying *The cities and boroughs in Ireland* (1832).
104. SR, 11 August 1827.
105. 7 January 1857.
106. Anderson had been appointed engineer to the works in 1856, and advised on more technical matters such as the setting of the retorts (see O'Sullivan 1992, 49).
107. CE, 2 March 1857.
108. CE, 3 June 1857; O'Sullivan 1992, 48.
109. James Reidy and Co. was Cork's main gasfitting firm, and won contracts for the Cavan Gaslight Co. The early gasworks at Trim, Enniscorthy, Lismore and Woodburne were also built by this Cork firm (see O'Sullivan 1987, 48).
110. CE, 6 January 1858.
111. Ibid., 3 March 1858.
112. Ibid., 8 September 1858, 19 March 1860.
113. Ibid., 22 August 1860.
114. Ibid., 6 March 1862.
115. Ibid., 13 May 1859; see O'Sullivan 1987, 51.
116. Ibid., 2 September 1867.
117. Ibid., 8 March 1875.
118. A further generating station was established by the Dublin Gas Company in Hawkins Street in 1891, and in 1892 Ireland's first city-based, local authority-controlled electricity-generating station was officially opened at Fleet Street in Dublin (Manning and McDowell 1984; O'Flanagan 1992). By the end of the 1890s all of the main urban centres in Ireland, with exception of Limerick, had electricity-generating stations, and of these only Cork and Galway were outside municipal control (Manning and McDowell 1984, 14). The Giant's Causeway, Portrush and Bush Valley Railway and Tramway Company were the first in the world to use electricity for traction on a commercial basis, opening in 1883 (see McGuigan 1964).
119. CC, 18 October 1890.
120. The circuits, alternating switches etc. were installed by Gerald Percival (Stratten and Stratten 1892, 145–6), who established Cork's first firm of electrical contractors. Percival and Brother Dominic Burke made an electric tramcar which ran at the 1889 exhibition at the Corn Exchange on Anglesea Street (see McGrath 1981, 26).
121. The third Earl of Rosse built the world's largest telescope in the 1840s and discovered that many galaxies were spiral-shaped, see Earl of Rosse 1985a, 83. Charles Parsons went on to found NEI Parsons of Newcastle, Earl of Rosse 1985b, 87.
122. CC, 24 October 1895.
123. CC, 21 December 1898; see also McGrath 1981, 98–100.
124. CC, 6 August 1896.
125. CE, 2 and 12 September 1898.
126. CC, 21 December 1898.
127. As note 126.
128. CC, 25 May 1917; see also Coakley 1919, 81.

GLOSSARY OF TECHNICAL TERMS

ashlar. A masonry technique in which large, smoothly faced square or rectilinear blocks, dressed by a stonecutter on all of the principal faces, are laid in regular courses.

Babcock and Wilcox boiler. An early form of watertube boiler used to raise steam. In watertube boilers it became possible to raise high pressure steam more safely than in the traditional **Lancashire boiler**.

bark mill. A device which employed edge runner stones for crushing bark, for use in the manufacture of tanning liquors. In Cork many bark mills were originally powered by horses.

barm. A term commonly applied to the yeasts used by brewers and distillers in the fermentation process.

beam engine. Early form of steam engine in which machinery was set in motion through the action of a rocking beam.

beetling. A finishing process in the manufacture of linen and cotton in which wooden pestles (beetles), powered by a waterwheel, were allowed to fall on a rotating drum of cloth, to create a sheen.

bends. In tanning, the term applied to the two separated sections of the **butt**.

blast furnace. A smelter for reducing ores, which employed water-powered (and later steam-powered) bellows to produce a continuous air blast. The air blast created temperatures sufficient to reduce the ores to a molten state, which enabled the molten metal to be run off into a casting bed and the slag to be tapped off separately.

bleach green. A textile-processing site at which raw cloth (usually brown linen) was bleached white.

bleaching. A process in which linen and cotton were bleached white, after which the cloth could be either be dyed or colour printed.

breastshot waterwheel. A waterwheel which receives incoming water about half way up its circumference.

buck house. In linen manufacture a building containing boilers, in which the cloth was steeped and boiled.

bundling room. In a flax-spinning mill a room in which dried hanks of yarn were arranged in bundles containing 60,000 yards.

butt. In tanning, the thickest and most prized section of a hide, which is divided into two sections called **bends**.

caisson. In bridge construction, a structure formed by driving piles into the river bed to form a free-standing box which is then pumped free of water. The box, thus formed, can then be used to lay the foundations of the bridge piers below water level.

calender. In linen manufacture a machine which subjected the cloth to pressure by passing it through pairs of rollers. The pressure exerted by these rollers not only ensured that the cloth was the same thickness throughout, but also imparted a smooth external finish.

calico printing. In cotton manufacture, the printing of coloured patterns on the cloth.

carbonisation. In the manufacture of town gas, a process in which bituminous coal was distilled in a **retort**.

carding. A process in which raw wool and cotton were prepared for spinning by separating the tangled fibres and paralleling them to form a **sliver**.

carding machine. A device for mechanically carding cotton, flax and wool fibres, in which wire rollers were used to form loose threads or **slivers**.

cast-iron. The product of the **blast furnace**. Contains 3–4% carbon and can be cast into intricate shapes, although it cannot be reheated and worked by a smith like **wrought iron**.

charcoal mill. In gunpowder manufacture, a water-powered installation in which charcoal is ground into a powder.

charge house. In gunpowder manufacture (at Ballincollig Gunpowder Mills) a small circular building in which pre-mixed ingredients of gunpowder (salpetre, charcoal and sulphur) are stored before being processed in the **incorporating mills**.

charring house. In gunpowder manufacture an installation in which charcoal is made by placing wood in metal tubes and inserting these into a furnace.

clasp arm. A form of waterwheel construction in which the spokes are clamped around the waterwheel's axle to form a square.

cockle cylinders. In grain milling, a mechanical device for separating foreign seeds from grain.

Coffey still. A form of **patent still** developed by a former Irish excise officer Aenas Coffey (1780–1852) and patented by him in 1830.

combing. In the manufacture of **worsted** cloth, a process in which the longer fibres or long staple wool or **tops** was separated from the short staple wool or **noils**. Originally carried out by hand, the process was not successfully mechanised until the 1840s.

composition mills. See **incorporating mills**.

compound engine. In steam engines a working principal involving two cylinders, which enabled high-pressure steam to be used, first in a high-pressure cylinder and then in a larger low-pressure cylinder, in which the steam continued to expand and perform useful work on the piston.

condenser. In the manufacture of town gas, a metal box containing cast-iron pipes in which gas was cooled.

copper. In brewing a large copper receptacle in which **wort** is boiled with hops and sugar.

corning house. In gunpowder manufacture a water-powered installation in which **press cake** is mechanically forced through sieves to form small granules of gunpowder.

Cornish boiler. A cylindrical steam boiler with a single firetube, developed by the Cornishman Richard Trevithick (1771–1833), in 1808, which enabled high-pressure steam of up to 50psi be used in steam engines.

couch frame. In malting, a wooden receptacle for piling heaps of swollen barley after its removal from the **steep**.

cullet. In glass-making, broken glass which is added to the ingredients of new glass to assist in the melting process.

culm. Anthracitic slack or coal dust traditionally used as fuel in lime-burning, malting, grain drying etc.

cupola furnace. A vertical furnace used in iron foundries, in which a blast of air from a steam-powered blowing engine was used to remelt pigs of cast-iron (and occasionally scrap iron), to make iron castings.

currying. The skilled finishing process in which tanned leather is dressed, impregnated with dubbin and pared down to the required thickness.

Curtis turbine. A form of impulse steam turbine developed in America by Charles Gordon Curtis (1860–1953).

cuts. In linen manufacture, a standard length of cloth, the equivalent of 300yds.

cutwaters. A bow or wedge-shaped projection on the pier of a bridge, which protects its foundations from the scouring action of the river, and from any large floating objects.

direct fire setting. In the manufacture of town gas, an arrangement of retorts in which the retorts are heated by a furnace set immediately below them.

doffers. In flax-spinning mills, female operatives who removed and replaced flyer bobbins, supervised by a 'doffing mistress'.

double-acting pump. A pump whose piston ejects a liquid on both the inward and outward strokes (i.e. where each stroke is a power stroke), in contrast to single-acting pumps where such movement is confined to the outward stroke.

drawing frame. In linen and cotton manufacture a machine which elongated the slivers created by a carding machine.

droppings room. In the malting process a room adjoining a malt kiln, into which the dried malt is shovelled downwards from the kiln floor.

dry spinning. In linen manufacture, the term given to the earliest form of water-powered flax spinning. This was only capable of producing coarser yarns and was eventually replaced by **wet spinning**.

drying room. In flax-spinning mills, a room often situated over the boiler house in which hanks of yarn were dried.

dusting house. In gunpowder manufacture, a water-powered installation in which excess dust was removed from the powder granules by tumbling it in gauze-covered rollers.

economiser. A device which uses the exhaust fumes of a steam engine to pre-heat the boiler's feed water.

exhauster. In the manufacture of town gas, a series of rotary pumps, powered by a steam engine, which pump gas from the **retorts** to the **condenser**.

feints. In whiskey distilling, the product of the low wines still.

filter tunnel. In municipal water supply a man-made circular tunnel which used sands in the river bed to naturally filter incoming water.

fining. In brewing, a process in which finings (a gelatinous substance made from the swim bladder of a sturgeon) were added to a cask of beer, to drag particles of sediment to the bottom of the cask and help to keep the beer clean.

floating dock. A man-made anchorage for ships, which was entered through a lock gate on the flow tide. When the lock gates are closed the dock remains full of water, which enabled ships to unload their cargoes safely, irrespective of the rise and fall of the tides.

flooring. In malting, the process in which the steeped barley is spread on wooden floors to germinate.

Fourneyron turbine. An early form of **reaction turbine** developed by the French engineer Benôit Fourneyron in 1827.

French burr millstone. A composite millstone (i.e. a millstone made from separate pieces of stone cemented together) made with stone from Le Ferté, near Paris.

fritting. In glass manufacture, a process in which the ingredients of glass were calcined in an oven to remove impurities.

fulling. In the manufacture of woollen cloth, a process in which the cloth is beaten in a trough filled with an alkaline solution (made with a clay called fuller's earth or with stale urine), which thickened the cloth and removed any grease or oils absorbed by the cloth during spinning and weaving.

gas engine. A form of internal combustion engine powered first by town gas and later with producer gas (i.e. gas made from low grade fuels, in Ireland generally turf).

gas holder. A receptacle for storing gas. Gasholders (or gasometers) with telescopic sections came into use in the 1820s.

glass-making cone. In glass-making, a tall, brick-built, truncated cone which provided an updraught for the glass-making furnaces and shelter for the glass workers.

Grand Jury. In Ireland, a local administrative body empowered to raise the *cess* (rates), and to use this money to repair and build roads, bridges, courthouses, lunatic asylums, etc. The Grand Juries were replaced by County Councils in 1899.

granulating house. In gunpowder manufacture, a machine with toothed rollers which granulated the **press cake**.

graving dock. A dry-dock, usually with lock gates, which enabled ships to be graved, i.e. cleaned of all accretions, and general repairs, re-painting and tarring to be undertaken.

green charge. In gunpowder manufacture, the pre-mixed ingredients of gunpowder: salpetre, charcoal and sulphur.

hackling. In a flax-spinning mill, a process in which the flax fibres were carefully combed out, first by a machine and then by skilled workers called hacklers in a sorting shop.

handling pits. In tanning, a series of pits with progressively stronger tanning liquors, in which the hides were laid flat and which, when the hides were moved from pit to pit, ensured that these were exposed to liquors of increasing strength.

hank. A length of yarn used to determine its count (i.e. the length of fibre required to make one pound in weight).

headrace. A man-made water channel directing water to a mill-wheel or water turbine.

hop back. In brewing, a false-bottomed vessel which collected the spent hops and allowed the beer to pass into the coolers.

hopper barge. A floating barge with bottom-opening doors, which allowed material excavated by a dredger to be floated out to sea and dumped.

horizontal engine. A form of stationary steam engine in which the cylinder and crankshaft are arranged horizontally, as opposed to those of **beam engines** and **vertical engines**.

house-built engine. An early form of beam engine which relied on the structure housing it for support.

house machine. In rope-making, a process by which ropes were manufactured with wheeled bogies called travellers, which hauled out rope of different diameters.

incorporating mills. In gunpowder manufacture, a water-powered mill in which the pre-mixed ingredients of gunpowder were ground together (incorporated) under millstones set on edge (i.e. edge-runner stones).

independent engine. A stationary steam engine which is entirely supported by its own framework, where the engine is no longer reliant on the structure housing it for support (see **house-built engine**).

inverted vertical engine. A stationary steam engine in which the cylinder is positioned above the crankshaft.

Jonval turbine. A form of **reaction turbine** developed by Feu Jonval in France in 1841.

kieve. In Ireland this a generic term for a large wooden receptacle, such as those using for mashing barley in the brewing and distilling processes, in tanning and in traditional bleaching.

Lancashire boiler. A variety of horizontal steam boiler with two internal fire tubes, patented by William Fairbairn and John Heatherington in 1844. Extensively used in Britain and Ireland to replace **cornish boilers**.

lap. In the manufacture of cotton, tufts of cotton fibres disentangled from bales of raw cotton.

layer pits. In the tanning process a pit in which hides are laid flat in between layers of bark.

laying and stranding. A process in rope-making in which strands of yarn were intertwined to form a single cord.

lehr or annealing arch. A long gallery through which pieces of newly fabricated glass were slowly drawn to allow them to cool slowly.

limepit. In tanning, a pit containing an alkaline liquor. Raw hides were immersed in these pits to facilitate the loosening of the hairs on the skin.

lime putty. Quicklime (i.e. lime which has been calcined in a kiln) which has been slaked in water to produce slaked or hydrated lime. When mixed with sand and water this produces a non-hydraulic cement which hardens on exposure to air.

line. In flax spinning, the long flax fibres separated from the short fibres or **tow** in the **hackling** process.

line shafting. In industrial buildings, the overhead shafting transmitting the power of a water or steam-powered prime mover to machinery.

low wines. In whiskey manufacture, the first distillate from a pot still.

lye. In traditional cloth bleaching, an alkaline solution comprising ashes mixed with water.

malt loft. In brewing a storage loft for malt, usually the upper storey of a malt tower (a tall building housing the malt screens and milling plant).

malt mill. In brewing and distilling a mill for grinding malt to grist.

mash tun. In brewing and distilling, a large circular vessel in which grist (ground malt) is mixed with hot water to make **worts**.

masher. In brewing and distilling a vessel with internally mounted rotating arms, in which grist and water were mixed before being admitted in to the **mash tun**.

McNaughting. A method of compounding low-pressure, single cylinder engines through the addition of a small high-pressure cylinder, patented by William McNaught in 1845.

meter house. In town gas manufacture a meter, usually contained in a separate building within the works, which monitored gas production.

mill cake. In gunpowder manufacture, the term given to the raw gunpowder after being processed in the **incorporating mills**.

millpond. A man-made reservoir in which water is stored for use by a water-powered installation.

mixing house. In gunpowder manufacture, a building in which the refined ingredients of gunpowder are mixed with water.

nap. In woollen cloth processing, raising the fibres of the cloth and shearing them off to a uniform length, to impart a soft feel to the surface of the cloth.

narrow gauge. In Ireland, a railway with a gauge of 3ft or less.

noils. The shorter woollen fibres (separated from the longer woollen fibres or **tops** by combing) used in the manufacture of **woollen** cloth.

overshot waterwheel. A waterwheel which receives incoming water on the upper part of its circumference.

Parsons turbine. A steam reaction turbine developed by Charles Parsons and patented by him in 1884.

patent slip. A device for hauling ships out of the water by means of a carriage pulled either by a manually operated capstan or a steam winch, along metal rails laid in the bottom of a man-made slipway.

patent still. In whiskey distillation, a still which enabled distillation to be undertaken continuously.

pot still. In whiskey distillation, a large flat-bottomed copper vessel, which initiates the separation of alcohol from the **wort** or **wash**, by heating it and converting it into a vapour.

Presentment. An order made by a **Grand Jury**, to raise money and allocate it to undertake various works such as road construction and repair, etc.

press cake. In gunpowder manufacture, the term applied to **mill cake** after it had been processed in the **press house**.

press house. In gunpowder manufacture, a water-powered installation in which **mill**

cake was processed in a hydraulic press, to remove residual moisture.

proofing house. In gunpowder manufacture, a building associated with testing the strength (i.e. proofing) of gunpowder.

quicklime. Lime which has been calcined in a lime kiln.

reaction turbine. A water or steam-powered turbine which is turned by the reaction of a water or steam jet being forced to change direction.

reeling room. In a flax-spinning mill the top floor of the mill were the yarn is wound onto reels.

retort. (a) In the manufacture of town gas, a D-sectioned refractory vessel in which bituminous coal was heated; (b) In charcoal manufacture a tube into which a piece of wood is placed and then inserted into a furnace.

retting. A process in which bundles of flax are soaked in water for two weeks so as to loosen the flax fibre from the shous, or waste portion of the plant.

roller milling. The manufacture of flour by passing the grain through a series of chilled iron or steel rollers.

rope race. A narrow compartment extending upwards through a spinning mill to accommodate the rope drive, which transmitted the motion of the engine to a series of line shafts on the individual mill floors.

rope walk. A long open or covered way used for laying out and stranding ropes.

rotative engine. A steam engine capable of transmitting rotary motion to machinery.

roughing room. In a flax-spinning mill, a building in which the ends of the flax fibre were given a rough combing and were squared off at the root end.

rough stuff. A department in a footwear maufacturing works in which the soles, insoles and heel lifts were cut out by means of a cutting press.

rounding. In tanning, the division of a hide into several parts.

roving frame. In a flax-spinning mill, a machine which both drew out the sliver and imparted a slight twist to it to create a roving.

saddle tank engine. A railway locomotive with its water tank curved over the boiler, effectively hanging over it like a saddle.

saggar. A fireproof ceramic vessel in which fine pottery or clay pipes are placed to protect them from the direct heat of the kiln.

Scherzer lifting bridge. A lifting bridge whose lifting span was raised by an electrically powered counterbalance.

scutching. A process in which flax fibre was separated from the shous by the action of rapidly rotating wooden scutching blades.

shearing. A finishing process for woollen cloth in which the nap is raised and sheared off to produce a smooth surface to the cloth.

shelling stones. In grain milling a pair of millstones used for shelling (i.e. the removal of the husks of the cereal grains), preparatory to grinding.

side lever engine. An early form of beam engine in which the rocking beam is set beside the cylinder, enabling significant savings in headroom.

side tank engine. A railway locomotive with a rectangular water tank which is set on frames on either side of the boiler.

slaked lime. Quick or calcined lime which has reacted with water to form a paste.

sliver. In textile spinning, a continuous strand of untwisted loose thread.

sour. In cloth bleaching, the steeping of the cloth in buttermilk which acted as a dilute acid or sour. The purpose of souring was to neutralise the cloth to facilitate grassing, during which the cloth was bleached by exposure to sunlight.

spade mill. A water-powered forge, equipped with a trip-hammer, forge bellows, grindstones, guillotines etc. in which spades, shovels and other small iron tools were manufactured.

sparging. In brewing a process in which the strength of the **worts** was reduced by sprinkling a **mash tun** with hot water.

spent grains. In brewing and distilling the residues of the bruised malt collected in the false bottom of a **mash tun**, and traditionally sold off as animal feed.

stack. A tall, vertical chimney used to provide a draught for boiler furnaces and to disperse exhaust fumes.

standard gauge. In Ireland, a railway built to a gauge of 5ft 3in.

steep. In the malting process a wooden or cast-iron tank in which barley is immersed in water, before **flooring**.

stock dying. In woollen manufacture, the dying of the raw wool.

stove house. In gunpowder manufacture, an oval boiler house, with drying houses on either side.

suspenders. In tanning, a series of pits containing a weak tanning liquor in which hides were suspended on poles.

suspension waterwheel. A cast-iron waterwheel which transmits power by means of a cast-iron gear (segment) bolted to its rim.

tailrace. A man-made channel which directs water away from a water-powered prime mover back to its source.

tanning. A series of processes in which raw hides are converted into leather.

tender engines. A railway locomotive whose supply of fuel and water is hauled behind it in a separate wheeled vehicle called a tender.

tentering. A finishing process for woollen cloth in which the fabric is stretched under tension.

tops. The longer fibres of wool, used in the manufacture of **worsted cloth** which are separated from the shorter fibres (**noils**) by **combing**.

tow. The shorter flax fibres, which are separated from the longer fibres or **line**, in the **hackling process**.

trip hammer. A water-powered forge hammer activated by cams set on the axle of the waterwheel. In Ireland these are generally employed in **spade mills**.

triple expansion engine. A stationary steam engine in which steam undergoes three successive expansions in three separate cylinders.

tuck mill. A fulling mill.

tun and stilling room. In late eighteenth-century Cork breweries, a room in which the porter or beer was stored in large wooden vats (tuns) before being poured into casks.

turnpike. A toll road constructed and maintained by a turnpike trust.

turn table. A manually operated rotating platform which enables railway locomotives to be turned through 360°.

undershot waterwheel. A waterwheel in which the incoming water is directed onto floats or paddles at the lowest part of its circumference.

voussoirs. A wedge-shaped stone or brick used to form part of an arch.

wagon boiler. A low-pressure steam boiler shaped like a covered wagon.

wash. In whiskey distilling the term applied to the fermented wort, from which alcohol is separated in a still.

weaving factory. In Ireland, the term applied to the buildings housing linen-weaving looms.

well tank engine. A railway locomotive in which the water tank is hung between the frames, an arrangement which gave the engine a lower centre of gravity.

wet spinning. In flax spinning, a mechanised process in which the flax fibre is passed through a trough of hot water. By this means the binding gums in the fibre could be dissolved, which enabled finer yarns to be drawn off than was possible in the **dry-spinning** process.

willeying. A mechanised process used in the preliminary sorting of wool and cotton, which cleans out the dirt and gently teased out the fibres preparatory to carding.

woollen cloth. Cloth made from the shorter woollen fibres or **noils**.

worm. A spiral copper coil connected to the head of a **pot still**, whose lower portion was placed in a **worm tub**.

worm tub. In whiskey distillation, a large circular wooden tub filled with water, in which a worm is coiled. The water condensed the warm vapours directed into the worm from the **pot still**.

worsted cloth. A variety of woollen cloth made from long woollen fibres or **tops**.

worts. In brewing and distilling, unfermented or raw beer.

wrought iron. Malleable iron containing a very low percentage of carbon. It can be forged by a smith when reheated. Stronger in tension than cast-iron.

BIBLIOGRAPHY

The bibliography is divided into sub-sections as follows:

Manuscript Sources
Printed Material 1) Newspapers 2) Parliamentary Papers 3) Books and Printed Papers
Directories
Theses

ABBREVIATIONS

HC	House of Commons
HMSO	His/Her Majesty's Stationery Office
IAR	Industrial Archaeology Review
JCHAS	Journal of the Cork Historical and Archaeological Society
JIRRS	Journal of the Irish Railway Record Society
JKAHS	Journal of the Kerry Archaeological and Historical Society
TNS	Transactions of the Newcomen Society
UJA	Ulster Journal of Archaeology

MANUSCRIPT SOURCES

Cork Archives Institute

Sunbeam-Wolsey Collection.
Beamish and Crawford Collection.
Irish Distillers Collection.
Cork Corporation Minute Book 1867–74, Pipe Water Committee.
Cork Corporation Waterworks and Fire Brigade Minute Books 1879–1910.
Cork Corporation Waterworks Resident Engineer's Report Books 1893–1900.

Cork City Library

Goad Insurance Plans, Cork City.

National Archives, Dublin

Valuation Survey books for the city of Cork, compiled 1849–51 and for the areas defined as the survey environs.

Birmingham Central Libraries

Boulton and Watt Collection.

Public Record Office, London

War Office records (1806–28) relating to Board of Ordnance's management of Ballincollig Gunpowder Mills

PRINTED MATERIAL

(1) Newspapers

The Corke Journal
The New Cork Evening Post
The Hibernian Chronicle
The Cork Evening Herald or Munster Advertiser
The Cork Constitution or The Cork Advertiser 1825–73; The Cork Constitution 1873–1922
The Cork Examiner
The Cork Mercantile Chronicle
The Cork Morning Intelligencer
The Southern Reporter and Cork Commercial Courier
The Cork Sun
The Cork Evening Echo
The Irish Times

(2) Parliamentary Papers

(a) Pre-1800

The Journals of the House of Commons of the Kingdom of Ireland [1613–1800], 19 vols., Dublin, 1796–1800.

(b) Post-1800

Fourth report of the Commissioners of Enquiry into the collection and management of the revenue arising in Ireland. HC, 1822 (634), xiii.
Accounts relating to distilling from malt and raw corn. HC, 1828 (217), xviii.
Report of the Commissioners of Inland Revenue. HC, 1829 (353), xii.
Report on roads made at the public expense in southern district of Ireland by Richard Griffiths. HC, 1831 (119), xii.
Public Works Ireland. HC, 1831, xvii.
Report of the select committee on turnpike roads in Ireland. HC, 1831–2 (645), xviii.
Second report of the Commissioners appointed to consider and recommend a general system of railways for Ireland. HC, 1837–8 (145), xxxv.
Report of the Commissioner appointed to enquire into the Turnpike Trusts, Ireland. HC, 1856 (2110), xix.
Report from the select committee on industries [Ireland]. HC, 1884–5 (288), ix.

(3) Books and Printed Papers

ANDERSON, E.B. 1984 *Sailing ships of Ireland*. Facsimile reprint of edition of 1951, Impact Printing, Coleraine.
ANDREWS, J.H. 1956 'Notes on the historical geography of the Irish iron industry', *Irish Geography* **3**, 139–49.
ANDREWS, J.H. 1964 'Road planning in Ireland before the railway age', *Irish Geography* **5** (1), 17–41.
ANON. 1873 *The celebrated brewery of Sir John Arnott & Co., Cork*. The Irish Porter Breweries (Sketch no. 2). Boole Library, University College, Cork, Munster Print collection, 677.
ANON. 1886 *Cork industrial exhibition report 1882*. Cork.
ANON. 1891 *The industries of Ireland. Part 1: Belfast and the towns of the north*. London.

Reprinted as *Industries of the north one hundred years ago: industrial and commercial life in the north of Ireland, 1888–91*, with an introduction by W.H. Crawford, Friar's Bush Press, Belfast, 1986.

ANON. 1956 *W & H.M. Goulding Ltd, Dublin, Ireland: 1856–1956.* Temple Press, Dublin.

ANON. 1977 *The first sixty years 1917–1977: Ford in Ireland.* Cork.

ARCHER, J. 1801 *Statistical survey of County Dublin.* Dublin.

ASPIN, C. 1987 *The woollen industry.* Shire Publications, Princes Risborough.

AYTO, E. G. 1987 *Clay tobacco pipes.* Shire Publications, Princes Risborough.

BARKER, T.C. 1977 *The glassmakers: Pilkington — the rise of an international company 1826–1976.* Weidenfeld and Nicolson, London.

BARNARD, A. 1887 *The whiskey distilleries of the United Kingdom.* London.

BARNARD, A. 1889–91 *The noted breweries of Great Britain and Ireland,* 4 vols. Sir Joseph Causton and Sons, London.

BARNARD, T.C. 1985 'Anglo-Irish industrial enterprise: iron-making at Enniscorthy, Co. Wexford, 1657–92', PRIA **85**C, no. 4, 101–44.

BARRY, M. 1985 *Across deep waters: bridges of Ireland.* Frankfort Press, Dublin.

BARRY, R. 1920 'The resources of Ireland', *Catholic Bulletin* **10**, February 1920, 101–7.

BARRY, W. 1895a 'Port of Cork steamships', *JCHAS* **1**, no. 4, April 1905, 433–46.

BARRY, W. 1895b 'Port of Cork steamships', *JCHAS* **1**, no. 10, October 1905, 145–73.

BARRY, W. 1917 'History of the Port of Cork steam navigation 1815–1915', *JCHAS* **23**, no. 113, 1–16, 79–93, 125–42, 185–99.

BARRY, W. 1919 *History of the Port of Cork steam navigation.* Cork.

BEAMISH, N.L. 1844 'Statistical report of the parish of St Michael', in *Report of the 13th meeting of the British Academy for the advancement of science.* London.

BELL, J. and WATSON, M. 1986 *Irish farming 1750–1900.* John Donald, Edinburgh.

BIANCONI, M. and WATSON, S.J. 1962 *Bianconi, king of the Irish roads.* Figgis, Dublin.

BIELENBERG, A. 1991 *Cork's Industrial Revolution 1780–1880: development or decline?* Cork University Press.

BIELENBERG, A. 1993 *Locke's Distillery: a history.* Lilliput Press, Dublin.

BINNIE, G.M. 1981 *Early Victorian water engineers.* Thomas Telford Ltd, London.

BOUCHER, C.T.G. 1963 *John Rennie, 1761–1821: the life and work of a great engineer.* Manchester.

BOWIE, G. 1978 'Early stationary steam engines in Ireland', *IAR* **2**, no. 1, 168–74.

BOWIE, G. 1979–80 'Surviving stationary steam engines in the Republic of Ireland', *IAR* **4**, no. 1, 81–90.

BOWIE, G.S. and JONES, D.H. 1978 'Regional variations in water powered grain mills in the British Isles', *Trans. International Molinological Soc.* **4**, 259–68.

BRADLEY, J. and HALPIN, A. 1993 'The topographical development of Scandinavian and Anglo-Norman Cork', in O'Flanagan, P. and Buttimer, C.G. (eds.), *Cork History and Society...*, 15–44. Geography Publications, Dublin.

BRUNICARDI, N. 1982 (2nd ed.) *Haulbowline, Spike and Rocky Islands in Cork Harbour.* Éigse Books, Fermoy.

BRUNICARDI, N. 1985 *The bridge at Fermoy.* Éigse Books, Fermoy.

BRUNICARDI, N. 1987 *John Anderson, Entrepreneur.* Éigse Books, Fermoy.

BRUNSKILL, R.W. 1990 *Brick building in Britain.* Batsford, London.

BUCHANAN, R.A. 1977 *Industrial archaeology in Britain.* Pelican, Harmondsworth.

BUSH, J. 1769 *Hibernia Curiosa.* Dublin.

CADOGAN, T. 1988 'Belvelly Brickworks', *Harbour Lights — Jour. of the Great Island Hist. Soc.* **1**, 31–40.

CALLAN MacARDLE, T. and CALLAN, W. 1902a 'The brewing industry in Ireland', in Coyne, W.P. (ed.), *Ireland: industrial and agricultural*, 451–93. Dublin.

CALLAN MacARDLE, T. and CALLAN, W. 1902b 'The distilling industry' in Coyne, W.P. (ed.), *Ireland: industrial and agricultural*, 494–511. Dublin.

CALVERT, F. 1807 *The first series of select views of Cork and its environs.* Cork.

CAMPBELL, T. 1778 *Philosophical survey of the south of Ireland, in a series of letters to John Watkinson MD.* Dublin.

CARR, J. 1806 (repr. 1970 with an introduction by L.M. Cullen) *The stranger in Ireland or a tour in the southern and western parts of that country in 1805.* London.

CASSERLEY, H.C. 1974 *Outline of Irish railway history.* David and Charles, Newton Abbot.

CAULFIELD, R. 1876 *The council book of the corporation of Cork.* Guildford.

CLARKE, P. 1992 *The Royal Canal: the complete story.* Elo Publications, Dublin.

CLEARY, R.M. 1985 'Excavation of wall and wooden pump (off Smith Street, Cork City)', *JCHAS* **90**, 120–26.

CLEMENS, P.G.E. 1976 'The rise of Liverpool 1665–1750', *Economic History Review* **29**, no. 2, 211–25.

CLEMENTS, P. 1970 *Marc Isambard Brunel.* Longmans, London.

COAKLEY, D.J. 1919 *Cork, its trade and commerce: official handbook of the Cork Incorporated Chamber of Commerce and Shipping.* Guy and Co., Cork.

COE, W.E. 1969 *The engineering industry of Northern Ireland.* David and Charles, Newton Abbot.

COLE, G.A.J. 1922 *Memoir and map of localities of minerals of economic importance and metalliferous mines in Ireland.* Memoir of the Geological Survey of Ireland. Mineral Resources, 2 vols. Stationery Office, Dublin.

COLLINS, J. T. 1958 'Gleanings from old Cork newspapers', *JCHAS* **63**, 95–102.

COOPER, J. 1986 'SERG goes Irish-Waterford to Cork', *Stationary Engine Research Group Bulletin* **8**, no. 2, 46–60.

CORCORAN, N. and MURPHY, E. (eds.) 1986 'Employees at the Board of Ordnance establishments in Ballincollig in 1815', *Jour. Ballincollig Community School Local Hist. Soc.*, 7–9.

CORRAN, H.S. 1970 'Spence of Cork Street', *Technology Ireland*, May 1970, 24.

CORRAN, T.H. 1975 *A history of brewing.* David and Charles, Newton Abbot.

COSSONS, N. 1987 *The B.P. book of industrial archaeology.* David and Charles, Newton Abbot.

COUGHLAN, A. and O'REILLY, F.D. 1992 'The North Cork coalfields', *Mallow Field Club Journal*, no. 10, 44–53.

COWMAN, D. and REILLY, T.A. 1988 *The lost mines of West Carberry.* Geological Survey of Ireland, Dublin.

COX, R.C. 1982 'Robert Mallet: engineering work in Ireland' in Cox, R.C. (ed.), *Robert Mallet 1810–1881*, 71–118. Centenary Seminar Papers. RIA and Irish Engineering Publications, Dublin.

COYNE, W. P. (ed.) (nd) *Ireland: industrial and agricultural.* Browne and Nolan, Dublin.

CRAIG, M. 1983 *The architecture of Ireland from the earliest times to 1880.* Batsford, London.

CRAWFORD, W.H. 1988 'The evolution of the linen industry in Ulster before industrialisation', *Irish Economic and Social History Review* **15**, 32–53.

CREEDON, C. 1960 *The Cork and Macroom Direct Railway.* Cork.

CREEDON, C. 1985 *Cork City railway stations 1849–1985: an illustrated history.* Privately published. Cork.

CREEDON, C. 1986 *The Cork, Bandon and South Coast Railway, vol. 1, 1849–1899.* Privately published. Cork.

CREEDON, C. 1989 *The Cork, Bandon and South Coast Railway, vol. 2, 1900–1950.* Privately published. Cork.

CREEDON, C. 1991 *The Cork, Bandon and South Coast Railway, vol. 3, 1951–1961–1976.* Privately published, Cork.

CREEDON, C. 1992 *The Cork, Blackrock and Passage Railway, 1850–1932.* Privately published, Cork.

CROCKER, G. 1986 *The gunpowder industry*. Shire, Princes Risborough.

CROFTON-CROKER, T. 1824 (repr. 1981) *Researches in the south of Ireland*. Irish Academic Press, Dublin.

CRONIN, M. 1993 'Work and workers in Cork City and County 1800–1900', in O'Flanagan, P. and Buttimer, G.G. (eds.), *Cork History and Society...*, 721–58. Geography Publications, Dublin.

CROSSLEY, D. 1990 *Post-medieval archaeology in Britain*. Leicester University Press.

CROSSMAN, V. 1994 *Local government in nineteenth-century Ireland*. Institute of Irish Studies, Queen's University of Belfast.

CROWLEY, T.E. 1986 *Beam engines*. Shire, Princes Risborough.

CULLEN, L.M. 1968 *Anglo-Irish trade, 1660–1800*. Manchester University Press.

CULLEN, L.M. 1977 'Eighteenth-century flour milling in Ireland', *Irish Economic and Social History Review* **4**, 5–52.

CULLEN, L.M. 1987 (2nd ed.) *An economic history of Ireland since 1660*. Batsford, London.

CULLEN, L.M. and SMOUT, T.C. (eds.) 1978 *Comparative aspects of Scottish and Irish economic and social history 1600–1900*. John Donald, Edinburgh.

d'ALTON, I. 1980 *Protestant society and politics in Cork 1812–1844*. Cork University Press.

DALY, M.E. 1985 *Dublin — the deposed capital: a social and economic history 1860–1914*. Cork University Press.

DALY, M.E. 1992 *Industrial development and Irish identity 1922–1939*. Gill and Macmillan, Dublin.

DALY, S. 1978 *Cork, a city in crisis: a history of labour conflict and social misery 1870–1872*. Tower Books, Cork.

DAVIES, C. 1938 'Kilns for flax-drying and lime-burning', *UJA* **3**, no. 1, 79–80.

DAVIS, W. 1985 'Aneas Coffey, excise man, distiller and inventor', in Mollan, C., Davis, W. and Finucane, B. (eds.), *Some people and places in Irish science and technology*, 22–3. Royal Irish Academy, Dublin.

DAY, R. 1898 'The St George Steam Packet Company's Ship "Sirius"', *JCHAS* **4**, no. 39, 243–4.

DELANEY, J.F. 1910 *City Engineer's report on the excessive consumption of water in the city and suburbs [of Cork] and filtration arrangements*. Guy and Co., Cork.

DELANEY, J.F. 1911 *Report on the general condition of the city water supply*. Guy and Co., Cork.

DELANEY, J.G. 1990 'Brickmaking in Gillen', *Folklife* **28**, 31–62.

DELANY, R. 1973 *The Grand Canal of Ireland*. David and Charles, Newton Abbot.

DELANY, R. 1988 *Ireland's inland waterways*. Appletree Press, Belfast.

DELANY, R. 1992 *Ireland's Royal Canal 1789–1992*. Lilliput Press, Dublin.

DELANY, V.T.H. and DELANY D.R. 1966 *The canals of the south of Ireland*. David and Charles, Newton Abbot.

DICKINSON, H.W. and JENKINS, R. 1927 (repr. 1989) *James Watt and the Steam Engine*. Encore Editions, London.

DICKSON, D. 1971 'A description of County Cork, *c.* 1741', *JCHAS* **76**, no. 224, 152–4.

DICKSON, D. 1978 'Aspects of the rise and decline of the Irish cotton industry', in Cullen, L.M. and Smout, T.C. (eds.), *Comparative aspects...*, 100–115. John Donald, Edinburgh.

DICKSON, D. 1983 'The place of Dublin in the eighteenth-century Irish economy', in Devine, T.M. and Dickson, D. (eds.), *Ireland and Scotland 1600–1850: parallels and contrasts in economic and social development*, 177–92. John Donald, Edinburgh.

DODSWORTH, R. 1984 *Glass and glassmaking*. Shire, Princes Risborough.

DONNACHIE, I. 1979 *A history of the brewing industry in Scotland*. John Donald, Edinburgh.

DONNELLY Jr, J. 1971 'Cork market: its role in the nineteenth-century Irish butter trade', *Studia Hibernica*, no. 11, 130–63.

DONNELLY Jr, J. 1975 *The land and people of nineteenth-century Cork: the rural economy and the land question*. Routledge and Kegan Paul, London.

DOWLING, D. 1972 'Glenmore brickyards: a forgotten industry', *Old Kilkenny Review*, no. 24, 42–51.

DUDLEY WESTROPP, M.S. 1978 (revised edition (ed.) Boydell, M.) *Irish glass: a history of glass-making in Ireland from the sixteenth century*. Albert Figgis, Dublin.

DUNLEVY, M. 1989 *Penrose glass*. National Museum of Ireland, Dublin.

EARL, B. 1978 *Cornish explosives*. Treithick Society, Penzance.

ELMAN, R. 1982 James Joyce. Oxford University Press, New York.

FAYLE, H. 1970 *Narrow gauge railways of Ireland*. East Ardsley.

FITZGERALD, J. 1981 'The Drogheda textile industry, 1780–1820', *County Louth Archaeological and Historical Journal* **20**, no. 1, 36–48.

FITZGERALD, W.A. 1984 *Cork City waterworks 1768–1984*. Cork.

FLANAGAN, P. 1972 *The Ballinamore and Ballyconnell Canal*. David and Charles, Newton Abbot.

FOLEY, C. 1991 *A history of Douglas*. Cork.

FRASER, R. 1801 *General view of the agriculture etc. of the County Wicklow*. Dublin.

GAILEY, R.A. 1970 'The typology of the Irish spade', in Gailey, R.A. and Fenton, A. (eds.), *The Spade in...*, 35–48. HMSO, Belfast.

GAILEY, R.A. 1982 *Spade-making in Ireland*. Holywood, Ulster Folk and Transport Museum, Belfast.

GAILEY, R.A. and FENTON, A. (eds.) 1970 *The Spade in Northern and Atlantic Europe*. HMSO, Belfast.

GIBSON, C.B. 1861 *The history of the county of Cork*, 2 vols. London.

GILES, C. and GOODALL, I.H. 1992 *Yorkshire textile mills: the buildings of the Yorkshire textile industry 1770–1930*. HMSO, London.

GILLIGAN, H.A. 1988 *A history of the port of Dublin*. Gill and Macmillan, Dublin.

G.M. 1917 'The Cork Improvement Act 1917', *JCHAS* **22**, part 3, 172–3.

GOURVISH, T.R. and WILSON, R.G. 1994 *The British brewing industry 1830–1980*. Cambridge University Press.

GREEN, E.R.R. 1949 *The Lagan Valley, 1800–50: a local history of the industrial revolution*. Faber and Faber, London.

GREEN, E.R.R. 1963 *The industrial archaeology of County Down*. HMSO, Belfast.

GRIBBON, H.D. 1969 *The history of water power in Ulster*. David and Charles, Newton Abbot.

GRIBBON, H.D. 1978 'The Irish Linen Board, 1711–1828', in Cullen, L.M. and Smout, T.C. (eds.), *Comparative aspects...*, 77–87. John Donald, Edinburgh.

GUTHRIE, J. 1971 *A history of marine engineering*. London.

HALL, J. 1813 *Tour through Ireland*, 2 vols. London.

HALL, Mr and Mrs S.C. 1841 *Ireland: its scenery, character etc.* 3 vols. London.

HAMOND, F. 1987 *Gunpowdermills, Ballincollig*. Appendix D, Reconstruction of incorporating mill no. 3, Ballincollig, Co. Cork. Cork County Council.

HAMOND, F. 1991 *Antrim coast and glens industrial heritage*. HMSO, Belfast.

HAMOND, F. and SCALLY, C. 1988 *The Greater Belfast industrial archaeology survey*. DOE Northern Ireland, Belfast.

HARRISON, R. S. 1991 *Cork City Quakers 1655–1939: a brief history*. Privately published, Cork.

HAY, G.D. and STELL, G.P. 1986 *Monuments of industry: an illustrated historical record*. HMSO, Glasgow.

HENCHION, R. 1974 'Some old wheeled mills of the Glashaboy', *Cork Holly Bough*.

HILL, H. H. 1943 'Cork architecture', *JCHAS* **48**, 95–8.

HILLS, R. L. 1988 *Papermaking in Britain 1488–1988: a short history*. Athlone Press, London.

HILLS, R. L. 1989 *Power from steam: a history of the stationary steam engine*. Cambridge University Press.

HOLLAND, M. 1917 'Survey of the town walls of Cork in 1733', *JCHAS* **23**, 199–205.

INCE, L. 1984 *The Neath Abbey iron company*. De Archaeologische Pres, Eindhoven.

INGLIS, H. D. 1834 *Ireland in 1834: a journey throughout Ireland during the spring, summer and autumn of 1834*, 2 vols. London.

JACKSON, J. 1987 'Mallow–Lombardstown Canal', *Mallow Field Club Journal*, no. 3, 22–9.

JACOBSON, D. 1977 'The political economy of industrial location: the Ford Motor Company at Cork, 1912–26', *Irish Economic and Social History* **4**, 36–55.

JENKINS, J.G. 1973 *The Rhaedr Tannery*. (n.p.)

JENKINS, S. C. 1992 *The Cork and Muskerry Light Railway*. Oakwood Press, Headington, Oxford.

JENKINS, S. C. 1993 *The Cork, Blackrock and Passage Railway*. Oakwood Press, Headington, Oxford.

KANEFSKY, J. 1979 'Motive power in British industry and the accuracy of the 1870 factory return', *Economic History Review*, 2nd ser., **32**, 360–75.

KELLEHER, G. D. 1992 *Gunpowder to guided missiles: Ireland's war industries*. Privately published, Belfast.

KENNEDY, L. 1981 'Regional specialisation, railway development and Irish agriculture in the nineteenth century', in Goldstrom, J.M. and Clarkson, L.A. (eds.), *Irish population, economy and society: essays in honour of the late K.H. Connell*, 173–94. Clarendon Press, Oxford.

KILROY, J. 1996 *Irish Trams*. Colourpoint, Dublin.

KINAHAN, G.H. 1889 'Economic geology of Ireland', *Jour. Geological Society Ireland* **8**.

KING, L. and KINSELLA, S. 1986 'Sir Thomas Tobin (1807–1881)', *Jour. Ballincollig Community School Local Hist. Soc.*, 21–4.

LAMPLUGH, G.W. *et al.* 1905 *The geology of the country around Cork and Cork Harbour*. HMSO, Dublin.

LANGFORD, P. and MULHERIN, S. 1982 *Cork City quay walls*. Institute of Civil Engineers of Ireland, Dublin.

LAW, R.J. 1986 *The steam engine*. HMSO, London.

LEWIS, S. 1837 *A topographical dictionary of Ireland*, 2 vols. Lewis and Co., London.

LINDSAY, J. 1968–71 'Falls Foundry 1900–14: a textile machinery firm in Belfast', *Textile History* **1**, 350–62. David and Charles, Newton Abbot.

LOCKWOOD, J.F. 1962 *Flour milling*. Henry Simon, Stockport.

LOHAN, R. 1994 *Guide to the archives of the Office of Public Works*. Stationery Office, Dublin.

LUCAS, A.T. 1968 'Cloth finishing in Ireland', *Folk Life* **6**, 18–67.

LUDLOW, C.G. 1989 'An outline of the salt industry in Ireland', in *The history of technology, science and society, 1750–1914*, 1–13. Jordanstown, University of Ulster.

LYNCH, P. and VAIZEY, J. 1960 *Guinness's Brewery in the Irish economy, 1759–1886*. Cambridge University Press.

MacCARTHY, C.J.F. 1983 'An antiquary's notebook 5', *JCHAS* **88**, 111–17.

MacCARTHY, C.J.F. 1985 'An antiquary's notebook 7', *JCHAS* **90**, 186–99.

MacCLEOD, C. 1978 ' "The land we live in": a toast in Cork decanters', *JCHAS* **88**, no. 237, 59–65.

McCRACKEN, E. 1957 'Charcoal-burning ironworks in seventeenth- and eighteenth-century Ireland, *UJA* **20**, 3rd series, 122–38.

McCRACKEN, E. 1971 *The Irish woods since Tudor times: their distribution and exploitation*. David and Charles, Newton Abbot.

McCRACKEN, J.L. 1973 'The age of the stage coach', in Nowlan, K. B. (ed.) *Travel and transport in Ireland*, 47–63. Gill and Macmillan, Dublin.

McCUTCHEON, W.A. 1965 *The canals of the north of Ireland*. David and Charles, Newton

Abbot.

McCUTCHEON, W.A. 1977 *Wheel and spindle aspects of Irish industrial history*. Blackstaff Press, Belfast.

McCUTCHEON, W.A. 1980 *The industrial archaeology of Northern Ireland*. HMSO, Belfast.

McCUTCHEON, W.A. 1990 'Belfast ropeworks' in Mollan, C., Davis, W. and Finucane, B., *Some people and places...*, 82–3. Royal Irish Academy, Dublin.

McDONAGH, O. 1964 'The origins of porter', *Economic History Review*, 2nd ser., **16**, no. 3, 530–35.

McGRATH, W. 1950 'Building of new bridges', *Cork Evening Echo*, 5th December.

McGRATH, W. 1955 'A century of service 1855–1955: the building of Cork's tunnel', *Cork Weekly Examiner and Holly Bough*.

McGRATH, W. 1974 'Cork's narrow gauge', *JIIRS* 2, no. 64, June, 210–23.

McGRATH, W. 1976 'Tomorrow is 65th anniversary of Brian Boru Bridges', *Cork Evening Echo*, 31 December.

McGRATH, W. 1980 'Sad end for bridge engines', *Cork Examiner*, 25 March.

McGRATH, W. 1981 *Tram tracks through Cork*. Tower Books, Cork.

McGRATH, W. 1984 'A Lower Glanmire Road mystery solved, a note', *Cork Holly Bough*.

McGUIGAN, J.H. 1964 *The Giant's Causeway tramway*. Oakwood Press, Headington, Oxford.

McGUIRE, E.B. 1973 *Irish whiskey: a history of distilling, the spirit trade and excise controls in Ireland*. Gill and Macmillan, Dublin.

McNEILL, D.B. 1969 and 1971 *Irish passenger steamship services*, 2 vols. David and Charles, Newton Abbot.

McPARLAN, J. 1802 *Statistical survey of the county of Leitrim*. Dublin.

McQUILLAN, J. 1993 *The railway town: the story of the Great Northern railway works and Dundalk*. Dundalgan Press, Dundalk.

MAGUIRE, J.F. 1853 *The industrial movement in Ireland as illustrated by the national exhibition of 1852*. John O'Brien, Cork.

MALCOLM, E. 1986 *Ireland sober, Ireland free: drink and temperance in nineteenth-century Ireland*. Dublin.

MANNING, M. and McDOWELL, M. 1984 *Electricity supply in Ireland: the history of the ESB*. Gill and Macmillan, Dublin.

MANNION, J. 1988 'The maritime trade of Waterford in the eighteenth century', in Smith, W.J. and Whelan, K. (eds.), *Common ground: essays on the historical geography of Ireland presented to T. Jones Hughes*, 208–33. Cork University Press.

MARMION, A. 1855 *The ancient and modern history of the maritime ports of Ireland*. J.H. Banks, London.

MARSHALL, J. 1978 *A biographical dictionary of railway engineers*. David and Charles, Newton Abbot.

MEASOM, G. S. 1866 *The official illustrated guide to the Midland Great Western and Dublin Drogheda Railway*. London.

MEGHAN, P.J. 1959 'The administrative work of the Grand Jury', *Administration* 6, no. 3, 247–64.

MESSENGER, B. 1988 *Picking up the linen threads*. Blackstaff Press, Belfast.

MIDDLEMASS, T. 1981 *Irish standard gauge railways*. David and Charles, Newton Abbot.

MOLLAN, C., DAVIS, W. and FINUCANE, B. (eds.) 1985 *Some people and places in Irish science and technology*. Royal Irish Academy, Dublin.

MOORE, M. 1996 *Archaeological inventory of County Wexford*. Stationery Office, Dublin.

MOSS, M. and HUME, J.R. 1986 *Shipbuilders to the world: 125 years of Harland and Wolff 1861–1986*. Blackstaff Press, Belfast.

MULCAHY, M. 1966 *A short history of Kinsale*. Privately published, Cork.

MULLINS, M.B. 1863 'An historical sketch of engineering in Ireland', *Trans. of the Institution of Civil Engineers of Ireland* 6, 1–181.

MURPHY, M. 1980 'The working classes of nineteenth-century Cork, *JCHAS* **89**, 26–51.

MURPHY, M. 1981 'The economic and social structure of nineteenth-century Cork' , in Harkness, D. and O'Dowd, M. (eds.), *The town in Ireland. Historical Studies* 13, 125–54. Appletree Press, Belfast.

MURPHY, S. 1986 *Stone mad*. Routledge and Kegan Paul, London.

MURRAY, K.A. 1981 *Ireland's first railway*. Irish Railway Record Society, Dublin.

MURRAY, K.A. and McNEILL, D.B. 1976 *The Great Southern and Western Railway*. Irish Railway Record Society, Wicklow.

NASH, R.C. 1985 'Irish Atlantic trade in the seventeenth and eighteenth centuries', *William and Mary Quarterly* **42**, 3, 229–356.

NEWENHAM, T. 1809 *A view of the natural, political and commercial circumstances of Ireland*. London.

NÍ CHINNÉIDE, S. 1973 'A new view of Cork City in 1790', *JCHAS* **78**, no. 227, 1–13.

O'BRIEN, J.B. 1985 'The Hacketts: glimpses of entrepreneurial life in Cork 1800–1870', *JCHAS* **90**, 150–57.

O'BRIEN, J.B. 1993 'Population, politics and society in Cork, 1780–1900', in O'Flanagan, P. and Buttimer, C.G. (eds.), *Cork History and Society...*, 699–720. Geography Publications, Dublin.

O'BRIEN, W. 1994a *Our mining past, the metal mining heritage of Cork*. Cork Public Museum.

O'BRIEN, W. 1994b *Mount Gabriel Bronze Age mining in Ireland*. Galway University Press.

O'CALLAGHAN, A. 1991 *Of timber, iron and stone*. Cork.

Ó CLÉIRIGH, N. 1992 *Valentia, a different Irish island*. Portobello Press, Dublin.

Ó DANACHAIR, C. 1970 'The use of the spade in Ireland', in Gailey, R.A. and Fenton, A. (eds.), *The Spade in...*, 49–56. HMSO, Belfast.

O'DONOVAN, D. 1984 'A Lower Glanmire Road mystery solved', *Cork Holly Bough*.

O'FLANAGAN, N. 1992 'Dublin's current history', *Technology Ireland* **24**, no. 5, 42–4.

O'FLANAGAN, P. and BUTTIMER, C. G. (eds.) 1993 *Cork history and society: interdisciplinary essays on the history of an Irish county*. Geography Publications, Dublin.

Ó GRÁDA, C. 1988 *Ireland before and after the Famine: explorations in economic history, 1800–1925*. Manchester University Press.

Ó GRÁDA, C. 1994 *Ireland: a new economic history 1780–1939*. Clarendon Press, Oxford.

O'KEEFFE, P.J. 1980 'Richard Griffiths: planner and builder of roads', in Herries Davies, G. L. and Mollan, C. R. (eds.), *Richard Griffiths 1784–1878*, 57–75. Royal Dublin Society, Dublin.

O'KEEFFE, P. and SIMINGTON, T. 1991 *Irish stone bridges: history and heritage*. Irish Academic Press, Dublin.

O'KELLY, M.J. 1970 'Wooden water mains at South Terrace, Cork', *JCHAS* **75**, 125–8.

OLLERENSHAW, P. 1985 'Industry, 1820–1914', in Kennedy, L. and Ollerenshaw, P. (eds.), *An economic history of Ulster 1820–1939*, 62–108. Manchester University Press.

Ó LUING, S. 1975 'Richard Griffith and the roads of Kerry I', *JKAHS* **8**, 89–113.

Ó LUING, S. 1976 'Richard Griffith and the roads of Kerry II', *JKAHS* **9**, 92–124.

O'MAHONY, C. 1984 'Bygone industries of Blarney and Dripsey', *JCHAS* **89**, 77–87.

O'MAHONY, C. 1986a *The maritime gateway to Cork: a history of the outports of Passage West and Monkstown, 1754–1942*. Tower Books, Cork.

O'MAHONY, C. 1986b 'The hazards of gunpowder manufacture at Ballincollig', *Jour. Ballincollig Community School Local Hist. Soc.* **2**, 10–12.

O'MAHONY, C. 1987 'Copper mining at Allihies, Co. Cork', *JCHAS* **92**, 71–85.

O'MAHONY, C. 1989 'Shipbuilding and repairing in nineteenth century Cork', *JCHAS* **94**, 74–87.

O'MAHONY, C. 1992 Review of Bielenberg, A., *Cork's Industrial Revolution 1780–1880* (see above), *JCHAS* **97**, 150–51.

Ó MURCHADHA, D. 1990 'The siege of Cork in 1690', *JCHAS* **95**, 1–19.

O'NEILL, T. P. 1973 'Bianconi and his cars', in Nowlan, K. B. (ed.), *Travel and transport in Ireland*, 82–95. Gill and Macmillan, Dublin.

O'NEILL, T. 1984 'Tools and things: machinery on Irish farms 1700–1981', in Gailey, A. and Ó Hogáin, D. (eds.), *Gold under the furze: studies in folk life tradition presented to Caoimhín Ó Danachair*, 101–14. Glendale Press, Dublin.

O'SULLIVAN, C. 1987 *The gasmakers historical perspectives on the Irish gas industry.* Irish Gas Association/O'Brien Press, Dublin.

O'SULLIVAN, C. 1992 'The gas question', *Technology Ireland* **24**, no. 26, 46–50.

O'SULLIVAN, J.C. 1969 'Wooden pumps', *Folk Life* **7**, 101–16.

O'SULLIVAN, S. 1975a 'An epic of bridges (no. 43)', *Cork Evening Echo*, 9th July.

O'SULLIVAN, S. 1975b 'Anglesea bridge (no. 44)', *Cork Evening Echo*, 30th July.

O'SULLIVAN, W. 1937 *The economic history of Cork City from the earliest times to the Act of Union.* Cork University Press.

PALMER, M. 1990 'Industrial archaeology: a thematic or period discipline', *Antiquity* **64**, no. 243, 275–85.

PATTERSON, E. M. 1988 *The Londonderry and Lough Swilly railway: a history of the narrow gauge railways of north-west Ireland.* David and Charles, Newton Abbot.

PERREN, R. 1990 'Structural change and market growth in the food industry: flour milling in Britain, Europe and America, 1850–1914', *Economic History Review*, 2nd ser., **43**, no. 3, 420–37.

POLLARD, S. 1986 *Peaceful conquest: the industrialisation of Europe 1760–1970.* Oxford University Press, New York.

POLLARD, S. and ROBERTSON, P. 1979 *The British shipbuilding industry 1870–1914.* Cambridge, Mass.

POWER, C. 1991 'Quarterstown Mills, Mallow', *Mallow Field Club Jour.*, no. 9, 5–17.

POWER, D. *et al.* 1992 *Archaeological inventory of County Cork, vol. 1 — West Cork.* Stationery Office, Dublin.

POWER, D. *et al.* 1994 *Archaeological inventory of County Cork, vol. 2 — East and South Cork.* Stationery Office, Dublin.

PRESS, J. 1989 *The footwear industry in Ireland 1922–1973.* Irish Academic Press, Dublin.

PRIDEAUX, J.D.C.A. 1981 *The Irish narrow gauge railway.* David and Charles, Newton Abbot.

READ, H. 1980 'The Penroses of Woodhill, Cork: an account of their property in the city', *JCHAS* **85**, 79–98.

REYNOLDS, M. 1983 *A history of the Irish post office.* MacDonnell Whyte, Dublin.

REYNOLDS, T.S. 1983 *Stronger than a hundred men: a history of the vertical waterwheel.* John Hopkins University Press, London.

ROBERTSON, C.J.A. 1983 *The origins of the Scottish railway system 1722–1844.* John Donald, Edinburgh.

ROBINS, J. 1980 *The lost children: a study of charity children in Ireland 1700–1900.* Dublin.

ROLLESTON, T.W. 1902 'The Irish leather and boot-making industry', in Coyne W. P. (ed.), *Ireland, industrial and agricultural*, 408–12. Dublin.

ROLT, L.T.C. 1980 *Isambard Kingdom Brunel.* Pelican, Harmondsworth.

ROLT, L.T.C. 1986 *Tools for the job: a history of machine tools to 1950.* HMSO, London.

ROLT, L.T.C. 1988 *George and Robert Stephenson: the railway revolution.* Penguin, London.

RONAYNE, J. R. 1854 *The supply of water to the city of Cork, and its application to the production of motive power within the city.* Cork.

ROSSE, EARL OF 1990a 'William, Third Earl of Rosse (1800–1867)', in Mollan, C., Davis, W. and Finucane, B., *Some people and places in Irish science and technology*, 83. Royal Irish Academy, Dublin.

ROSSE, EARL OF 1990b 'Charles Parsons 1854–1931', in Mollan, C., Davis, W. and Finucane, B., *Some people and places in Irish science and technology*, 87. Royal Irish Academy, Dublin.

ROTHERY, E.J. 1968 'Aneas Coffey', *Annals of Science* **23**, 53–71.

RUSSELL, P. 1980–81 'John Frederic La Trobe-Bateman (1810–1889) Water Engineer', *TNS* **52**, 119–38.

RYAN, J. 1985 *Aspects of building construction in Cork*. University College Cork Seminar. N.p.

RYAN, J.H. and DAVEY, H. 1902 *Corporation of Cork Waterworks Committee report on works, plant and machinery at pumping station with special reference to the efficiency of the filter tunnel*. Guy and Company, Cork.

RYAN, N. 1992 *Sparkling granite: the story of the granite working people of the Three Rock region of County Dublin*. Stone Publishing, Dublin.

RYNNE, C. 1986 'An early turbine at Ballincollig Gunpowder Mills', *Jour. Ballincollig Community School Local Hist. Soc.* **2**, 13–17.

RYNNE, C. 1989a *The industrial archaeology of Cork City and its environs: a pilot study*. Royal Irish Academy, Cork.

RYNNE, C. 1989b 'Early water turbines: an Irish history', *Technology Ireland* **21**, no. 3, 19.

RYNNE, C. 1989c 'The influence of the linen industry in the south of Ireland on the adoption of the water turbine', in *The History of Technology, Science and Society 1750–1914* , 19–32. Jordanstown, New University of Ulster.

RYNNE, C. 1991 *The industrial archaeology of Cork City and its environs: a sites and monuments record*. Royal Irish Academy, Cork.

RYNNE, C. 1993 *The archaeology of Cork City and harbour from the earliest times to industrialisation*. Collins Press, Cork.

SHAW MASON, W. 1814–19 *A statistical account or parochial survey of Ireland*, 3 vols. Graisberry and Campbell, Dublin.

SHEPHERD, W.E. 1984a 'The Cork, Bandon and South Coast Railway—1', *JIRRS* **15**, no. 14, June, 209–18.

SHEPHERD, W.E. 1984b 'The Cork, Bandon and South Coast Railway—2', *JIRRS* **15**, no. 15, October, 286–94.

SIMINGTON, R.C. (ed.) 1942 *The civil survey vol. VI: valuations c. 1663–4 Waterford and Cork Cities*. Dublin.

SKEMPTON, A.W. 1975–6 'A history of the steam dredger 1797–1830', *TNS* **47**, 97–116.

SMITH, C. 1750 (repr. 1815) *The ancient and present state of the county and city of Cork*, 2 vols. Cork.

SMYTH, W.J. 1988 'Flax cultivation in Ireland: the development and demise of a regional staple', in Smyth, W.J. and Whelan, K. (eds.), *Common ground: essays on the historical geography of Ireland*, 129–44. Cork University Press.

SPROULE, J. (ed.) 1854 *The industrial exhibition of 1853*. Dublin.

STARK, A.G. 1850 *The south of Ireland in 1850*. Dublin.

STEPHEN, L. and LEE, S. (eds.) 1917 *Dictionary of national biography* **17**. London.

STORCK, J. and TEAGUE, W.D. 1952 *Flour for man's bread: a history of milling*. Minneapolis.

STRETTON, C.E. 1896 (1986 repr.) *The development of the locomotive: a popular history 1803–6*. Bracken Books, London.

SWANTON, W.A. 1992 *Cork's early buses: the story of Southern Motorways and its times*. Privately published, Cork.

SWEETMAN, R. 1988 'The development of the port', in Beckett, J.C. *et al.* (eds.), *Belfast, the making of the city 1800–1914*, 57–70. Appletree Press, Belfast.

TAKEI, A. 1994 'The first Irish linen mills', *Irish Economic and Social History Review* **21**, 28–38.

TANN, J. and GWYN JONES, R. 1996 'Technology and transformation: the diffusion of the roller mill in the British flour milling industry, 1870–1907', *Technology and Culture* **37**, no. 1, 36–69.

TAYLOR, G. and SKINNER, A. 1778 (1968 repr. with an introduction by J.H. Andrews)

Maps of the roads of Ireland. Irish University Press, Shannon.

THOMSON, R.S. 1981 'Leather manufacture in the post medieval period with special reference to Northhamptonshire', *Post Medieval Archaeology* **15**, 161–75.

THOMSON, R.S. 1981–2 'Tanning: man's first manufacturing process', *TNS* **53**, 139–56.

TOWNSEND, H. 1815 *A general and statistical survey of the county of Cork*, 2 vols. Cork.

TREBILCOCK, C. 1981 *The industrialisation of the continental powers*. London.

TUCKEY, F. H. 1837 (repr. 1980) *The county and city of Cork Remembrancer*. Tower Books, Cork.

UNDERWOOD, A.J.V. 1935 *Historical development of distilling plant*. London.

Von TUNZELMAN, G.N. 1978 *Steam power and British industrialisation to 1860*. Oxford.

WAKEFIELD, E. 1812 *An account of Ireland, statistical and political*, 2 vols. Longman, London.

WALLER, M.H. and WALLER, P. 1992 *British and Irish tramway systems since 1945*. Ian Allen, Runnymede.

WARREN, P. 1981 *Irish glass: Waterford–Cork–Belfast in the age of exuberance*. Faber and Faber, London.

WATKINS, G. 1971 *The textile mill engine*, 2 vols. David and Charles, Newton Abbot.

WATTS, M. 1983 *Corn milling*. Shire, Princes Risborough.

WEIR, R.B. 1978 'The patent still distillers and the role of competition in nineteenth-century Irish economic history', in Cullen, L.M. and Smout, T.C. (eds.), *Comparative aspects of Scottish and Irish economic and social history 1600–1900*, 129–44. John Donald, Edinburgh.

WEIR, R.B. 1995 *The history of the Distillers Company 1877–1939: diversification and growth in whisky and chemicals*. Clarendon Press, Oxford.

WHITEHOUSE, P.B. and SNELL, J.B. 1984 *Narrow gauge railways of the British Isles*. Bracken Books, London.

WILKINSON, N.B. 1975–6 'An American powdermaker in Great Britain: Lammot du Pont's journal, 1858', *TNS* **47**, 85–96.

WILLIAMS, M. 1985 *Ford and and Fordson tractors*. Farming Press, London.

WILLIAMS, M. 1991 *Tractors since 1889*. Farming Press, Ipswich.

WILLIAMS, M. and FARNIE, D.A. 1992 *Cotton mills in Greater Manchester*. Carnegie Publishing, Preston.

WILLIAMS, R. 1989 *Limekilns and limeburning*. Shire, Princes Risborough.

WILLIAMS, R.A. 1991 *The Berehaven copper mines, Allihies, Co. Cork, S.W. Ireland*. Northern Mine Research Society, Worsop.

WILLIAMS, T.I. 1981 *A history of the British gas industry*. Oxford University Press.

WILSON, C.A. 1975 'Burnt wine and cordial waters: the early days of distilling', *Folklife* **13**, 54–65.

WILSON, G.B.L. 1973–4 'The small country gasworks', *TNS* **40**, 33–43.

WILSON, P.N. 1955–7 'The waterwheels of John Smeaton', *TNS* **30**, 24–48.

WINDELE, J. 1843 *Historical and descriptive notices of the city of Cork and its vicinity*. Cork.

YOUNG, A. 1780 (repr. 1970, ed. A.W. Hutton) *A tour in Ireland with general observations on the present state of that kingdom*, 2 vols. London.

DIRECTORIES

(Note only those Cork City and County directories cited in the text are listed here)

ALDWELL, A. (ed.) 1844 *The county and city of Cork Post Office General Directory 1844–5*. Cork.

ANON. *Commercial Directory of Ireland, Scotland... for years 1820–1821–1822*.

Guy's Directory of Munster. Cork, 1893.

Holden's Triennial directory of 1805 (1805–1806–1807). London.

LUCAS, R. 'The Cork directory for the year 1787', *JCHAS* **72**, 135–57.
Pigot and Company's City of Dublin and Hibernian Provincial Directory. Manchester, 1824.
Slater's Royal National Commercial Directory of Ireland. London, 1856.
STRATTEN and STRATTEN 1892 *Dublin, Cork and the South of Ireland.* London.
WEST, W. 1809 *The Cork Directory 1809–1810.* Cork.

THESES

BOWIE, G. 1975 *Watermills, windmills and stationary steam engines In Ireland.* PhD, QUB.
COSGRAVE, M.B., 1989 *A history of Beamish and Crawford.* MA thesis, UCC.
DICKSON, D. 1977 *The economic history of the Cork region in the eighteenth century.* PhD, Trinity College, Dublin.
LANE, S. 1980 *Clay tobacco pipes from Cork City.* MA, UCC.
McCARTHY, P.J. 1949 *An economic history of the port of Cork 1813–1900.* MEconSc thesis, UCC.
NOLAN, D. 1974 *The County Cork Grand Jury 1836–1899.* MA, UCC.
O'KEEFE, S. 1974 *Commercial and industrial change in Cork 1800–1825.* MA, Maynooth.

TOPOGRAPHICAL INDEX

Note on contents:
Names of towns, streets, rivers etc. are included in this index.
For Bridges, Quays and Railway companies/lines — see under those headings in Subject
Index

NAMES INDEX

Note on contents:
This index contains personal names, names of companies, mills, societies etc. mentioned in the text.
Authors cited are **not** included, except where their work is discussed in the text.
Bridges and Quays are listed under 'Bridges' and 'Quays' in the *Subject Index*.
Railway lines are listed in the *Subject Index* under 'Railway Companies/Lines'.
Railway stations are listed in the *Subject Index* under 'Railway Stations'.
Ships' names are listed in the *Subject Index* under 'Ships'.

SUBJECT INDEX

Note: **Treatment of names**; Names of persons, companies, mills, foundries, societies etc. are listed in the **Names Index**; names of mills etc. are **also** listed in this index *under* their subject-matter – e.g. 'Breweries', 'Iron foundries'; mills etc. given extensive treatment in the text appear in this index in their own right e.g. 'Donnybrook Spinning Mill'; names of **bridges** and **quays** are listed here under 'Bridges' and 'Quays'; **railway lines** are listed under 'Railway Companies/Lines'; **railway stations** are listed under 'Railway stations'; **road routes** are listed under 'Roads'; **ships' names** are listed under 'Ships'; **places** are indexed in the separate Topographical Index.